028.12
K64b

142607

DATE DUE			

Best Encyclopedias:
A Guide to General and Specialized Encyclopedias

Best Encyclopedias:
A Guide to General and Specialized Encyclopedias

by Kenneth F. Kister

ORYX PRESS
1986

The rare Arabian Oryx is believed to have inspired the myth of the unicorn. This desert antelope became virtually extinct in the early 1960s. At that time several groups of international conservationists arranged to have 9 animals sent to the Phoenix Zoo to be the nucleus of a captive breeding herd. Today the Oryx population is over 400, and herds have been returned to reserves in Israel, Jordan, and Oman.

Copyright © 1986 by Kenneth F. Kister
Published by The Oryx Press
2214 North Central at Encanto
Phoenix, AZ 85004-1483

Published simultaneously in Canada

Printed and Bound in the United States of America

∞ The paper used in this publication meets the minimum requirements of American National Standard for Information Science—Permanence of Paper for Printed Library Materials, ANSI Z39.48, 1984.

Library of Congress Cataloging-in-Publication Data

Kister, Kenneth F., 1935–
  Best encyclopedias.

  Includes index.
  1. Encyclopedias and dictionaries—Book reviews.
  2. Encyclopedias and dictionaries—Miscellanea.
  3. Encyclopedias and dictionaries—Bibliography.
  I. Title.
  AE1.K57   1986   028.1'2   85-43370
  ISBN 0-89774-171-4

You ask what is the use of classification, arrangement, systematization? I answer you: order and simplification are the first steps toward the mastery of a subject—the actual enemy is the unknown.

Thomas Mann's Settembrini
The Magic Mountain

Contents

Introduction

Practically everyone has used an encyclopedia at one time or another and knows how valuable a good one can be for quickly locating basic factual information or an understandable overview of an unfamiliar or complicated subject. But finding the best encyclopedia—the one that most effectively meets *your* particular needs—is not so easy. Few people know offhand how one encyclopedia differs from another. How, for instance, does the *New Standard Encyclopedia* stack up against the *Encyclopedia Americana*? The *Merit Students Encyclopedia*? The *Young Students Encyclopedia*? What are the strengths of these encyclopedias? Their limitations? Are the two best-known encyclopedias in North America, namely the *New Encyclopaedia Britannica* and the *World Book Encyclopedia,* works of exemplary quality or are their reputations inflated by high-powered advertising? How do newcomers like the *Academic American Encyclopedia,* the *Concise Columbia Encyclopedia,* and the *Knowledge Encyclopedia* compare with the older, established titles? When might a specialized encyclopedia like *Grzimek's Animal Life Encyclopedia* or the *Harvard Encyclopedia of American Ethnic Groups* be preferable to any general encyclopedia?

Best Encyclopedias—subtitled *A Guide to General and Specialized Encyclopedias*—provides authoritative answers to such questions. The guide is designed to help any interested consumer in the United States or Canada distinguish good encyclopedias from bad and mediocre ones and ultimately determine which encyclopedia among the many available will best serve the specific informational needs of that consumer. No single encyclopedia is best for everyone. The encyclopedia most appropriate for, say, a journalist or university professor will almost certainly not be the first choice for a family with school-age children.

General English-language encyclopedias receive the most attention in the guide, simply because this type of encyclopedia is, by its very nature, of greatest interest to the largest number of North American consumers. Specifically, *Best Encyclopedias* reviews 52 general encyclopedias in English, ranging from large multivolume sets for adults, such as the *New Encyclopaedia Britannica* and *Collier's Encyclopedia,* to small works for children such as *Nelson's Encyclopedia for*

Young Readers and *Purnell's Pictorial Encyclopedia.* The guide also includes an extensive section on specialized encyclopedias for those seeking encyclopedic depth on a particular subject (see Appendix B). The *Encyclopedia of World Literature in the 20th Century,* the *Encyclopedia of American Foreign Policy,* and the *New York Botanical Garden Illustrated Encyclopedia of Horticulture* are but a few examples of the growing number of fine specialized encyclopedias currently available. Finally, this guide identifies major foreign-language encyclopedias of potential interest to North Americans (see Appendix C). In all, *Best Encyclopedias* furnishes information about more than 500 encyclopedias and encyclopedic works.

Most encyclopedias covered in *Best Encyclopedias* are in print; that is, publishers or distributors have a stock on hand and the books can be purchased in retail bookstores, through book wholesalers, or directly from a representative of the publisher or distributor. However, this guide also includes some titles no longer in print and therefore no longer available through normal retail channels. Such works—limited to substantial or well-known encyclopedias now discontinued (for example, *Encyclopedia International,* 1963–82)—receive notice because they may be encountered on the secondhand book market or as remainder items in bookstores or discount stores. The possibility also exists that an out-of-print encyclopedia will be reprinted or revised and offered for sale at any time, sometimes under a different title. Old editions of *Encyclopedia International,* for instance, have appeared in recent years under various titles, including *Webster's New Family Encyclopedia, Webster's New Age Encyclopedia,* and *New Age Encyclopedia.* In addition, out-of-print encyclopedias of substance are often found in library reference collections, and users of this guide might want an evaluation.

Reviews of general English-language encyclopedias in *Best Encyclopedias* are arranged alphabetically by title, as shown in the Table of Contents. Each review provides basic data about the encyclopedia (such as publisher, editor, price, number of volumes, pages, articles, words, cross-references, etc.); critical comments with examples; a note comparing the encyclopedia with other titles of similar size, price, and intended usership; sales information; and citations to reviews in other publications. An additional comparative feature is the chart at the end of the reviews (see Appendix A). The specialized encyclopedias, each briefly described in Appendix B, are grouped by subject: "Architecture," "Art (General)," "Astronomy and Space Science," "Biology (General) and Zoology," and so on. And the foreign-language encyclopedias, listed in Appendix C, are organized by language.

To find a specific encyclopedia in this guide, always turn first to the index at the back of the book. The index affords easy and complete alphabetical access to all encyclopedias reviewed or otherwise mentioned in this guide. In addition, the index includes entries for former and variant titles. For example, the review of the one-volume *University Desk Encyclopedia* notes that the work has also been published in three volumes as the *Concord Desk Encyclopedia*; users of this guide seeking information about the *Concord Desk Encyclopedia* will find an entry in the index under that title leading to the *University Desk Encyclopedia* review. The index also provides necessary cross-references, such as "*Britannica.* See NEW ENCYCLOPAEDIA BRITANNICA"; "*Encyclopedia Britannica.* See NEW ENCYCLOPAEDIA BRITANNICA"; "*Americana.* See ENCYCLOPEDIA AMERICANA." Likewise, subject entries in the index help access the many specialized encyclopedias covered in this guide. The index entry "Plants," for instance, refers users to a number of pertinent titles, including the aforementioned *New York Botanical Garden Illustrated Encyclopedia of Horticulture.*

Following customary practice, the words *encyclopaedia* and *encyclopaedic* are alphabetized throughout this guide as if they were spelled *encyclopedia* and *encyclopedic.*

Cross-references, printed in SMALL CAPITAL LETTERS, frequently appear in the encyclopedia reviews, directing users to competing or related titles. For example, a reference to FUNK & WAGNALLS NEW ENCYCLOPEDIA in the review of the *Academic American Encyclopedia* indicates that *Funk & Wagnalls* has its own review in this guide. Users of this guide should also be aware of the distinction between a new *printing* and a new *edition* of an encyclopedia. Briefly, a new printing implies relatively minor or routine revision on a continuous (usually annual) basis, whereas a new edition suggests substantial change on a scale well beyond the ordinary continuous revision program.

Best Encyclopedias is an entirely new work. It is current as of March 1, 1986, the closing date for adding new titles, review citations, price changes, and the like.* Encyclopedias reviewed in this guide are 1984–85 editions, or the latest edition published; for example, the 1975 (fourth) edition of the *New Columbia Encyclopedia* is reviewed because it is the most recent edition of that encyclopedia. In most instances, encyclopedia statistics reported in this guide (number of pages, articles, words, illustrations, etc.) are actual counts or estimates furnished by the publisher or distributor and verified (via sampling) by the author of *Best Encyclopedias.* Responsibility for all descriptive matter and unattributed opinion in the book rests with the author, a nationally known authority on reference materials.

Finally, a personal word about the numerous other people who have contributed in one way or another to the making of this book: I am especially indebted to Norman Horrocks, director of the School of Library Service at Dalhousie University in Nova Scotia, for kindly sending me reviews and articles about encyclopedias I might otherwise have missed; to the many reviewers whose criticisms are incorporated in the book; to my students in the "Basic Information

---

*Please check with publishers for all prices, as they are subject to change.

Sources and Services" course at the School of Library and Information Science at the University of South Florida in Tampa for their helpful suggestions; to those publishers and distributors who generously sent me examination copies of their encyclopedias; to Anne Thompson and Christine Ferdinand, diligent and discerning editors, and the rest of the Oryx Press editorial and production staffs for their conscientious work; and to Clarice Ruder, my wife and colleague, who helped in more ways than I can say.

Kenneth F. Kister
Tampa, Florida

Questions and Answers about Encyclopedias

WHAT IS AN ENCYCLOPEDIA?

Perhaps Henry David Thoreau put it most simply in his classic *Walden* when he referred to an encyclopedia as "an abstract of human knowledge." More precisely, an encyclopedia is a reference source in either print or electronic form that summarizes basic knowledge and information on all important subjects or, in the case of a specialized encyclopedia, a particular subject. An encyclopedia is an attempt to encompass, or encircle, that knowledge and information deemed essential or universally worth knowing—the word *encyclopedia* coming to us from the Greek *enkyklios* (circle) and *paideia* (of learning).

Encyclopedias are always arranged in a systematic manner, usually alphabetically but sometimes by subject in a classified, or topical, sequence. Retrieval of the encyclopedic contents is normally facilitated by an index and/or cross-references. Physical size and intended readership determine an encyclopedia's range and depth. For example, a multivolume set designed for adult use will naturally provide broader and deeper coverage than a single-volume work for children. But no encyclopedia, no matter how large or detailed it might be, can include everything there is to know about any topic. The article on the opera in a general encyclopedia, for instance, will almost certainly trace the history of the musical form and identify its most notable practitioners, but such an account cannot be expected to treat relatively minor or secondary matters like feuds among divas or the recent innovation of projecting subtitles on a screen above the stage during foreign-language productions. Encyclopedias deal only in the bare bones of knowledge and information.

Historically, encyclopedias date back to antiquity when they served the educated elite as codifications of existing knowledge and informed speculation. However, with the advent of the printing press and accompanying growth of literacy and intellectual enlightenment, encyclopedias broadened their scope to accommodate a rush of new ideas, new theories, new vocations, new inventions, and new discoveries, a trend that culminated with the publication of the famous eighteenth-century French *Encyclopédie* of Diderot and d'Alembert. This vast undertaking, comprising 70 volumes issued between 1751 and 1772, challenged the established thought of the day and helped pave the way for the French Revolution. Hans Koning describes its impact in an article in the *New Yorker* (March 2, 1981, p. 67): "The Encyclopédie raised a storm that blew away the smells of powdered wigs, love potions, and alchemists' retorts; shook the salons of the court and the chambers of bishops and parliamentarians still meeting in the shadow of stake and rack; and astounded the still humble new middle class." Moreover, the *Encyclopédie* inspired the compilation of similar works in other countries, including the best known of all English-language encyclopedias, the *Encyclopaedia Britannica* (now *New Encyclopaedia Britannica*), which first appeared in three volumes during 1768–71.

Contemporary encyclopedias rarely fan the flames of revolution. Rather, they tend to be works of strict, objective scholarship tailored to satisfy the most basic informational and educational needs of the now dominant (and no longer humble) middle classes, particularly the student population at all levels. It should come as no surprise, then, that today's encyclopedias customarily have shorter entries and are more popularly written and heavily illustrated than those of the past. Indeed, encyclopedias have always mirrored the civilizations that produce them, and present-day encyclopedias are no exception.

One final note about what an encyclopedia is—and is not. Consumers should understand that encyclopedias are sometimes called "dictionaries," "handbooks," etc. By way of example, Mark Boatner's *Civil War Dictionary* is actually an encyclopedia, as its subtitle ("A Concise Encyclopedia") makes clear. Nor is every reference work with "encyclopedia" in its title really an encyclopedia. The *Encyclopedia of Associations,* for instance, is a directory, and the *Encyclopedia of Ghosts* has been described this way: "Misleadingly titled, this so-called encyclopedia is not a traditional reference book in either organization or approach, but rather an entertainingly written foray into the realm of the supernatural." (Quoted from *Booklist,* January 15, 1985, p. 667.)

WHO NEEDS AN ENCYCLOPEDIA?

Many students and professional people—doctors, lawyers, journalists, business executives, the clergy, teachers, and, of course, librarians—look upon encyclopedias as extremely valuable or even indispensable sources of information. But practically all literate people, no matter what their educational or occupational status, can benefit from the services of a quality encyclopedia. Such works provide convenient access to a wealth of factual information (How tall is the World Trade Center? What is the weight of a football? When was Nellie Ross, the first female governor in the United States, born?). They also analyze, synthesize, and summarize complex ideas and phenomena, putting them into language that the average reader can understand (What is DNA, or deoxyribonucleic acid, and what is its role in the genetic process? How does the polygraph, or lie detector, work? What are the main principles of capitalism? Keynesian economics? Which philosophers are classified as existentialists and what do they believe?).

Encyclopedias are also useful as a means of keeping abreast of significant advances in knowledge. The day when a single individual, even the greatest of geniuses, could know everything worth knowing has long since passed. Furthermore, experts calculate that the world's knowledge and information is now doubling approximately every ten years. A recent study by the Massachusetts Institute of Technology, for instance, estimates that over two billion books, six billion magazines, and 22 billion newspapers roll off the presses each year in the United States alone, twice the number published just a decade ago. Add to this what the M.I.T. study terms the "extraordinary rates of growth in the transmission of electronic communication," and the problem of keeping pace with new developments in any field assumes almost heroic proportions. This explosion of knowledge and information, which began in earnest with the onset of the Industrial Revolution more than two centuries ago, is evident in all subject areas, but none so insistently as science and technology, where progress in agriculture, medicine, communication, transportation, and space exploration has been nothing short of spectacular. Consider the remarkably short time, historically speaking, between the invention of the steam engine and human beings landing on the moon, or the discovery of the circulation of the blood and the first artificial heart.

As already noted, no encyclopedia can possibly include everything every educated reader might want to know, nor does any make such a claim. But in a very real sense, our best encyclopedias stand as small bulwarks against the onrushing tide of ever-increasing knowledge and information. Encyclopedias offer an intellectual framework or perspective through which the average person can begin to study and comprehend where we have been and where we are going in this or that field of knowledge. As Louis Shores, a distinguished encyclopedist, once observed, the encyclopedia is "one of the few generalizing influences in a world of over-specialization. It serves to recall that knowledge has unity."

From a practical standpoint, however, not everyone needs to own an encyclopedia. Consumers considering the purchase of a set mainly for the use of their school-age children should bear in mind that public and school libraries normally have at least several decent encyclopedias available. (On the other hand, the libraries may not be open when the children need to consult the encyclopedias, or the libraries may be inconveniently located.) Parents should also realize that, despite the blandishments of some encyclopedia sales representatives, having an encyclopedia in the house will not necessarily transform little Sam or Sally into an "A" student (although the suspicion exists that children from homes with books in abundance generally do better in school than their classmates who lack such resources). In addition, some teachers discourage or prohibit student use of encyclopedias, believing that students will copy the encyclopedia and neglect the rest of the library's materials. Not everyone agrees with this reasoning, including the author of this book; nevertheless, consumers thinking seriously about buying an encyclopedia for use in their children's schoolwork would be wise to check with teachers before making a final decision.

Who needs an encyclopedia? Without question, any inquisitive, literate person, young or old, will benefit from having a good encyclopedia handy. But who should buy an encyclopedia? Ultimately, individual consumers must answer for themselves, after carefully considering these basic questions: Can we afford an encyclopedia? Can we afford the *best* encyclopedia—that is, the one that best meets our needs? Who will actually use the encyclopedia? Will the encyclopedia be used enough to justify the expense? This last question is particularly important. To be a wise investment, an encyclopedia must be used, the more the better. Buying an encyclopedia, writes Tyler Mathisen in *Money* magazine (October 1983, p. 210), "is like buying a whole cow to get the ribs; much of the material inevitably goes unread." Unfortunately, some people buy an encyclopedia and the whole thing, ribs and all, goes to waste. To repeat: Any encyclopedia, no matter how fine it might be, is a poor bargain if it is not used.

WHO MAKES AND SELLS ENCYCLOPEDIAS?

The general encyclopedia market in North America is dominated by four well-known, highly respected publishers. The Big Four and their encyclopedias are:

1. Encyclopaedia Britannica, Inc. (and its sister company Encyclopaedia Britannica Educational Corporation—EBEC), which publishes and sells the 32-volume *New Encyclopaedia Britannica,* the largest and most prestigious encyclopedia in the English language; the 26-volume *Compton's Encyclopedia,* aimed at the family and young adult market; and the 16-volume *Young Children's Encyclopedia* (also published under the title *Compton's Precyclopedia*), for beginning readers. Recently, Britannica discontinued publication of the *Britan-*

nica Junior Encyclopedia, a 15-volume set for children in the elementary grades.

2. Grolier, Inc. (and its subsidiary, Grolier Educational Corporation), which publishes and sells the 30-volume *Encyclopedia Americana,* a major work for adults and the first multivolume encyclopedia of any significance produced in the United States (1829); the 21-volume *Academic American Encyclopedia,* the newest (1980) general multivolume encyclopedia on the North American scene; and the 21-volume *New Book of Knowledge,* a longtime favorite with young readers. In 1982, Grolier suspended publication of the 20-volume *Encyclopedia International,* a set designed for the family and older student market. Earlier, in 1976, the company discontinued the *American Peoples Encyclopedia,* a 20-volume work for adults.

3. Macmillan, Inc. (and its subsidiary, Macmillan Educational Company), which publishes and sells two general encyclopedias of relatively recent vintage, the 24-volume *Collier's Encyclopedia,* a large set for adults that first appeared in 1950, and the 20-volume *Merit Students Encyclopedia,* a set for family and older student use first published in 1967.

4. World Book, Inc. (a subsidiary of the Scott and Fetzer Company), which publishes and sells the 22-volume *World Book Encyclopedia,* indisputably the best-selling encyclopedia in North America, and the 15-volume *Childcraft,* a topically arranged set for preschool and elementary school children.

Actual figures concerning encyclopedia sales, either in terms of dollar volume or units sold, are not available. But according to informed estimates, these four publishers account for roughly 90–95 percent of all sales of general encyclopedias in the United States and Canada each year, with World Book the leader, commanding a 32 percent share of the market. The remaining 5–10 percent of the market is divided among such companies as Funk & Wagnalls, Inc., publisher of the 29-volume *Funk & Wagnalls New Encyclopedia* and the 15-volume *Charlie Brown's 'Cyclopedia,* both sold principally in supermarkets; the Standard Educational Corporation, which publishes the *New Standard Encyclopedia,* a 17-volume work for adults and older students; Pergamon Press, distributor of the *New Caxton Encyclopedia,* a profusely illustrated 20-volume set prepared in Great Britain; and Fitzhenry & Whiteside in Ontario, which sells the 12-volume British-made *Everyman's Encyclopaedia* exclusively in Canada. (This encyclopedia is not sold in print form in the United States because its publisher, the English firm of J.M. Dent & Sons Ltd., lacks copyright clearance in the U.S. for the set's photographs; *Everyman's* is available in the U.S., however, in electronic form via the Dialog computer database system.)

Publishers of one- and two-volume general encyclopedias also claim a small share of the market. The leading publishers are the

Columbia University Press, which produces and sells the *New Columbia Encyclopedia* and the *Concise Columbia Encyclopedia*; Random House, Inc., publisher of the *Random House Encyclopedia* and the *New Universal Family Encyclopedia*; the Frontier Press Company, publisher of the *Lincoln Library of Essential Information*; and the Southwestern Company, publisher of the *Volume Library*.

Specialized encyclopedias, which can be viewed as either complements or alternatives to general encyclopedias, are made and sold by a great variety of publishers and distributors in North America. Among the most prominent and prolific of these are (with examples):

*Cambridge University Press: *Cambridge Encyclopedia of Archaeology; Cambridge Encyclopedia of Earth Sciences; Cambridge Encyclopedia of Russia and the Soviet Union; Popular Encyclopedia of Plants.*

*Crown Publishers, Inc.: *Encyclopedia of Painting; Harmony Illustrated Encyclopedia of Rock; Illustrated Encyclopedia of Space Technology; International Center of Photography Encyclopedia of Photography; Official Encyclopedia of Bridge.*

*Facts on File: *Encyclopedia of Alcoholism; Encyclopedia of American Crime; Encyclopedia of American Journalism; World Encyclopedia of Political Systems & Parties; World Press Encyclopedia.*

*Greenwood Press: *American Educators' Encyclopedia; Dictionary of American Communal and Utopian History; Dictionary of Mexican American History; Encyclopedia of American Agricultural History; Kabuki Encyclopedia.*

*Harper & Row: *Complete Outdoors Encyclopedia; Encyclopedia of American History; Encyclopedia of Anthropology; Encyclopedia of Military History; Worldmark Encyclopedia of the States.*

*Macmillan, Inc.: *Baseball Encyclopedia; Encyclopedia of Educational Research; Encyclopedia of Philosophy; International Encyclopedia of the Social Sciences; Wyman's Gardening Encyclopedia.*

*McGraw-Hill Book Company: *Encyclopedia of Black America; Encyclopedia of North American Railroading; Encyclopedia of World Art; McGraw-Hill Encyclopedia of Science and Technology; New Catholic Encyclopedia.*

*Oxford University Press: *Encyclopedia of the Musical Film; Oxford Companion to American Literature; Oxford Companion to Ships and the Sea; Oxford Encyclopedia of Trees of the World; World Christian Encyclopedia.*

*Prentice-Hall: *Concise Encyclopedia of Information Technology; Encyclopedia of Accounting Systems; Encyclopedia of Archaeological Excavations in the Holy Land; Encyclopedia of Integrated Circuits; Prentice-Hall Encyclopedia of Mathematics.*

*Charles Scribner's Sons: *Dictionary of American History; Dictionary of the History of Ideas; Dictionary of the Middle Ages; Encyclopedia of American Foreign Policy; Encyclopedia of World Costume.*

*Van Nostrand Reinhold Company: *Color Encyclopedia of Gemstones; Encyclopedia of Computer Science and Engineering; Grzimek's Animal Life Encyclopedia; International Encyclopedia of Psychiatry, Psychology, Psychoanalysis, and Neurology; Van Nostrand's Scientific Encyclopedia.*
*John Wiley & Sons: *Encyclopedia of Industrial Chemical Analysis; Encyclopedia of Polymer Science and Technology; Encyclopedia of Psychology; Kirk-Othmer Encyclopedia of Chemical Technology; Worldmark Encyclopedia of the Nations.*

For further information about who makes and sells all types of encyclopedias, see Appendix E at the back of this book for a directory of North American encyclopedia publishers and distributors and their products.

HOW TRUSTWORTHY ARE ENCYCLOPEDIA SALESPEOPLE?

The adage that encyclopedias are "sold not bought" contains more than a grain of truth. Most people perceive encyclopedias, unlike automobiles or toothpaste, to be a discretionary, or luxury, item. Hence, most potential customers must be convinced that an encyclopedia, which can cost as much as $1,250 or more, is a desirable investment. The person who normally does the convincing (or tries to) is the encyclopedia representative—a figure often portrayed in cartoons and movies as the worst sort of huckster. And, indeed, because encyclopedias rarely sell themselves, and because encyclopedia salespeople customarily work on commission, hard-sell tactics are not uncommon. According to one former encyclopedia representative (quoted in the article "All About Encyclopedias" in *Money,* October 1983, p. 209), "We were trained to play on guilt by telling parents their children might grow up to be dummies if they didn't have an encyclopedia."

And sometimes encyclopedia salespeople cross the line from hard sell to fraudulent and deceptive practices, such as misrepresenting the purpose of their call or using false advertising. In an old but still valid article entitled "Buying an Encyclopedia" in *Consumers' Research Magazine* (February 1975, p. 12), W.T. Johnston and Joy B. Trulock discuss the techniques of the unscrupulous sales representative, warning, "Don't be caught in the trap of the claim that he has only one bargain or 'demo' sample set left. The prices on most standard and good encyclopedias are fairly rigid. Watch, too, that he hasn't quoted you an inflated price and then makes the offer to throw in a dictionary and an atlas free of charge when in reality these volumes were included in the price he gave you to begin with. And last, don't accept a 'free' set and then sign a contract agreeing to pay $400 for an annual updating service for the next 10 years."

Fortunately, the most blatant encyclopedia sales abuses have declined in recent years. Much of the credit for this improvement belongs to the Federal Trade Commission (FTC), a regulatory agency of the U.S. government, which instituted several consumer protection measures during the 1970s designed to curb the crooked or overzealous encyclopedia representative. The most effective of these measures has been the so-called cooling-off regulation, which permits consumers to cancel a contract for any door-to-door purchase of $25 or more within three business days after signing the contract. Moreover, during the past decade the FTC has investigated the whole encyclopedia industry for questionable sales methods, resulting in regulatory action against most of the major companies, including Encyclopaedia Britannica, Grolier, and Macmillan. All of this public attention has helped persuade encyclopedia publishers and distributors to clean up their sales act.

But instances of shady and illegal sales practices continue to be reported, and consumers would be wise to heed these suggestions when dealing with any encyclopedia representative:

- Do not be pressured into making a purchase decision until you are ready. As consumer advocate Herbert Denenberg has observed (in *Caveat Emptor,* August–September 1979, p. 19), "The surest earmark of a phony salesman with a lousy deal is the one who insists you have to buy right now or you'll miss a monumental bargain. What you'll probably miss if you don't buy in a hurry is a monumental rip-off."
- Do not sign a blank or incomplete contract.
- Do not talk with a salesperson when you are tired or not feeling well.
- Do not fall for come-ons like "free" gifts or prizes.
- Do not buy an encyclopedia unless it will be used sufficiently to justify the expense.
- If you do invest in an encyclopedia, do not automatically sign up for the yearbooks, traditionally part of the package. Although some are excellent, yearbooks (or annual supplements) are usually expensive, only indirectly relate to the encyclopedia, and are often never used.

WHAT ABOUT A SECONDHAND ENCYCLOPEDIA?

New encyclopedias are expensive, ranging from $500 to $1,250 and up for a quality multivolume set. *Collier's Encyclopedia,* for instance, now costs about $1,100 to individual consumers and over $700 to schools and libraries (educational institutions customarily receive a healthy discount); the *Academic American Encyclopedia* goes for nearly $800 to individuals and $600 to schools and libraries; the *World Book Encyclopedia* is priced around $600 to individuals and over $400 to schools and libraries; and the *New Encyclopaedia Britannica* starts at $1,250 for individuals and sells for $950 to schools and libraries. Specialized encyclopedias of comparable size are equally or more expensive. For example, the current edition (1982) of the *McGraw-Hill Encyclopedia of Science and Technology,* a 15-volume set, costs well over $900. One way around the high cost of encyclopedias is to buy a secondhand set. Substantial savings—sometimes more than 50 percent—can be realized by investing in an older, used encyclopedia.

Like most products, encyclopedias begin to lose value the minute they are purchased. The general rule of thumb is that an encyclopedia depreciates between 15 and 20 percent the first year and 10 percent each year thereafter. By way of example, the Literary Mart, a New York City bookseller, recently offered a 1982 printing of *Encyclopedia Americana* for $450 (in good condition); the current retail price of the *Americana* is about $1,000 to individuals (and just under $800 to schools and libraries). Similarly, a 1982 set of the *New Book of Knowledge* was priced at $250, whereas today the encyclopedia retails for approximately $650 ($450 to schools and libraries). Literary Mart listed the current, sixth edition (1983) of *Van Nostrand's Scientific Encyclopedia* at $85; new, the two-volume set retails for about $138.

Naturally, a secondhand encyclopedia will not be as current as a new set. How important a consideration should up-to-dateness be when buying an encyclopedia? If the informational needs of those who will be using the set are mainly in the areas of history, literature, music, philosophy, religion, etc., where knowledge is not as volatile and readily discarded as in the sciences, then a used encyclopedia several years old can be a good buy. If, on the other hand, the encyclopedia's users will be consulting the set principally for information in the physical, technical, biological, or behavioral sciences, where knowledge changes very rapidly and currentness is vital, a secondhand encyclopedia makes little sense, no matter how inexpensive it might be. Generally speaking, any encyclopedia over ten years old should be avoided.

Who sells secondhand encyclopedias? Sometimes they can be found in the classified advertisements of the local newspaper, but the best place to locate a used or older encyclopedia is through a bookstore that specializes in such materials. Most large cities have at least one bookstore that trades in secondhand and remainder books, including large reference sets. Two of the most active dealers in North America are the Reference Book Center (175 Fifth Avenue, New York, NY 10010; 212-677-2160) and the aforementioned Literary Mart (1261 Broadway, New York, NY 10001; 212-684-0588). These and similar booksellers provide current catalogs upon request.

WON'T COMPUTERS REPLACE ENCYCLOPEDIAS?

Computers have become an increasingly influential, even dominating, force in our lives during the past ten years or so. But, no, computers will not replace encyclopedias anytime soon. The familiar set of printed books covering basic knowledge from A to Z that we call an encyclopedia will continue to be a fixture for the foreseeable future. The computer revolution, however, is creating an entirely new form of encyclopedia that consumers should know about and understand—the electronic encyclopedia (also called the automated or online encyclopedia). At present, the electronic encyclopedia (as opposed to the customary print version) is in its infancy. Only two encyclopedias of any significance, the *New Encyclopaedia Britannica* and the *Academic American Encyclopedia,* are currently available in electronic form, and usership is quite limited. But by the 1990s, as more and more homes, libraries, schools, and offices become equipped with computer terminals, information analysts expect automated encyclopedias to compete more or less on an equal footing with print encyclopedias.

Print and electronic encyclopedias differ in a number of important ways. In terms of physical format and appearance, the two could not be more unalike. The print encyclopedia consists of bound volumes on a bookshelf, whereas the automated version is made up of electronic hardware (keypads, video display units, etc.) that links the user to a remote computer system. In terms of organization and accessibility of material, the print encyclopedia is typically arranged in alphabetical order, with access enhanced by cross-references and/or a general index. The electronic encyclopedia, on the other hand, is a machine-readable database that can be programmed to scan and retrieve any word or word combinations in the encyclopedic text. Called full-text searching, this feature utilizes Boolean logic (the linking of search terms in AND/OR/NOT relationships) to zero in on the desired information. As far as size is concerned, the print encyclopedia is limited to a predetermined number of volumes or pages, whereas the computerized encyclopedia has the capability of expanding its contents to accommodate practically limitless quantities of data. In the vital area of keeping current, the print encyclopedia is normally revised once a year, whereas the computerized version can easily be updated every month, every week, or even, if necessary, every day.

The two types of encyclopedias are also very different in the manner in which they are merchandised and priced. The print encyclopedia is usually sold by a publisher's representative, with the customer paying a fixed price for the set (often on an installment plan). The electronic version, however, is usually sold via subscription, with user charges calculated on the basis of computer connect-time, similar to the long-distance telephone billing procedure. Consumers should be aware that, given the present pricing structure, electronic encyclopedias can be quite expensive. An online search for information on, say, the Civil War may cost $25 or $30 or more, depending on the type of question involved and the skill and discipline of the searcher. At that rate, an entire encyclopedia could be acquired in print form for the price of as few as 20 or 30 searches.

Which is preferable, the traditional print encyclopedia or the innovative electronic version? Should a consumer considering the purchase of an encyclopedia today go with the tried and true or kick over the traces and opt for the new? Actually, both types of encyclopedias have their strong and weak points. As the foregoing discussion indicates, print encyclopedias lack the great storage, retrieval, and updating capabilities of their automated counterparts, but encyclopedias in electronic form can be wildly expensive, and they require much more training to be used effectively. Perhaps a wait-and-see attitude concerning electronic encyclopedias is the wisest course for the average consumer at this time. It almost goes without saying that automated encyclopedias will change and improve with new developments. One such promising development is delivery of encyclopedic information by compact laser disc. Laser discs, which can be accessed via a home computer, are capable of providing not only the text of encyclopedia articles but moving pictures and sound as well. The entry on Mozart, for instance, may be supplemented by recorded music from *Don Giovanni* or the unfinished *Requiem* coordinated with a visual display of the score. The first encyclopedia to become available on compact disc is Grolier's *Academic American Encyclopedia,* which appeared in disc form in late 1985 at $199. According to the article "Encyclopedia on a Disk" in *Time* magazine (July 29, 1985, p. 64), the compact disc encyclopedia "works on personal computers like the IBM PC once they are equipped with a special compact-disk drive. This spins the CD platter and translates the digital information into words with a laser beam. The first such hookups ... will cost about $2,000."

For additional information about electronic and compact disc encyclopedias, see these articles:

"Coming Soon: Encyclopedias That Can Talk" by Daniel Machalaba in the *Wall Street Journal,* February 18, 1981, p.29.

"Computerized Encyclopedias" by John Free in *Popular Science,* June 1983, pp. 138–39.

"Online Encyclopedias: Are They Ready for Libraries? Are Libraries Ready for Them?" by Gordon Flagg in *American Libraries,* March 1983, pp. 134–36.

"Online Encyclopedias: The Potential" by Stephen P. Harter and Kenneth F. Kister in *Library Journal,* September 1, 1981, pp. 1600–02.

"Short Circuiting Reference Books: Students are Beginning to Tap into On-Screen Encyclopedias" by Robert T. Grieves in *Time,* June 13, 1983, p. 76.

WHAT TO LOOK FOR WHEN CHOOSING AN ENCYCLOPEDIA

Obviously, not all encyclopedias are of equal quality or worth. Given the large number and variety of titles available (both general and specialized), how does the ordinary person go about deciding which encyclopedia to buy or consult? A simple solution is to check this edition of *Best Encyclopedias* for the title that seems most suitable, based on such fundamental considerations as physical size, intended readership, quality, and price. For example, after looking over the reviews in *Best Encyclopedias,* a family of modest means with several school-age children might conclude that a reasonably priced, medium-size general encyclopedia of good repute like the *New Standard Encyclopedia* or the *World Book Encyclopedia* is the best buy. On the other hand, a college student majoring in American history might decide that the best choice is not a general encyclopedia at all but, rather, a specialized work like the eight-volume *Dictionary of American History* or the much less expensive, single-volume *Encyclopedia of American History.*

This expedient method of choosing an encyclopedia will satisfy most casual consumers who lack the time and/or inclination to formulate their own opinions about specific titles. Serious consumers (such as teachers, librarians, journalists, researchers, and advanced students), however, are urged to inspect *firsthand* any encyclopedia being considered for purchase or extensive use in preparing a term paper, thesis, article, or similarly important project. Nothing beats personal examination when it comes to selecting reference materials, and this is particularly true in the case of encyclopedias, where the expense involved can be quite high.

How, then, does the interested consumer go about personally evaluating an encyclopedia? What qualities or features distinguish an outstanding encyclopedia from one that is second-rate? The author of *Best Encyclopedias* recommends this general procedure: After locating an examination set or copy at a library or bookstore or from the publisher, ask the encyclopedia some questions that it might reasonably be expected to answer—and demand clear, accurate, up-to-date, easily retrievable information in return. Interrogate the encyclopedia as if you were Mike Wallace on the trail of a hot story. Ask the encyclopedia, for instance, about sodium pentothal, popularly known as "truth serum." How effective is sodium pentothal at eliciting the truth? How does it work biochemically? Are there different kinds of truth serum? Are confessions obtained with the use of truth serum admissible as evidence in a court of law? Does the encyclopedia reveal who first used or developed truth serum? Still in search of the truth (appropriately enough), you might next ask the encyclopedia similar questions about the polygraph, or lie detector, test.

The object, of course, is to discover the encyclopedia's range, depth, strengths, weaknesses, and idiosyncrasies through actual use. And when possible, the encyclopedia's chief competitors should be asked the same questions for the purpose of head-to-head comparison. It is interesting to note, for example, that the *Academic American Encyclopedia* provides only two very brief references to truth serum in the articles *Sedative* and *Sodium Pentothal,* neither of which contains much general information (and only one of which is found under the entry "Truth Serum" in the index), whereas the competing *World Book Encyclopedia* includes a concise, informative discussion of the subject in the article *Sodium Pentothal* that should satisfy most questions most readers might have. Another encyclopedia in the same size and user class, *Funk & Wagnalls New Encyclopedia,* informs the reader that the drug scopolamine can be used as a truth serum, but there is nothing about sodium pentothal in the encyclopedia. The larger, more advanced *Encyclopedia Americana* includes a paragraph about sodium pentothal in the articles *Anesthesia* and *Barbiturates,* but information about truth serum is nowhere to be found. This hardly means that the *Academic American Encyclopedia, Funk & Wagnalls New Encyclopedia,* and *Encyclopedia Americana* lack merit as general encyclopedias. It does mean, however, that in this particular instance they failed to deliver. Too many such failures will lead the user to question the encyclopedia's dependability, just as the clock that strikes 13 once too often is suspect.

Hence, the more questions you ask the encyclopedia the better. In the case of the reviews in *Best Encyclopedias,* the author preselected questions, or topics, that represent major areas of knowledge and cover information likely to be found in general encyclopedias. Thirty-five topics were systematically checked in each encyclopedia for adults and older students: *abortion; acquired immune deficiency syndrome* (AIDS); *adoption; apartheid; asbestos; breakdancing; Canadian Constitution; capital punishment; circumcision; computers; cruelty to animals* (or *animal rights*); *dimethyl sulfoxide* (DMSO); *D'Oyly Carte; Dresden, Germany; earthquakes; Falkland Islands; gambling; health maintenance organizations* (HMOs); *John Maynard Keynes; Nicaragua; Olympic Games; Pearl Harbor; polygraph test* (or *lie detector test*); *Ayn Rand; Rainer Maria Rilke; robots; Nellie Tayloe Ross; Sacco and Vanzetti; Scientology; Shroud of Turin; Sikhism; Switzerland; truth serum* (or *sodium pentothal*); *Vietnam War*; and *Richard Wagner.*

General encyclopedias for children and younger students are naturally less detailed and sophisticated than those intended for adults and older readers. The 20 topics checked in the encyclopedias for young people reviewed in *Best Encyclopedias* reflect this distinction: *adoption; animals; Argentina; Paul Bunyan; Canada; card games; computers; earthquakes; health; Martin Luther King, Jr.; Nicaragua; Olympic Games; religion; Paul Revere; robots; Betsy Ross; sexual reproduction; Switzerland; Harry S. Truman*; and *World War II.*

To repeat: Ask the encyclopedia questions, the more the better. Cross-examine it, checking topics like those above, but ones based on your own knowledge and interests. Very quickly you will begin to learn whether or not the encyclopedia is clearly written, intelligently organized, reasonably current, and so on.

To achieve a full and fair sense of the overall quality of the total encyclopedia, carefully consider these 14 points during the evaluation process:

Does the Encyclopedia Provide the Material You and Others Who Will Be Using It Are Likely to Need? How extensive is the encyclopedia's coverage? How deep is the coverage? Are there any noticeable or glaring gaps in the coverage? If you or the encyclopedia's principal users are mainly interested in a particular subject or field of knowledge (such as history or art or general science), shouldn't a specialized encyclopedia be considered?

Is the Encyclopedia Comprehensible to You and Others Who Will Be Using It? For whom is the encyclopedia intended? Adults? Young people? Children? The introduction or preface to the work should make this plain, but unfortunately encyclopedia makers have a habit of exaggerating reader suitability claims. Is the writing style clear and interesting? Are technical and potentially unfamiliar terms defined or explained? Is jargon avoided? Is the style relatively consistent throughout, or does it vary from article to article? To evaluate the encyclopedia's clarity and reader suitability, read several articles on subjects about which you have little or no knowledge. Then ask yourself: Do I understand what is being said? Do the same with others who will be using the encyclopedia heavily, including children.

Is the Encyclopedia Produced by Reputable People? Who made the encyclopedia? What are the credentials of the contributors and chief editors? Such information should be provided in the front matter, or introductory material. Has the encyclopedia achieved recognition over the years as a work of quality? If it is a comparatively new or little-known work, has it received favorable notice in such review publications as *American Reference Books Annual, Booklist,* and *Best Encyclopedias*? What is the reputation of the publisher or distributor? For an informed opinion on this last question, check with your local public or school librarian.

Is the Encyclopedia Reliable? Are the facts right most of the time? Is the encyclopedia's explanation, or interpretation, of factual material in accord with responsible contemporary scholarship? No encyclopedia is entirely without error or misinterpretation, but users have a right to expect a reasonably high level of accuracy. Check a number of topics on which you are well versed to test the encyclopedia's reliability. You might also ask a friend or neighbor who has some particular expertise to read an article or two.

Is the Encyclopedia Free from Bias and Stereotyping? Are such widely debated issues as the Arab-Israeli conflict, prayer in the schools, abortion, circumcision, homosexuality, marijuana, communism, and evolution treated as fairly and objectively as possible? Are differing points of view on all major sides of such questions represented, or does the encyclopedia simply avoid controversial issues (a form of bias)? Do the contributors bring an impartiality to their work, or are they open to charges of bias, as in the case of, say, a consultant to the nuclear power industry writing about the 1979 accident at the Three Mile Island plant? Bias and stereotyping of any kind—racial, sexual, political, religious, etc.—have no place in a quality encyclopedia.

Is the Encyclopedia Reasonably Current? Encyclopedias cannot be expected to be as current as the daily newspaper. On the other hand, an encyclopedia boasting a recent copyright should be fairly up-to-date. (The latest date on the reverse side of the title page indicates the most recent copyright edition.) An encyclopedia with a 1986 copyright, for example, ought to include information on such 1980s concerns as microcomputers, artificial body parts and organ transplants, the recently diagnosed diseases of chlamydia and acquired immune deficiency syndrome (AIDS), laser disc technology, the space shuttle, telephone deregulation, and spouse and child abuse. As a rule, at least ten percent of the contents of a continuously published encyclopedia should be revised each year. With regard to so-called encyclopedia updating supplements or yearbooks, consumers should understand that these annual publications, though sometimes useful as a chronology of events, do not really keep an encyclopedia current, despite vigorous claims to the contrary by many encyclopedia sales representatives.

Are the Encyclopedia's Contents Readily Accessible? How is the encyclopedia arranged? Is it easy to use? If arranged alphabetically, is the filing letter by letter (in which case *Newspaper* precedes *New York*) or word by word (*New York* precedes *Newspaper*)? Are cross-references furnished in sufficient quantity? Is there a comprehensive general index? Is the index analytical? That is, are broad entries like "Canada" broken down into more specific subentries, such as "Canada—Agriculture," "Canada—Art and Architecture," "Canada—Climate," and "Canada—Constitution"? To determine how well the encyclopedia performs in the crucial area of accessibility, search for information on both a broad subject like evolution, mass transportation, or energy conservation, and a quite specific one like truth serum or asbestos.

Does the Encyclopedia Include Well-Selected Bibliographies? An encyclopedia is frequently the first—but not the last—place one looks for information. Hence, good encyclopedias include bibliographies, or lists of recommended publications that may be consulted for additional information on a subject. Are the bibliographies, which are usually located at the end of the encyclopedia's articles, reasonably up-to-date? Do they include the most important or best-known works on the subject? Are both print and nonprint materials listed?

Is the Encyclopedia Adequately Illustrated? Does the encyclopedia's pictorial matter—photographs, drawings, diagrams, reproductions of paintings and other works of art, transparencies, maps, and the like—complement and enhance the written text, or are the illustrations merely pretty page fillers? Are the illustrations large enough? Are they clearly and sharply reproduced? Are they of recent vintage? Or are the illustrations too often small, out-of-register visual images that bespeak another era? Browse through several volumes of the encyclopedia with an eye to judging how well the words and illustrations interact with each other.

Is the Encyclopedia Physically Well Made and Aesthetically Pleasing? Is the page layout uncrowded and attractive to the eye? Is the print large and legible enough for those who will be using the encyclopedia, including children? Does the binding seem sturdy enough to hold up under heavy use? Do the volumes lie flat when open (for easy consultation on a desk or stand), or are they so tightly bound that they spring shut? Spend some time examining the physical makeup of the encyclopedia.

Does the Encyclopedia Have any Special or Unique Features? If so, do these features add to the informational value of the encyclopedia from your standpoint, or are they largely promotional gimmicks? Some encyclopedias, for instance, include study guides, dictionaries, atlases, and the like as supplements to the basic work. Others offer research services to customers. Others have distinctive illustrations (as in the case of the art reproductions in the *New Caxton Encyclopedia*) or a unique arrangement (the *New Encyclopaedia Britannica*). In other instances, the encyclopedia is available in both print and electronic form (see, for example, the *Academic American Encyclopedia, Everyman's Encyclopaedia,* and the *New Encyclopaedia Britannica*); in the case of the *Kussmaul Encyclopedia,* the work is sold only in electronic form.

Is the Encyclopedia Fairly Priced? What is the encyclopedia's lowest retail price? Do educational institutions receive a discount? If so, how much? Is the price equitable for an encyclopedia of this type, size, and quality? (See Appendix A at the back of this book for a comparison chart of general encyclopedias that includes price information.) Consumers should be aware that the price of an encyclopedia can vary greatly depending on the type of binding, even though the encyclopedia's contents are exactly the same. For the overwhelming majority of consumers, the least expensive binding will serve their needs just as well as a higher-priced one. Prices may also be affected by "package deals," wherein the consumer must agree to buy not only the encyclopedia but a number of extra items, such as anthologies of children's stories, yearbooks, dictionaries, atlases, globes, bookcases, and research services. If you only want the encyclopedia, do not be cajoled or dunned into buying unneeded extras.

What Do Published Reviews Say about the Encyclopedia? Has the encyclopedia received positive notices from responsible critics? Are the reviews mostly in agreement? Mixed? How do they square with your own findings? The major sources of encyclopedia reviews in North America are *American Reference Books Annual* (*ARBA*), published each year since 1970 by Libraries Unlimited in Littleton, Colorado; *Booklist,* a twice-monthly review journal published since 1905 by the American Library Association; and the book you are now reading, *Best Encyclopedias* by Kenneth F. Kister, published by Oryx Press in 1986 (first edition). Several other review journals include criticisms of specialized encyclopedias, such as *Choice, Library Journal, RQ, School Library Journal,* and *Wilson Library Bulletin.* For further information about these and other sources of encyclopedia reviews, see Appendix D ("Encyclopedia Bibliography") at the back of this book.

How Does the Encyclopedia Compare with Its Major Competitors? Which encyclopedias compete directly with the one under review? (See the comparison chart in Appendix A that groups general encyclopedias by size and intended readership.) How do these encyclopedias match up in terms of coverage? Readability? Authority? Reliability? Objectivity? Recency? Bibliographies? Illustrations? Physical format? Special features? Price? Reviewer opinion? Comparative analysis of competing encyclopedias can be a time-consuming as well as frustrating business, but the serious consumer will find it well worth the effort. Only through this process can one begin to appreciate fully an encyclopedia's strengths, weaknesses, and, if you will, personality.

Reviews of General English-Language Encyclopedias

Academic American Encyclopedia

FACTS

Academic American Encyclopedia. Also published in North America as the *Lexicon Universal Encyclopedia;* published abroad as the *Grolier Academic Encyclopedia.* Bernard S. Cayne, Editorial Director; K. Anne Ranson, Editor in Chief. Danbury, CT: Grolier, Inc. 21 volumes. First edition published in 1980; new printing with revisions each year. Lowest retail price: $850 plus shipping and handling; with discount to schools and libraries: $650 plus shipping and handling.

The 21-volume *Academic American Encyclopedia* is intended "for students in junior high school, high school, or college and for the inquisitive adult" (preface). The encyclopedia contains 9,696 pages, 28,500 articles, and approximately 9 million words. The articles, most of which are of the short-entry type, average about 325 words in length (or a third of a page). They are accompanied by 16,616 illustrations (75 percent in full color), plus 1,080 maps. Some 2,400 editors and contributors are noted at the front of Volume 1. About 75 percent of the articles are signed. The encyclopedia is arranged alphabetically word by word (*New York* precedes *Newspaper*), with access to specific information enhanced by 67,000 cross-references in the text and an analytical index of more than 200,000 entries. The encyclopedia's printed text is completely machine-readable; as a result, the *Academic American* is available in electronic form from a number of vendors, including Bibliographic Retrieval Services (BRS), CompuServe, Dialog, and Dow Jones News/Retrieval. (For additional information about the electronic version of the *Academic American,* see the section on purchasing the encyclopedia below.)

EVALUATION

First published in 1980, the *Academic American* is the newest major multivolume general English-language encyclopedia on the market. It was created from scratch in the late 1970s by the Aretê Publishing Company of Princeton, New Jersey, an American subsidiary of Verenigde Nederlandse Uitgeversbedrijven (VNU), a giant publishing company in the Netherlands. Although financed by Dutch money, the encyclopedia was prepared from the outset with North American readers principally in mind. In 1982, Grolier, Inc., one of the leading

U.S. encyclopedia publishers, acquired the set. During its brief history, the *Academic American* has achieved a solid reputation as one of our five or six premier general encyclopedias. The editors and contributors, most of whom are U.S. college professors, bring respectable credentials to the work.

The encyclopedia's coverage is fairly well balanced, although scientific and technical subjects, which account for roughly 35 percent of the text, tend to stand out. Such articles as *Animal, Animal Behavior, Animal Communication, Animal Courtship and Mating, Animal Experimentation, Animal Husbandry,* and *Animal Migration* exemplify the encyclopedia's close attention to scientific topics. Conversely, geographical subjects are often slighted. The *Academic American*'s article on Nicaragua, for example, is limited to two pages, whereas such competing encyclopedias as FUNK & WAGNALLS NEW ENCYCLOPEDIA, the NEW STANDARD ENCYCLOPEDIA, and the WORLD BOOK ENCYCLOPEDIA provide two or three times as much coverage. The same is true of articles on the U.S. states, Canadian provinces, and places in both countries. Moreover, the *Academic American*'s coverage in many areas suffers from lack of sufficient depth, due largely to the encyclopedia's emphasis on short articles. As noted in *Choice* (March 1981, p. 912), "The AAE's most serious shortcoming is the brevity of its entries. Undergraduates looking for articles that will put their subjects into historical and philosophical perspective will usually find their needs better met by consulting another encyclopedia." James Rettig's review in *Wilson Library Bulletin* (February 1982, p. 460) makes a similar point, complaining that the articles "leave the reader wishing the skeleton of facts carried more meat and connecting tissue. They give a teasing, tantalizing taste of their subjects but do not impart enough of its real flavor."

Information in the *Academic American* is usually accurate, objective, and current. Many of the minor errors spotted by critics in the first (1980) edition have since been corrected, but some small inaccuracies remain. Articles dealing with controversial issues normally give both sides of the argument, although sometimes controversy is merely noted but not discussed. For example, in the article *Scientology* the reader learns that the religion "has been the subject of much controversy" but not what the controversy involves. As might be expected in the case of a relatively new work, the *Academic American* tends to be quite current in terms of both facts and perspective. Since acquiring the set in 1982, Grolier has put a high priority on keeping it as up-to-date as possible. The 1985 printing, for instance, includes more than 1,400 new or revised articles, 100 or so new photographs, and 50 revised maps—all entailing changes in over 1,750 of the encyclopedia's nearly 10,000 pages. Such articles as *Asbestos, Canada, Computer, Computer Memory, Earthquakes, Health-Care Systems, Olympic Games, Robot,* and *Sacco and Vanzetti Case* are as current as can be expected. Consumers may be interested to know that whereas the *Academic American* in print form is revised once a year, the electronic version is updated four times a year.

The encyclopedia's writing style and readability have evoked widespread disagreement among users and critics. The review in *Choice* (March 1981, p. 914), for instance, states that "the prose style in the AAE is commendable. It is well written, concise, and informative without being condescending or obscure." Jovian Lang, in *Reference Sources for Small and Medium-sized Libraries* (1984, p. 25), characterizes the articles as "written in a light, captivating style." On the other hand, a review in *Booklist* (December 1, 1982, p. 517) observes that the "information is presented clearly and briefly, if, on the whole, in an unduly pedestrian fashion. Sometimes, particularly in science and mathematics articles, the effect may prove too dense for some readers." In the same vein, Gary Barber, in *Reference Services Review* (Summer 1982, p. 48), refers to the encyclopedia's "generally undistinguished writing style." The author of *Best Encyclopedias* has found the *Academic American*'s style in most instances to be clear but dry and stilted—a bit too formal or academic (the encyclopedia's title notwithstanding). Consider, for example, the first two paragraphs of the article *Earthquakes*:

> An earthquake is a naturally induced shaking of the ground, caused by the fracture and sliding of rock within the Earth's crust. Of the 6,000 earthquakes detected throughout the world each year, 5,500 are either too small or too far from populated areas to be felt directly. Another 450 are felt but cause no damage, and 35 cause only minor damage. The remaining 15, however, can exact great tolls in death and suffering, besides heavily damaging houses, buildings, and other structures.
>
> The size of an earthquake is determined by the dimensions of the rupturing fracture, or FAULT, and by the total amount of slip, or displacement, that takes place on it. The larger the fault surface and slip, the greater the energy released during the earthquake. In addition to deforming the rock near the fault, this energy produces the shaking that occurs at the time of the earthquake and a variety of seismic waves that radiate throughout the Earth. While small earthquakes involve a few centimeters of slip on faults only tens or hundreds of meters long, a great earthquake may involve meters of slip on a fault hundreds of kilometers long.

Under normal circumstances, the *Academic American* will best serve college and advanced high school students, along with better-educated adults. The encyclopedia will usually be beyond the capabilities of most junior high, or middle school, students. The encyclopedia does not write down to its readers, nor does it always define or explain potentially difficult or unfamiliar terms (such as *seismic waves* and *radiate*). Moreover, the syntax, or sentence structure, is overly complex for young or slow readers.

The contents of the *Academic American* are easily retrievable. A variety of cross-references in the text helps point the user in the right direction. For example, in the excerpt from the article *Earthquakes* quoted above, the word FAULT is printed in SMALL CAPITAL LETTERS, indicating that the encyclopedia has an article entitled *Fault* where related information can be found. In other instances, *See also* references appear at the end of an article, as in the case of *Asbestos,* which includes references to *Mining and Quarrying* and *Silicate Minerals.* But the set's principal finding device is a large, 640-page analytical index of over 200,000 entries. The index is outstanding. In terms of the ratio of index entries to total words in the encyclopedia (9 million), the *Academic American* provides one index entry for every 45 words of text, or a ratio of 1:45. No other general encyclopedia currently offers such a detailed index. Only COLLIER'S ENCYCLOPEDIA, with a ratio of 1:50, comes close.

The illustrations, which make up approximately a third of the total text, add much to the encyclopedia's informational content. Mostly in color, the illustrations include photographs, reproductions of artwork, maps, and innovative cutaway diagrams. The article *Computer,* for instance, has nine illustrations, including a drawing showing how a digital computer works. Also noteworthy are the illustration captions, which furnish much additional—and informative—textual information. The article on Rainer Maria Rilke, for example, includes a portrait with the caption: "Rilke was one of the foremost German poets of his time and one of the most influential of the 20th century. His search for objective lyric expression and mystical vision was manifested in works that convey a sense of sublime tragedy by using subtle and highly refined language complemented by soaring rhythm. Rilke expounded his theories of life and art in *Letters to a Young Poet* (1929)." Another valuable feature of the encyclopedia is its bibliographies, or references for further study. Appended to nearly half of the articles, the bibliographies are carefully selected and reasonably current. The encyclopedia's physical format is both well made and appealing to the eye. Of particular note is the attractive page design, which includes the contemporary "ragged right" (wherein the right-hand margin of each column of type is not justified, or even), a style that not only looks good but improves reading ease by reducing the amount of hyphenation and maintaining even spacing between words.

For the most part, encyclopedia critics have received the *Academic American* enthusiastically. A recent review in *Booklist* (December 15, 1984, p. 566) notes that the encyclopedia "continues to present a broad spectrum of up-to-date information that adults and high school students need—and presents it accurately, objectively and concisely." Wendy Pradt Lougee, reviewing the first printing (1980) in *College and Research Libraries* (January 1982, p. 90), concludes that, "while some users may find the dictionary-like format disconcerting, *AAE* serves superbly as a quick reference tool. *Academic American* is rich in detail and is excitingly attractive, thus reaffirming that less *can* be more." And *Library Journal* (May 15, 1982, p. 959), in naming the set as one of its best reference books for 1981, calls the *Academic American* "a superior, short-article encyclopedia."

To Summarize: The *Academic American,* the newest multivolume general English-language encyclopedia on the market, has many strengths, the most conspicuous being the easy accessibility and relative currentness of its contents, its fine illustrations and bibliographies, and its attractive format. Another plus is the encyclopedia's wide availability in electronic (as opposed to print) form. On the negative side, the *Academic American* 's articles sometimes lack sufficient depth and the writing style tends to be dry. In addition, potentially confusing or unfamiliar terms are not always defined in context.

In Comparison: The *Academic American,* published in 21 volumes containing 9 million words, is a middle-sized encyclopedia for adults and older students. Generally speaking, it compares favorably with other in-print encyclopedias in that category, namely COMPTON'S ENCYCLOPEDIA (26 volumes; 8.5 million words), FUNK & WAGNALLS NEW ENCYCLOPEDIA (29 volumes; 9 million words), MERIT STUDENTS ENCYCLOPEDIA (20 volumes; 9 million words), the NEW CAXTON ENCYCLOPEDIA (20 volumes; 6 million words), the NEW STANDARD ENCYCLOPEDIA (17 volumes; 6.4 million words), and the WORLD BOOK ENCYCLOPEDIA (22 volumes; 10 million words). Without question, the *Academic American* 's chief competitor is the WORLD BOOK, a quality encyclopedia that offers many of the same features as the *Academic American* but is designed to serve a somewhat broader audience (from upper elementary to adult readers). The *Academic American* is sometimes unfairly compared with the three large adult encyclopedias: COLLIER'S ENCYCLOPEDIA (24 volumes; 21 million words), ENCYCLOPEDIA AMERICANA (30 volumes; 31 million words), and the NEW ENCYCLOPAEDIA BRITANNICA (32 volumes; 44 million words). These encyclopedias are in another league from the *Academic American* in terms of size, price, and intended readership.

To Purchase the *Academic American Encyclopedia*: If you are an individual consumer and wish to order the encyclopedia, contact Grolier, Inc., at Sherman Turnpike, Danbury, CT 06816 or telephone toll-free 1-800-243-7256. Your name will be forwarded to a sales representative in your area who will handle the transaction. Note that the encyclopedia is also sold in homes by independent distributors under the title *Lexicon Universal Encyclopedia.* The sales representative will most likely attempt to sell you additional publications along with the encyclopedia, including an annual called the *Encyclopedia Yearbook.* You need not buy any extras unless you want them. In the case of the *Encyclopedia Yearbook,* this so-called updating service has no editorial connection with the encyclopedia and should be avoided unless you are absolutely sure it will be used.

If you are ordering the *Academic American* for a school or library, contact Grolier Educational Corporation at the address or telephone number given above. Your order will be processed immediately.

As already noted, the *Academic American* is also available in electronic (or online) form. The electronic version is prepared by Grolier Electronic Publishing, Inc. (95 Madison Avenue, New York, NY 10016; 212-696-9750). A number of vendors of online database services currently offer the electronic encyclopedia for use in homes, businesses, and libraries. For access and price information, contact these vendors:

- Bibliographic Retrieval Services, Inc. (BRS), 1200 Route 7, Latham, NY 12110; 1-800-833-4747 (outside New York State); in New York State call collect 518-783-7251.

- CompuServe, Inc., 5000 Arlington Centre Boulevard, P.O. Box 20212, Columbus, OH 43220; 1-800-848-8990 (outside Ohio); in Ohio call 614-457-8600.

- Dialog Information Services, Inc., 3460 Hillview Avenue, Palo Alto, CA 94304; 1-800-227-1927 (outside California); in California call 1-800-982-5838.

- Dow Jones News/Retrieval, P.O. Box 300, Princeton, NJ 08540; 1-800-257-5114 (outside New Jersey); in New Jersey call 609-452-2000.

- VU/TEXT Information Services, Inc., 1211 Chestnut Street, Philadelphia, PA 19107; 1-800-258-8080 (outside Pennsylvania); in Pennsylvania call 215-665-3300.

Finally, note that, as of late 1985, Grolier began marketing its compact disc (CD) version of the *Academic American*. The disc, which measures exactly 4.72 inches in diameter, is available at $199 and contains the entire encyclopedia, excluding illustrations. However, costly special computer hardware is required. For further information about the CD encyclopedia, contact Grolier Electronic Publishing, Inc. (see address and telephone above).

For More Information about the *Academic American Encyclopedia* See: *American Reference Books Annual,* 1984, pp. 10–12 (review by G. Edward Evans); *Booklist,* December 15, 1984, pp. 565–66 (unsigned review); *Booklist,* April 15, 1984, pp. 1164–68 (unsigned review of electronic version only); *Booklist,* July 1, 1981, pp. 1402–05 (unsigned review); *Choice,* March 1981, pp. 912–16 (unsigned review); *College and Research Libraries,* January 1982, pp. 87–90 (review by Wendy Pradt Lougee); *Introduction to Reference Work* by William A. Katz (4th ed., New York: McGraw-Hill, 1982), vol. 1: *Basic Information Sources,* pp. 187–89; *Library Journal,* May 15, 1982, p. 959 (unsigned review); *Library Journal,* September 1, 1981, pp. 1618–20 (review by Thomas A. Karel and James E. Bobick);

Library Journal, September 1, 1981, pp. 1600–02 (article by Stephen P. Harter and Kenneth F. Kister entitled "Online Encyclopedias: The Potential"); *New York Times,* May 30, 1980, pp. 1-D (article by N.R. Kleinfield entitled "Encyclopedia with New Twist"); *Popular Science,* June 1983, pp. 138–39 (article by John Free entitled "Computerized Encyclopedias"); *Reference Services Review,* Summer 1982, pp. 43–49 (review by Gary D. Barber); *Reference Sources for Small and Medium-sized Libraries* (4th ed., Chicago: American Library Association, 1984), pp. 25–26 (review by Jovian P. Lang); *RQ,* Winter 1983, pp. 221–22 (review by Toni Risoli of electronic version only); *RQ,* Fall 1981, pp. 87–88 (review by Dennis Thomison); *Time,* June 13, 1983, p. 76 (article by Robert T. Grieves entitled "Short Circuiting Reference Books"); *Wilson Library Bulletin,* February 1982, pp. 459–60 (review by James Rettig); *Wilson Library Bulletin,* March 1981, pp. 436–41 (article by Kenneth Kister entitled "The Making of the *Academic American Encyclopedia*").

American Educator

FACTS

American Educator: A Comprehensive Encyclopedia to Meet the Needs of Home, School, and Library. Donald E. Lawson, Editor in Chief. Lake Bluff, IL: United Educators, Inc. 20 volumes. Former titles: *Hill's Practical Encyclopedia* (1901); *Hill's Practical Reference Library of General Knowledge* (1902–06); *New Practical Reference Library* (1907–18). First published as the *American Educator* in 1919; out of print since 1977 (last priced at approximately $250).

The *American Educator,* which ceased publication in 1977, intends to be "a source of essential knowledge ... carefully designed to serve every member of the family, with particular attention to the needs of elementary and high school students" (foreword). When last published, the 20-volume encyclopedia contained 7,750 pages, 13,000 articles, and roughly 5 million words. The articles, most of which are quite brief, average just under 400 words in length (or less than half a page). They are accompanied by 12,000 illustrations (15 percent in color), plus 693 maps. Most of the articles are unsigned. The encyclopedia is arranged alphabetically letter by letter (*Newspaper* precedes *New York*), with access to specific information enhanced by 16,000 cross-references. The set has no index.

EVALUATION

The *American Educator* (1919–77) traces its origins to the six-volume *New Practical Reference Library* (1907–18), which in turn derived from the four-volume *Hill's Practical Reference Library of General Knowledge* (1902–06) and *Hill's Practical Encyclopedia* (1901). Soon after United Educators, Inc. acquired the *American Educator* in 1931, it was expanded to ten volumes. Later, in 1957, the editors added four more volumes, and in 1972, after its last major revision, the set reached its final size of 20 volumes. Throughout its history, the *American Educator* has never been considered a first-class encyclopedia, despite its boast of having more Nobel Prize winners as contributors "than any other encyclopedia in the world." By the time it went out of print in the late 1970s, the encyclopedia was totally outclassed by the competition.

The *American Educator* suffers from a number of conspicuous weaknesses. Specifically, subject coverage is often superficial or incomplete, particularly in the social and behavioral sciences. The encyclopedia is not always factually accurate, nor are controversial issues always treated adequately. For instance, the subject of abortion is never mentioned. Even during the years it was published and revised on an annual basis, the encyclopedia was often out of date, the result of a lax and inconsistent approach to continuous revision. Today, many of the articles read like relics from another era, and naturally such contemporary topics as acquired immune deficiency syndrome (AIDS), breakdancing, and health maintenance organizations (HMOs) are not covered. Access to the encyclopedia's contents is hampered by erratic cross-references and, most of all, by the lack of any sort of index. The predominately black-and-white illustrations, which account for about 35 percent of the total text, range from mediocre to poor. Likewise, the physical format is drab and uninviting. On the plus side, the writing style is clear and economical; normally, the encyclopedia will be suitable for adults and students who read at the junior and senior high school levels.

To Summarize: The now defunct *American Educator* was summed up before its demise in this way: "It is distinguished in neither its illustrative matter nor its style of presentation, especially when compared to the leading young people's encyclopedias of similar price range and scope" (*American Reference Books Annual,* 1973, p. 104). Today, the *American Educator* is a poor excuse for an encyclopedia. Occasionally a set will appear on the secondhand book market. Prospective purchasers should beware.

In Comparison: The *American Educator*'s principal competition came from general encyclopedias aimed at the family and older students, such as COMPTON'S ENCYCLOPEDIA, MERIT STUDENTS ENCYCLOPEDIA, the NEW STANDARD ENCYCLOPEDIA, and the WORLD BOOK ENCYCLOPEDIA. All of these encyclopedias were superior to the *American Educator* when it lived and, of course, still are.

For More Information about the *American Educator* See: *American Reference Books Annual,* 1973, pp. 103–04 (review by Christine L. Wynar); *Booklist,* December 15, 1965, pp. 369–76 (unsigned review).

American Peoples Encyclopedia

FACTS

The American Peoples Encyclopedia: A Modern Reference Work. Also published as the *University Society Encyclopedia.* Wallace S. Murray, Editorial Director; Edward Humphrey, Supervisory Editor. New York: Excelsior Trading Corp., a subsidiary of Grolier, Inc. 20 volumes. First published in 1948; out of print since 1976 (last priced at $325.50).

The *American Peoples Encyclopedia,* which ceased publication in 1976, is said to be a "compendium of information designed to be helpful to the present-day nonspecialist" (introduction). When last published, the 20-volume encyclopedia for adults and older students contained 11,125 pages, 35,500 articles, and 10 million words. The articles, most of which are of the specific-entry variety, average 300 words in length (or a third of a page). They are accompanied by 13,200 illustrations (10 percent in color), plus 1,142 maps. Roughly 1,700 contributors are noted in Volume 1. Most articles, however, are not signed. The encyclopedia is arranged alphabetically letter by letter (*Newspaper* precedes *New York*), with access to specific information enhanced by 72,000 cross-references and an index of some 126,000 entries.

EVALUATION

Based loosely on material derived from the old *Nelson's Encyclopedia* (1905–40), *American Peoples* first appeared in 1948 under the imprint of Spencer Press of Chicago. Until 1958, the encyclopedia was sold solely by Sears, Roebuck through the company's stores and its mail-order catalog division. In 1961, Grolier, Inc., one of the major U.S. encyclopedia publishers, acquired the rights to *American Peoples,* revitalizing the set under the direction of Lowell Martin, a well-known librarian and experienced encyclopedia editor. But over the years, the encyclopedia was allowed to deteriorate and by the mid-1970s it went out of print. Toward the end, *American Peoples* was also distributed under the title *University Society Encyclopedia* by the University Society, Inc. of Midland Park, New Jersey.

American Peoples has never been considered a top-notch encyclopedia, but neither is it a disgracefully bad work. Among its strengths are concise, accurate articles on people and places (which account for the majority of entries) and reasonably good access to the set's contents. In the latter instance, ample cross-references are complemented by a detailed index that provides one entry for every 80 words of text, or a quite respectable ratio of 1:80. On the other hand, the encyclopedia has a number of readily discernible faults, including dull illustrations, sparse bibliographies, a bland writing style, and superficial coverage of many topics. In addition, even when it was being published and revised each year, *American Peoples* was not always up-to-date. As noted in a review in *Booklist* (July 15, 1974, p. 1208), "The encyclopedia may be satisfactory for coverage of historical topics and those where new interpretations have not been made, but it unevenly meets the needs of users for current up-to-date coverage of names, events, and statistics. Revision in page layout has been extremely scanty for the last eight years." Today, after being defunct for ten years, *American Peoples* is badly dated, lacking recent material on such subjects as abortion, the Canadian Constitution, capital punishment, computers, the Falkland Islands, Nicaragua, robots, and the Vietnam War, to say nothing of 1980s concerns like acquired immune deficiency syndrome (AIDS) and health maintenance organizations (HMOs).

To Summarize: Out of print now for a decade, *American Peoples* (1948–76) is an undistinguished encyclopedia for adults and older students. Secondhand sets of the encyclopedia surface now and then at garage sales or stores that carry old books. In almost all instances, prospective purchasers would be wise to consider another encyclopedia, new or used.

In Comparison: As a middle-sized, modestly priced, multivolume encyclopedia for the family, *American Peoples* competed directly with such sets as COMPTON'S ENCYCLOPEDIA, FUNK & WAGNALLS NEW ENCY-

CLOPEDIA, MERIT STUDENTS ENCYCLOPEDIA, the NEW STANDARD ENCY-
CLOPEDIA, and the WORLD BOOK ENCYCLOPEDIA. When compared
head-to-head with any of these encyclopedias, *American Peoples* almost always came out second best.

For More Information about the *American Peoples Encyclopedia*
See: *American Reference Books Annual,* 1973, pp. 104–05 (review by
Bohdan S. Wynar); *Booklist,* July 15, 1974, pp. 1206–08 (unsigned
review); *Library Journal,* February 15, 1966, pp. 1080–81 (review by
James W. Stanford).

Britannica Junior Encyclopaedia

FACTS

Britannica Junior Encyclopaedia for Boys and Girls. Marvin Martin,
Editor. Chicago: Encyclopaedia Britannica, Inc. 15 volumes. Former
title: *Weedon's Modern Encyclopedia* (1931–32). First published as
Britannica Junior: An Encyclopaedia for Boys and Girls in 1934; out
of print since 1984 (last priced at $279).

The *Britannica Junior Encyclopaedia,* which has recently been
discontinued by the publisher, aims "to provide a simple, accurate,
and easy-to-use reference work for the elementary school student"
(preface). Despite its name, *Britannica Junior* is not an abridged or
juvenile version of the old *Encyclopaedia Britannica* (1768–1973) or
its successor, the NEW ENCYCLOPAEDIA BRITANNICA. When last issued
in 1984, the 15-volume *Britannica Junior* contained 8,000 pages,
4,200 main articles, and approximately 5.4 million words. The articles, which are of the broad-entry type, average 1,300 words in length
(or two full pages). They are accompanied by 11,800 illustrations
(about 40 percent in color), plus 1,066 maps, including those in a
separate atlas section in the final volume. Some 800 editors and
contributors are noted at the front of Volume 1, but none of the
articles is signed. The encyclopedia is arranged alphabetically letter by
letter (*Newspaper* precedes *New York*), with access to specific information enhanced by 5,800 cross-references in the text and an
analytical index of 57,000 entries. Unlike most encyclopedia indexes,
Britannica Junior 's is placed at the beginning of the set in Volume 1
rather than at the end in the final volume. Another unusual feature of
the index—appropriately called the Ready Reference Index—is its

inclusion of some 25,000 brief factual entries covering topics (mostly of a biographical and geographical nature) not found in the main articles.

EVALUATION

The encyclopedia first appeared in 1931–32 as an eight-volume set entitled *Weedon's Modern Encyclopedia* published by the S.L. Weedon Company of Cleveland. Encyclopaedia Britannica, Inc. then obtained the rights to the set, which reappeared in 1934 in 12 volumes as *Britannica Junior: An Encyclopaedia for Boys and Girls.* In 1947, the set was expanded to its present 15 volumes. *Britannica Junior* was also published in an inexpensive 25-volume supermarket binding during the 1970s, but this edition has long since disappeared from the market. Over the years, *Britannica Junior* has achieved a reputation as one of the better multivolume encyclopedias for children. Recently, however, the set began to look shopworn and to fall behind the pace of changing knowledge. Thus, in 1984, it was, in the words of a Britannica editor, "temporarily discontinued" with no indication of when, if ever, it would be published again. (Actually, the last revised printing occurred in 1982; the 1984 printing was without revision of any kind.)

On balance, *Britannica Junior* adequately meets the needs of young people in the upper elementary and junior high school grades. Coverage reflects the elementary school curriculum in the United States and Canada, although out-of-school interests, such as hobbies and games, are also included. The encyclopedia is conscientiously edited, and as might be expected, its information is normally trustworthy. The aforementioned Ready Reference Index, which is simply constructed and easy to use, furnishes good access to the encyclopedia's contents. In fact, *Britannica Junior*'s index compares quite favorably with the NEW BOOK OF KNOWLEDGE's Dictionary Index and COMPTON'S ENCYCLOPEDIA's Fact-Index, both of which are similar in purpose to the Ready Reference Index. Other commendable features found in *Britannica Junior* include fine maps, particularly those by Hammond in the atlas section in Volume 15, and the encyclopedia's large readable type.

But *Britannica Junior* also has a number of glaring weaknesses. Most obvious perhaps is the set's lack of up-to-dateness, which not only shows in articles on such topics as computers, Nicaragua, and the Olympic Games, but in the illustrations that accompany them. As pointed out in *American Reference Books Annual* (1982, p. 26), "Detracting from the internal attractiveness of the encyclopedia are old-fashioned pictures, small in detail and garish in color." In addition, this same review notes that the illustrations "are also decidedly sexist, with men pictured more than women, and women pictured mostly in homemaker or similar roles." Sensitive issues such as abortion and homosexuality—topics of concern to young people—are often ignored completely or relegated to superficial entries in the Ready Reference Index. The encyclopedia's writing style, although usually clear, is sometimes well beyond the reading capabilities of elementary and junior high school students. Moreover, the style tends to be dull. "While the text is generally readable and suitable for the intended audience," observes a reviewer in *Booklist* (May 15, 1983, p. 1234), "the set's style is not very interesting and 'liveliness' cannot be called a hallmark of *BJ*." Jovian Lang, in *Reference Sources for Small and Medium-sized Libraries* (1984, p. 26), also comments on the set's "unexciting style." Like its writing style, the encyclopedia's format and design are flat and uninspiring, lacking the visual appeal a children's encyclopedia should have.

To Summarize: *Britannica Junior,* a well-known multivolume encyclopedia for young people first published in 1934, has been discontinued, at least for the time being, as of 1984. Although still a creditable work in many respects, *Britannica Junior* has a faded, shopworn air about it. The publisher indicates that remaining sets of the encyclopedia on hand will not be sold, but may be used in "special promotions" and the like. Secondhand sets published within the last ten years and priced under $100 would be a good buy for someone in the market for a children's encyclopedia (especially when considering that such an encyclopedia will most likely be outgrown in a few years).

In Comparison: When it was being published, *Britannica Junior* competed head-to-head with the NEW BOOK OF KNOWLEDGE and the YOUNG STUDENTS ENCYCLOPEDIA, all substantial multivolume sets aimed directly at the elementary and junior high school student. Of the three, the NEW BOOK OF KNOWLEDGE is the most impressive, albeit the most expensive. Also competitive in this age group are the larger COMPTON'S ENCYCLOPEDIA, MERIT STUDENTS ENCYCLOPEDIA, and the WORLD BOOK ENCYCLOPEDIA. These sets, however, are more appropriate for a somewhat older readership.

For More Information about the *Britannica Junior Encyclopaedia* See: *American Reference Books Annual,* 1982, pp. 26–27 (review by Barbara Sproat); *Booklist,* May 15, 1983, pp. 1233–35 (unsigned review); *Introduction to Reference Work* by William A. Katz (4th ed., New York: McGraw-Hill, 1982), vol. 1: *Basic Information Sources,* pp. 191–92; *Reference Sources for Small and Medium-sized Libraries* (4th ed., Chicago: American Library Association, 1984), p. 26.

Cadillac Modern Encyclopedia

FACTS

The Cadillac Modern Encyclopedia: The World of Knowledge in One Volume. Max S. Shapiro, Executive Editor. New York: Cadillac Publishing Company, Inc. One volume. Electronic version: KUSSMAUL ENCYCLOPEDIA. First edition published in 1973; out of print since 1980 (last priced at $24.95).

The *Cadillac Modern Encyclopedia,* published in 1973 and now out of print, is designed to serve adults and older students and covers "those subjects most often included in American school curricula at all levels, from junior high school through college" (preface). The single-volume encyclopedia contains 1,954 pages, 18,000 articles, and approximately 2.5 million words. The articles, most of which are quite brief, average 150 words in length (or about nine articles per page). They are accompanied by 1,110 illustrations (almost all in black-and-white), plus 300 maps. Nearly 100 editors and contributors are identified at the front of the volume, but none of the articles is signed. The encyclopedia is arranged alphabetically letter by letter (*Newspaper* precedes *New York*), with access to specific information enhanced by 50,000 cross-references in the text. There is no index. In the early 1980s, General Videotex Corporation of Cambridge, Massachusetts, acquired the rights to the encyclopedia and created an electronic version called the KUSSMAUL ENCYCLOPEDIA .

EVALUATION

Although published only once (in 1973) and never revised, *Cadillac Modern* remains a fairly useful source of information about people, places, events, and concepts up to the early 1970s. The work is especially strong in the physical and biological sciences. The editor and moving force behind *Cadillac Modern,* the late Max Shapiro, who died in 1981, was also the author of the highly successful *Mathematics Made Simple,* published by Doubleday in 1943 and still in print. In 1977, Doubleday published the mathematics articles in *Cadillac Modern* under the title *Mathematics Encyclopedia.* In addition to its strong scientific coverage, the encyclopedia includes nearly 4,000 biographies, numerous book and opera plot summaries, and a 300-page Special Reference Section that consists of 232 tables, charts, and documents on such diverse subjects as first aid, Supreme Court cases, inventions, chemical elements, spelling rules, and foreign currencies. The encyclopedia is reasonably accurate and objective, and its contents are usually accessible.

On the negative side, *Cadillac Modern* is obviously no longer current, as such topics as abortion, acquired immune deficiency syndrome (AIDS), Canada, capital punishment, computers, Nicaragua, and the Vietnam War readily attest. Furthermore, treatment of many topics is superficial, even by one-volume encyclopedia standards. The article on abortion, for example, is limited to ten lines. And the illustrations, including the maps, are unexceptional.

To Summarize: The one-volume *Cadillac Modern,* now more than a decade old, has been out of print for a number of years. Its contents are severely dated, but for material prior to the early 1970s it remains a viable reference work. An updated version of *Cadillac Modern* is the KUSSMAUL ENCYCLOPEDIA, available only in electronic form via home or business computer.

In Comparison: In its day, *Cadillac Modern* was one of the top small-volume general encyclopedias for adults and older students, competing strongly with such leading titles as the LINCOLN LIBRARY OF ESSENTIAL INFORMATION, the NEW COLUMBIA ENCYCLOPEDIA, the RANDOM HOUSE ENCYCLOPEDIA, and the VOLUME LIBRARY. Today, however, all of these works, along with newcomer CONCISE COLUMBIA ENCYCLOPEDIA, are preferable to *Cadillac Modern.*

For More Information about the *Cadillac Modern Encyclopedia* See: *American Reference Books Annual,* 1975, pp. 31–32 (unsigned review); *Booklist,* January 1, 1979, pp. 767–68 (unsigned review); *Booklist,* February 15, 1975, pp. 623–24 (unsigned review); *Choice,* April 1975, p. 195 (unsigned review); *Library Journal,* March 1, 1974, pp. 642–43 (review by Annette Hirsch).

Chambers's Encyclopaedia

FACTS

Chambers's Encyclopaedia. M.D. Law and M. Vibart Dixon, Managing Editors. London, England: International Learning Systems Corporation Ltd. 15 volumes. Fourth revised edition with corrections published in 1973; out of print since 1979 (last priced at $325.50).

Chambers's Encyclopaedia, last published in 1973 and now discontinued, is "primarily a British production and therefore no doubt reflects to some extent the intellectual atmosphere of post-war Britain" (preface). Intended for (again in the words of the preface) "the educated layman," the 15-volume encyclopedia contains 12,600 pages, 28,000 articles, and 14.5 million words. The articles, some of which are quite long, average slightly more than 500 words in length (or half a page). They are accompanied by 4,500 illustrations (most in black-and-white), plus 416 maps. Some 3,000 contributors are noted in the final volume. All but the briefest articles are signed. The encyclopedia is arranged alphabetically letter by letter (*Newspaper* precedes *New York*), with access to specific information enhanced by approximately 10,000 cross-references in the text and an index of 225,000 entries.

EVALUATION

Chambers's originated in the nineteenth century when the firm of W. & R. Chambers of Edinburgh, Scotland, issued the encyclopedia in 520 weekly parts between 1859 and 1868. The parts were eventually cumulated into a ten-volume set. Between then and the onset of World War II, the encyclopedia established a secure reputation as a work of quality. Revised editions appeared periodically, including one reprinted in the United States under the title *Library of Universal Knowledge* (1880–81). In point of fact, after the *Encyclopaedia Britannica* (now NEW ENCYCLOPAEDIA BRITANNICA) became American-owned and -produced at the turn of the century, *Chambers's* assumed the position of the largest and most distinguished general multivolume encyclopedia published in the United Kingdom. In 1944, the firm of George Newnes Ltd. acquired the rights to the set and, in 1950, issued a radically revised edition in 15 volumes: "The second world war eventually made imperative a completely new work—new in plan, in method of treatment, in content and even in outward appearance" (preface). Further revised editions appeared in 1955, 1959, and 1966. The 1966 (fourth) revised edition was reprinted with corrections in 1973, marking the last time the encyclopedia was published. A fifth edition has been contemplated, but the cost to do the job right—it has been more than 20 years since the set was last updated—is estimated at between $6 and $10 million, a prohibitive figure for the publisher under present conditions.

Despite its age and out-of-print status, *Chambers's* is still a formidable encyclopedia. Traditionally, the set has been known for its accurate, objective articles and authoritative tone. Or as *Choice* (October 1967, p. 793) put it, *Chambers's* is "stolid, serious, and scholarly." It is especially valuable for historical background on British topics. A review in *Booklist* (February 1, 1979, p. 883), for instance, notes that "the caliber of *Chambers's* is predictably best in those areas associated with the British heritage. The British Civil War (rebellion of the parliamentarians against Charles I) is better described than the U.S. Civil War. Heraldry receives four times the space devoted to economics." Another useful feature of *Chambers's* is its atlas section. Found in Volume 15, the atlas contains 114 maps by the highly regarded cartographic firm of John Bartholomew & Sons Ltd. of Edinburgh, along with a gazetteer-index.

The encyclopedia's greatest limitation, of course, is its lack of up-to-dateness. Such topics as abortion, acquired immune deficiency syndrome (AIDS), apartheid, capital punishment, computers, the Falkland Islands, Nicaragua, robots, Switzerland, and the Vietnam War are either not current or not covered. The maps, including those in the aforementioned atlas, are also considerably dated. It should be stressed that, unlike practically all North American general multivolume encyclopedias, *Chambers's* was never revised continuously on an annual basis but, rather, kept current by new revised editions issued every five or so years. Because the last of these revisions occurred in 1966, *Chambers's* is now drastically dated. Other conspicuous limitations include a dull format, unsatisfactory illustrations (they are too few in number and those that are included tend to be too small and too dark), a writing style that is too academic or learned for most North American readers (with the exception of college-educated adults), and skimpy, incomplete bibliographies.

To Summarize: Last published in 1973 and out of print since 1979, *Chambers's,* once the premier British general encyclopedia, remains useful as a source of historical information, particularly about people, places, and events in the United Kingdom. But much of the text is so dated that only a thorough revision of the encyclopedia's total contents can restore the set to its former eminence. At this time, such a revision appears unlikely.

In Comparison: *Chambers's* replaced the *Encyclopaedia Britannica* (now NEW ENCYCLOPAEDIA BRITANNICA) as the leading British-made general encyclopedia when *Britannica* passed into American hands in the early 1900s. Today, however, the top British sets are EVERYMAN'S ENCYCLOPAEDIA and the NEW CAXTON ENCYCLOPEDIA, both smaller, more up-to-date, and more popularly constructed encyclopedias than *Chambers's.*

For More Information about *Chambers's Encyclopaedia* See: *Booklist,* February 1, 1979, pp. 882–83 (unsigned review); *Choice,* October 1967, pp. 793–95 (unsigned review); *Library Journal,* April 15, 1967, pp. 1601–02 (review by Allan Angoff).

Charlie Brown's 'Cyclopedia

FACTS

Charlie Brown's 'Cyclopedia: Super Questions and Answers and Amazing Facts. New York: Random House, Inc.; Toronto: Random House of Canada Ltd. Copyright by United Features Syndicate, Inc. Distributed by Funk & Wagnalls, Inc. 15 volumes. First edition published in 1980–81. Lowest retail price: $38.35.

The 15-volume *Charlie Brown's 'Cyclopedia* is intended, according to an advertisement for the set, to make "looking things up a lot of fun." Aimed at beginning readers and children in the primary grades, the encyclopedia contains 720 pages, some 1,000 articles, and approximately 180,000 words. The articles, which consist of questions and answers, are usually brief, averaging 180 words in length (or half a page or more). They are accompanied by 900 illustrations (all in color) that feature characters from Charles Schulz's "Peanuts" comic strip. No editors or contributors are listed, nor are the articles signed. The set is arranged topically, each volume dealing with a broad subject: *Your Body* (Volume 1); *All Kinds of Animals from Fish to Frogs* (Volume 2); *All Kinds of Animals from Dinosaurs to Elephants* (Volume 3); *Cars and Trains and Other Things that Move* (Volume 4); *Boats and Other Things that Float* (Volume 5); *Planes and Other Things that Fly* (Volume 6); *Space Travel* (Volume 7); *Stars and Planets* (Volume 8); *The Earth, Weather and Climate* (Volume 9); *People Around the World* (Volume 10); *What We Wear* (Volume 11); *Holidays* (Volume 12); *Machines and How They Work* (Volume 13); *Sound, Light and Air* (Volume 14); and *Electricity and Magnetism* (Volume 15). Access to specific information is enhanced by an index of 1,500 entries. There are no cross-references in the text.

EVALUATION

Charlie Brown's 'Cyclopedia, published a volume at a time between 1980 and 1981 strictly for the supermarket trade, is based on a series of five books entitled *Charlie Brown's Super Book of Questions and Answers, Charlie Brown's Second Super Book of Questions and Answers,* etc. (Random House, 1976–81). Like other encyclopedic works designed for very young readers (such as CHILDCRAFT, COMPTON'S PRECYCLOPEDIA, and the TALKING CASSETTE ENCYCLOPEDIA), the

'Cyclopedia attempts to stimulate the child's innate curiosity about the world and its wonders. Unlike its competitors, however, the *'Cyclopedia* is heavily oriented toward science, as the titles of the volumes listed above indicate. The subject of earthquakes, for instance, receives two full pages of coverage ("What is an earthquake?" "Can an earthquake change the surface of the earth?" "How can you protect yourself from earthquakes?"), whereas countries (such as Argentina and Nicaragua), people (Paul Revere and Harry Truman), and sports and games (baseball and football) are not covered at all.

Information in the *'Cyclopedia* is usually accurate and objective, albeit quite simplistic. A short item on computers ("Which is smarter—a computer or the human brain?"), for example, informs the reader that "the human brain is smarter, but a computer works faster. Computers can do only what people tell them—or 'program' them—to do. They cannot think of anything new, while the human brain is always coming up with new ideas. However, a computer is very fast. It can, for example, solve in a few minutes a mathematical problem that might take a person many, many years to figure out." Information in the set is current as of the late 1970s, as in the case of "What is Martin Luther King, Jr., Day?" (in *Holidays*), which notes that "many states honor the memory of Martin Luther King, Jr., on January 15, his birthday," but fails to mention that King's birthday is now also a federal holiday.

The writing style, befitting the intended audience, is both elementary and vivid. For instance, in answer to the question "Can an earthquake change the surface of the earth," the *'Cyclopedia* states:

> Yes. A big earthquake can break off part of a mountain, which then tumbles down onto the land below it. An earthquake can tear open the ground. It can shove huge blocks of land around. Any of these things can happen in just a few minutes.
>
> Big earthquakes cause a lot of damage. Buildings fall down. Gas pipes burst and start fires. Whole cities sometimes start burning. Water pipes break, so there is no water to put out the fires. Many people are killed by the falling buildings or the fire. Luckily, most earthquakes are small. They do very little damage.

In addition, potentially new or difficult terms are often defined and pronounced in context. For example, the discussion following the material on earthquakes which asks, "How were the mountains made?" defines the word *sediment* and gives its pronunciation in parentheses (SED-uh-mint).

Information on specific topics like earthquakes and computers is easily located in the *'Cyclopedia* via the index in the final volume. There is, however, one glaring problem with the index. The encyclopedia is consecutively paged from Volume 1 (pages 1–48) through Volume 15 (pages 673–720), and although the index gives page numbers, it does not include volume numbers. Hence, the index entry "earthquake, 390–91," for example, leads the user to the right pages, but in which volume are pages 390–91? The illustrations, which consist of photographs and drawings, are dominated by Schulz's familiar comic strip characters. They add interest and visual appeal to the set.

To Summarize: *Charlie Brown's 'Cyclopedia* is a colorful, inexpensive set for preschoolers and primary school students. Published on a volume-a-month basis in 1980–81, the *'Cyclopedia* emphasizes scientific information and features characters from the "Peanuts" comic strip.

In Comparison: The *'Cyclopedia,* published in 15 volumes containing 180,000 words, is most similar in concept and format to DISNEY'S WONDERFUL WORLD OF KNOWLEDGE (20 volumes; 750,000 words), published by Grolier, Inc. in 1973. Topically arranged and utilizing Disney characters much as the *'Cyclopedia* makes use of the "Peanuts" gang, DISNEY'S WONDERFUL WORLD OF KNOWLEDGE is a mediocre set no longer heavily promoted by the publisher. The *'Cyclopedia* also competes with two other multivolume encyclopedic sets for beginning readers: CHILDCRAFT (15 volumes; 750,000 words) and COMPTON'S PRECYCLOPEDIA (16 volumes; 325,000 words), also published as the YOUNG CHILDREN'S ENCYCLOPEDIA. Both CHILD-CRAFT and COMPTON'S PRECYCLOPEDIA, like DISNEY'S WONDERFUL WORLD OF KNOWLEDGE, are much larger and more expensive than the *'Cyclopedia.* On balance, CHILDCRAFT is the best of these works. One other set, the NEW TALKING CASSETTE ENCYCLOPEDIA (10 volumes; 100,000 words), is also aimed at the beginning reader. A unique work in that it is published on cassette tape rather than in print form, the NEW TALKING CASSETTE ENCYCLOPEDIA is limited almost solely to classroom use, because of its high price ($695) and unusual format.

To Purchase *Charlie Brown's 'Cyclopedia*: The *'Cyclopedia* is sold only in supermarkets in North America. According to the distributor, Funk & Wagnalls, Inc., the set is unavailable except in those supermarkets currently selling it a volume at a time.

No other reviews of *Charlie Brown's 'Cyclopedia* are available at this time.

Childcraft

FACTS

Childcraft: The How and Why Library. William H. Nault, Editorial Director; Robert O. Zeleny, Executive Editor. Chicago: World Book, Inc. 15 volumes. First edition published in 1934; revised periodically, most recently in 1985. Lowest retail price: $199.00 plus $14.50 shipping and handling; with discount to schools and libraries: $170.00 delivered.

Childcraft is "a 15-volume resource library designed especially for preschool and primary-grade children and for the older child who needs high-interest, easy-to-read materials" (preface). The set contains approximately 5,000 pages, 3,000 articles (including many literary selections), and 750,000 words. The articles, some of which are quite long for a work aimed at beginning readers, average 250 words in length (or nearly two pages). They are accompanied by 4,500 illustrations (over 50 percent in color). There are no maps. Most of the material is staff-written and unsigned, although all the literary selections (poems, stories, and the like) are signed. The set is arranged topically, each volume dealing with a broad subject or theme: *Once Upon a Time* (Volume 1), a collection of nursery rhymes, poems, stories, etc., intended for reading aloud to preschoolers; *Time to Read* (Volume 2), a collection of literary works geared chiefly for children in the primary grades; *Stories and Poems* (Volume 3), a collection for young readers ages eight and up; *World and Space* (Volume 4); *About Animals* (Volume 5); *The Green Kingdom* (Volume 6), which covers the plant world; *How Things Work* (Volume 7); *About Us* (Volume 8), an introduction to the children of the world; *Holidays and Birthdays* (Volume 9); *Places to Know* (Volume 10); *Make and Do* (Volume 11), which covers practical arts and crafts for young people; *Look and Learn* (Volume 12), which introduces the visual world; *Mathemagic* (Volume 13); *About Me* (Volume 14), an exploration of the child as a physical and social being; and *Guide for Parents* (Volume 15), which includes articles on child development and an A-to-Z medical guide written for adults. Access to specific information is enhanced by an index of 20,000 entries in Volume 15. In addition, Volumes 1–3 have their own author and titles indexes, and Volumes 4–14 include individual subject indexes. There are no cross-references in the text.

EVALUATION

Childcraft, which first appeared in 1934 in seven volumes, recently celebrated its fiftieth birthday. In the beginning, the set was more about children than for them, but as it grew and evolved over the years, *Childcraft* became almost exclusively a collection of self-discovery materials for the young reader, Volume 15 (*Guide for Parents*) being the obvious exception. In 1964, *Childcraft* absorbed the six-volume *How and Why Library* (1912–59), at which time the set's full title became *Childcraft: The How and Why Library.* Over the past 50 or so years, *Childcraft* has received universal recognition as an outstanding reference and enrichment source for children from the ages of four to ten. The set, including an annual supplement entitled *Childcraft Annual,* is produced by a full-time staff of well-qualified editors and artists, some of whom also work on the WORLD BOOK ENCYCLOPEDIA, the publisher's excellent school and family encyclopedia. Evidence of the overwhelming acceptance of *Childcraft* can be seen in the number of foreign-language editions of the set. Specifically, *Childcraft* has been published in nine other languages over the years, beginning in 1949 in Portuguese (*O Mundo da Criança*) and then in Spanish (*El Mundo de los Niños*), Swedish (*Barnens Basta*), Italian (*I Quindici*), German (*Kinderzeit*), and French (*Je veux savoir*). There have also been Hebrew, Japanese, and Korean versions.

Childcraft manages to cover many areas of interest and concern to preschoolers and beginning readers, as the volume titles noted above plainly show. Moreover, the supplement, *Childcraft Annual,* treats a new topic each year. Recent annuals have been devoted to birds, dogs, Indians, words, and the sea. But users and prospective purchasers of *Childcraft* should bear in mind that the set is not an encyclopedia in the traditional sense, nor does it claim to provide encyclopedic coverage of people, places, events, etc. For instance, the set has nothing on such important figures as Harry Truman and Louis Pasteur or places like Nicaragua and Tokyo. It does offer, however, much material designed to stir children's curiosity and imagination about the world and their place in it, along with an impressive amount of basic factual information.

Childcraft's contents are accurate, unbiased, easily accessible, and reasonably current. An elementary article on computers in Volume 7 (*How Things Work*), for example, is as timely as can be expected. A conspicuous strength of the set is its fine illustrations. They make up roughly 60 percent of the total text and are nicely varied, informative, and almost always well reproduced. Happily, *Childcraft* is printed on high-quality offset paper manufactured specially to obtain the best color reproduction possible. Lillian Biermann Wehmeyer, in a review in *American Reference Books Annual* (1980, p. 28), has this to say about the set's illustrations: "Perhaps the set's most striking feature is the graphics—colorful, well-designed pages presenting a wide range of media and styles, including work of Caldecott winners [an award given annually by the American Library Association for the best children's picture book] and widely recognized photographers. Nearly every page is illustrated, and one should not overlook the effective use of white space, yielding uncluttered pages that direct the eye to visuals or text." Likewise, the page layout is extraordinarily appealing, designed to capture the reader's attention immediately and hold it.

The writing style conveys the same creative spirit. The first of two articles on earthquakes in Volume 4 (*World and Space*), for instance, begins this way:

> "The mountains seemed to walk!"
>
> That is what a Chinese writer said about a terrible earthquake he saw. During the worst earthquakes, the ground shivers and shakes and rumbles. Whole sections of land get pushed out of place, so that mountains truly seem to "walk."
>
> Earthquakes begin in the earth's rocky crust. Pressure builds up and begins to push. The force of this push actually bends the rocks, just as you bend a stick. And, suddenly, the rocks snap and break, just as the stick would snap if you kept bending it. This sends shivers through the ground making it quiver and quake.

As previously mentioned, *Childcraft* is appropriate for children ages four to ten. Somewhat older youngsters with reading problems might also find it useful.

Childcraft is not without some faults. Foremost among these is the set's pervasive middle-class orientation. Slums, litter, bullies, child abuse, evil—all are unknown in the bright, neat world of *Childcraft,* where the faces of the children are predominately white and almost always smiling. A reviewer in *Booklist* (June 15, 1975, p. 1083) makes the same criticism: "Various ethnic groups are included, though not widely. The reader is not aware of various economic groups, for the total impression is of clean, shining, well-dressed children." Another major problem—shared by *Childcraft*'s competitors, namely CHARLIE BROWN'S 'CYCLOPEDIA, COMPTON'S PRECYCLOPEDIA, DISNEY'S WONDERFUL WORLD OF KNOWLEDGE, and the TALKING CASSETTE ENCYCLOPEDIA —is that the set is quickly outgrown. As young readers mature, they will find *Childcraft* increasingly babyish. Prospective purchasers of the set, particularly those considering it for use in the home, should be aware of this natural limitation.

The most recent reviews of *Childcraft* have, on the whole, been quite favorable. William A. Katz, in his *Introduction to Reference Work* (1982, vol. 1, p. 192), writes, "The set includes stories and factual material about practically everything of interest to a young child, from animals and art to the body. With excellent illustrations and well-thought-out texts, the volumes are useful for preschool and early grades." Lillian Biermann Wehmeyer, in her review in *American Reference Books Annual* (1980, p. 28), concludes that "Overall, *Childcraft* is best seen as a motivator, designed to evoke a sense of wonder, rather than as an information source. Still, because it is generally readable and accurate, the set is a good starting place for primary-grade readers." And *Booklist* (June 15, 1975, p. 1083) recommends the work "for home purchase and for school and public libraries serving young children."

To **Summarize:** Not strictly an encyclopedia, *Childcraft* is a 15-volume "resource library" for young children first published in 1934 and frequently revised since that time. The set includes informational articles, as well as numerous literary selections, such as stories, poems, nursery rhymes, and folktales. The illustrations, which account for well over half the total text, are first-rate, and the writing style is captivating. On the negative side, the set overemphasizes middle-class atitudes and values, and it is quickly outgrown. In the final analysis, *Childcraft* is highly recommended for public, school, day-care, and kindergarten libraries, as well as those families with young children that can readily afford it.

In **Comparison:** *Childcraft,* published in 15 volumes containing 750,000 words, is unquestionably the best encyclopedic set available for children ages four to ten. The set's chief rival is COMPTON'S PRECYCLOPEDIA (16 volumes; 325,000 words), also published as the YOUNG CHILDREN'S ENCYCLOPEDIA. Arranged alphabetically (whereas *Childcraft* is topical), COMPTON'S PRECYCLOPEDIA possesses a number of appealing features, but it lacks *Childcraft* 's superior design and vitality. Also aimed at roughly the same age group are CHARLIE BROWN'S 'CYCLOPEDIA (15 volumes; 180,000 words), DISNEY'S WONDERFUL WORLD OF KNOWLEDGE (20 volumes; 750,000 words), and the NEW TALKING CASSETTE ENCYCLOPEDIA (10 volumes; 100,000 words). In terms of quality, however, none of these titles is in the same class as *Childcraft* or, for that matter, COMPTON'S PRECYCLOPEDIA.

To **Purchase** *Childcraft:* If you are either an individual consumer or representing an educational institution and wish to order the set, consult the yellow pages of the local telephone directory under "Encyclopedias" for the World Book, Inc., sales representative in your area. If the company is not listed in the directory, contact World Book, Inc. at Merchandise Mart Plaza, Chicago, IL 60654 or telephone toll-free 1-800-621-8202. Your name will be forwarded to the sales representative nearest you who will handle the transaction. The sales representative will most likely attempt to sell you additional publications along with *Childcraft,* including *Childcraft Annual,* the *Childcraft Dictionary,* and the WORLD BOOK ENCYCLOPEDIA. You need not buy any extras unless you want them. Purchasers of *Childcraft,* however, should seriously consider taking *Childcraft Annual,* which is an excellent supplement to the set. It should also be mentioned that when *Childcraft* is purchased in combination with the WORLD BOOK ENCYCLOPEDIA, it costs $159 to individuals—a savings of $40 off the retail price. Consumers interested in any of the various foreign-language editions of *Childcraft* noted earlier in this review should contact the home office of World Book, Inc. in Chicago for the latest sales information. Generally, these foreign-language editions are not sold in the United States or Canada.

For More Information about *Childcraft* See: *American Reference Books Annual,* 1980, pp. 27–28 (review by Lillian Biermann Wehmeyer); *Booklist,* June 15, 1975, pp. 1080–83 (unsigned review); *Introduction to Reference Work* by William A. Katz (4th ed., New York: McGraw-Hill, 1982), vol. 1: *Basic Information Sources,* p. 192; *Reference Sources for Small and Medium-sized Libraries* (4th ed., Chicago: American Library Association, 1984), p. 26 (review by Jovian P. Lang).

Collier's Encyclopedia

FACTS

Collier's Encyclopedia with Bibliography and Index. William D. Halsey, Editorial Director; Emanuel Friedman, Editor in Chief. New York: Macmillan Educational Company, a division of Macmillan, Inc. 24 volumes. First edition published in 20 volumes in 1950–51; new printings with revisions each year. Lowest retail price: $1,099.50 delivered; with discount to schools and libraries: $749.00 plus $20.00 shipping and handling.

Collier's Encyclopedia, which "has been designed and built to fill the needs of the most exacting school and home users" (preface), serves adults and college and advanced high school students. The 24-volume encyclopedia contains 19,700 pages, 25,000 articles, and roughly 21 million words. The articles, many of which are of the broad-entry type, average about 1,000 words in length (or nearly one full page). They are accompanied by 17,350 illustrations (2,000 in color), plus 1,450 maps. Some 5,000 editorial advisers and contributors are identified in Volume 1. Practically all (98 percent) of the articles are signed. The encyclopedia is arranged alphabetically letter by letter (*Newspaper* precedes *New York*), with access to specific information enhanced by 12,000 cross-references in the text and an analytical index of more than 400,000 entries.

EVALUATION

Collier's first appeared in 1950–51 in 20 volumes. In 1962, a major revision expanded the set to its present size of 24 volumes. During its almost 40 years of existence, *Collier's* has achieved a reputation as one of the five or six leading general encyclopedias published in English. The founding editor, the late Louis Shores, brought outstanding credentials to the work, as does the present editor, Emanuel Friedman. The contributors, most of whom are North American professors and scholars, are also well qualified.

The encyclopedia's coverage tends to be well balanced, with important people, places, events, and concepts in the major knowledge areas all receiving adequate attention. The set also includes much practical information. The article *Insurance,* for example, provides a down-to-earth discussion of the various types of insurance available (such as automobile, home, health, etc.) and what to look for when considering each type. Similarly, the article *Child Psychology and Development* was recently expanded to include a section called "Practical Problems of Childhood," which provides information on such matters as divorce, child abuse, sibling rivalry, fears and nightmares, bed-wetting, and the effects of too much television on children.

Information in *Collier's* is normally accurately and objectively presented. Sometimes, however, controversial or sensitive issues are ignored or glossed over, as in the case of the article *Circumcision,* which notes that the procedure is "practiced as a religious rite by Jews, Muslims, and many primitive peoples" and that it is "also extensively practiced in modern medicine as a sanitary measure," but fails to mention any of the contemporary arguments against circumcision. The set's contents are quite current in most areas, the result of an energetic and consistent approach to annual revision over the years. For instance, during the five-year period between 1980 and 1984, 276 new articles and 1,137 illustrations were added to the encyclopedia; 157 articles were completely rewritten; and 7,217 articles and over 500 maps were revised in some manner—all involving changes in 13,165 (or well over half) of the set's 19,700 pages. Such articles as *Acquired Immune Deficiency Syndrome (AIDS), Computer, Nicaragua, Robot,* and *Shroud of Turin* are admirably up-to-date.

The encyclopedia's writing style is typically clear and to-the-point. Normally the text will be comprehensible to adults and college and high school students who possess good reading skills.

Consider, for example, the first paragraph of the article on earthquakes:

> EARTHQUAKE, a vibratory shaking of the ground caused by some sudden disturbance of natural origin within the earth. The vibrations are elastic waves traveling at high speed through the earth. The largest earthquakes are sometimes felt more than 1,000 miles (1,600 km) from the source of the shock and can be detected on seismographs, sensitive earthquake recording instruments, on the other side of the world. The point from which the vibrations start is the focus of the earthquake and the point on the surface of the earth directly above the focus is the epicenter. The foci of most earthquakes are within 10 miles (1.6 km) [sic] of the earth's surface. However, there are some areas in which earthquake foci have occasionally occurred as deep as 450 miles (720 km). Thousands of earthquakes occur each day, but only a small proportion of them are felt.

As this example indicates, *Collier's* does not write down to its readers. Usually, however, it does define or explain in context potentially difficult or unfamiliar terms (such as *seismograph* and *epicenter*). To repeat: *Collier's* will best serve a literate adult and older student readership.

Locating specific information in *Collier's* frequently requires use of the general index in the final volume because many of the set's articles are, as previously noted, of the broad-entry type. Broad-entry (as opposed to specific-entry) simply means that related topics are treated under one large or all-embracing heading rather than separately. An example is the *Collier's* article *Savoy Opera,* which covers Richard D'Oyly Carte, the D'Oyly Carte Opera Company, and the various Gilbert and Sullivan comic operas. In a specific-entry encyclopedia (such as ENCYCLOPEDIA AMERICANA), D'Oyly Carte (the man and the company) and individual operas like the *Pirates of Penzance* each have their own entries, whereas in *Collier's* they do not. Fortunately, *Collier's* possesses an excellent index, an indication of which is its enviable number of entries (400,000) per total number of words in the encyclopedia (21 million). In other words, *Collier's* provides approximately one index entry for every 50 words of text (a 1:50 ratio). Among the major general English-language encyclopedias, only the ACADEMIC AMERICAN ENCYCLOPEDIA has a better ratio. Hence, even though *Collier's* lacks separate articles on D'Oyly Carte and the *Pirates of Penzance,* these subjects can be readily located through the index, which leads the user to the *Savoy Opera* article.

The encyclopedia's bibliographies, most of which are found at the beginning of Volume 24, add a valuable dimension to the set. About 12,000 carefully selected titles recommended for further reading are listed by subject. The encyclopedia's illustrations, on the other hand, are not as impressive. The numerous black-and-white drawings and diagrams are customarily informative, nicely complementing the written text, but some of the photographs are drab and appear dated. Several years ago, encyclopedia critic Harvey Einbinder quite rightly pointed out (in his article "Encyclopedias: Some Foreign and Domestic Developments" in *Wilson Library Bulletin,* December 1980, p. 261) that "readers who peruse the pages of *Collier's* today are carried back three decades in a time machine—viewing a 1950 black-and-white kinescope instead of a bright, multi-colored video image." To their credit, the makers of *Collier's* recognize the problem and are currently adding new color illustrations to the set at the rate of 150 per year. From a physical standpoint, *Collier's* is well constructed and aesthetically appealing.

Collier's generally receives high marks from critics in most areas. In the current edition of his *Introduction to Reference Work* (1982, vol. 1, p. 187), William A. Katz, a prominent authority on reference materials, says, "In terms of words, *Collier's* has 21 million, ranking third behind the *Britannica* and *Americana.* However, it is in first place when it comes to the index, with the best index volume of any of the sets. Another feature of the final volume is the excellent section on bibliographies." Janet Littlefield, in *American Reference Books Annual* (1982, p. 30), concludes that *Collier's* "is carefully prepared and edited," but adds, "Certainly not flashy, it could use more color illustrations." And Jovian Lang, in a short but incisive review in *Reference Sources for Small and Medium-sized Libraries* (1984, p. 26), notes that articles in *Collier's* "encompass content of interest to secondary school and college students as well as to the public at large, with key facts about the physical, life, and earth sciences, humanities, and arts clearly set forth in language accessible to the general reader. Large-scale articles, such as those on psychology, Dostoyevsky, and ballet, are exemplary."

To Summarize: *Collier's* is a first-rate general encyclopedia for adults and older students with good reading skills. It is usually accurate, unbiased, authoritative, clearly written, and as up-to-date as can be expected. An outstanding analytical index facilitates quick and easy retrieval of specific information. The encyclopedia's conspicuous weakness—lack of abundant color illustrations—is being corrected, albeit slowly.

In Comparison: *Collier's,* published in 24 volumes containing 21 million words, is a large encyclopedia for adults and older students who have serious informational needs. It compares quite favorably with the other two large general adult encyclopedias currently available, namely ENCYCLOPEDIA AMERICANA (30 volumes; 31 million words) and the NEW ENCYCLOPAEDIA BRITANNICA (32 volumes; 44 million words). Obviously, *Collier's* is the smallest of these encyclopedias, but it is also the most current, best indexed, easiest to read, and least expensive of the three. On the other hand, the NEW ENCYCLOPAEDIA BRITANNICA is the largest, most scholarly, and most prestigious of the three, and ENCYCLOPEDIA AMERICANA, which runs second in just about every evaluative category (size, readability, accessibility, up-to-dateness, prestige, price, etc.), offers expecially good coverage of North American people, places, and events. Each of these large sets is, on balance, an excellent work that can be recommended without hesitation to those who truly require a large, costly, adult encyclopedia. Because of the expense involved (each of these encyclopedias costs more than $1,000 at retail), consumers are urged to examine all three sets closely prior to making a final purchase decision.

To Purchase *Collier's Encyclopedia:* If you are an individual consumer and wish to order the encyclopedia, contact P.F. Collier, Inc. (the publisher's retail sales organization), at 866 Third Avenue, New York, NY 10022 or telephone toll-free 1-800-257-9500 Ext. 485. Your name will be forwarded to a sales representative in your area who will handle the transaction. The salesperson will most likely attempt to sell you additional publications along with the encyclopedia, including the company's two yearbooks, *Collier's Year Book* and *Health and Medical Horizons.* The whole package, called Collier's Home Educational Program, currently sells for around $1,400. You need not buy these or any other extras unless you want them. In the case of the yearbooks, these so-called updating services have little direct connection with the encyclopedia and should not be purchased unless you are sure they will be used.

If you are ordering the encyclopedia for a school or library, contact Macmillan Professional Books at 866 Third Avenue, New York, NY 10022 or telephone toll-free 1-800-257-5755. Your order will be processed immediately.

For More Information about *Collier's Encyclopedia* **See:** *American Reference Books Annual,* 1982, pp. 27–30 (review by Janet Littlefield); *Booklist,* December 15, 1984, pp. 566–68 (unsigned review); *Booklist,* September 1, 1983, p. 62 (unsigned review); *Introduction to Reference Work* by William A. Katz (4th ed., New York: McGraw-Hill, 1982), vol. 1: *Basic Information Sources,* pp. 186–89; *Reference Sources for Small and Medium-sized Libraries* (4th ed., Chicago: American Library Association, 1984), p. 26 (review by Jovian P. Lang); *Wilson Library Bulletin,* December 1980, p. 261 (article by Harvey Einbinder entitled "Encyclopedias: Some Foreign and Domestic Developments").

Collins Gem Encyclopedia

FACTS

Collins Gem Encyclopedia. Ian Crofton, Editor. London, England: William Collins Sons & Company Ltd. Distributed in North America by Simon & Schuster, Inc. 2 volumes. Based on and abridged from *Collins Concise Encyclopedia* (1933–76). First edition published in 1979; revised in 1980. Lowest retail price: $7.90 (each volume at $3.95).

The two-volume *Collins Gem Encyclopedia,* a pocket-sized work (the volumes measure 3¼ by 4¾ in.; 8 by 12 cm.) for adults and older students, is said to be a "reference guide to all fields of human activity and knowledge ... from the birth of civilization in Sumeria to the furthest reaches of space exploration, from ancient Greek tragedy to pop art" (preface). The little encyclopedia, which is British-made, contains 1,125 pages, 14,000 articles, and approximately 450,000 words. The articles, which are extremely brief, average 32 words in length (or about 12 or 13 articles per page). The encyclopedia has no illustrations whatsoever, including maps. An editorial staff of five is listed, but no contributors are identified, nor are the articles signed. The encyclopedia is arranged alphabetically letter by letter (*Newspaper* precedes *New York*), with access to specific information enhanced by roughly 5,000 cross-references in the text. There is no index.

EVALUATION

First published in 1979 and revised the following year, *Collins Gem,* according to a note in the front matter, "is based on and abridged from *Collins Concise Encyclopedia,*" a larger work of no great reputation that has been on the British scene since 1933. Although *Collins Gem* is produced in Great Britain, its text "has been particularly tailored to the needs of the English-speaking world" (preface), including readers in the United States and Canada. The encyclopedia emphasizes people, places, historical events and movements, and scientific topics. Some important subjects are apparently not covered at all. At least, nothing was found on such topics as adoption, gambling, polygraph (or lie detector) tests, robots, and the Shroud of Turin. Nevertheless, the coverage is quite broad, considering the size of the work. More often the problem is not whether a topic is covered but the superficiality of the coverage, the articles generally being little more than dictionary-style entries. The 40-word article *Abortion,* for instance, merely defines the term as it is used in medicine. Likewise, the subject of Pearl Harbor is limited to a parenthetical note ("attacked by Japanese in 1941 bringing US into WWII") in the article on Hawaii. But sometimes the coverage is surprisingly generous, as in the article *Capital Punishment,* which furnishes an informative account of the status of the death penalty in the United States and Europe.

Information in *Collins Gem* is accurately and objectively presented. The article *Vietnam War,* for example, gives an impartial account of the conflict's resolution: "Despite formal conclusion of war (1973), guerrilla activities continued in South, which capitulated with capture of Saigon (April, 1975). Length of war, high US casualties, corruption of South Vietnam govt. contributed to opposition of war within US." Sometimes, however, controversy is either completely ignored (as in the case of the aforementioned article on abortion) or simply acknowledged without any explanation as to the nature of the debate (as in the case of *Scientology,* which informs the reader that "controversial practices have led to official inquiries in some countries," but nothing more). Information in *Collins Gem* is quite current as of the mid-1970s, as the article on the Vietnam War mentioned above shows. Obviously, the encyclopedia lacks material on happenings prior to 1981. For instance, the article *Falkland Islands* notes, "Entire area claimed by Argentina," but there is nothing about the recent war over the Falklands.

The encyclopedia's writing style is straightforward and economical, often using abbreviations and omitting nonessential words. The article on earthquakes, for example, begins this way:

> EARTHQUAKE, shaking or trembling of the Earth's crust originating naturally below the surface. Consists of series of shock waves generated at focus or foci, which may cause changes in level, cracking or distortion of surface. Often accompanied by volcanic activity, landslides, giant sea waves (*tsunamis*). Associated with younger fold-mountain regions of Earth, esp. fault lines; prob. the result of stresses caused by movement of crustal plates (*see* PLATE TECTONICS). Severity measured by various scales, *eg* Richter, Mercalli.

Plainly, *Collins Gem* is written for a literate adult and older student audience. Potentially difficult or unfamiliar terms are not defined or explained in context—what, for instance, are *fault lines* or *fold-mountain regions*?—and the syntax, or sentence structure, will pose problems for those without good reading skills.

The encyclopedia's contents are reasonably accessible, due largely to the specificity of the entries and the judicious use of cross-references, which usually appear in SMALL CAPITAL LETTERS, as in the case of PLATE TECTONICS in the excerpt from the article on earthquakes quoted in the preceding paragraph. As mentioned at the beginning of this review, *Collins Gem* lacks illustrations entirely. Like all titles in the "Gem" pocketbook series, the encyclopedia has soft, or flexible, covers. Also, the print is very small and hard on the eyes.

To Summarize: *Collins Gem,* an abridgment of the larger *Collins Concise Encyclopedia,* is a pocket-sized general encyclopedia for adults and older students published in Great Britain in two volumes in 1979 and revised the following year. It lacks depth (the articles average only 32 words in length) and currentness (revised only once in 1980), and the print is extremely small. But this tiny encyclopedia is very inexpensive and might serve as a useful quick reference source for the traveler or the person whose informational needs are not great.

In Comparison: *Collins Gem,* published in two volumes containing 450,000 words, is a small encyclopedia for adults and older students. It cannot compare with the leading one- and two-volume general adult encyclopedias, namely the LINCOLN LIBRARY OF ESSENTIAL INFORMATION (two volumes; 3.5 million words), the NEW COLUMBIA ENCYCLOPEDIA (one volume; 6.6 million words), the RANDOM HOUSE ENCYCLOPEDIA (one volume; 3 million words), and the VOLUME LIBRARY (two volumes; 3.5 million words). All of these encyclopedias, as the figures indicate, offer much more information than *Collins Gem.* Also, they are much more expensive. More in the same league with *Collins Gem* are the CONCISE COLUMBIA ENCYCLOPEDIA (one volume; one million words), the KNOWLEDGE ENCYCLOPEDIA (one volume; 300,000 words), PEARS CYCLOPAEDIA (one volume; 1.2 million words), and the QUICK REFERENCE HANDBOOK OF BASIC INFORMATION (one volume; 750,000 words). Among these smallest of the small general encyclopedias for adults, the CONCISE COLUMBIA ENCYCLOPEDIA is the standout choice for North Americans. In the final analysis, the only thing *Collins Gem* has going for it, comparatively speaking, is its low, low price.

To Purchase *Collins Gem Encyclopedia:* The encyclopedia is sold in North American retail bookstores. If it is not in stock (and it may well not be), most bookstores will order it for you. You can also order the encyclopedia directly from the distributor, Simon & Schuster, Inc. at 1230 Avenue of the Americas, New York, NY 10020 or telephone 212-245-6400.

No other reviews of *Collins Gem Encyclopedia* are available at this time.

Compton's Encyclopedia

FACTS

Compton's Encyclopedia and Fact-Index. Michael Reed, Editor. Chicago: F.E. Compton Company, a division of Encyclopaedia Britannica, Inc. 26 volumes. Former title: *Compton's Pictured Encyclopedia* (1922–67). First published as *Compton's Encyclopedia* in 1968; new printing with revisions each year. Lowest retail price: $699 delivered; with discount to schools, libraries, and teachers: $499 delivered.

The 26-volume *Compton's Encyclopedia,* which intends to be "an innovative, forward-looking reference work for young people" (preface), is a curriculum-oriented encyclopedia that generally serves the needs of the whole family and specifically those of students from the ages of nine to 18. The encyclopedia contains approximately 11,000 pages, 10,000 main articles, and 8.5 million words. The main articles, of which about 4,000 are quite long, average 850 words in length (or more than a full page). The set also includes nearly 30,000 very brief articles, or fact entries, in the index in the final volume (called the Fact-Index). The main articles are accompanied by 20,500 illustrations (20 percent in full color), plus some 2,000 maps. The Fact-Index is not illustrated (although until recently it was). Roughly 600 editors, advisers, artists, and contributors are listed in Volume 1. Most of the main articles are not signed, nor are any of the fact entries in the Fact-Index signed. The encyclopedia is arranged alphabetically letter by letter (*Newspapers* precedes *New York*), with access to specific information enhanced by more than 35,500 cross-references and an analytical index (the aforementioned Fact-Index) of 150,000 entries.

EVALUATION

Compton's first appeared in 1922 in eight volumes under the title *Compton's Pictured Encyclopedia,* so called because no other encyclopedia at the time offered so many and such a great variety of illustrations. Published by F.E. Compton Company of Chicago, the set was expanded to 15 volumes in 1932. In 1961, Encyclopaedia Britannica, Inc., long one of the most prominent names in encyclopedia publishing, acquired *Compton's* and generally upgraded the set. In 1968, the encyclopedia grew to 24 volumes and was retitled simply

Compton's Encyclopedia, the word "Pictured" no longer deemed necessary. In 1974, two more volumes were added and the set attained its present size of 26 volumes. For the most part, *Compton's* has enjoyed the reputation of a first-class encyclopedia for students and the family. During the 1970s, however, the set was not adequately maintained, failing to keep pace with its chief competitors, MERIT STUDENTS ENCYCLOPEDIA and the WORLD BOOK ENCYCLOPEDIA. Happily, in the early 1980s, the publisher decided to revitalize the set, a process that is now well established under the editorial direction of Michael Reed, an experienced encyclopedia hand who previously worked on the ACADEMIC AMERICAN ENCYCLOPEDIA and *Science Year,* a World Book, Inc. publication.

The encyclopedia's contents loosely reflect the curricula of junior and senior high schools in the United States and Canada. Out-of-school topics—camping, fishing, games, gardening, pets, etc.—are also covered. Subjects in the area of science and technology receive especially strong coverage in *Compton's,* as such long and substantive articles as *Aerospace, Agriculture, Air Conditioning, Airplane, Algebra, Animal, Animal Behavior, Animal Migration, Antibiotic, Apes and Monkeys, Aquarium, Arithmetic, Astronomy, Atomic Particles, Automation, Automobiles,* and *Aviation* attest. Major places, particularly the U.S. states and Canadian provinces, also receive generous coverage. On the other hand, topics in the social and behavioral sciences tend to be less well covered. For example, information about capital punishment is relegated to three short paragraphs at the end of the article *Prisons,* and the subjects of homosexuality, missing children, and religious cults are not treated at all.

Compton's is a conscientiously edited encyclopedia. Information in the set is normally accurate, although occasionally small factual errors will be encountered, as in the article *Abortion,* which states that abortion became legal in the United States in 1971 when in fact legalization did not occur until 1973, when the Supreme Court decided the landmark case *Roe* v. *Wade.* Information in *Compton's* is usually objectively presented. Again, the article *Abortion* is a good example: "In the United States abortion was made legal in 1971 over the objections of some groups, the Roman Catholic Church in particular. Those opposed to abortion feel it is the taking of a human life. Those in favor of legalized abortion cite overpopulation, the problems of unwanted children, and the dangers of illegal abortion." Sometimes, however, controversial or sensitive subjects are simply ignored, as in the cases of circumcision and homosexuality.

As mentioned earlier, the encyclopedia was neglected during much of the 1970s and, as a result, some of the text, including many illustrations, became noticeably dated. But the present effort to revitalize the set, which entails thorough revision of several volumes each year, is making good headway, and such articles as *Abortion, Adoption, Argentina, Asbestos, Canada,* and *Falkland Islands* are now as current as can be expected. *Compton's* still has a way to go until it is as up-to-date as such rivals as the ACADEMIC AMERICAN ENCYCLOPE-DIA, MERIT STUDENTS ENCYCLOPEDIA, and the WORLD BOOK ENCY-CLOPEDIA, but discernible progress is being made. As noted in a recent review in *Booklist* (December 15, 1984, p. 568), "If *Compton's* continues to revise heavily at least four volumes a year, the ency-clopedia will have a new look in a few years."

Compton's advertises itself as "the one that's fun to read.... Our articles are written to be *read,* understood and remembered from start to finish." Generally speaking, the encyclopedia's articles are written in a clear and interesting fashion. The first two paragraphs of the article *Earthquake* typify the *Compton's* style:

> EARTHQUAKE. An earthquake is a shaking of the ground. It occurs when masses of rock change position below the earth's surface. The shifting masses send out shock waves that may be powerful enough to wreck buildings, roads, and bridges. They may even alter the surface of the earth, thrusting up cliffs and opening fissures in the ground.
>
> Earthquakes, or *temblors,* go on almost continuously. It is es-timated that perhaps one million earthquakes occur each year. Fortunately, most of them can be detected only by sensitive instru-ments called *seismographs.* Others are felt as small tremors. Some of the rest, however, cause major catastrophes. They produce such tragic and dramatic effects as destroyed cities, broken dams, earth slides, giant sea waves, and volcanic eruptions. A very great earth-quake usually occurs at least once a year in some part of the world.

Note that potentially difficult or unfamiliar terms (in this case *temblors* and *seismographs*) are italicized and defined in context.

Another useful (though less apparent) feature of *Compton's* is its "pyramid" writing style—that is, the article begins with the simplest or most elementary material and then gradually becomes more de-tailed or complex as the text progresses. For example, toward the end of *Earthquakes,* the article's content, vocabulary, and syntax (or sen-tence structure) are clearly more advanced than at the beginning:

> Some of the side effects of earthquakes cause the most damage. Fires break out and rage unchecked over wide areas, since water mains are often broken. Seismic sea waves are another danger. These are known by the Japanese name of *tsunamis,* though they are often inaptly called tidal waves. They are not caused by the tides but are probably the result of vertical fault movements or landslides under the sea. In the deep ocean the waves travel at speeds of over 600 miles an hour but remain low in height. As the tsunamis approach shore they build up into powerful walls of water 90 feet or more in height.

Like its chief competitors (MERIT STUDENTS ENCYCLOPEDIA and the WORLD BOOK ENCYCLOPEDIA), *Compton's* is most appropriate for users with reading skills from the seventh- to twelfth-grade levels. In addition, the set can be comprehended by above-average readers in the upper elementary grades.

Access to the encyclopedia's contents is quite good, due in part to an abundance of cross-references in the text but mostly to the excellent Fact-Index, which serves the dual function of a finding device and a source of quick reference information not included in the main text of the set. For example, the Fact-Index entry "Capital punishment" refers the user to page 506 in the "P" volume where information on capital punishment can be found in the article *Prisons*. However, the next entry in the Fact-Index ("Capital University") provides no page and volume references but, rather, a six-line description of the subject. Cross-references in the main text alert readers to such entries in the Fact-Index. Recently, the Fact-Index underwent some major changes. Symbols are no longer used to denote subentries, which are now indicated by the more conventional means of indentation, and the Fact-Index is no longer illustrated (as it had been since the set first appeared in 1922). The Fact-Index is published as a single unit in Volume 26 (called the Master Fact-Index) and in sections at the end of each of the first 25 volumes, each section covering that part of the alphabet that corresponds to the volume itself. One minor problem that sometimes occurs when using the Master Fact-Index is that index references give only the letter and page number of the volume, e.g., P-506. But in a number of instances, individual letters, such as "P," are split into two consecutively paged volumes, as in the case of "P-Phil" (Volume 18) and "Phill-Pytho" (Volume 19). The problem is, of course, which volume contains page 506?

Black-and-white illustrations predominate in *Compton's*. They are plentiful, appearing on almost every page of the set (except for Volume 26), but they are also frequently dreary and dated, especially the photographs. Marda Woodbury, reviewing the encyclopedia in *American Reference Books Annual* (1982, p. 30), put it this way: "Browsing through, one gets a pervasive feeling that many illustrations, though usually pertinent to the article, show hairdos, clothes, and cars that are 15, 20, or more years out of date." Presumably, as efforts to revitalize *Compton's* proceed, dated illustrations will be systematically replaced. Physically, the encyclopedia is well made and designed, although the preponderance of old, dark illustrations is a drawback.

In recent years, critics have given *Compton's* mixed reviews. *Booklist* (December 15, 1984, p. 568) concludes that the encyclopedia's "emphasis on practical and curriculum-related information makes it an attractive set for children and young people," but only after pointing out that *Compton's* has been guilty of "insufficient currentness" in the past. Jovian Lang, in *Reference Sources for Small and Medium-sized Libraries* (1984, p. 27), says of the encyclopedia:

"Geography, nature study, U.S. history, sports and games, biography, and basic science are especially well handled in *Compton's.* Interpretations of women's roles in society have been conscientiously brought into line with contemporary egalitarian thinking. Controversial topics are avoided. Continuous revision has kept the material fresh, particularly the science, geography, and social sciences articles. However, lack of currency in certain areas is a weakness." And Marda Woodbury, in *American Reference Books Annual* (1982, p. 31), sums up the set in this manner: "*Compton's,* though outdated in some respects, has kept its science articles (particularly its biology and physics) very current, and offers a format that lends itself to browsing and classroom use."

To Summarize: *Compton's,* a well-known general encyclopedia for the family generally and students between the ages of nine and 18 specifically, provides especially strong coverage in the area of science and technology. The encyclopedia is normally reliable and interestingly written. On the negative side, it sometimes avoids controversial issues, is not always up-to-date, and its illustrations, once the set's greatest strength, are now often too dark and too old. The editors, however, are aware of these deficiencies, and steps are currently being taken to correct them, although that process will require a number of years.

In Comparison: *Compton's,* published in 26 volumes containing 8.5 million words, falls roughly into the category of encyclopedias for adults and older students, although in some instances the set will also be useful to younger readers. Generally speaking, *Compton's* competes with the ACADEMIC AMERICAN ENCYCLOPEDIA (21 volumes; 9 million words), FUNK & WAGNALLS NEW ENCYCLOPEDIA (29 volumes; 9 million words), MERIT STUDENTS ENCYCLOPEDIA (20 volumes; 9 million words), the NEW STANDARD ENCYCLOPEDIA (17 volumes; 6.4 million words), and the WORLD BOOK ENCYCLOPEDIA (22 volumes; 10 million words). Over the years, *Compton's* has competed head-to-head with the WORLD BOOK, a quality encyclopedia that offers many of the same features as *Compton's* and, more recently, MERIT STUDENTS, another quality set aimed at exactly the same readership as *Compton's.* On balance, WORLD BOOK and MERIT STUDENTS are today better encyclopedias than *Compton's,* although the latter's revitalization program now under way could change that judgment in the years to come.

To Purchase *Compton's Encyclopedia:* If you are an individual consumer and wish to order the encyclopedia, consult the white pages of the local telephone directory under "Encyclopaedia Britannica, Inc." for the sales representative in your area. If the company is not listed in the directory, contact Encyclopaedia Britannica, Inc. at Britannica Centre, Customer Service Department, 310 South Michigan Avenue, Chicago, IL 60604 or telephone collect 312-347-7298. Your name will be forwarded to a sales representative in your area who will handle the transaction. Note that schoolteachers receive a $100 discount off the retail price. The sales representative will most likely attempt to sell you additional publications along with the encyclopedia, including two annuals entitled *Compton's Yearbook* and the *Yearbook of Science and the Future.* You need not buy any extras unless you want them. In the case of the yearbooks, these so-called updating services have no real editorial connection with the encyclopedia and should be avoided unless you are absolutely certain they will be used.

If you are ordering *Compton's* for a school or library, contact Encyclopaedia Britannica Educational Corporation at the address above or call toll-free 1-800-554-9862. Your order will be processed immediately.

For More Information about *Compton's Encyclopedia* See: *American Reference Books Annual,* 1982, pp. 30–31 (review by Marda Woodbury); *Booklist,* December 15, 1984, p. 568 (unsigned review); *Introduction to Reference Work* by William A. Katz (4th ed., New York: McGraw-Hill, 1982), vol. 1: *Basic Information Sources,* pp. 189–91; *Reference Sources for Small and Medium-sized Libraries* (4th ed., Chicago: American Library Association, 1984), p. 27 (review by Jovian P. Lang).

Compton's Precyclopedia

FACTS

Compton's Precyclopedia: Based on the Young Children's Encyclopedia. Also published as the YOUNG CHILDREN'S ENCYCLOPEDIA. Howard L. Goodkind, Editor in Chief; Margaret Sutton, Managing Editor. Chicago: F.E. Compton Company, a division of Encyclopaedia Britannica, Inc. 16 volumes (plus a 110-page paperbound volume entitled *Teaching Guide and Index*). Former title: *Compton's Young Children's Precyclopedia* (1971). First published as *Compton's Precyclopedia* in 1973; revised periodically, most recently in 1985. Lowest retail price: $249 delivered; with discount to schools and libraries: $239 delivered.

Compton's Precyclopedia, called a "training" encyclopedia by the publisher, provides "topics of high interest to young children that are described in a variety of styles—fictional, conversational and poetic" (advertisement). The 16-volume set contains 2,944 pages, 650 articles (plus an activity, or "Things to Do," section at the beginning of each volume), and approximately 325,000 words. The articles, which are normally quite lengthy, average 500 words in length (or just under five full pages). They are accompanied by 2,400 illustrations (all in color), plus 20 maps. A small editorial and production staff is listed in Volume 1. None of the articles is signed, but the last page of each volume does identify those responsible for the text in that volume. The set is arranged alphabetically letter by letter (*Newspapers* precedes *New York*), with access to specific information enhanced by some 500 cross-references and an index of 800 entries (in the paperbound volume entitled *Teaching Guide and Index*).

EVALUATION

Compton's Precyclopedia first appeared in 1971 under the title *Compton's Young Children's Precyclopedia*. Two years later the title was shortened to *Compton's Precyclopedia*. As its subtitle indicates, the *Precyclopedia* derives from the YOUNG CHILDREN'S ENCYCLOPEDIA, first published in 1970 as a mail-order and supermarket item. The two sets are exactly the same except for these minor differences: The *Precyclopedia* includes a 24-page activity, or "Things to Do," section at the beginning of each volume, whereas the YOUNG CHILDREN'S ENCYCLOPEDIA does not; the *Precyclopedia* comes with a 110-page paperbound *Teaching Guide and Index* volume, whereas the YOUNG CHILDREN'S ENCYCLOPEDIA does not; and the *Precyclopedia* is usually sold in conjunction with COMPTON'S ENCYCLOPEDIA, whereas the YOUNG CHILDREN'S ENCYCLOPEDIA is sold with the NEW ENCYCLOPAEDIA BRITANNICA. Both the *Precyclopedia* and YOUNG CHILDREN'S ENCYCLOPEDIA have a reputation of being among the best beginning encyclopedias available for children between the ages of four and ten.

Like its chief competitor, CHILDCRAFT, the *Precyclopedia* comprises stories, folktales, games, riddles, jingles, jokes, and factual articles on subjects likely to be of interest to young readers. For example, Volume 1 includes a story set in Africa (*Amos Wins the Big Race*), biographical information about Louisa May Alcott (*Tales of Happy Families*), an adventure piece about the Amazon (*Exploring the Amazon River*), and three articles about astronauts (*Doing the Job, A Walk in Space,* and *More about Astronauts*). Users and prospective purchasers of the *Precyclopedia* should understand that no effort has been made to provide comprehensive coverage of the world's knowledge, and that in the strictest sense the *Precyclopedia* is not really an encyclopedia but a browsing set. As a review in *Booklist* (November 1, 1979, p. 454) observes, "There will be users who will question some of the subject headings, the exclusion of some topics and inclusion of others. For example, there is an article about baseball but none about football, basketball, or soccer. There is a major article about marsupials but not about mammals. Information is included about polar bears but not about pandas or teddy bears. The story of *Red Riding Hood* is told; that of the *Three Bears* is not."

Information in the *Precyclopedia* is accurately and objectively presented. Likewise, the material is reasonably current, although timeliness is not as crucial in a work of this type as it is in a true encyclopedia. Occasionally, however, the addition of new information would improve an article. The two-page entry on the Panama Canal, for instance, lacks any mention of the recently negotiated treaties involving the Canal Zone. In the set's latest revision (1985), five new articles have been added, all dealing with famous women (including Louisa May Alcott, Susan B. Anthony, and Emily Dickinson), six articles have been dropped, and 25 articles have been rewritten or updated and, in some cases, reillustrated (among them, the articles on computers, space, and the ocean).

The *Precyclopedia*'s writing style is normally clear, interesting, and informal. Reading levels vary from article to article, but in most instances the text will be comprehensible to beginning readers in the primary grades. Consider, for example, the last portion of the article *Inside the Earth,* which deals with earthquakes:

> Sometimes a big layer of rock that is deep, deep down slips and rubs against another layer of rock. This causes a shaking and rumbling called an *earthquake* .

> Scientists learn something about what's inside the Earth by using special earthquake instruments.

> What's inside the Earth is a riddle. Nature gives us some hints when volcanoes shoot out melted rock and there are earthquakes. It lets us know that in some places there is solid rock, and in other places hot melted rock, and in still other places hot melted iron. But we still need to know a lot more than we do.

Access to specific information in the *Precyclopedia* is good, facilitated by the index portion of the aforementioned *Teaching Guide and Index,* which locates the main subjects treated in the set. Also, cross-references appear at the end of many articles. For instance, at the end of *Inside the Earth* there is this notation: "*Want to know more? Read* Fossils *in Volume 6 and* Volcanoes *in Volume 16.*" The guide portion of the *Teaching Guide and Index* provides a broad topical approach to the contents of the *Precyclopedia* for teachers or parents who might want to use the set for instructional purposes. For example, the guide brings together articles in the set under such headings as "Health and Safety," "The Community Is People," "Communications," "Transportation," "Exploring," "Our Earth," "Animals," and "Plants."

Illustrations, all in color, make up about half the set's total text. Mostly drawings, the illustrations add much to both the instructional and visual appeal of the *Precyclopedia.* The set's physical format is satisfactory, except for these problems: Guide words (or running heads) are not included at the top of each page, thus making it difficult to locate an article by browsing; some pages lack numbers, which may confuse or frustrate young users; and, the most serious complaint, the volumes do not always lie flat when open, thus rendering the set physically awkward to use for reference purposes. Sally Wynkoop, in a review in *American Reference Books Annual* (1975, p. 33), describes the situation this way: "Each volume contains a total of 184 pages, side-sewn in a flat-backed binding. Because of this, the volumes actually snap shut if not held tightly. The binding results also in very deep gutters [inner margins], so that illustrations that are fully bled across two pages are often quite distorted."

The *Precyclopedia* has not been heavily reviewed over the years, and the criticisms that have appeared have been mixed. The Wynkoop review in *American Reference Books Annual* (1975, pp. 33–34) quoted from in the preceding paragraph is almost entirely negative. On the other hand, a more recent review by the Reference and Subscription Books Review Committee (now Reference Books Bulletin Editorial Board) in *Booklist* (November 1, 1979, p. 456) is mostly positive, concluding in this manner: "Distinctive and effective presentations of concepts and very clear explanations of complicated natural phenomena make *Precyclopedia* valuable for home use, for use in nursery schools, Headstart groups and in kindergartens. It is recommended." And Jovian Lang, in *Reference Sources for Small and Medium-sized Libraries* (1984, p. 27), commends the set's "storytelling style and excellent graphics."

To Summarize: A "training" set designed to introduce beginning readers to the ins and outs of encyclopedias and reference work, *Compton's Precyclopedia* is more a collection of stories than a real encyclopedia, although it is arranged alphabetically and does have cross-references and an index. The *Precyclopedia,* which has practically the same text as the YOUNG CHILDREN'S ENCYCLOPEDIA, offers an interesting writing style and imaginative illustrations, but the coverage is highly eclectic, there are several problems with the physical format, and the set will be quickly outgrown.

In Comparison: *Compton's Precyclopedia,* published in 16 volumes (plus the paperbound *Teaching Guide and Index*) containing 325,000 words, is an attractive work for children ages four to ten. The *Precyclopedia*'s main competition is CHILDCRAFT (15 volumes; 750,000 words). Arranged topically (whereas the *Precyclopedia* is alphabetical), CHILDCRAFT is the outstanding encyclopedic set for beginning readers. Although the *Precyclopedia* possesses a number of appealing features, it lacks CHILDCRAFT's superior design and vitality. Also aimed at roughly the same age group are CHARLIE BROWN'S

'CYCLOPEDIA (15 volumes; 180,000 words), DISNEY'S WONDERFUL WORLD OF KNOWLEDGE (20 volumes; 750,000 words), and the NEW TALKING CASSETTE ENCYCLOPEDIA (10 volumes; 100,000 words). In terms of quality, however, none of these titles comes close to CHILDCRAFT, or for that matter, the *Precyclopedia* (also published as the YOUNG CHILDREN'S ENCYCLOPEDIA).

To Purchase *Compton's Precyclopedia:* If you are an individual consumer and wish to order the *Precyclopedia,* consult the white pages of the local telephone directory under "Encyclopaedia Britannica, Inc." for the sales representative in your area. If the company is not listed in the directory, contact Encyclopaedia Britannica, Inc. at Britannica Centre, Customer Service Department, 310 South Michigan Avenue, Chicago, IL 60604 or telephone collect 312-347-7298. Your name will be forwarded to a sales representative in your area who will handle the transaction. The *Precyclopedia* is normally sold in the home as part of a package deal involving COMPTON'S ENCYCLOPEDIA, a larger work for older students and the whole family. (Note that the *Precyclopedia*'s counterpart, the YOUNG CHILDREN'S ENCYCLOPEDIA, is usually sold with the NEW ENCYCLOPAEDIA BRITANNICA.) Of course, you need not buy COMPTON'S ENCYCLOPEDIA or any other Britannica products in order to purchase the *Precyclopedia.*

If you are ordering the *Precyclopedia* for a school or library, contact Encyclopaedia Britannica Educational Corporation at the address above or call toll-free 1-800-554-9862. Your order will be processed immediately.

For More Information about *Compton's Precyclopedia* **See:** *American Reference Books Annual,* 1975, pp. 33–34 (review by Sally Wynkoop); *Booklist,* November 1, 1979, pp. 453–56 (unsigned review); *Introduction to Reference Work* by William A. Katz (4th ed., New York: McGraw-Hill, 1982), vol 1: *Basic Information Sources,* pp. 192–93; *Reference Sources for Small and Medium-sized Libraries* (4th ed., Chicago: American Library Association, 1984), p. 27 (review by Jovian P. Lang).

Concise Columbia Encyclopedia

FACTS

The Concise Columbia Encyclopedia. Also published as the *Concise Columbia Encyclopedia in Large Print* (eight volumes; 1984). Judith S. Levey and Agnes Greenhall, Editors. New York: Columbia University Press (hardbound edition); New York: Avon Books (paperbound edition). One volume. Based on and abridged from the NEW COLUMBIA ENCYCLOPEDIA (1975). First edition published in 1983. Lowest retail price: $29.95 (hardbound); $14.95 (paperbound). Large print edition: $275.00.

The *Concise Columbia Encyclopedia,* a desk-sized work for adults and older students based on the NEW COLUMBIA ENCYCLOPEDIA (1975), intends to be "an up-to-date one-volume general encyclopedia of convenient size presenting a substantial body of information in compact form" (preface). The encyclopedia contains 943 pages, 15,000 articles, and more than a million words. The articles, which are of the specific-entry type, average 70 words in length (or roughly 15 articles per page). They are accompanied by approximately 75 illustrations (all black-and-white line drawings), plus 34 maps. An editorial staff of 75, including 53 contributors, and 33 academic consultants are noted at the front of Volume 1. None of the articles is signed. The encyclopedia is arranged alphabetically letter by letter (*Newspaper* precedes *New York*), with access to specific information enhanced by 50,000 cross-references in the text. There is no index. Note that the encyclopedia has also been published in an eight-volume large-print edition in 1984.

EVALUATION

Issued in 1983 in a single volume and not revised since that time, the *Concise Columbia* is a partial abridgment of the much larger NEW COLUMBIA ENCYCLOPEDIA (3,000 pages; 50,000 articles; 6.6 million words), an outstanding one-volume work published in 1975 as the retitled fourth edition of the *Columbia Encyclopedia,* which initially appeared in 1935 and in revised editions in 1950 and 1963. In concept and size, the *Concise Columbia* closely resembles an earlier, now defunct work entitled the *Columbia-Viking Desk Encyclopedia,* an abridged version of the 1963 (third) edition of the *Columbia*

Encyclopedia. The *Columbia-Viking Desk Encyclopedia*, published in 1968, consisted of 1,200 pages, 33,000 concise entries, and about a million and a half words. The name "Columbia" has come to stand for quality small-volume encyclopedias (both general and specialized), and the *Concise Columbia*, the latest in the line, carries on the tradition admirably. It should be pointed out that, although the encyclopedia has no official connection with Columbia University, more than half of its consultants are affiliated with the school.

The *Concise Columbia* 's coverage is fairly well balanced, although biographical, geographical, and scientific subjects predominate. For example, nearly a third of the encyclopedia's 15,000 articles describe people, both living and dead. Countries, states, provinces, and major cities, rivers, lakes, mountains, deserts, and the like are equally well covered. Among the 3,000 articles in the area of science are excellent, concise treatments of the current electronics revolution. See, for instance, *Artificial Intelligence (AI), Boolean Algebra, Computer, Computer Graphics, Computer Program, Computer Terminal, Electronic Game, Logical Circuit, Microprocessor, Programmed Instruction (or Programmed Learning), Programming Language, Robotics,* and *Videotex.*

In many instances, articles in the *Concise Columbia* are abbreviated versions of those appearing in the older NEW COLUMBIA ENCYCLOPEDIA. Frequently, historical detail found in the NEW COLUMBIA has been reduced or eliminated in the *Concise Columbia*, and the bibliographies in the former have been dropped entirely. A review in *Booklist* (March 1, 1984, p. 952) observes: "Most articles appear to have been condensed or rewritten using material in the older work. Much information provided in the longer *New Columbia Encyclopedia* has had to be sacrificed, and technical topics understandably suffer since explanations are shorter; cultural entries lose some of the details of contextual descriptions." But the *Concise Columbia* does offer considerable information not found in the older NEW COLUMBIA ENCYCLOPEDIA, including approximately 500 new entries covering such contemporary subjects as Alzheimer's disease and health maintenance organizations (HMOs) and people like Lech Walesa and Pete Rose.

The *Concise Columbia* is normally accurate and objective in its presentation of information. The article *Abortion,* for example, informs the reader that, although "attitudes toward abortion have generally become more liberal in the 20th cent.," the subject "remains a controversial issue in the U.S., however, and in 1977 Congress barred the use of Medicaid funds for abortion except for therapeutic reasons and in certain other specified instances." Information in the encyclopedia is current as of 1982, as indicated in such articles as *Canada,* which discusses the constitutional changes that occurred that year, and *Falkland Islands,* which refers to the 1982 war between Great Britain and Argentina over the Falklands. Other articles on present-day subjects—*Black English, Gentrification, Greenhouse Effect, In Vitro Fertilization, Money-Market Fund, Videotex,* etc.—are as current as could be wished. Overall, the *Concise Columbia* is as up-to-date as any single-volume general encyclopedia currently on the North American market.

The encyclopedia's writing style is clear, direct, and spare. Or, in the words of the editors, articles in the *Concise Columbia* "are written to be both succinct and easy to understand." Ordinarily, the text will be comprehensible to adults and high school and college students with good reading skills. The first part of the article *Earthquake* typifies the encyclopedia's style:

> Earthquake, trembling or shaking movement of the earth's surface. Great earthquakes usually begin with slight tremors, rapidly increase to one or more violent shocks, and diminish gradually. The immediate cause of most shallow earthquakes is the sudden release of stress along a FAULT, or fracture, in the earth's crust, resulting in the movement of opposing blocks of rock past one another. This causes vibrations to pass through and around the earth in wave form (see TSUNAMI). The subterranean origin of an earthquake is its focus; the point on the surface directly above the focus is the epicenter.

Note that technical terminology, such as *fault, focus,* and *epicenter,* is defined or explained in context.

The contents of the *Concise Columbia* are fairly easy to retrieve, thanks in large part to numerous cross-references within or at the end of articles. These *See* and *See also* references, printed in SMALL CAPITAL LETTERS, direct the user to related information in the encyclopedia. Examples (FAULT and TSUNAMI) can be seen in the excerpt from the article *Earthquake* quoted above. Also, many *See* references are provided in the A-to-Z listing, such as "*Lamb. See Sheep.*" Occasionally, however, the cross-reference system malfunctions. For instance, although the encyclopedia has an article entitled *Lie Detector,* there is no "*Polygraph. See Lie Detector*" reference. Likewise, the article on Harrisburg, Pennsylvania, mentions the 1979 nuclear power plant accident at Three Mile Island (which is near Harrisburg) but does not refer the reader to the article *Three Mile Island.* In such instances, a general index would be welcome.

The *Concise Columbia,* like its parent, the NEW COLUMBIA ENCYCLOPEDIA, is not a heavily illustrated volume. The relatively few illustrations that are included, however, add significantly to the informational value of the encyclopedia. All black-and-white line drawings, the illustrations deal almost exclusively with scientific and technical matters, such as diagrams of the human ear, nucleic acid, continental drift, and a poisonous mushroom. A few simple, black-and-white, staff-drawn maps of major countries appear throughout the text. In addition, 16 pages of physical maps by Rand McNally are included in the center of the book. These maps, all in color, depict the continents and Atlantic and Pacific Ocean floors. (In the Avon paperbound edition of the *Concise Columbia,* these Rand McNally maps are reproduced in black-and-white and are located at the back of the book; in the eight-volume large-print edition, these maps are integrated with the text and, like the paper edition, reproduced in black-and-white.) A great deal of information in the encyclopedia is presented in concise, convenient tabular form. Specifically, there are 41 tables on subjects ranging from African and American Indian languages and the dynasties of ancient Egypt to the Olympic Games and Shakespeare's plays. Physically, the *Concise Columbia* is a well-made book, with readable type and a clean layout. Desk-sized (7½ by 10¼ in.; 19 by 27 cm.), the volume is portable and reasonably easy to handle, weighing in at 4½ pounds (or less than half of what the NEW COLUMBIA ENCYCLOPEDIA weighs).

Critical reaction to the *Concise Columbia* has been overwhelmingly favorable. Harry Whitmore, in *Library Journal* (December 15, 1983, pp. 2323–24), concludes that the "*Concise Columbia* continues the high standards of its predecessors and is a useful ready reference and supplementary information source. There is no comparable work within its price range. Recommended for home and office purchase and for public, academic, school, and some special libraries." Samuel Rothstein, in *American Reference Books Annual* (1984, p. 13), says, "For the many people who want an encyclopedia that will be the counterpart of a good 'desk dictionary'—compact, inexpensive, authoritative, and up to date—the *Concise Columbia Encyclopedia* will be just the ticket." James Rettig ends his review in *Wilson Library Bulletin* (December 1983, p. 305) with these words: "Giving balanced subject coverage in clear, objective articles, the *Concise Columbia* merits accolades and frequent use as a desk reference." And a reviewer in *Booklist* (March 1, 1984, p. 952) finds the encyclopedia "a reasonably priced reference tool for all types of libraries and for home use as well. As such, it is an attractive alternative to other (and much heavier) one-volume encyclopedias."

To Summarize: The *Concise Columbia,* a desk-sized general encyclopedia based on and abridged from the older and larger NEW COLUMBIA ENCYCLOPEDIA, is an excellent work for adults and older students. Within the strictures of a single volume, the encyclopedia provides reliable, unbiased, and reasonably current coverage of essential knowledge, with emphasis on biographical, geographical, and scientific subjects. It is available in three different editions: hardbound, paperbound, and large print (the latter in eight volumes).

In Comparison: The *Concise Columbia,* published in one volume containing approximately one million words, is a small encyclopedia for adults and high school and college students. It cannot compare, at least in terms of quantity, with the leading one- and two-volume general adult encyclopedias currently on the market, namely, the

LINCOLN LIBRARY OF ESSENTIAL INFORMATION (two volumes; 3.5 million words), the RANDOM HOUSE ENCYCLOPEDIA (one volume; 3 million words), the VOLUME LIBRARY (two volumes; 3.5 million words), and the NEW COLUMBIA ENCYCLOPEDIA (one volume; 6.6 million words), from which the *Concise Columbia* derives. All of these encyclopedias, as the figures indicate, offer much more information than the *Concise Columbia*. Also, they are considerably more expensive. More in the *Concise Columbia* 's league are COLLINS GEM ENCYCLOPEDIA (two volumes; 450,000 words), the KNOWLEDGE ENCYCLOPEDIA (one volume; 300,000 words), PEARS CYCLOPAEDIA (one volume; 1.2 million words), and the QUICK REFERENCE HANDBOOK OF BASIC KNOWLEDGE (one volume; 750,000 words). Among these smallest of the small general encyclopedias for adults, the *Concise Columbia Encyclopedia* is hands down the best buy.

To Purchase the *Concise Columbia Encyclopedia:* If you are an individual consumer and wish to buy the encyclopedia, first check the retail bookstores in your area. If the encyclopedia is not in stock and no store will order it for you, you can order the encyclopedia directly from the publisher by contacting Columbia University Press at 136 South Broadway, Irvington, NY 10533 or telephone 914-591-6471. Both the hardbound edition (one volume; $29.95) and the large-print edition (eight volumes; $275.00) are handled by Columbia University Press. For the paperbound edition (one volume: $14.95), order directly from Avon Books, 1790 Broadway, New York, NY 10019 or telephone 212-399-4500. If you are ordering the encyclopedia for a school or library, place the order with your local book wholesaler.

For More Information about the *Concise Columbia Encyclopedia* See: *American Reference Books Annual,* 1984, p. 13 (review by Samuel Rothstein); *Booklist,* March 1, 1984, pp. 951–52 (unsigned review); *Library Journal,* December 15, 1983, pp. 2323–24 (review by Harry E. Whitmore); *Publishers Weekly,* April 1, 1983, p. 29 (unsigned article entitled "Erudition and Humor in Two from Avon"); *Wilson Library Bulletin,* December 1983, p. 305 (review by James Rettig).

Disney's Wonderful World of Knowledge

FACTS

Disney's Wonderful World of Knowledge. Originally published in Italian as *Enciclopedia Disney* (16 volumes; 1970). New York: Danbury Press, a division of Grolier, Inc. 20 volumes. First English-language edition published in 1973. Lowest retail price: $229.50.

    Disney's Wonderful World of Knowledge, aimed chiefly at beginning readers and primary school students, is described as "a library of human knowledge for children that masterfully combines learning with the magic of vivid color and imagination in 20 beautiful volumes" (advertisement). The set contains approximately 2,500 pages, 1,200 articles, and 750,000 words. The articles average 600 words in length (or about two pages). They are accompanied by 4,000 illustrations (all in color), plus 50 maps. The set is arranged topically, each volume dealing with a broad subject or theme: *Animals* (Volume 1); *Natural Wonders* (Volume 2); *Inventions* (Volume 3); *Transportation* (Volume 4); *Caves to Skyscrapers* (Volume 5); *Birds, Fish, and Insects* (Volume 6); *Exploration and Discovery* (Volume 7); *Treasures of the Earth* (Volume 8); *Science and Technology* (Volume 9); *Myths and Legends* (Volume 10); *Holidays Around the World* (Volume 11); *A Tour Through Time* (Volume 12); *The Continents* (Volume 13); *Stories* (Volume 14); *The Human Body* (Volume 15); *The Far West* (Volume 16); *Great Capitals* (Volume 17); *Great Leaders* (Volume 18); and *Art Through the Ages* (Volume 19). Access to specific information is enhanced by an index (Volume 20) of some 12,000 entries. There are no cross-references in the text.

EVALUATION

Disney's originated abroad in 1970 as a 16-volume Italian-language set entitled *Enciclopedia Disney.* In 1973, Grolier, a leading North American publisher of encyclopedias, issued a revised and enlarged version of the work in English under the title *Disney's Wonderful World of Knowledge.* Not revised since it first appeared and sold mainly via mail order, *Disney's* has never been considered more than a marginal item for young children.

    Like CHILDCRAFT and COMPTON'S PRECYCLOPEDIA (two quality works aimed at the same audience as *Disney's*), the set covers a broad range of topics of potential interest to beginning readers, but it is not an encyclopedia in the strictest sense, nor does it claim to provide encyclopedic coverage of people, places, events, etc. Promotional literature for the set explains: "*Disney's Wonderful World of Knowledge* fills the gap before the young reader is ready for conventional reference sets by adding that special dimension of entertainment and adventure to the fascinating world of fact. With an irrepressible host of Disney's best-loved characters as guides, each enchanting volume takes the young reader on a personal 'tour' of the breathtaking wonders of the world." In reality, the set's coverage leaves much to be desired, as a reviewer in *Booklist* (July 15, 1975, p. 1202) emphatically points out: "Sometimes information one would expect to find is not included. A child wanting to learn more about robins, a very familiar bird to children, would find only one reference.... Most of the information, while interesting and accurate, is miscellaneous in nature and not organized in such a way as to be useful in writing reports at school or in satisfying individual curiosity at home."

Information in *Disney's* is normally reliable and unbiased. Indeed, in some instances the material is taken verbatim from the NEW BOOK OF KNOWLEDGE, a highly regarded set for elementary and junior high school students also published by Grolier. Recency of information is not so important in a juvenile set like *Disney's* as it is in a true encyclopedia, but nonetheless, *Disney's* is now well over a decade old and some of the volumes—*Inventions, Transportation, Science and Technology,* and *Great Leaders* in particular—are beginning to show their age. The set's writing style is often quite informal, especially when the Disney characters are speaking ("Oh, dear, sorry about that scientific stuff, but I thought you needed to catch your breath"), and readability levels vary from volume to volume. Generally speaking, the text will be understandable to children ages six to ten who possess good reading skills, but some of the articles in *Disney's,* especially those in the science area, require reading capabilities beyond those of most primary school students.

The contents of the set are reasonably accessible by means of the master index in Volume 20. (Individual volumes also have their own indexes.) The index, however, contains a high error rate and many of the set's illustrations are not indexed. The illustrations, which make up an estimated 65 percent of the total text, are all in color and usually informative and well reproduced. They include 3,000 photographs, art reproductions, diagrams, and drawings. There are also some 1,000 cartoon drawings featuring Disney characters (Mickey and Minnie Mouse, Donald Duck, et al.) as storytelling guides. A review in *Booklist* (July 15, 1975, p. 1203) criticizes this approach: "The mixture of Disney cartoon art and the illustrations is incompatible and also makes for [a] cluttered and unattractive page. Children who appreciate the fine pictures will be insulted by the babyish cartoon characters running across the pages and often on top of the pictures detracting from their visual impact." Physically, *Disney's* is pleasant to look at and sturdily bound, although the volumes do not lie flat when open.

To Summarize: *Disney's Wonderful World of Knowledge* is a second-rate browsing set for young children. Published in 1973 and never revised, the set is colorful and interestingly written but it lacks consistent reading levels, accurate indexing, and current information.

In Comparison: *Disney's Wonderful World of Knowledge*, a 20-volume set for young readers containing 750,000 words, is most similar in concept and format to CHARLIE BROWN'S 'CYCLOPEDIA (15 volumes; 180,000 words), a supermarket item distributed by Funk & Wagnalls, Inc. Topically arranged and utilizing the "Peanuts" gang much as *Disney's* makes use of Walt Disney characters, CHARLIE BROWN'S 'CYCLOPEDIA is more current and less expensive than *Disney's*. *Disney's* also competes with two other multivolume encyclopedia sets for beginning readers: CHILDCRAFT (15 volumes; 750,000 words) and COMPTON'S PRECYCLOPEDIA (16 volumes; 325,000 words), also published as the YOUNG CHILDREN'S ENCYCLOPEDIA. Both of these sets are superior to *Disney's* in practically every way. On balance, CHILDCRAFT is the best of these works. One other set, the NEW TALKING CASSETTE ENCYCLOPEDIA (10 volumes; 100,000 words), is also aimed at the beginning reader. A unique work in that it is published on cassette tape rather than in print form, the NEW TALKING CASSETTE ENCYCLOPEDIA is limited almost solely to classroom use, because of its high price ($695) and unusual format.

To Purchase *Disney's Wonderful World of Knowledge:* *Disney's* has been sold over the years almost exclusively as a mail-order product. However, if you are an individual consumer and wish to order the set, contact Grolier, Inc. at Sherman Turnpike, Danbury, CT 06816 or telephone toll-free 1-800-243-7256. If the set is available, your name will be forwarded to a sales representative in your area who will handle the transaction. The possibility exists, however, that *Disney's* may no longer be in stock. For some time, Grolier has been reporting that the set will soon be discontinued. In the past, the publisher has also sold *Disney's* to schools and libraries in a reinforced binding. To determine the status and price of this edition, contact Grolier Educational Corporation at the address or telephone number given above.

For More Information about *Disney's Wonderful World of Knowledge* See: *Booklist,* July 15, 1975, pp. 1202–23 (unsigned review).

Encyclopedia Americana

FACTS

The Encyclopedia Americana. Bernard S. Cayne, Editorial Director; Alan H. Smith, Editor in Chief. Danbury, CT: Grolier, Inc. 30 volumes. Former title: *The Americana* (1907–12). International edition published in 1918–20; new printing with revisions each year since 1936. Lowest retail price: $1,200 plus shipping and handling; with discount to schools and libraries: $799 plus shipping and handling.

The 30-volume *Encyclopedia Americana,* the first multivolume general encyclopedia of any consequence to be published in North America (first edition, 1829–33), is currently the second largest English-language encyclopedia available (after the NEW ENCYCLOPAEDIA BRITANNICA). Intended for adults and college and advanced high school students, the *Americana* aims to be "a bridge between the worlds of the specialist and the general reader" (preface). The encyclopedia contains 26,690 pages, 52,000 articles, and an estimated 31 million words. The articles, many of which are of the specific-entry type, average about 600 words in length (or half a page). They are accompanied by 22,425 illustrations (2,200 in full color), plus 1,270 maps. Approximately 6,400 editors, advisers, and contributors are listed at the beginning of Volume 1. About 75 percent of the articles are signed. The *Americana* is arranged alphabetically word by word (*New York* precedes *Newspaper*), with access to specific information enhanced by 40,000 cross-references in the text and a general index of 353,000 entries.

EVALUATION

The *Americana* first appeared between 1829 and 1833 in 13 volumes. Edited by Francis Lieber, a well-known scholar, the work was loosely based on a translation of the seventh edition of *Konversations-Lexikon,* a popular German encyclopedia familiarly known as *Brockhaus,* after its publisher Friedrich Arnold Brockhaus. At the turn of the century, the set expanded to 16 volumes under the editorship of Frederick Converse Beach, who also edited the magazine *Scientific American.* The *Americana* reached its present size of 30 volumes with the publication of the International edition in 1918–20, the last entirely new edition of the encyclopedia. Over the years, the *Americana* has met with great favor in North America and throughout the English-speaking world. The publisher, Grolier, Inc. is a leading publisher of reference materials, and the set's current editors are experienced hands. An impressive roster of contributors adds to the set's authority, although a relatively high number of those listed are retired or deceased.

As might be expected, the *Americana* covers all important subjects and areas of knowledge. While international in scope, its coverage has traditionally emphasized U.S. and Canadian geography, biography, history, and institutions. In recent years, however, many less important historical figures and smaller places in North America have been systematically excised from the set, the space gained used to expand or add articles on topics of greater significance. In point of fact, over the past 20 years or so, the total number of articles in the *Americana* has dropped from around 60,000 to 52,000, dramatic evidence of the encyclopedia's changing contents. The *Americana* has also long been noted for its substantial coverage of scientific and technical subjects, an emphasis that remains as strong today as in the past. Another valuable feature is the encyclopedia's many separate articles on famous works of art, literature, and music, such as the *Mona Lisa,* F. Scott Fitzgerald's *Great Gatsby,* and Gilbert and Sullivan's *Pirates of Penzance.*

Information in the *Americana* is normally accurate and unbiased. For example, the article *Capital Punishment* includes a long and balanced discussion under the subheading "Debate on the Value of Capital Punishment." Such articles as *Abortion, Circumcision,* and *Sacco-Vanzetti Case* are equally objective. Information in the encyclopedia is reasonably current in most instances. The article on Richard D'Oyly Carte, for example, notes that his famous D'Oyly Carte Opera Company, established in 1881 to perform Gilbert and Sullivan operettas, "folded on Feb. 27, 1982." Not all major encyclopedias have yet recorded this important fact. Similarly, articles on acquired immune deficiency syndrome (AIDS), asbestos, circumcision, Nicaragua, Ayn Rand, and robots are very much up-to-date. On the other hand, some articles are dated, as in the case of *Group Insurance* and *Health Insurance.* But overall efforts to keep the *Americana* current have improved measurably during the 1980s. The 1984 printing, for example, includes approximately 380 entirely new articles, 600 completely rewritten articles, and 1,000 revised articles, along with 445 new photographs and 325 new or revised maps—all involving changes in more than 2,400 of the set's 26,690 pages. Much of the revision effort centers on what the editors call the "rebuilding program," wherein one or two volumes of the encyclopedia are thoroughly overhauled each year. Twenty-five of the set's 30 volumes (1–19, 21–26) have been rebuilt thus far since the program was initiated in 1967. As noted in the preceding paragraph, numerous short biographical and geographical articles have been eliminated during this long, comprehensive volume-by-volume revision.

The *Americana*'s writing style is customarily clear and functional. Consider, for example, the first two paragraphs of the article *Earthquake:*

> EARTHQUAKE, a shaking of the ground caused by the breaking and shifting of subterranean rock under immense pressure. The vibrations that constitute an earthquake are at times sufficiently severe to damage or destroy man-made structures and to effect visible changes in the earth's surface. Often the vibrations are felt by people but cause no destruction. In the great majority of cases their existence is known only through records of their passage obtained on instruments called seismographs, designed to register this kind of ground movement.
>
> When earthquake waves are recorded by seismographs at distant points, the patterns indicate that the waves originated within a limited region, called the *focus* of the earthquake. It is thought that many foci are in the range of 30 miles (50 km) in length and breadth, but a few of the largest may measure up to 500 or 600 miles (800 to 960 km). Foci have been located at depths down to a little more than 1/10 of the earth's radius (about 400 miles, or 640 km). An important question for seismologists is why they are no deeper.

As this example clearly shows, the *Americana* is written for adults and older students who possess good reading skills. Although technical terms such as *focus* and *seismograph* are explained or defined in context, the encyclopedia is not normally appropriate for children or young students.

The contents of the encyclopedia are readily accessible in most instances. Cross-references are used sparingly (considering the size of the set). For example, the eight-page article *Earthquake* contains not a single cross-reference, even though articles like *Fault* and *Seismograph* offer much related information. Fortunately, the *Americana* does have an effective index. Found in Volume 30, the 838-page analytical index consists of over 350,000 entries. In terms of the ratio of index entries to total words in the encyclopedia (31 million), the *Americana* provides one index entry for every 90 words of text, or a ratio of 1:90. Among the *Americana*'s chief competitors, COLLIER'S ENCYCLOPEDIA has a much better ratio (1:50), whereas the NEW ENCYCLOPAEDIA BRITANNICA is not as impressive (1:110).

Illustrations in the *Americana,* well over half of which are photographs, tend to be dark and uninspiring. Harvey Einbinder, in an article entitled "Encyclopedias: Some Foreign and Domestic Developments" in *Wilson Library Bulletin* (December 1980, p. 261), hits the nail on the proverbial head when he states: "Revising an encyclopedia is a thankless task. Editors generally have little freedom and authority. They are often forced to utilize continuous revision and are unable to introduce new visual methods of presenting factual information. This handicap is quite noticeable in *Collier's* and the *Americana*. These encyclopedias rely on black-and-white illustrations and rarely use line drawings, diagrams, charts, or colored pictures to supplement their text. As a result, they exude a staid, antiquarian languor, rather than the bustling excitement of a vital repository of contemporary knowledge." Efforts are currently under way to improve this situation, however slowly. For example, in 1983 the *Americana* article *Painting* included 28 black-and-white and only six color reproductions of famous artwork, but in 1984 the article was completely revised and now has nearly 100 illustrations, all in color. Bibliographies in the encyclopedia, appended to some 10,000 articles, are also undistinguished, mainly because so many of them are dated and hence do not always represent the best sources to consult for further information. From a physical standpoint, the encyclopedia is well made but lacks aesthetic appeal.

On balance, recent reviews of the *Americana* have been favorable. Bohdan Wynar, a knowledgeable critic, writes in *American Reference Books Annual* (1984, p. 15): "In conclusion, we would like to repeat that in spite of certain shortcomings, *Americana* remains a well-edited and comprehensive work, which is highly recommended to all types of libraries as well as for home use." A review in *Booklist* (December 1, 1983, p. 546) concludes that the *Americana* "remains a very good, all-purpose encyclopedia for American users. Its standards are high, its coverage is broad, its language is clear, and its announced policy of continuous revision is consistently and conscientiously carried out." And William A. Katz, another highly regarded critic, notes in his *Introduction to Reference Work* (1982, vol. 1, p. 185), "As the title implies, the strength of this work is the emphasis on American history, geography, and biography. This encyclopedia unquestionably places greater emphasis on this area than any of the other sets, and it is particularly useful for finding out-of-the-way, little-known material about the United States."

To Summarize: The *Americana,* the first major general encyclopedia published in North America (1829–), is a well-established, ably edited set for adults and older students. It has a number of conspicuous strengths, most notably a clear writing style, accurate and unbiased presentation of information, and strong coverage of U.S. and Canadian topics (despite the deletion of many minor biographical and geographical articles in recent years). In addition, its contents are easily accessible, due mainly to the set's effective index. On the debit side, the *Americana* has lackluster illustrations and bibliographies, and the set is sometimes not as current as it might be, although much improvement has been made in this area during the 1980s.

In Comparison: The *Americana,* published in 30 volumes containing 31 million words, is a large encyclopedia for adults and college and high school students with serious informational needs. It compares quite favorably with the other two large general adult encyclopedias currently available, namely COLLIER'S ENCYCLOPEDIA (24 volumes; 21 million words) and the NEW ENCYCLOPAEDIA BRITANNICA (32 volumes; 44 million words). Of these three large sets, COLLIER'S ENCYCLOPEDIA is the smallest, but it is also the most current, best indexed, easiest to read, and least expensive. On the other hand, the NEW ENCYCLOPAEDIA BRITANNICA is the largest, most scholarly, and most prestigious of the three. The *Americana* tends to come off second-best in just about every evaluative test (size, readability, accessibility, up-to-dateness, prestige, price, etc.), although its coverage of North American people, places, and events is superior. Each of these large sets is, on balance, an excellent work that can be recommended without hesitation to those who truly require a large, costly adult encyclopedia. Because of the expense involved (each of these encyclopedias costs more than $1,000 at retail), consumers are urged to examine all three sets closely prior to making a final purchase decision.

To Purchase the *Encyclopedia Americana:* If you are an individual consumer and wish to order the encyclopedia, contact Grolier, Inc. at Sherman Turnpike, Danbury, CT 06816 or telephone toll-free 1-800-243-7256. Your name will be forwarded to a sales representative in your area who will handle the transaction. The sales representative will most likely attempt to sell you additional publications with the encyclopedia, including a yearbook entitled the *Americana Annual.* You need not buy any extras unless you want them. In the case of the *Americana Annual,* the book is a solid chronicle of the year's events but it has minimal relationship to the encyclopedia.

If you are ordering the encyclopedia for a school or library, contact Grolier Educational Corporation at the address or telephone number given above. Your order will be processed immediately.

For More Information about the *Encyclopedia Americana* See: *American Reference Books Annual,* 1984, pp. 13–15 (review by Bohdan S. Wynar); *Booklist,* December 15, 1984, pp. 568–70 (unsigned review); *Booklist,* December 1, 1983, pp. 554–46 (unsigned review); *Introduction to Reference Work* by William A. Katz (4th ed., New York: McGraw-Hill, 1982), vol. 1: *Basic Information Sources,* pp. 182–86; *Reference Sources for Small and Medium-sized Libraries* (4th ed., Chicago: American Library Association, 1984), pp. 27–28 (review by Jovian P. Lang); *Wilson Library Bulletin,* December 1980, p. 261 (article by Harvey Einbinder entitled "Encyclopedias: Some Foreign and Domestic Developments").

Encyclopedia International

FACTS

Encyclopedia International. Also published as the *New Age Encyclopedia, Webster's New Age Encyclopedia,* and *Webster's New Family Encyclopedia.* Bernard S. Cayne, Editorial Director; Edward Humphrey, Editor in Chief. Danbury, CT: Lexicon Publications, a subsidiary of Grolier, Inc. 20 volumes. First published in 1963–64; out of print since 1982 (last priced at $450).

The *Encyclopedia International,* which has recently been discontinued by Grolier, Inc. "is intended to serve both the cultural and practical interests of the whole family, and it is especially concerned with the needs of students on the various school levels" (preface). The set has also been published in recent years as the *New Age Encyclopedia, Webster's New Age Encyclopedia,* and *Webster's New Family Encyclopedia,* and it may currently be on the North American market under any or all of these titles. When last issued by Grolier in 1982, the 20-volume encyclopedia contained 11,927 pages, 29,728 articles, and 9.5 million words. The articles, most of which are of the short-entry type, average about 300 words in length (or roughly a third of a page). They are accompanied by 12,836 illustrations (20 percent in color), plus 875 maps. Some 2,000 editors and contributors are identified, the latter listed in the final volume. All except the briefest articles are signed. The encyclopedia is arranged alphabetically letter by letter (*Newspaper* precedes *New York*), with access to specific information enhanced by 15,000 cross-references and an analytical index of 126,000 entries.

EVALUATION

The first few volumes of the *International* appeared in 1963, with the rest of the set following early the next year. Designed to replace the old, worn-out *Grolier Encyclopedia* (1944–61), the *International* served as the publisher's middle-sized general encyclopedia for secondary school students and the family as a whole, standing between the larger ENCYCLOPEDIA AMERICANA, intended for adults and advanced students, and the smaller NEW BOOK OF KNOWLEDGE, aimed at children and younger students. In 1965, Grolier issued an inexpensive abridged version of the *International* under the title *Grolier Universal*

Encyclopedia, but the set failed to catch on and it expired in 1972. In recent years, the *International* has not been adequately maintained, the rate of annual revision falling well below acceptable standards. Finally, in 1982, Grolier discontinued publication. At about the same time, Grolier acquired the rights to publish the ACADEMIC AMERICAN ENCYCLOPEDIA, an excellent general work of recent vintage that is roughly the same size as the *International.* As previously noted, however, older printings of the *International* may currently be available under such titles as the *New Age Encyclopedia, Webster's New Age Encyclopedia,* and *Webster's New Family Encyclopedia.* Usually distributed through door-to-door or mail-order sales campaigns, these titles should not be purchased at any price without first very carefully examining the set, especially for currentness of material.

The *International,* though no longer published, is not a shamefully bad encyclopedia. Its coverage, which consists chiefly of short articles on specific topics, emphasizes people, places, and events. It also devotes considerable space to practical subjects, such as mortgages, medical problems, fire safety, and recreational activities. Information in the set is normally reliable, and there are few instances of bias or stereotyping. Likewise, the information is usually accessible, due principally to an effective system of cross-references and a good general index. The writing style is, in the words of a review in *Booklist* (December 15, 1978, p. 709), "lucid and concise," though sometimes the prose lacks vitality. The text, which has been tested for readability by Dr. Jeanne Chall using the Dale-Chall formula, will be comprehensible to adults and older students reading at the junior high school level or beyond. As might be expected, potentially difficult or unfamiliar terms are defined or explained in context.

The encyclopedia's greatest liability in recent times has been lack of up-to-dateness. As William A. Katz observes in his *Introduction to Reference Work* (1982, vol. 1, p. 188), "While the material [in the *International*] is accurate and clear, it is too often dated." The most recent review of the set in *Booklist* (December 15, 1978, p. 710) echoes this criticism, finding "the currency of *International*'s articles to be uneven," and the bibliographies to be "too old and too few." And Janet Littlefield, in a lengthy and informative review in *American Reference Books Annual* (1982, p. 36), describes the situation this way: "Unfortunately, *International*'s major fault is its datedness. Grolier's editorial department indicates that some 1,000 articles are new or revised for the 1981 edition. Although *International* indicates that it is continuously revised, the 3% revision of the 1981 edition is below the revision rate of 10% per year recommended by most authorities." Another glaring problem that plagues the encyclopedia is its frequently dreary illustrations, the large majority of which are reproduced in black-and-white. In some cases, the illustrations are so dark as to be of little or no informational value.

To Summarize: The *Encyclopedia International,* a well-known multivolume set for the family generally and secondary school students in particular, first appeared in 1963–64 and was discontinued, at least for the time being, in 1982. Although still a respectable encyclopedia in many ways, the *International* suffers conspicuously from out-of-date material and illustrations that are dull and sometimes poorly reproduced. Older printings of the *International* may be found on the secondhand book market. In addition, the encyclopedia has been distributed under a variety of other titles, specifically the *New Age Encyclopedia, Webster's New Age Encyclopedia,* and *Webster's New Family Encyclopedia.* These titles, which date from the mid-1970s or before, are not recommended. Consumers are advised to see a note in the January 1, 1983, issue of *Booklist* (p. 633) pointing out that advertising for *Webster's New Family Encyclopedia* "is both false and misleading."

In Comparison: When it was being published, the *International* competed directly with the major sets for young adults and the family, namely COMPTON'S ENCYCLOPEDIA, MERIT STUDENTS ENCYCLOPEDIA, and the WORLD BOOK ENCYCLOPEDIA. All three of these encyclopedias are superior to the *International* in practically every respect. Note that the *International* (20 volumes; 9.5 million words) has been replaced in the Grolier family of encyclopedias by the similarly sized ACADEMIC AMERICAN ENCYCLOPEDIA (21 volumes: 9 million words).

For More Information about the *Encyclopedia International* See: *American Reference Books Annual,* 1982, pp. 35–37 (review by Janet H. Littlefield); *Booklist,* January 1, 1983, p. 633 (note by Helen K. Wright regarding advertising for *Webster's New Family Encyclopedia* ; see also a follow-up note in *Booklist,* February 1, 1983, p. 738); *Booklist,* December 15, 1978, pp. 709–11 (unsigned review); *Introduction to Reference Work* by William A. Katz (4th ed., New York: McGraw-Hill, 1982), vol 1: *Basic Information Sources,* pp. 187–88.

Everyman's Encyclopaedia

FACTS

Everyman's Encyclopaedia. David A. Girling, Editor. London, England: J.M. Dent & Sons Ltd. Distributed in Canada by Fitzhenry & Whiteside Publishers (the encyclopedia is not sold in the United

States in printed form). 12 volumes. Former title: *Everyman Encyclopaedia* (first edition, 1913–14). Former titles in North America: *Macmillan Everyman's Encyclopedia* (fourth edition, 1958); *International Everyman's Encyclopedia* (fifth edition, 1967). Sixth edition published in 1978. Lowest retail price in Canada: $401.50; recommended retail price in the United Kingdom: £195.00.

Everyman's Encyclopaedia, which intends to be "an authoritative source of facts and information" (advertisement), is a medium-sized general encyclopedia of British origin for adults and older students. The 12-volume encyclopedia contains 8,896 pages, 51,000 articles, and approximately 9 million words. The articles, the large majority of which are of the specific-entry type, average under 200 words in length (or roughly a fifth of a page). They are accompanied by about 5,000 illustrations (all in black-and-white), plus 600 maps, including a 64-page color atlas in the final volume. Some 400 editors and contributors are noted, although none of the articles is signed. The encyclopedia is arranged alphabetically word by word (*New York* precedes *Newspaper*), with access to specific information enhanced by nearly 15,000 cross-references. The set has no index. The encyclopedia is also available in electronic form through Dialog Information Services, Inc., a leading database vendor located in Palo Alto, California. (For additional information about the electronic version of *Everyman's,* see the section on purchasing the encyclopedia below.)

EVALUATION

The British-made *Everyman's,* published by the highly respected London firm of J.M. Dent & Sons Ltd., has been part of the English-language encyclopedia scene for three-quarters of a century, the first edition appearing in 1913–14 in 12 volumes, with thorough revisions issued at irregular intervals: second edition, 1931–32; third edition, 1950; fourth edition, 1958; fifth edition, 1967; and, most recently, the sixth edition in 1978, prepared at a reputed cost of £1 million. The 1958 (fourth) edition was distributed in North America under the title *Macmillan Everyman's Encyclopedia* and the fifth (1967) edition as the *International Everyman's Encyclopedia* (an Americanized version of the encyclopedia in 20 volumes that contained approximately one million words more than the British edition). Both of these titles have long since disappeared from the market. The current, sixth (1978) edition is distributed in North America only in Canada by the firm of Fitzhenry & Whiteside Publishers of Ontario. The encyclopedia is not sold in print form in the United States mainly because, in the words of a Dent representative, "we did not acquire the picture rights for the U.S.A." As noted above, however, *Everyman's* is available in the United States in electronic form. Basically, *Everyman's* is produced in Great Britain chiefly by Britons for Britons, but the encyclopedia is well known and regarded throughout the English-speaking world.

It should come as no surprise, then, that the encyclopedia's coverage, though nominally international in scope, heavily emphasizes British and European people, places, events, and developments. A.J. Walford, reviewing the sixth edition in the *Library Association Record* (September 1979, p. 439), notes that "the British slant is reflected in such contributions as that on Medical education: London boroughs and London, Oxford and Cambridge colleges and institutes each have entries. Hull received nearly three pages; Hamburg, about two-thirds of a page." Biographical entries, which range from Aristotle to Zola, account for roughly 25 percent of the total contents. The large majority of articles are quite brief. As Nicholas Bagnall observes in a review in the "Books of the Week" section of the London *Sunday Times* (December 31, 1978, p. 12), "Instead of trying, as the old 'Britannicas' successfully did, to make us swallow a subject like architecture or international trade in a single, huge gulp, they [the editors of *Everyman's*] have divided it into tasty bits. So international trade can be studied under 'Devaluation,' 'Free Trade,' 'Balance of Payments,' 'Protection' or whatever, according to requirements: the total sum of information is more impressive than it looks."

Everyman's has a well-deserved reputation as an authoritative, accurate, and unbiased encyclopedia. Another strength is the set's clear, straightforward writing style. Technical terms are often italicized and defined at the point of use. In addition, articles about things and events customarily begin with a definition, an aid to clarity. For instance, the article *Armada, Spanish* begins, "Armada is a Spanish word meaning simply an armed force, but is now applied especially to the great Spanish fleet fitted out against England in 1588." Consumers should understand, however, that *Everyman's* is strictly for adults and older students who possess average or better reading skills. The encyclopedia will not normally be comprehensible to children or younger students.

Everyman's also has a number of conspicuous weaknesses. Perhaps the most glaring is the encyclopedia's lack of continuous revision. Unlike practically all of the better general multivolume encyclopedias produced in North America (such as the ACADEMIC AMERICAN ENCYCLOPEDIA, COLLIER'S ENCYCLOPEDIA, COMPTON'S ENCYCLOPEDIA, ENCYCLOPEDIA AMERICANA, MERIT STUDENTS ENCYCLOPEDIA, the NEW ENCYCLOPAEDIA BRITANNICA, and the WORLD BOOK ENCYCLOPEDIA), *Everyman's* is not updated on an annual basis. Rather, the publisher issues an entirely new edition when it is determined that the present one has become excessively dated. But knowledge is now changing so rapidly that an encyclopedia that is revised only every eight or ten years, as has been the case with *Everyman's* since 1950, is woefully out-of-date most of the time. For example, users of the current, sixth edition, published in 1978, will search in vain for any mention of such contemporary topics as acquired immune deficiency syndrome (AIDS), the development of the artificial heart, and the Falkland Islands conflict between Great Britain and Argentina. Nor will articles on such subjects as abortion, apartheid, Canada, capital punishment, and computers provide anything approaching current information.

Another problem that affects the encyclopedia's peformance as an effective source of information is its lack of an index. Cross-references, printed in SMALL CAPITAL LETTERS within the text of articles, help steer the user in the right direction sometimes, but they hardly compensate for a good analytical index. Still another limitation is *Everyman's* relatively dull, staid appearance, due in large part to the lack of color among the set's 5,000 or so illustrations. In some instances, black-and-white illustrations are just as instructive as ones in color, but that is not so in the case of flags, flowers, art work, etc.

To Summarize: *Everyman's,* a British-made general encyclopedia that dates back to 1913–14, is both authoritative and reliable as a source of information for adults and older students. Unfortunately, the set is revised too infrequently; it lacks a needed index; and it has unexciting illustrations and a dull design. Another negative point, at least in the eyes of most North American consumers, is the encyclopedia's strong British flavor.

In Comparison: *Everyman's,* published in 12 volumes containing 9 million words, is one of two major British general multivolume encyclopedias for adults currently on the market. The other is the NEW CAXTON ENCYCLOPEDIA (20 volumes; 6 million words), a more popularly written and aesthetically appealing work than *Everyman's.* The only other multivolume adult British encyclopedia of any consequence is CHAMBERS'S ENCYCLOPAEDIA (15 volumes; 14.5 million words), which regrettably is now very dated and has been out of print since the late 1970s. North American consumers seeking a middle-sized encyclopedia for the family would be well advised to forget about *Everyman's* (and the NEW CAXTON ENCYCLOPEDIA) and look toward such quality sets as the ACADEMIC AMERICAN ENCYCLOPEDIA, COMPTON'S ENCYCLOPEDIA, MERIT STUDENTS ENCYCLOPEDIA, and the WORLD BOOK ENCYCLOPEDIA, all made on this side of the Atlantic. Indeed, one of the reasons the publisher of *Everyman's* has given for not selling the current edition in the United States is that "there are really too many American encyclopedias for us to publish an edition there" (see *Publishers Weekly,* January 8, 1979, p. 44).

To Purchase *Everyman's Encyclopaedia:* As previously noted, *Everyman's* is sold in North America in print form only in Canada. Interested consumers should contact Fitzhenry & Whiteside Publishers at 195 Allstate Parkway, Markham, Ontario L3R 4T8 or telephone 416-477-0030. The encyclopedia is not sold in the United

States in print form, but the text is available in electronic (or online) form. For access and price information concerning the electronic version of *Everyman's,* contact Dialog Information Services, Inc. 3460 Hillview Avenue, Palo Alto, CA 94304 or telephone toll-free 1-800-227-1927 (outside California); in California call 1-800-982-5838. Finally, *Everyman's* is published in Great Britain by J.M. Dent & Sons Ltd. at Aldine House, 33 Welbeck Street, London W1M 8LX. Any questions about acquiring the encyclopedia that cannot be answered by either Fitzhenry & Whiteside or Dialog should be sent directly to Dent in London.

   For More Information about *Everyman's Encyclopaedia* **See:** *Library Association Record,* September 1979, p. 439 (review by A.J. Walford); *Sunday Times* (London), December 31, 1978, "Books of the Week" section, p. 12 (review by Nicholas Bagnall).

Finding Out: Silver Burdett's Children's Encyclopedia

FACTS

Finding Out: Silver Burdett's Children's Encyclopedia. John Paton, Editor. Morristown, NJ: Silver Burdett Company. Copyright by Grisewood & Dempsey Ltd. of London, England. Ten volumes. First edition published in 1980 in England; 1981 printing adapted for and published in the United States. Lowest retail price: $140.00 plus shipping and handling; with discount to schools and libraries: $105.00 plus shipping and handling.

   The ten-volume *Finding Out: Silver Burdett's Children's Encyclopedia,* originally published in Great Britain and adapted for use in the United States, is aimed specifically at elementary school students in grades three to six. The encyclopedia contains 816 pages, approximately 1,300 articles, and 250,000 words. The articles, which tend to be quite brief, average just under 200 words in length (or one and a half articles per page). They are accompanied by 2,000 illustrations (almost all in color), plus 100 simple maps. Twenty-four editors and contributors are listed at the front of each volume, although none of the articles is signed. The encyclopedia is arranged alphabetically letter by letter (*Newspaper* precedes *New York*), with access to specific information enhanced by 1,500 cross-references in the text and two indexes totaling 6,000 entries, one alphabetical (4,400 entries) and the other topical (1,600 entries).

EVALUATION

The British-made *Finding Out* first appeared in 1980 under the imprint of the London publisher Grisewood & Dempsey Ltd. The following year, the encyclopedia was "adapted and published in the United States" (title page) by the Silver Burdett Company of Morristown, New Jersey, a firm best known for its distribution of Time-Life books in durable library bindings. The editor of *Finding Out,* John Paton, is an experienced hand, having also edited the KNOWLEDGE ENCYCLOPEDIA and RAND McNALLY'S CHILDREN'S ENCYCLOPEDIA, both one-volume items also originally published by Grisewood & Dempsey. The late Michael Dempsey (of Grisewood & Dempsey) is well known in Great Britain as a publisher and editor of encyclopedias for young people, such as the 16-volume HARVER JUNIOR WORLD ENCYCLOPEDIA (which resembles *Finding Out* in many ways) and single-volume works like the *Great World Encyclopedia* (1975) and *Purnell's First Encyclopedia in Colour* (1974). Dempsey has also written many books for children on scientific subjects, which perhaps accounts for *Finding Out*'s heavy emphasis on the natural and technical sciences.

Finding Out selectively covers knowledge of potential interest to young readers ages seven to twelve. Volume 3, for instance, begins with these articles: *Commonwealth; Communism; Compass; Compounds; Computers; Concrete; Confucius; Congo; Congress; Conifers; Connecticut; Constantinople; Constitution, American; Continental Shelf;* and *Continents.* Overall, roughly half of the articles deal with scientific topics. Significant people, places, and events in the United States are covered, including a brief entry for each state. Similar Canadian subjects, however, are largely ignored. Not surprisingly, British historical events and personalities receive considerable coverage, as in the articles *Victoria, Queen; Waterloo, Battle of; Wellington, Duke of; William the Conqueror*; and *William of Orange.*

Information in *Finding Out* is normally accurate and presented in an objective manner. For example, the article on Vietnam states, "Vietnam used to be divided into two countries, North Vietnam and South Vietnam. Hanoi was the main city in the north and Saigon (now called Ho Chi Minh City) in the south. From the 1950s until 1975, the two countries were at war. South Vietnam was supported by the United States. North Vietnam was communist. Now the whole country is communist." Information in the set is also reasonably current as of the late 1970s, as the foregoing example shows. The writing style is usually clear, simple, and interesting. Most of the text will be comprehensible to elementary school students in grades three through six, and precocious beginning readers as well as slow junior high school students may also find much of the material understandable. Consider, for instance, the first two paragraphs of the article *Earthquake:*

> People often use the saying "safe as houses." But in certain lands houses sometimes topple over because the ground starts trembling. This trembling is called an earthquake. About half a million earthquakes happen every year. Most are so weak that only special instruments called *seismographs* show that they have happened. Only one earthquake in 500 does any damage. But some earthquakes can cause terrible damage and suffering. Three-quarters of a million people are thought to have died when an earthquake hit the Chinese city of Tangshan in 1976.
>
> Small tremors can happen when VOLCANOES erupt, when there is a landslide, or when the roof of an underground cave falls in. The largest earthquakes occur when one huge piece of the Earth's crust slips suddenly against another piece. This slipping may take place deep underground. But the shock travels up through the crust and sets the surface quaking.

The contents of *Finding Out* are readily accessible. Some 1,500 cross-references throughout the text assist users in locating additional information. For example, in the excerpt from the article *Earthquake* quoted above, the word VOLCANOES is printed in SMALL CAPITAL LETTERS, indicating that the encyclopedia has an article entitled *Volcanoes* where more or related material on the subject can be found. The set also has two indexes, both found at the end of Volume 10. The first and most important index is an alphabetical list of 4,400 entries that provides access to specific information in the set. This index is reliable and useful, but occasionally it fails to deliver. As pointed out in a review of *Finding Out* in *Booklist* (September 1, 1983, pp. 64–66), "Some entries in the index lead to very meager information. For example, there is no article on Lebanon; yet the country appears in the Index, but the citation leads only to its appearance on a map of the Middle East and a picture of its flag." The other index, which contains about 1,600 entries, lists subjects covered in the encyclopedia under 16 broad headings, such as "Animals," "Art and Music," "Your Body," "Our Earth," "Eating and Drinking," and "History."

The illustrations, which make up approximately 50 percent of the set's total text, are almost all in color and most are drawings. With few exceptions, they add to the informational content of the encyclopedia. Of particular value are the captions that accompany most of the illustrations. By way of example, the article on computers includes a drawing of a silicon chip next to a pinhead; the caption reads: "The silicon chip is a tiny computer in its own right. The pinhead next to it shows how small it is. A silicon chip this size can work a wristwatch or a small pocket caculator [sic]." Physically, the set is well made, bright, and attractive.

To Summarize: *Finding Out,* a British encyclopedia for children adapted for use in the United States (but not Canada), is acccurate, authoritative, well written, easily acessible, and physically appealing. Its greatest drawback is the selectivity of its coverage, which very much favors scientific subjects, and the brevity of many of its articles. In essence, a pleasing work for children that lacks depth.

In Comparison: *Finding Out: Silver Burdett's Children's Encyclopedia,* published in ten volumes containing 250,000 words, is intended for students in the upper elementary grades. The set is considerably smaller than the other multivolume general encyclopedias currently on the North American market for the same readership, namely the NEW BOOK OF KNOWLEDGE (21 volumes; 6.8 million words), the NEW KNOWLEDGE LIBRARY (35 volumes; 2 million words), and the YOUNG STUDENTS ENCYCLOPEDIA (24 volumes; 1.5 million words). Unquestionably, the NEW BOOK OF KNOWLEDGE, the largest of these titles, is the best—but it is also the most expensive. *Finding Out,* though attractively put together, lacks substance when compared head-to-head with the other encyclopedias in its category. In terms of size, style, appearance, content, and intended usership, *Finding Out* closely resembles the HARVER JUNIOR WORLD ENCYCLOPEDIA (16 volumes; one million words), another set for young people originally produced in Great Britain by Michael Dempsey. *Finding Out* also has much the same text (including illustrations) as the one-volume KNOWLEDGE ENCYCLOPEDIA (300,000 words), also edited by John Paton, except the latter is written for a more advanced readership.

To Purchase *Finding Out: Silver Burdett's Children's Encyclopedia:* If you wish to order the encyclopedia for personal use or for a school or library, contact the Silver Burdett Company in Morristown, NJ 07960 or telephone toll-free 1-800-631-8081 (outside New Jersey); in New Jersey call collect 201-285-7700. Your order will be processed immediately. Note that schools and libraries receive a discount of approximately 25 percent.

For More Information about *Finding Out: Silver Burdett's Children's Encyclopedia* **See:** *Booklist,* September 1, 1983, pp. 64–66 (unsigned review).

Funk & Wagnalls New Encyclopedia

FACTS

Funk & Wagnalls New Encyclopedia. Leon L. Bram, Editorial Director; Robert S. Phillips, Editor in Chief. New York: Funk & Wagnalls, Inc. 29 volumes. Former titles: *Funk & Wagnalls Standard Encyclopedia of the World's Knowledge* (1912–30); *Funk & Wagnalls New Standard Encyclopedia of Universal Knowledge* (1931–48); *New Funk & Wagnalls Encyclopedia* (1949–53); *Universal Standard Encyclopedia* (1954–58); *Funk & Wagnalls Standard Reference Encyclopedia* (1959–70). First published as *Funk & Wagnalls New Encyclopedia* in 1971; new printings with revisions each year. Lowest retail price (sold in supermarkets only): $139.80; to schools and libraries: $199.50 (suggested price).

Funk & Wagnalls New Encyclopedia, a 29-volume adult set intended for "the homes and students of the U.S. and Canada" (preface), is sold chiefly in North American supermarkets on the book-a-week plan. The encyclopedia contains 13,024 pages, 25,000 articles, and an estimated 9 million words. The articles, most of which are of the specific-entry type, average about 350 words in length (or about half a page). They are accompanied by 9,175 illustrations (35 percent in color), plus 317 maps. Well over 1,000 editors, consultants, and contributors are identified at the beginning of Volume 1. Most of the articles are not signed. The encyclopedia is arranged alphabetically letter by letter (*Newspapers* precedes *New York*), with access to specific information enhanced by 85,000 cross-references in the text and an analytical index of some 130,000 entries.

EVALUATION

Funk & Wagnalls, Inc. is an old, established name in North American reference book publishing that dates back to 1876. Since 1912, the firm has continuously published a general multivolume encyclopedia under a variety of titles, the latest being *Funk & Wagnalls New Encyclopedia* (1971–), which is actually the sixth edition in the line. Earlier titles in the Funk & Wagnalls encyclopedia series are: *Funk & Wagnalls Standard Reference Encyclopedia* (fifth edition, 1959–70); *Universal Standard Encyclopedia* (fourth edition, 1954–58); *New Funk & Wagnalls Encyclopedia* (third edition, 1949–53); *Funk & Wagnalls*

New Standard Encyclopedia of Universal Knowledge (second edition, 1931–48); and *Funk & Wagnalls Standard Encyclopedia of the World's Knowledge* (first edition, 1912–30).

Since the early 1950s, the encyclopedia has been sold almost exclusively through supermarket chains in the United States and Canada. This marketing strategy has no doubt been profitable over the years for Funk & Wagnalls. Indeed, a recent advertisement noted that the firm has sold more encyclopedias "through supermarkets than anyone else." But the supermarket connection has not done the encyclopedia's reputation much good. There is a strong tendency among knowledgeable encyclopedia consumers and critics to dismiss any set associated with supermarkets as automatically inferior. In the case of *Funk & Wagnalls New Encyclopedia,* however, this prejudice is unwarranted. In recent years, the encyclopedia has earned the grudging approval (if not the affection) of reviewers, librarians, teachers, and others as a reference work to be reckoned with, especially when price is taken into account. In 1983, *Funk & Wagnalls* underwent an exhaustive revision that consolidated and built upon earlier improvements. The set's current editorial team and contributors bring very respectable qualifications to their work.

Entries in *Funk & Wagnalls* are, for the most part, quite brief, but there are also a goodly number of longer survey articles, such as *American Literature, Computer, Health Insurance, Nuclear Energy, Olympic Games,* and *Vietnam War.* The encyclopedia's coverage is fairly well balanced, although biographical and geographical topics predominate, accounting for roughly 40 percent of all articles. Scientific subjects are also well covered, with 25 percent of the articles. Conversely, the arts and humanities receive short shrift. Newly established artists, writers, and performers tend to be ignored. Likewise, current developments in the area of religion are neglected. For instance, controversial movements such as Scientology and Hare Krishna lack coverage, and the Shroud of Turin is limited to one sentence in the article *Turin.* The far-reaching 1983 revision did, however, increase the set's international coverage in an effort to correct what the editors perceived to be an "Anglo-American bias." By way of example, new articles on Islamic religion, culture, and politics have been added.

Information in *Funk & Wagnalls* is normally reliable and unbiased. The excellent article *Abortion,* for example, includes a section entitled "Resistance and Controversy" that objectively describes the current debate on the subject. Likewise, information in the encyclopedia is reasonably current. The aforementioned 1983 revision, which expanded the set from 27 to 29 volumes, updated the contents from beginning to end, resulting in 58 percent of the articles being new, completely rewritten, or revised. This massive overhaul, the most extensive since the sixth edition appeared in 1971, plus regular semiannual revisions, ensure that most of the material in *Funk &*

Wagnalls is relatively up-to-date. Certainly such articles as *Abortion, Adoption, Asbestos, Canada, Circumcision, Health Insurance,* and *Nicaragua* are as timely as can be expected. In a few instances articles are not as current as they might be. The article *Sacco-Vanzetti Case,* for instance, fails to incorporate recent official actions that have significantly affected the case. Fortunately, such omissions are rare.

Funk & Wagnalls is intended for an adult and older student readership. It is usually written in clear, albeit unexciting prose. In most cases, the encyclopedia will be comprehensible to users reading at the seventh- or eighth-grade level, although scientific articles tend to be written at a somewhat higher level. The first paragraph of the article *Earthquake* illustrates the point:

> EARTHQUAKE, vibrations produced in the earth's crust when rocks in which elastic strain has been building up suddenly rupture, and then rebound. The vibrations can range from barely noticeable to catastrophically destructive. Six kinds of shock waves are generated in the process. Two are classified as body waves—that is, they travel through the earth's interior—and the other four are surface waves. The waves are further differentiated by the kinds of motions they impart to rock particles. Primary (compressional) waves send particles oscillating back and forth in the same direction as the waves are traveling, whereas secondary (shear, or transverse) waves impart vibrations perpendicular to their direction of travel.

The editors of *Funk & Wagnalls* recognize the need to provide easy, effective access to the set's contents: "The various information-finding devices are essential supporting networks to the articles. The index and internal cross-references ensure that all the information in the articles is accessible to the reader and that information need not be repeated in several places, occupying valuable space" (preface). As might be expected, the encyclopedia includes ample *See* and *See also* references within the articles. But the set's main finding device is a 480-page analytical index of approximately 130,000 entries. Found in the final volume (prior to 1983 it was split between the final two volumes), the index is excellent. Prepared under the direction of Barbara M. Preschel, who also supervised the making of the original index for the ACADEMIC AMERICAN ENCYCLOPEDIA , *Funk & Wagnalls'* index furnishes about one entry for every 70 words of encyclopedic text, or a quite favorable ratio of index entries to text words of 1:70. Among *Funk & Wagnalls'* major competitors, only the ACADEMIC AMERICAN ENCYCLOPEDIA (1:45) and MERIT STUDENTS ENCYCLOPEDIA (1:65) have better ratios; the WORLD BOOK ENCYCLOPEDIA (1:70) is on par with *Funk & Wagnalls*.

The encyclopedia's illustrations are not as impressive as its index. The extensive 1983 revision greatly improved the set's lackluster illustrations by adding numerous new color photographs. As noted in Marilyn Strong-Noronha's informative review of the 1983 edition in

American Reference Books Annual (1984, p. 15), "One of the most positive changes from previous editions is the increase in illustrations. The use of four-color illustrations was doubled, and Hammond provided complete updates on all Hammond maps and indexes." Nevertheless, *Funk & Wagnalls* still has a way to go before its illustrations can honestly be called anything but mediocre. James Rettig, in a review of the 1983 set in *Wilson Library Bulletin* (October 1983, p. 146), rightly observes that "some of the black-and-white photographs still lack resolution and some of them are dated—photographs of San Salvador and Chicago, for example." A related criticism concerns the encyclopedia's unattractive and sometimes confusing page layout. Specifically, there is no extra leading (or spacing) between the end of one article and the beginning of another. Again, James Rettig in *Wilson Library Bulletin* (October 1983, p. 146) puts his finger on the problem: "Despite an appealing typeface, one must fault the graphic design on one point. The lack of a line or two of white space between articles makes them appear to run into one another and renders subheadings almost indistinguishable from main headings." Yet another problem with the physical format is the set's cheap binding. After only minimal use, pages may begin to fall out.

As the criticisms quoted in the preceding paragraph indicate, *Funk & Wagnalls* has come in for its share of disapproving comments. But, on balance, the encyclopedia has been well received in recent years by the reviewers. Herbert Denenberg, a consumer advocate, has called *Funk & Wagnalls* "dollar for dollar the best encyclopedia" (in *Caveat Emptor,* August-September 1979, p. 19). William A. Katz, a well-known authority on reference materials, writes in his *Introduction to Reference Work* (1982, vol. 1, p. 186), "Anyone who looks at it [*Funk & Wagnalls New Encyclopedia*] carefully will conclude that it is one of the best buys for the average family where a set may not be used often." *Booklist* (December 15, 1984, p. 570) concludes that " *Funk & Wagnalls* is an excellent encyclopedia for homes, useful for both adults and older children. It is also a practical purchase for libraries." And Marilyn Strong-Noronha, in *American Reference Books Annual* (1984, p. 18), asserts that *Funk & Wagnalls* is "by far the best of the 'supermarket encyclopedias.'"

To Summarize: *Funk & Wagnalls* is an inexpensive, well-maintained family encyclopedia that has risen above the "supermarket" stigma. On the negative side, the encyclopedia's coverage is weak in the arts and humanities, the illustrations (though upgraded recently) remain mediocre at best, and the set is physically unappealing and poorly bound.

In Comparison: *Funk & Wagnalls,* published in 29 volumes containing approximately 9 million words, is a medium-sized general encyclopedia for adults and older students. In terms of quality alone, the encyclopedia comes out second-rate when compared head-to-head with most of the available sets in this category, namely the ACADEMIC AMERICAN ENCYCLOPEDIA (21 volumes; 9 million words), COMPTON'S ENCYCLOPEDIA (26 volumes; 8.5 million words), MERIT STUDENTS ENCYCLOPEDIA (20 volumes; 9 million words), the NEW CAXTON ENCYCLOPEDIA (20 volumes; 6 million words), the NEW STANDARD ENCYCLOPEDIA (17 volumes; 6.4 million words), and the WORLD BOOK ENCYCLOPEDIA (22 volumes; 10 million words). On the other hand, when price is taken into account, *Funk & Wagnalls,* which sells for well below any of its competitors, is often chosen as the best buy.

To Purchase *Funk & Wagnalls New Encyclopedia:* If you are an individual consumer, the encyclopedia can be purchased only at a participating supermarket. Unfortunately, no one (including the publisher) is able to advise consumers when or if the encyclopedia might be sold in a supermarket in their locality. In other words, if you are a retail customer who wants to buy *Funk & Wagnalls* and it is not currently being sold in a supermarket in your area, you are out of luck. The set is not sold in-home or by mail order.

If you wish to order the encyclopedia for a school or library, contact Proteus Enterprises, Inc. at 961 West Thorndale, Bensenville, IL 60106 or telephone 312-766-5544. Your name and institution will be forwarded to a distributor in your area who will handle the transaction. Note that Proteus Enterprises deals only with school and library sales.

For More Information about *Funk & Wagnalls New Encyclopedia* See: *American Reference Books Annual,* 1984, pp. 15–18 (review by Marilyn Strong-Noronha); *Booklist,* December 15, 1984, p. 570 (unsigned review); *Booklist,* December 15, 1983, pp. 609–10 (unsigned review); *Caveat Emptor,* August-September 1979, pp. 119–20 (review by Herbert S. Denenberg); *Introduction to Reference Work* by William A. Katz (4th ed., New York: McGraw-Hill, 1982), vol. 1: *Basic Information Sources,* p. 186; *School Library Journal,* May 1984, p. 22 (unsigned review); *Wilson Library Bulletin,* October 1983, p. 146 (review by James Rettig).

Golden Book Encyclopedia

FACTS

The Golden Book Encyclopedia in Sixteen Accurate, Fact-filled Volumes Dramatically Illustrated with More Than 6,000 Pictures. Bertha Morris Parker and Alice F. Martin, Editors. New York: Golden Press, a division of Western Publishing Company, Inc. 16 volumes. Third revised edition published in 1969; out of print since 1978 (last priced at $75).

The *Golden Book Encyclopedia,* "especially designed for young grade-school children" (title page), was discontinued in the late 1970s. The 16-volume encyclopedia contains 1,536 pages, 1,375 articles, and approximately 600,000 words. The articles, most of which are quite brief, average 425 words in length (or about a full page). They are accompanied by 6,250 illustrations (all in color), plus 375 maps. A staff of 15 editors and 99 illustrators is listed on the back of the title page. None of the material is signed. The encyclopedia is arranged alphabetically letter by letter (*Newspapers* precedes *New York*), with access to specific information enhanced by 2,000 cross-references in the text and an index of some 3,500 entries.

EVALUATION

The first edition of the *Golden Book Encyclopedia,* a heavily illustrated work for children, appeared in 1959, followed by a revised second edition in 1961 and a third (and final) edition in 1969. Sold mostly in supermarkets and to schools and libraries, the encyclopedia was never recognized as more than a second-string reference work, and in 1978, after deciding not to revise the set again, the publisher withdrew it from the market. The publisher, Golden Press, is chiefly known for its colorfully illustrated books for children.

Not surprisingly, then, the most noteworthy feature of the *Golden Book Encyclopedia* is its profusion of bright, prominent illustrations, which account for roughly half of the set's total text. The illustrations—all full-color drawings—were created exclusively for the encyclopedia by artists commissioned for the work. Although the drawings are usually striking, they are by no means picture perfect. The color, which is often brassy and florid, is sometimes out of alignment; in other instances, the drawings contribute little or nothing to the informational value of the text, serving instead as window dressing and page fillers. As a reviewer of the first edition (1959) of *Golden Book* in *Library Journal* (January 15, 1960, p. 360) remarked concerning the illustrations, "The quality ranges from the 'very good' (as of flora, fauna, and other natural phenomena) to others that can only be classed as poor, ineffective, gaudy, or faded out. For example, photographs of such people as Franklin Roosevelt and the art works of Raphael, Renoir, and other artists would have been infinitely preferable to the poorly drawn representations used here."

Another serious problem with *Golden Book* is its superficial and sometimes eccentric coverage. For instance, the encyclopedia includes articles on the goatsucker (a bird) and diatom (an algae), but nothing on Martin Luther King, Jr. Likewise, topics of great interest to elementary school students, such as popular music, drug use and abuse, and human sexuality are entirely ignored. A valuable review of the third edition (1969) of the set in *Booklist* (December 15, 1970, p. 317) notes that *Golden Book* "does not meet the overall requirements of a general encyclopedia for serious school reference. Science is the only field which approximates adequate coverage. There are deficiencies both in the comprehensiveness and quality of coverage for the other fields of knowledge." Other weaknesses in the encyclopedia include a poorly constructed index and lack of up-to-date information. About the only point in *Golden Book*'s favor is its simple, readable style. The text, which is limited to a basic vocabulary of 7,500 words, will be comprehensible to children ages seven to twelve.

To Summarize: Out of print now for nearly a decade, *Golden Book* (1959–78) is an inferior encyclopedia for young people. Secondhand sets of the work occasionally surface at garage sales or used bookstores. In practically every instance, consumers would be wise to steer clear of this old, now disreputable encyclopedia.

In Comparison: As a multivolume general encyclopedia for children and younger students, *Golden Book* competed with such established works as the NEW BOOK OF KNOWLEDGE and the YOUNG STUDENTS ENCYCLOPEDIA, both of which are still on the market, and the BRITANNICA JUNIOR ENCYCLOPAEDIA, the HARVER JUNIOR WORLD ENCYCLOPEDIA, and the OXFORD JUNIOR ENCYCLOPAEDIA, all now (like *Golden Book*) discontinued. When compared directly with any of these titles, *Golden Book* inevitably comes off second best. Consumers in search of an inexpensive multivolume encyclopedia about the same size as *Golden Book* would do well to look into FINDING OUT: SILVER BURDETT'S CHILDREN'S ENCYCLOPEDIA.

For More Information about the *Golden Book Encyclopedia* See: *Booklist,* December 15, 1970, pp. 313–17 (unsigned review); *Library Journal,* January 15, 1960, pp. 360–61 (review by Lucille R. Menihan).

Harver Junior World Encyclopedia

FACTS

Harver Junior World Encyclopedia. Originally published in Great Britain as the *Junior World Encyclopedia* (12 volumes; 1960). Michael W. Dempsey, Editor in Chief. Freeport, NY: Harver Educational Services, Inc. Copyright by British Printing Corporation Publishing Ltd. of London, England. 16 volumes. Revised edition adapted for and published in the United States in 1972; out of print since 1977 (last priced at $70.50).

In their introduction to the set, the editors state that "few skills are more important than the ability to use reference works. The *Harver Junior World Encyclopedia* is designed to help young people develop this skill at an early age." Specifically, *Harver Junior,* which was discontinued in 1977, serves children and younger students from the ages of seven to twelve. Despite its name, *Harver Junior* is not an abridged or juvenile version of the larger HARVER WORLD ENCYCLOPE-DIA, a set for adults and older students. When last published in 1972, the 16-volume encyclopedia contained 1,344 pages, 1,550 articles, and about a million words. The articles, most of which are of the specific-entry type, average slightly more than 600 words in length (or just under a full page). They are accompanied by some 2,000 illustrations (90 percent in color), plus 65 maps, including those in an atlas section in the final volume. Fifty-five editors, consultants, and contributors are identified at the front of Volume 1. None of the articles is signed. The encyclopedia is arranged alphabetically letter by letter (*Newspaper* precedes *New York*), with access to specific information enhanced by more than 1,000 cross-references in the text and an index of roughly 20,000 entries.

EVALUATION

Harver Junior first appeared in 1960 in Great Britain under the title *Junior World Encyclopedia* in 12 volumes. In 1972, the publisher, Macdonald Educational Ltd. of London (and member of the giant British Printing Corporation) rewrote and retitled the set for readers in the United States. Distributed in North America in 16 very thin volumes as the *Harver Junior World Encyclopedia* under the imprint of Harver Educational Services, Inc. of Freeport, New York, the encyclopedia was sold principally in supermarkets and to the school and library trade. It made little impact on the U.S. or Canadian market and was declared out of print in 1977. Macdonald Educational, the set's maker and British publisher, has since indicated that the encyclopedia will be revised in the future, but the latest word from a Macdonald representative is, "Regrettably, no progress was made on the revision of the *Harver Junior World Encyclopedia.* All our editors have been fully occupied on many other projects" (letter dated February 13, 1984). The editor of the 1972 edition is the late Michael W. Dempsey, a prolific producer of reference works for young people (see, for example, FINDING OUT: SILVER BURDETT'S CHILDREN'S ENCYCLOPEDIA, which closely resembles *Harver Junior*) and books on scientific subjects for children.

As the foregoing suggests, *Harver Junior* is hardly an encyclopedia of first importance. At the present time, the set's most conspicuous weakness is, of course, its lack of up-to-dateness. But just as serious is the inherent problem of superficial and imbalanced coverage. Subjects of great curiosity to elementary school students, such as human sexuality and drug use, are ignored or given short shrift. On the other hand, the encyclopedia includes numerous articles on exotic topics like earwigs, loess, nails and claws, pupa, and slow worms. Nearly 60 percent of all articles are devoted to science and geography, whereas art and literature receive scant attention. Likewise, controversial subject matter is excluded. Another weakness concerns the set's poor accessibility of information. A reviewer in *Booklist* (February 15, 1979, p. 946) quite rightly calls *Harver Junior* 's cross-references "inadequate" and further observes that the index "is shallow and fails to pick up many of the general topics embedded in articles. Incorrect page references were also noted." On the plus side, the encyclopedia's illustrations are plentiful and usually informative, especially the diagrams of technical subjects. Also, the writing style is usually simple (if not always entirely clear). Potentially unfamiliar or difficult terms are often (but not always) italicized and defined in context.

To Summarize: *Harver Junior,* a British-produced children's encyclopedia adapted for the North American market, is a substandard work that has been out of print for a number of years. The British publisher, however, has indicated that eventually the set will be revised and presumably made available to the U.S. and Canadian encyclopedia-buying public.

In Comparison: As a multivolume general encyclopedia for children and younger students, *Harver Junior* competed with such established works as the NEW BOOK OF KNOWLEDGE and the YOUNG STUDENTS ENCYCLOPEDIA, both of which are still on the market, and the BRITANNICA JUNIOR ENCYCLOPAEDIA, the GOLDEN BOOK ENCYCLOPEDIA, and the OXFORD JUNIOR ENCYCLOPAEDIA, all now (like *Harver Junior*) discontinued. When compared directly with any of these titles, *Harver Junior* inevitably comes out second best, except in the case of the GOLDEN BOOK ENCYCLOPEDIA, a wretchedly bad set. As Christine Wynar wrote in her review of *Harver Junior* in *American Reference Books Annual* (1973, p. 106), the set "can not compete with the major children's encyclopedias.... It is not recommended." Consumers in search of an inexpensive multivolume encyclopedia about the same size as *Harver Junior* would do well to look into FINDING OUT: SILVER BURDETT'S CHILDREN'S ENCYCLOPEDIA, a ten-volume work that looks and sounds somewhat like *Harver Junior* but is all around a much better work (and it is currently in print).

For More Information about the *Harver Junior World Encyclopedia* See: *American Reference Books Annual, 1973,* pp. 105–06 (review by Christine L. Wynar); *Booklist,* February 15, 1979, pp. 946–47 (unsigned review); *Booklist,* November 1, 1973, pp. 245–49 (unsigned review).

Harver World Encyclopedia

FACTS

Harver World Encyclopedia: Alphabetical Encyclopedia in 20 Volumes. Martin Self, Editor in Chief. New York: Harver Educational Services, Inc. 20 volumes. Second edition published in 1975; out of print since 1981 (last priced at $375.50).

The *Harver World Encyclopedia,* last published in 1975 and now apparently discontinued, "is designed primarily as a reference book to supply answers to specific questions" (preface). Intended for adults and older students, the 20-volume encyclopedia contains 5,855 pages, 20,000 articles, and approximately 7.5 million words. The articles, most of which are of the specific-entry type, average 375 words in length (or about a third of a page). They are accompanied by more than 16,000 illustrations (over 50 percent in color), plus 470 maps. An editorial and production staff of 34, plus 135 contributors and advisers, is listed at the front of Volume 1. None of the articles is signed. The encyclopedia is arranged alphabetically letter by letter (*Newspaper* precedes *New York*), with access to specific information enhanced by 30,000 cross-references in the text. The set has no index.

EVALUATION

The first edition of *Harver World,* an entirely new encyclopedia, appeared in 1973. Produced abroad especially for a North American audience, the set drew most of its editors and writers from the United Kingdom and its illustrations from the Netherlands and the vast picture resources of the Elsevier Company of Amsterdam, publisher of the heavily illustrated *Grote Winkler Prins* (See Appendix C), a standard Dutch multivolume encyclopedia. In 1975, a second edition of *Harver World* appeared, marked by the addition of a so-called "Instant Reference Supplement," which in actuality is nothing more than a very old unabridged English-language dictionary split among the encyclopedia's 20 volumes. The North American publisher, Harver Educational Services, Inc., eventually went out of business, and the encyclopedia, after being sold off by various distributors, is now out of print with no prospects of a new revised edition on the horizon.

The appearance of *Harver World* in the early 1970s, then a brand-new multivolume general encyclopedia on the North American scene, had little impact on the reference-book buying public (unlike, for instance, the publication of the ACADEMIC AMERICAN ENCYCLOPEDIA a decade later). Only the set's plentiful and colorful illustrations generated much enthusiasm. A review of the first (1973) edition in *Booklist* (April 1, 1974, p. 831) put it this way: "The most striking feature of *Harver World Encyclopedia* is its illustrations. More than 12,000 illustrations [grown to 16,000 in the second edition], most of them in full color, are used throughout the set. Illustrations include photographs, drawings, diagrams, and charts. Although in many cases photographs and drawings are rather small because of space limitations, they are uniformly clear, easily understood, and sharply reproduced. Color reproduction is particularly outstanding in both photographs and color illustrations." Today, the set's illustrations are still quite good (though sometimes dated), but they are no match for those found in two competing works, the aforementioned ACADEMIC AMERICAN ENCYCLOPEDIA and the British-made NEW CAXTON ENCYCLOPEDIA. *Harver World* is also noteworthy for its clear, nontechnical writing style. Comprehensible to users reading at the junior high school level and up, the text customarily italicizes difficult or unfamiliar terms and defines them in context.

But beyond these two conspicuous strengths, *Harver World* has little to offer the discerning encyclopedia user. The set's coverage lacks balance, with overemphasis on scientific and technical material at the expense of the arts and humanities. In addition, many articles provide overly simplistic treatment of complex subject matter. Information in the encyclopedia is not always reliable, nor is access to that information as effective as it might be if the set had an index.

(For the record, the publisher frequently promised that an index would be forthcoming, but it never appeared.) Another deficiency is the lack of bibliographies, or references for further study. And, naturally, information in the set is now woefully out-of-date.

To Summarize: *Harver World,* a completely new work when first published in 1973, is a mediocre encyclopedia for adults and older students. Now out of print (and likely to remain so), the set has very good illustrations and stylistic clarity but little else to recommend it. The possibility of encountering *Harver World* on the secondhand or remainder book market is quite good.

In Comparison: When it was in print, *Harver World* competed directly with the ACADEMIC AMERICAN ENCYCLOPEDIA, FUNK & WAGNALLS NEW ENCYCLOPEDIA, the NEW CAXTON ENCYCLOPEDIA, and the NEW STANDARD ENCYCLOPEDIA, all middle-sized sets for the family and students at the secondary school and college levels. Other competitors included COMPTON'S ENCYCLOPEDIA, MERIT STUDENTS ENCYCLOPEDIA, and the WORLD BOOK ENCYCLOPEDIA, sets also useful for the whole family but aimed at a slightly lower reading level. *Harver World* almost always appears second best when compared with any of these rivals, except where illustrations are concerned, and even then, as noted earlier, the ACADEMIC AMERICAN ENCYCLOPEDIA and NEW CAXTON ENCYCLOPEDIA, as well as the WORLD BOOK ENCYCLOPEDIA, are easily superior in this regard.

For More Information about the *Harver World Encyclopedia* **See:** *Booklist,* April 1, 1974, pp. 830–35 (unsigned review).

Illustrated World Encyclopedia

FACTS

Illustrated World Encyclopedia. Roger Bobley, Editor in Chief. Woodbury, NY: Bobley Publishing Corporation. Copyright by Mer-Fried Corporation. One volume. Former titles: *Illustrated Encyclopedia of Knowledge* (1954–57); *Illustrated Home Library Encyclopedia* (1955–57). First published as the *Illustrated World Encyclopedia* in 1958 in 15 volumes. One-volume abridged edition published in 1977; out of print since 1983 (last priced at $19.95).

The single-volume *Illustrated World Encyclopedia,* recently declared out of print by its publisher, is said to include "practically all the factual reference material you and your family will ever need" (preface). Intended mainly for adults and older students, the encyclopedia contains 1,619 pages, 7,300 articles, and roughly 2.5 million words. The articles, which are mostly short, average slightly more than 300 words in length (or a quarter of a page). They are accompanied by some 2,000 illustrations (all in black-and-white), plus 158 maps, including an eight-page atlas. A small editorial staff and 105 contributors and consultants are listed at the front of Volume 1. None of the articles is signed. The encyclopedia is arranged alphabetically letter by letter (*Newspaper* precedes *New York*), with access to specific information enhanced by 2,500 cross-references in the text. The encyclopedia has no index, although a separate "Index & Study Guide" volume has been advertised.

EVALUATION

The *Illustrated World Encyclopedia* originated in 1954 as a 20-volume set entitled the *Illustrated Encyclopedia of Knowledge,* described by Padraig Walsh in his *Anglo-American General Encyclopedias, 1703–1967* (p. 82) as an "extremely poor" work that "was, apparently, designed to be offered as a premium through chain and department stores and food supermarkets, and, in at least one instance, it was offered as an inducement to purchase a television set." Exactly the same set with an atlas volume added appeared around the same time under the title *Illustrated Home Library Encyclopedia.* In 1958, the Bobley Publishing Corporation acquired the rights to the set, revising it and changing the title to *Illustrated World Encyclopedia.* Between 1958 and 1973, Bobley published various editions in 15 and 21 volumes, selling them in retail stores at enticingly low prices. In 1977, Bobley issued a one-volume abridgment of its 21-volume set published in 1973. The rationale for this move is explained in the preface to the abridged work: "Until now ... *Illustrated World Encyclopedia* was, like most fine encyclopedias, available only in large, multivolume editions. But, by eliminating all but the best and most important illustrations and by making certain other changes in format, this remarkable one-volume edition was made possible. In fact, for the very first time, virtually the entire encyclopedic content of a well-known, 6,720-page, 21-volume encyclopedia has been re-published in a single 1,600-page volume." Despite these claims, *Illustrated World* is and always has been an inferior encyclopedia, no matter what its size or format.

Indeed, *Illustrated World* could appropriately serve as a model for how not to make an encyclopedia. Its coverage is wildly uneven and often superficial. The article *Football,* for instance, is three pages long, whereas *Feminism,* the only place in the volume where women's rights are mentioned, is limited to 250 words. *Backgammon,* at 1,500 words, is more than four times as long as *Art* (350 words). The encyclopedia contains numerous factual and typographical errors, as well as questionable assertions, as in the case of the article on fainting, which states that "almost always doctors consider that there is nothing serious, and nothing to worry about, in fainting." Access to information in the volume is poor, due to unreliable cross-references and the lack of an index. The writing style, which fluctuates from juvenile to erudite, has been characterized as "at times unclear, even ludicrous" (*Booklist,* January 15, 1978, p. 836). The illustrations, which should be something special in an encyclopedia with the word "illustrated" in its title, are frequently too small, too dark, and of minimal informational value. And, of course, *Illustrated World* is dreadfully out-of-date, a criticism just as true the day the volume was published in 1977 as it is today. Only the encyclopedia's consistently low price can account for whatever success it has had in the marketplace over the years.

To Summarize: *Illustrated World,* a one-volume abridgment of a multivolume set for family and student use, is a totally inadequate reference work. Published in 1977 and recently allowed to go out of print, the encyclopedia will no doubt reappear in due course in a "revised" edition of one or many volumes. In either case, buyer beware.

In Comparison: When it was on the market, *Illustrated World* competed with other small-volume adult encyclopedias, the most prominent being the LINCOLN LIBRARY OF ESSENTIAL INFORMATION, the NEW COLUMBIA ENCYCLOPEDIA, the RANDOM HOUSE ENCYCLOPEDIA, and the VOLUME LIBRARY. All of these titles are currently in print and greatly preferable to *Illustrated World.* Interested consumers should also check out the CONCISE COLUMBIA ENCYCLOPEDIA, the newest single-volume work.

For More Information about the *Illustrated World Encyclopedia* See: *Booklist,* December 1, 1978, pp. 635–37 (unsigned review); *Booklist,* January 15, 1978, pp. 836–38 (unsigned review).

Junior Encyclopedia of General Knowledge

FACTS

The Junior Encyclopedia of General Knowledge. Theodore Rowland-Entwistle and Jean Cooke, Editors. London, England: Octopus Books Ltd. Distributed in North America by W.H. Smith Publications, Inc. One volume. First edition published in 1978. Lowest retail price: $9.95.

The *Junior Encyclopedia of General Knowledge,* a one-volume reference work produced in Great Britain for children ages seven to fourteen aims to provide elementary facts on basic subjects and to stimulate the reader's intellectual awareness: "You won't find all human knowledge in an encyclopedia; but in this one you will find all you want to know at first glance—until your curiosity leads you further" (foreword). The encyclopedia contains 224 pages, 103 articles, and approximately 100,000 words. The articles, which are all of the broad-entry type, average 1,000 words in length (or two full pages). They are accompanied by 400 illustrations (all in color), plus 11 maps. None of the material is signed. The encyclopedia is arranged topically, the articles grouped by subject under 11 broad headings ("The Earth in Space," "Plants," "Animals," "Lands of the World," "The Arts," "Science and Technology," "Transport and Communications," "History of the World," "Sports and Games," "Emblems," and "People at Work"), with access to specific information enhanced by a five-page index of some 1,100 entries.

EVALUATION

Published in 1978 by the British firm of Octopus Books, the *Junior Encyclopedia* is distributed in North America by W.H. Smith Publications, Inc. in New York, which took over the book stock of the original distributor, Mayflower Books. The encyclopedia, which has never been revised, is edited by the husband-and-wife team of Theodore Rowland-Entwistle and Jean Cooke, who have worked together on other encyclopedias for children, including PURNELL'S PICTORIAL ENCYCLOPEDIA. As might be expected, coverage in the *Junior Encyclopedia* is quite selective, limited to basic information likely to be of interest or value to young readers. For example, under the broad heading "Science and Technology," there are 12 articles, all heavily illustrated in two-page spreads: *The Particles of Matter, Waves and Energy, Molecules and Matter, Chemistry in Everyday Life, Life, The Human Body, Creating a Family, Mathematics in Action, Ideas in Action, The Feats of Man, Energy and Power,* and *Fingertip Facts.* Obviously, the encyclopedia is intended, in the words of the foreword, as simply a "first glance" source of information.

What information there is in the encyclopedia is accurate, unbiased, and, notwithstanding the book's date of publication, as current as it needs to be. The article *World Wars and After* (in the "History of the World" section), for instance, informs the reader that "the United Nations, to which nearly all countries belong, has helped to keep the peace. It stopped Communist North Korea from conquering South Korea, but a similar attempt by the United States to stop the Communists of North Vietnam from taking over South Vietnam failed." The writing style, as the excerpt above indicates, is usually clear and direct, without patronizing the young reader. The text will be comprehensible to students reading at the third-grade level and beyond. Access to the encyclopedia's contents is reasonably good, despite the book's topical arrangement and lack of cross-references. The small index locates most specific topics covered in the volume. Likewise, the encyclopedia's illustrations, which constitute roughly half of the total text, are effective from both the informational and aesthetic standpoints. Mostly photographs and all in full color, the illustrations customarily include substantial captions.

To Summarize: The British-made *Junior Encyclopedia* is an attractive, informative, and inexpensive one-volume work for young children and students in the elementary and junior high school grades. Due to space limitations, however, the encyclopedia's coverage is highly selective and the treatment of what is covered is quite superficial.

In Comparison: The *Junior Encyclopedia of General Knowledge,* published in a single volume containing 100,000 words, is a small item for children. It competes with the JUNIOR PEARS ENCYCLOPAEDIA (one volume; 280,000 words), NELSON'S ENCYCLOPEDIA FOR YOUNG READERS (two volumes; 350,000 words), PURNELL'S PICTORIAL ENCYCLOPEDIA (one volume; 75,000 words), and RAND McNALLY'S CHILDREN'S ENCYCLOPEDIA (one volume; 15,000 words). None of these titles can be enthusiastically recommended, although NELSON'S ENCYCLOPEDIA FOR YOUNG READERS and the JUNIOR PEARS ENCYCLOPAEDIA are the best of the lot. Macmillan, Inc., a leading North American publisher of encyclopedias (COLLIER'S ENCYCLOPEDIA; MERIT STUDENTS ENCYCLOPEDIA), is currently preparing a small-volume encyclopedia for young children and students in the primary grades, but at this time it is far from ready for publication. There is a real need for a substantial one- or two-volume encyclopedia for young people.

To Purchase the *Junior Encyclopedia of General Knowledge:* The encyclopedia is sold in North American retail bookstores. If it is not in stock (and it may well not be), most bookstores will order it for you. You can also order the encyclopedia directly from the distributor, W.H. Smith Publications, Inc. at 112 Madison Avenue, New York, NY 10016 or telephone 212-532-6600. If W.H. Smith no longer has the book in stock (and it might not), interested consumers should contact Pergamon Press, Inc., which specializes in obtaining reference works published abroad. Contact Pergamon in the United States at Maxwell House, Fairview Park, Elmsford, NY 10523 or telephone 914-592-7700; in Canada write to Pergamon Press Canada Ltd., Suite 104, Consumers Road, Willowdale, Ontario M2J 1P9 or telephone 416-497-8337.

No other reviews of the *Junior Encyclopedia of General Knowledge* are available at this time.

Junior Pears Encyclopaedia

FACTS

Junior Pears Encyclopaedia. Edward Blishen, Editor. London, England: Pelham Books Ltd. Distributed in North America by Merrimack Publishers' Circle. One volume. First edition published in 1961; new revised edition each year. Lowest retail price: $14.95.

A single-volume work produced in Great Britain for children ages seven to fourteen, the *Junior Pears Encyclopaedia* is the young person's answer to PEARS CYCLOPAEDIA, a popular British annual for adults. According to the editor's introduction, *Junior Pears'* basic goal "is to provide information," but, he adds, "we've never wanted the book to be merely a bulging collection of facts. We've tried to make it pleasant to read as well as easy to consult." The encyclopedia contains 650 pages, approximately 1,500 articles, and 280,000 words. The articles, which include lists, chronologies, glossaries, etc., are usually brief, averaging less than 200 words in length (or half of a page). They are accompanied by 330 illustrations (all in black-and-white), plus 12 maps. The editor and 14 illustrators are noted at the front of the volume. None of the material is signed. The encyclopedia is arranged topically, the contents grouped by subject under 17 broad headings ("The World: Its History; Its Geography; Its Famous People"; "A Dictionary of Science and Mathematics"; "A Dictionary of Radio and Television"; "A Dictionary of Aircraft, Rockets and Missiles"; "Motor Cars, Motorcycles, Three-Wheelers, Scooters and Mopeds"; "Railways"; "Ships"; "The English Language"; "Music and the Arts"; "Sport"; "Something to Join"; "The Armed Services, the Police and Fire Brigades"; "The Law"; "Natural History"; and "Miscellany"), with access to specific information enhanced by a detailed table of contents at the front of the book and 100 or so cross-references in the text. The volume has no index.

EVALUATION

Junior Pears first appeared in 1961, edited by Edward Blishen, who remains in that position today, a remarkable feat of editorial dedication and longevity. The encyclopedia, which is revised every year, is loosely modeled on the older and larger PEARS CYCLOPAEDIA, an annual institution among British reference book users since 1897. *Junior Pears'* coverage is not well balanced, nor does it pretend to be comprehensive. Scientific and technical subjects, particularly in the areas of transportation and communication, receive considerable attention, whereas the arts and humanities by comparison receive short shrift. But by any measure, *Junior Pears,* like its big brother, PEARS CYCLOPAEDIA, crams an enormous amount of information into relatively little space. Most of the book's contents are typically encyclopedic—that is, basic facts about important people, places, events, and things. But it also includes much information not usually found in encyclopedias, and certainly not in single-volume works for children, such as a list of the world's busiest airports, a world map showing country size by population rather than land area, a detailed and nicely illustrated manual on how motorcycles work, and a dissertation on the garden hedge. In addition, a topic of contemporary concern—computers, the arms race, the environment, etc.—is often covered in a special chapter each year.

The chief problem for users of *Junior Pears* in North America is its unremitting emphasis on British history, personalities, geography, institutions, and culture. The geography chapter, for example, includes lists of the largest cities, highest mountains, and most important rivers in Great Britain, but no other countries; the entire chapter on sports is from the British perspective (cricket yes, baseball no); the chapter on the law deals almost exclusively with British laws, courts, and lawyers. A reviewer in *Booklist* (January 1, 1981, p. 643) observes, "Because of its British approach, this volume would have limited use in most American libraries." And Jim Roginski, reviewing *Junior Pears* in *American Reference Books Annual* (1979, p. 34), flatly states that the encyclopedia "holds little interest except for the staunchest Anglophile."

Information in *Junior Pears* is normally reliable and presented in an objective manner. Likewise, the book is admirably current, undergoing a rigorous reexamination each year. The writing style varies considerably from section to section. Some of the material is presented in an informal, even chatty fashion reminiscent of Mr. Rogers, the television friend to children ("I am always thrilled to see a humming-bird hawk-moth come darting into my garden"), but in the main the articles and definitions are written in clear, straightforward, nontechnical prose that will be understandable in most instances to readers at the upper elementary or junior high school level. The article *Earthquakes and Volcanoes* (in "The World: Its Geography") is a good example of the book's more formal style. Here is the first paragraph:

> Earthquakes and volcanic eruptions occur at the edges of the plates in the earth's crust. When plates are forced to move and grind against each other, a series of violent jerks and shudders occur. Like the waves which spread from the centre when a stone is thrown into a pond, the vibrations of an earthquake travel out from a centre called the epicentre. Earthquakes cause great damage and can start landslides and floods. The Richter Scale is used to measure the strength of the shock waves.

Another problem that all users of *Junior Pears* experience, no matter where they live, is grossly inadequate access to the book's contents. As already noted, the encyclopedia, which is arranged topically and not alphabetically, has very few cross-references and no index. There are extensive tables of contents both at the beginning of the book and in many of the individual sections, but this device hardly compensates for the lack of a detailed index and sufficient *See* and *See also* references. For example, the article on earthquakes quoted from in the preceding paragraph was easily located on page B13 through the table of contents for "The World: Its Geography" section. But only by browsing or luck will the user discover that additional information on earthquakes is available on page B52. There are no cross-references to guide the user from one entry to the other. Jim Roginski, in his sharply negative review of *Junior Pears* in *American Reference Books Annual* (1979, p. 34), asserts that "this volume is virtually unusable for those used to standardized pagination and organization." Likewise, Nicholas Bagnall, reviewing the encyclopedia in the London *Sunday Telegraph* (November 30, 1980), bemoans "the absence of a general index, which is a nuisance if one wants something in a hurry. All encyclopedias arranged thematically, as this one is, ought to have an index."

The encyclopedia's 330 illustrations, all small black-and-white line drawings, are well executed, especially those accompanying scientific and technical subjects. For instance, "The World: Its Geography" section includes a series of drawings that simply but clearly depicts various geographical features, such as an atoll, a butte, a delta, a fjord, an isthmus, a strait, and so on. The book's physical format is less satisfactory. The print, though legible, is quite small, a drawback particularly since the book is intended for children. The lack of color and somewhat crowded page layout also may discourage young readers. Moreover, the binding, which is glued rather than sewn, will not stand up to heavy use. On the other hand, the volume's small size (4½ by 7¼ in.; 12 by 19 cm.) is ideal for children.

To Summarize: *Junior Pears,* a one-volume encyclopedia modeled after the larger PEARS CYCLOPAEDIA, provides much material of interest and value to children and younger students. Its contents are accurate, objective, and current, but coverage is uneven and, from a North American point of view, overly British in emphasis.

In Comparison: *Junior Pears,* published in a single volume containing approximately 280,000 words, is a desk-sized work for children. It competes with the JUNIOR ENCYCLOPEDIA OF GENERAL KNOWLEDGE (one volume: 100,000 words), NELSON'S ENCYCLOPEDIA FOR YOUNG READERS (two volumes; 350,000 words), PURNELL'S PICTORIAL ENCYCLOPEDIA (one volume; 75,000 words), and RAND McNALLY'S CHILDREN'S ENCYCLOPEDIA (one volume; 15,000 words). None of these titles can be enthusiastically recommended to North American consumers, although NELSON'S ENCYCLOPEDIA FOR YOUNG READERS and *Junior Pears* (despite its heavy British bias) are the best of the lot. Macmillan, Inc., a leading North American publisher of encyclopedias (COLLIER'S ENCYCLOPEDIA; MERIT STUDENTS ENCYCLOPEDIA), is currently preparing a small-volume encyclopedia for young children and students in the primary grades, but at this time it is far from ready for publication. There is a real need for a substantial one- or two-volume encyclopedia for young people.

To Purchase the *Junior Pears Encyclopaedia:* The encyclopedia is sold in North American retail bookstores. If it is not in stock (and it might not be), most bookstores will order it for you. You can also order the encyclopedia directly from the distributor, Merrimack Publishers' Circle at 99 Main Street, Salem, NH 03079 or telephone 617-887-2440.

For More Information about the *Junior Pears Encyclopaedia* See: *American Reference Books Annual,* 1979, pp. 34–35 (review by Jim Roginski); *Booklist,* January 1, 1981, p. 643 (unsigned review); *Sunday Telegraph* (London), November 30, 1980 (review by Nicholas Bagnall).

Knowledge Encyclopedia

FACTS

Knowledge Encyclopedia. John Paton, Editor. New York: Arco Publishing, Inc. Copyright by Grisewood and Dempsey Ltd. of London, England. One volume. First edition published in 1979 in England; 1984 printing published in North America. Lowest retail price: $16.95.

The *Knowledge Encyclopedia,* a single-volume reference book originally published in Great Britain, is intended as "a work for all members of the family" (preface). The encyclopedia contains 415 pages, 2,500 articles, and approximately 300,000 words. The articles, most of which are very brief, average 120 words in length (or about six articles per page). They are accompanied by some 600 illustrations (almost all in color), plus 15 maps. Sixteen editors and contributors are listed at the front of the volume. None of the material is signed. The encyclopedia is arranged alphabetically letter by letter (*Newspaper* precedes *New York*), with access to specific information enhanced by nearly 4,000 cross-references in the text and an index of about 5,000 entries.

EVALUATION

The *Knowledge Encyclopedia* first appeared in 1979, a product of the London firm of Grisewood & Dempsey, a well-known publisher of encyclopedias for young people (see, for example, FINDING OUT: SILVER BURDETT'S CHILDREN'S ENCYCLOPEDIA and RAND McNALLY'S CHILDREN'S ENCYCLOPEDIA). In 1981, the volume was updated, and in 1984 Arco Publishing, Inc. of New York issued it for distribution in North America. The editor, John Paton, is an experienced hand, having worked on a number of other encyclopedias, including the NEW CAXTON ENCYCLOPEDIA and the two children's works mentioned above.

The *Knowledge Encyclopedia*'s coverage emphasizes biographical, geographical, and scientific and technical subjects. Conversely, the arts, humanities, and social issues receive cursory attention. The encyclopedia's coverage also exhibits a rather strong British bias. For example, the British Parliament is covered, whereas its U.S. and Canadian counterparts are not. Likewise, there is an article on English literature, but none on American or Canadian literature. The encyclopedia also contains an inordinate number of articles on strictly Australian topics, such as the black swan (a bird native to Australia and emblem of Western Australia), the echidna (an egg-laying mammal indigenous to Australia), Matthew Flinders (a British explorer credited with naming Australia), Ned Kelly (a famous Australian outlaw), the Murry-Darling system (an Australian river system), Newcastle (an Australian port city of some 363,000), and the wattle (a plant whose flower is the Australian national emblem). Whatever the topic, the articles in the *Knowledge Encyclopedia* are usually extremely short, rarely more than a paragraph in length. And, as might be expected, treatment of the subjects covered is quite superficial. Frequently, the articles are little more than dictionary definitions. A reviewer in *Booklist* (February 15, 1985, p. 844) correctly observes, "Students needing a goodly amount of resource material will have to turn to a standard encyclopedia or other nonfiction source; but if they just want to learn a little about a lot of topics, this wide-ranging volume will suit their purposes."

Information in the *Knowledge Encyclopedia* is normally accurate and objectively presented, although many controversial subjects are avoided. By way of example, the encyclopedia lacks coverage of such polemical issues as abortion, adoption, capital punishment, circumcision, and religious cults. In most areas of human sexuality, however, the book furnishes impartial (albeit very limited) information about sexual intercourse, birth control, homosexuality, and venereal disease. Ordinarily, information in the encyclopedia is current as of the late 1970s or, occasionally, the early 1980s. For example, the article *Vietnam* includes 1979 population data and *European Economic Community (EEC)* records Greece's entry into the organization in 1981. But numerous articles are less current than they might be. *Canada,* for instance, notes that "in the 1970s Quebec's provincial government announced that a vote would be held to discover whether its people wanted to break away from Canada and set up their own independent French-speaking nation," but fails to inform the reader that such a referendum was in fact held (and defeated) in 1980.

The encyclopedia's writing style is designed to accommodate the whole family, including young people in the upper elementary and junior high school grades who possess good reading skills. Generally speaking, however, the text is most appropriate for adults and older students at the secondary school level. The article *Earthquake,* quoted here in its entirety, is typical:

> A tremor in the Earth's crust. Earthquakes occur when there are sudden movements along FAULTS beneath the surface. They are most common near the edges of the moving plates, into which the Earth's crust is split. They may cause great damage and loss of life. One earthquake in China killed about 800,000 people in 1556.

Eugenia Schmitz, in a review in *American Reference Books Annual* (1985, p. 15), sums up the encyclopedia's readability this way: "Simple enough in style for a grade school audience without using controlled vocabulary, and yet interesting to their parents, this is definitely a browsing encyclopedia. It is a perfect lure for the reluctant student in a school library."

The contents of the *Knowledge Encyclopedia* are easily retrievable in most instances. Cross-references, printed in SMALL CAPITAL LETTERS, appear throughout the text (see the article *Earthquake* above for an example), and there is an adequate index at the back of the volume. However, articles that use British terminology, such as *Tyre* and *Motor Car,* would be more accessible to North American users if cross-references (for example, "*Tire.* See *Tyre*") were provided in either the text or the index or both. On the other hand, the encyclopedia's illustrations, which account for roughly a third of the total text, are virtually without fault. Colorful, informative, and well reproduced, they are clearly the best feature of what is otherwise an undistinguished work.

To Summarize: The *Knowledge Encyclopedia* is a small, British-made reference work for "all members of the family" (preface). Its illustrations are first-class, but beyond that the encyclopedia has little to offer the discriminating North American consumer.

In Comparison: The *Knowledge Encyclopedia,* published in one volume containing approximately 300,000 words, is a mediocre encyclopedia for adults and older students. Its format and style are suggestive of the larger UNIVERSITY DESK ENCYCLOPEDIA (one volume; 2 million words), which has been out of print for several years. The *Knowledge Encyclopedia* cannot compare with the leading one- and two-volume general adult encyclopedias, namely, the LINCOLN LIBRARY OF ESSENTIAL INFORMATION (two volumes; 3.5 million words), the NEW COLUMBIA ENCYCLOPEDIA (one volume; 6.6 million words), the RANDOM HOUSE ENCYCLOPEDIA (one volume; 3 million words), and the VOLUME LIBRARY (two volumes; 3.5 million words). All of these encyclopedias, as the figures indicate, offer much more information than the *Knowledge Encyclopedia.* Also, they are much more expensive. More in the *Knowledge Encyclopedia*'s league are COLLINS GEM ENCYCLOPEDIA (two volumes; 450,000 words), the CONCISE COLUMBIA ENCYCLOPEDIA (one volume; one million words), PEARS CYCLOPAEDIA (one volume; 1.2 million words), and the QUICK REFERENCE HANDBOOK OF BASIC INFORMATION (one volume; 750,000 words). Among these small, desk-sized general encyclopedias for adults, the CONCISE COLUMBIA ENCYCLOPEDIA is the standout choice for U.S. and Canadian consumers. In the final analysis, the only things the *Knowledge Encyclopedia* has going for it, comparatively speaking, are its excellent illustrations and reasonable price.

To Purchase the *Knowledge Encyclopedia:* The encyclopedia is sold in North American retail bookstores. If it is not in stock (and it might not be), most bookstores will order it for you. You can also order the encyclopedia directly from the publisher, Arco Publishing, Inc. at 215 Park Avenue South, New York, NY 10003 or telephone 212-777-6300.

For More Information about the *Knowledge Encyclopedia* See: *American Reference Books Annual,* 1985, p. 15 (review by Eugenia E. Schmitz); *Booklist,* February 15, 1985, p. 844 (unsigned review); *Booklist,* February 1, 1985, p. 774 (unsigned review); *Wilson Library Bulletin,* October 1984, p. 147 (review by James Rettig).

Kussmaul Encyclopedia

FACTS

Kussmaul Encyclopedia. J. Wesley Kussmaul, Editorial Director. Cambridge, MA: General Videotex Corporation. Encyclopedia is an electronic database, part of the Delphi information system offered by General Videotex Corporation. Print version: CADILLAC MODERN EN-CYCLOPEDIA. Inclusive dates: 1981 to present; updated irregularly. Contact General Videotex Corporation (3 Blackstone Street, Cambridge, MA 02139; telephone toll-free 1-800-544-4005) for price and availability information.

The *Kussmaul Encyclopedia* is an electronic (or online) encyclopedia based on the CADILLAC MODERN ENCYCLOPEDIA, a one-volume work for adults and older students published in 1973 and now out of print. The *Kussmaul Encyclopedia* consists of a machine-readable database that contains approximately 20,000 files and 3 million words. The files, which correspond to articles in the print version (that is, the CADILLAC MODERN ENCYCLOPEDIA), are normally quite brief, averaging 150 words in length. The *Kussmaul Encyclopedia* has no illustrations (by contrast, the print version has 1,110 black-and-white illustrations, plus 300 maps). The file content of the electronic encyclopedia is searchable by assigned subject headings, with access to specific information enhanced by 50,000 cross-references in the text. At the present time, the encyclopedia does not provide full-text searching (the capability of accessing any important word or word combinations in the database using Boolean logic).

EVALUATION

In 1983, J. Wesley Kussmaul, a bright young entrepreneur from the Boston area, began marketing Delphi, an electronic information service accessible via home computer. Today, Delphi, a product of General Videotex Corporation located in Cambridge, Massachusetts, has over 10,000 subscribers and is growing. (Delphi competes directly with two other major electronic information services for the home consumer, CompuServe and The Source.) A company brochure describes Delphi this way:

> Delphi is the information, communications and entertainment system that takes your home computer far beyond the limitations of disks or cartridges. With a simple phone call, Delphi connects you to the world's most sophisticated databases. With a simple phone call, you can get the latest news, weather and sports stories. Check the stock commodities and money markets. Do your banking. Go shopping. Make airline reservations.

> You can post messages on an electronic bulletin board, send and receive electronic mail, "talk" with other subscribers. Or you can go to the library and use a 20,000-entry encyclopedia or access an enormous research library.

The encyclopedia referred to here is, of course, the *Kussmaul Encyclopedia,* which derives from the old (1972) one-volume CADILLAC MODERN ENCYCLOPEDIA. In the early 1980s, well before he put the Delphi system together, Kussmaul acquired the electronic publishing rights to the CADILLAC MODERN ENCYCLOPEDIA, converted its text to machine-readable form, and marketed it as an online information service. In 1983, when Delphi was created, the encyclopedia naturally became part of the larger utility. Kussmaul reports that the encyclopedia is heavily used by subscribers, although it is now "a couple of steps down the menu" in importance to the overall system.

As noted, the *Kussmaul Encyclopedia* has about 20,000 files, or entries. The large majority of these have been taken directly from the CADILLAC MODERN ENCYCLOPEDIA, an accurate, impartial, competently prepared short-entry encyclopedia that provides strong coverage of topics in the physical and biological sciences (with particular emphasis on mathematics), as well as some 4,000 biographies, numerous book and opera plot summaries, and much tabular information. Over the years, Delphi has added some 2,000 files to the original database, and many entries have been updated. When the *Kussmaul Encyclopedia* initially went online, it was advertised as "Always up to the minute.... Everything you look up is absolutely current. In fact, don't be surprised to see something that appeared on yesterday's Evening News!" Unfortunately, this claim is no longer valid. At the time, Delphi editors were linking United Press International (UPI) wire stories with appropriate encyclopedia files. For example, a major development reported by UPI in, say, the war between Great Britain and Argentina over the Falkland Islands would be added to the Falkland Islands file in the encyclopedia. But for a variety of reasons (including UPI's recent financial problems), the encyclopedia no longer provides this creative updating feature. At present, according to Kussmaul, the encyclopedia is not updated as regularly or as frequently as he would like.

The encyclopedia's writing style is clear, spare, and nontechnical. Normally, the text will be comprehensible to users reading at the junior high school level and up. The encyclopedia's contents are readily accessible via assigned subject headings, or descriptors, which function much like an index in a print source. In addition, the encyclopedic text includes abundant cross-references that help steer the user in the right direction. Unlike the ACADEMIC AMERICAN ENCY-CLOPEDIA and the NEW ENCYCLOPAEDIA BRITANNICA, the two major general encyclopedias currently available in North America in auto-mated form, the *Kussmaul Encyclopedia* is not programmed for full-text searching—that is, the capability of electronically scanning all the files in a database and retrieving any nontrivial word or combination of words using Boolean logic (the linking of search terms in AND/OR/NOT relationships). Considering the relatively small size of its database, the *Kussmaul Encyclopedia* hardly needs the full-text searching feature, but it would make the file contents just that much more accessible. As pointed out earlier, the encyclopedia has no illustrations, although tentative plans exist for adding both pictures and sound to the database eventually. (For more on the subject of the encyclopedia of the future, see "Won't Computers Replace Encyclope-dias?" in the Questions and Answers section at the beginning of this book.)

To Summarize: The *Kussmaul Encyclopedia* is an electronic (as opposed to print) encyclopedia. Online since 1981, it is part of the Delphi information system produced by General Videotex Corpora-tion of Cambridge, Massachusetts. The encyclopedia, which is based on the old (1973) one-volume CADILLAC MODERN ENCYCLOPEDIA, pro-vides brief, accurate, objective, fairly current information on some 20,000 subjects. The *Kussmaul Encyclopedia* is both a useful reference source for Delphi subscribers and an interesting pioneering venture in electronic information storage and retrieval.

In Comparison: The electronic *Kussmaul Encyclopedia* contains roughly 20,000 files (or entries) and 3 million words. At this writing, only three other general encyclopedias are available electronically in North America, namely, the ACADEMIC AMERICAN ENCYCLOPEDIA (29,000 files; 9 million words), EVERYMAN'S ENCYCLOPAEDIA (51,000 files; 9 million words), and the NEW ENCYCLOPAEDIA BRITANNICA (62,300 files; 44 million words). Obviously, the *Kussmaul Encyclope-dia* is the smallest and least impressive of the four. The ACADEMIC

AMERICAN ENCYCLOPEDIA, on the other hand, is the leader among electronic encyclopedias, because of its ready availability through a number of information vendors, including the popular Dialog (see the ACADEMIC AMERICAN ENCYCLOPEDIA review for a complete list), and its full-text searching capability. The NEW ENCYCLOPAEDIA BRITANNICA, marketed by Mead Data Central, also offers full-text searching, but the Mead service is not available to individuals, schools, or libraries (at least at this time).

To Purchase the *Kussmaul Encyclopedia:* As noted, the encyclopedia is part of the Delphi electronic information system and therefore is available only to Delphi subscribers. The system is easily accessible via home computer and is said to be more affordable than its chief competitors, CompuServe and The Source. Consumers who wish to order Delphi (and the encyclopedia), or who simply seek more information, should contact General Videotex Corporation at 3 Blackstone Street, Cambridge, MA 02139 or telephone toll-free 1-800-544-4005.

No other reviews of the *Kussmaul Encyclopedia* are available at this time.

Lincoln Library of Essential Information

FACTS

The Lincoln Library of Essential Information. William H. Seibert, Editor in Chief. Columbus, OH: Frontier Press Company. Two volumes. Former title: *New Lincoln Library Encyclopedia* (1978–80). First edition published in 1924; new printing with revisions every two years (most recently in 1985). Lowest retail price: $139.98 delivered.

The *Lincoln Library of Essential Information,* a general encyclopedic work for adults and older students, intends to pack as much useful information into two volumes as possible. The encyclopedia contains approximately 2,500 pages, 25,000 articles, and 3.5 million words. The articles, many of which are very short, average 150 words in length (or about 11 articles per page). They are accompanied by 1,200 illustrations (most in black-and-white), plus 140 maps, including a 48-page color atlas. Some 150 editors and contributors are identified at the front of the first volume. None of the articles is signed. The encyclopedia is arranged topically, the contents grouped by subject in 12 sections, or "departments" ("Geography," "History," "Government," "Business and Economics," "Education and Human Studies," "English," "Literature," "Fine Arts," "Mathematics," "Science," "Biography," and "Miscellany"), with access to specific information enhanced by a detailed table of contents, 8,800 cross-references, and an index (printed at the end of both volumes) of some 75,000 entries.

EVALUATION

The *Lincoln Library,* named for Abraham Lincoln ("whose inspiring example demonstrated the possibilities of self-education"—title page), was first published in 1924 and has been issued at regular intervals, either annually or biennially, ever since. A supermarket edition entitled the *Encyclopedia of World Knowledge* appeared in 14 slim volumes in 1969, but it quickly went out of print. The *Lincoln Library* is well known to librarians and others who work with reference materials, but in recent years it has not kept pace with the times and is no longer considered an encyclopedia of first importance.

Within its 12 subject divisions, the *Lincoln Library* includes numerous survey articles, more than 50 specialized dictionaries (on such topics as art terms, chemical substances, and synonyms and antonyms), and some 200 tables and charts (on all sorts of subjects from coal production to verb forms). As might be expected, historical and statistical material predominates. The encyclopedia's subject coverage is a bit of a hodgepodge, with the sciences, social studies, and visual and literary arts emphasized to one degree or another while such important areas of knowledge as philosophy, religion, sociology, psychology, and psychiatry are all but ignored. Information in the *Lincoln Library* is usually reliable, although occasional inaccuracies do occur. Likewise, the encyclopedia usually presents its material in an objective manner, although controversial or sensitive issues such as abortion, adoption, birth control, and religious cults tend to be avoided.

As already noted, the encyclopedia is revised with each new printing, which normally appears every two years. Unfortunately, these revisions are not always as thorough or consistent as they might be. As a result, the encyclopedia lacks up-to-dateness in many areas. William A. Katz, in his authoritative *Introduction to Reference Work* (1982, vol. 1, p. 196) pinpoints the problem: "The difficulty with the *Lincoln* is its revision policy. Although it claims a policy of constant revision, a cursory glance at the 1980 printing will show it is best on current events, but slower on updating standard material in the social sciences, arts, and humanities. The specific-entry short items are more likely to reflect the year's past events than are the longer, more detailed survey articles." These criticisms are also true of printings after 1980, although a substantial revision in 1981 did temporarily improve the situation.

The *Lincoln Library*'s writing style is clear, albeit textbookish. Most of its articles, dictionary entries, and tabulations will be comprehensible to users reading at the junior high school level and up. Potentially difficult or unfamiliar terms are sometimes (but not always) defined or explained in context. The first paragraph of the article *Earthquake* (in the "Geography" department) typifies the encyclopedia's style:

> EARTHQUAKE. A trembling or shaking of the earth, varying from a slight tremor, perceptible only with the aid of delicate instruments, to a tremendous convulsion which may cause immense destruction of life and property. Great earthquakes may or may not be heralded by preliminary tremors. The principal shock or series of shocks usually continues over a few minutes, during which buildings are demolished and huge fissures appear in the earth. After the main shock, a series of minor disturbances, gradually decreasing in intensity, may continue for a period of many weeks, or even for several years. A seismograph, or seismometer, measures and records the intensity of earth vibrations, and a reading of 6.0 or more on the Richter scale indicates a major earthquake.

The encyclopedia's contents are reasonably accessible, thanks to an exhaustive index found at the end of Volume 1 and reprinted (for the sake of convenience) at the end of Volume 2. The set's illustrations are mostly black-and-white photographs, except for various color plates scattered throughout. As a rule, the illustrations add little to the informational value of the work, being dull and insufficiently detailed. It should be stated, however, that the editors make no claims on behalf of the illustrations: "Following the concept of presenting essential information, it has not been the aim to provide a heavily illustrated reference work" (preface). Physically, the encyclopedia is well made and will stand up under heavy use, but aesthetically it lacks appeal. The page layout has a cramped, uninviting look about it, and the old-fashioned typeface gives the impression of being straight out of the nineteenth century.

To Summarize: The two-volume *Lincoln Library,* intended for adults and older students, is an old standby dating back to 1924. In recent years, however, the encyclopedia has fallen on hard times. At present, it is an old-fashioned looking hodgepodge of somewhat dated information. Moreover, it has mediocre illustrations and tends to ignore controversial subjects.

In Comparison: The *Lincoln Library,* published in two volumes containing approximately 3.5 million words, is a small encyclopedia for adults and students at the secondary school and college levels. It compares directly with three other substantial small-volume adult encyclopedias, namely, the NEW COLUMBIA ENCYCLOPEDIA (one volume; 6.6 million words), the RANDOM HOUSE ENCYCLOPEDIA (one volume; 3 million words), and the VOLUME LIBRARY (two volumes; 3.5 million words). Also to be reckoned with in this category is the smaller CONCISE COLUMBIA ENCYCLOPEDIA (one volume; one million words), a recently published abridgment of the NEW COLUMBIA ENCYCLOPEDIA. Among these titles, the NEW COLUMBIA ENCYCLOPEDIA and the RANDOM HOUSE ENCYCLOPEDIA represent the best buys, along with the CONCISE COLUMBIA ENCYCLOPEDIA if a smaller (and less expensive) work will do. The *Lincoln Library,* though well known, has little to offer the wise consumer, comparatively speaking. Note also that the *Lincoln Library* is the most expensive encyclopedia in its category.

To Purchase the *Lincoln Library of Essential Information:* The encyclopedia is sold chiefly to schools and libraries by independent distributors. The publisher, Frontier Press, has no sales force of any size, and the two-volume set is not ordinarily available in retail bookstores. If you are either an individual consumer who wishes to order the *Lincoln Library* or are ordering the work for a school or library, the most expedient approach is to contact the Frontier Press Company at P.O. Box 1098, Columbus, OH 43216 or telephone 614-864-3737. Your order will be processed immediately.

For More Information about the *Lincoln Library of Essential Information* **See:** *American Reference Books Annual,* 1973, p. 106 (review by Bohdan S. Wynar); *Booklist,* January 1, 1979, pp. 768–69 (unsigned review); *Introduction to Reference Work* by William A. Katz (4th ed., New York: McGraw-Hill, 1982), vol. 1: *Basic Information Sources,* pp. 194–96; *Reference Sources for Small and Medium-sized Libraries* (4th ed., Chicago: American Library Association, 1984), p. 29 (review by Jovian P. Lang).

Merit Students Encyclopedia

FACTS

Merit Students Encyclopedia. William D. Halsey, Editorial Director; Emanuel Friedman, Editor in Chief. New York: Macmillan Educational Company, a division of Macmillan, Inc. 20 volumes. First edition published in 1967; new printing with revisions each year.

Lowest retail price: $1,099.50 delivered; with discount to schools and libraries: $525.00 plus $16.00 shipping and handling.

Merit Students Encyclopedia is intended for "the student at the fifth-grade, where the use of the encyclopedia begins in most schools, and continues to serve him as he moves through elementary school and secondary school" (preface). The 20-volume encyclopedia contains 12,300 pages, 21,000 articles, and 9 million words. The articles, many of which are of the short-entry type, average 425 words in length (or roughly half of a page). They are accompanied by 19,200 illustrations (25 percent in full color), plus 1,570 maps. Two hundred and twenty-five editors and advisers are identified at the front of Volume 1; in addition, some 2,300 contributors and reviewers are listed in Volume 20. Almost all of the articles are signed, either by the contributor or a reviewer (an authority who "vouches for the accuracy and completeness of the article but did not write it"). The encyclopedia is arranged alphabetically letter by letter (*Newspaper* precedes *New York*), with access to specific information enhanced by 10,600 cross-references in the text and an analytical index of more than 140,000 entries.

EVALUATION

In 1960, Macmillan, Inc., one of North America's premier encyclopedia publishers (COLLIER'S ENCYCLOPEDIA, the *Great Soviet Encyclopedia,* the *International Encyclopedia of the Social Sciences,* the *Encyclopedia of Philosophy,* etc.), began planning a new general encyclopedia that would serve students at the fifth grade level and up as well as the whole family. What eventually emerged in 1967 was *Merit Students Encyclopedia,* a junior version (but not an abridgment) of the larger, more advanced COLLIER'S ENCYCLOPEDIA. During the two decades of its existence, *Merit Students* has achieved recognition as a first-class reference source for both students and adults. The set's editor, Emanuel Friedman, who also oversees COLLIER'S ENCYCLOPEDIA, brings excellent qualifications to the work, as do most of the other editors and editorial advisers. However, a review by Heather Cameron and Ann Hartman in *American Reference Books Annual* (1982, p. 37) correctly points out that information provided about the makers of the encyclopedia is not always accurate: "A spot check of the biographical information for these editors given at the beginning of Volume 1 ... revealed that information was often incorrect or outdated, leaving us to wonder at the ongoing involvement of certain individuals in the revision process." Another criticism of the encyclopedia along the same lines is that an inordinate number of the 2,300 contributors and reviewers noted in the final volume are college and university officials who have done nothing but verify brief articles about their schools, a practice that uncharitably might be called padding the contributors' list. *Merit Students* is unquestionably an authoritative encyclopedia, but its authority lists need to be reworked.

The encyclopedia's coverage is well balanced among the major knowledge areas. The preface advises, "The scope and content of the encyclopedia were developed after analysis of the published curriculum material available from all the states of the United States, from the provinces of Canada, and from parochial school systems. Classroom teachers and curriculum experts in all subject areas were consulted as the list of articles was developed." Today, the set continues to reflect the curricula of North American schools. Befitting an encyclopedia designed specifically with educational instruction in mind, articles in *Merit Students* provide not only hard facts but, when appropriate, succinctly explain major concepts, themes, and trends, in an effort to put the subject into a broader intellectual perspective for the user. For example, the article on Sir William Gilbert (of Gilbert and Sullivan) informs the reader, "Gilbert made his plots deliberately absurd as a satire on the implausible situations of French and Italian opera. Although the settings of the operettas were different, the targets of his satire were always the English upper classes and the pompous, hypocritical values of the Victorian age."

The encyclopedia also furnishes good coverage of biographical and geographical topics, with emphasis on people and places in the United States and Canada. Articles on the U.S. states and Canadian provinces, for example, are uniformly excellent. Accredited colleges and universities in the United States (but not Canada) are likewise well covered, each institution accorded its own brief entry. Out-of-school, or extracurricular, subjects also receive considerable attention, as demonstrated by substantial articles on such topics as antiques, archery, baseball, boats and boating, the Boy Scouts, etiquette, first aid, gardening, houseplants, insurance, lifeguards, the Marine Corps, the Olympic Games, pensions, sewing, television, tennis, weight control, and wine.

Information in *Merit Students* is normally accurate and unbiased. The article on abortion, for instance, clearly and objectively presents arguments on both sides of this sensitive issue. The same is true of the articles *Birth Control, Homosexuality,* and *Sex Education.* The encyclopedia's contents are reasonably current in most instances. William A. Katz, in his *Introduction to Reference Work* (1982, vol. 1, p. 190), comments on *Merit Students'* "aggressive" approach to updating its material. Indeed, the encyclopedia has one of the most active and successful continuous revision programs of any set currently on the market. The 1984 printing, for example, includes 78 completely new or rewritten articles along with 837 others that have been updated to one degree or another. In all, 1,241 of the encyclopedia's 12,300 pages were revised in some manner in 1984. Such articles as

Acquired Immune Deficiency Syndrome (AIDS), Capital Punishment, Computer, Microprocessor (new in 1985), *Shroud of Turin,* and *Wordprocessor* (also new in 1985) are admirably current and attest to the editors' commitment to keep the set as up-to-date as possible. On the negative side, some of the college and university articles are in need of revision. For instance, Shippensburg (PA) University, which has had university status now for some time, is still identified as Shippensburg State College.

The encyclopedia's writing style tends to be clear and businesslike. The first paragraph of the article *Earthquake* is representative of *Merit Students'* style:

> EARTHQUAKE (Ėrth' kwk'), a naturally caused shaking of a part of the earth's surface. Earthquakes occur more than a thousand times a day. Their movements may be so slight as to go undetected or so violent that they cause widespread destruction and loss of life. One of the greatest natural disasters of all time—the earthquake of 1556 in Shensi province, China—is estimated to have taken more than 800,000 lives. In modern times, earthquakes continue to cause much damage and destruction. It is not yet possible to predict or control earthquakes. (*See also* DISASTERS.)

A useful technique that expands the encyclopedia's readability level is its simple-to-complex, or "pyramid," writing style—that is, the article begins with the simplest or most elementary material and then gradually becomes more detailed or complex as the text progresses. For example, toward the end of *Earthquake,* the article's content, vocabulary, and syntax (or sentence structure) are clearly more advanced than at the beginning:

> The study of earthquakes is called seismology. Seismologists determine the occurrence and intensity of earthquakes with instruments called seismographs, which record the different shock waves of the earthquake. The greater the amplitude, or height of the waves, the stronger the earthquake. (*See also* SEISMOGRAPH; SEISMOLOGY.)
>
> By measuring the amplitude of the waves, seismologists can determine the numerical strength of the earthquake, using the Richter magnitude scale. On this scale each successive number stands for an earthquake about 10 times stronger than the one represented by the preceding number. For example, an earthquake of magnitude 6 (moderately destructive) releases about 100 times more energy than an earthquake of magnitude 4 (slight damage). The largest earthquakes score higher than 8 on the Richter scale.

Like its principal competitors (COMPTON'S ENCYCLOPEDIA and the WORLD BOOK ENCYCLOPEDIA), *Merit Students* is most appropriate for users with reading skills from the seventh to twelfth grade levels. In addition, the encyclopedia can be comprehended by above-average readers in the upper elementary grades. A review in *Booklist*

(September 15, 1983, p. 151) characterizes *Merit Students'* readability as "that of the weekly adult newsmagazine," a fair assessment.

Information in *Merit Students* is fairly easy to find. More than 10,000 cross-references appear throughout the text to assist the user (the several references in the article on earthquakes quoted from above are typical). But to be truly effective, many more cross-references are needed. (Note that COMPTON'S ENCYCLOPEDIA has more than 35,000 cross-references and the WORLD BOOK ENCYCLOPEDIA 100,000.) The article *Turin* (the Italian city), for example, lacks a *See also* reference to *Shroud of Turin* and vice versa. Similarly, the biographical articles on Richard D'Oyly Carte, William Gilbert, and Arthur Sullivan all lack references to the article *Savoy Theatre* and vice versa. Unhappily, these are not isolated examples. As Heather Cameron and Ann Hartman remark in their instructive review of *Merit Students* in *American Reference Books Annual* (1982, p. 39), "The inadequacy of cross-referencing, noted in our review of the 1978 edition, continues to be a weakness of this [1981] edition." In many instances, however, the set's excellent 444-page index compensates for the cross-reference problem. In terms of the ratio of index entries (140,000) to total words in the encyclopedia (9 million), *Merit Students* furnishes one index entry for roughly every 65 words of text, or a ratio of 1:65. Among *Merit Students'* competitors, only the ACADEMIC AMERICAN ENCYCLOPEDIA has a better ratio (1:45).

The encyclopedia's bibliographies have been criticized as being too few and too old. The editors are apparently aware of the problem and are acting to correct it, albeit slowly. The set's illustrations, including the maps (by Rand McNally), are usually quite good, being clearly reproduced and carefully selected. "In each case the type of illustration was selected to provide the best visual communication. Trees are drawn in simple black and white to show the shape of the tree, leaf, flower, and fruit as aids to identification. Flowers and birds are shown in full color because color is of importance in identifying these subjects" (preface). Nonetheless, in some instances black-and-white illustrations are used where color is plainly called for, as in the case of the artwork accompanying the article on the painter Rubens. The text says that "Rubens' vibrant use of color influenced many 18th-century and 19th-century artists," but the painting that illustrates the article is in black-and-white. Physically, *Merit Students* is an exceptionally well made and attractively produced encyclopedia. Particularly noteworthy are the set's inviting page layout, legible typefaces, and clean, appealing design.

For the most part, encyclopedia critics have enthusiastically endorsed *Merit Students* as a work of high quality. Jovian Lang, for instance, in *Reference Sources for Small and Medium-sized Libraries* (1984, p. 28), commends the set as "exceptionally objective in its handling of sensitive political and social issues." The latest review in *Booklist* (December 15, 1984, p. 570) finds the set "useful and attractive" and "recommends it for advanced junior and senior high school students and adults." On the other hand, the latest review in *American Reference Books Annual* (1982, p. 39) offers a mixed verdict: "While *Merit Students Encyclopedia* is on the whole a well-indexed, well-illustrated, and well-written work, treating the broad range of young adults' interests, we were disappointed at times with the unevenness of revision."

To Summarize: *Merit Students* is a relatively new (1967–) multivolume general encyclopedia for students and the whole family. The set has numerous strengths, the most conspicuous being its balanced coverage, accurate and objective presentation of information, aggressive program of annual revision, and aesthetically pleasing format. Another plus is the encyclopedia's highly readable text. Weaknesses include inadequate cross-references and second-rate bibliographies.

In Comparison: *Merit Students,* published in 20 volumes containing 9 million words, falls mainly into the category of encyclopedias for adults and older students, although in some instances it will also be appropriate for younger readers (the set's editors claim a readability level of fifth grade and up). Generally speaking, *Merit Students* competes with the ACADEMIC AMERICAN ENCYCLOPEDIA (21 volumes; 9 million words), COMPTON'S ENCYCLOPEDIA (26 volumes; 8.5 million words), FUNK & WAGNALLS NEW ENCYCLOPEDIA (29 volumes; 9 million words), the NEW STANDARD ENCYCLOPEDIA (17 volumes; 6.4 million words), and the WORLD BOOK ENCYCLOPEDIA (22 volumes; 10 million words). Since its publication in 1967, *Merit Students'* major rivals have been COMPTON'S ENCYCLOPEDIA and the WORLD BOOK ENCYCLOPEDIA, both quality works that offer many of the same features as *Merit Students.* On balance, *Merit Students* is today a better encyclopedia than COMPTON'S (which is currently undergoing a thorough overhaul to correct a period of neglect) and in most areas it holds its own against WORLD BOOK, the acknowledged leader.

To Purchase *Merit Students Encyclopedia:* If you are an individual consumer and wish to order the encyclopedia, contact P.F. Collier, Inc. (the publisher's retail sales organization) at 866 Third Avenue, New York, NY 10022 or telephone toll-free 1-800-257-9500 Ext. 485. Your name will be forwarded to a sales representative in your area who will handle the transaction. The salesperson will most likely attempt to sell you additional publications along with the encyclopedia, including two yearbooks, *Merit Students Year Book* (which has practically the same contents as *Collier's Year Book,* an annual supplement to COLLIER'S ENCYCLOPEDIA) and *Health and Medical Horizons.* The whole package, called Merit Students Home Educational Program, currently sells for around $1,400.00. You need not buy these or any other extras unless you want them. In the case of the yearbooks, these so-called updating services have little direct connection with the encyclopedia and should not be purchased unless you are sure they will be used.

If you are ordering the encyclopedia for a school or library, contact Macmillan Professional Books at 866 Third Avenue, New York, NY 10022 or telephone toll-free 1-800-257-5755. Your order will be processed immediately.

For More Information about *Merit Students Encyclopedia* **See:** *American Reference Books Annual,* 1982, pp. 37–39 (review by Heather Cameron and Ann Hartman); *Booklist,* December 15, 1984, p. 570 (unsigned review); *Booklist,* September, 15, 1983, pp. 151–52 (unsigned review); *Introduction to Reference Work* by William A. Katz (4th ed., New York: McGraw-Hill, 1982), vol. 1: *Basic Information Sources,* pp. 189–91; *Reference Sources for Small and Medium-sized Libraries* (4th ed., Chicago: American Library Association, 1984), p. 28 (review by Jovian P. Lang).

Nelson's Encyclopedia for Young Readers

FACTS

Nelson's Encyclopedia for Young Readers. Laurence Urdang, Editor in Chief. Nashville, TN: Thomas Nelson Publishers. Two volumes (in slipcase). First edition published in 1980. Lowest retail price: $34.95.

Nelson's Encyclopedia for Young Readers, a small work for children ages seven to fourteen, intends to "answer many of your questions about the world in which you live" (publisher's introduction). The two-volume encyclopedia contains 973 pages, approximately 2,000 articles, and 350,000 words. The articles, which are uniformly brief, average 175 words in length (or about half a page). They are accompanied by 1,500 illustrations (50 percent in color), plus 200 maps. An editorial staff of 11, including four consulting editors, are listed at the front of both volumes. All of the articles are staff-written and unsigned. The encyclopedia is arranged alphabetically letter by letter (*Newspapers* precedes *New York*), with access to specific information enhanced by some 2,500 cross-references in the text and an index of 5,700 entries.

EVALUATION

Nelson's was issued in 1980 by Thomas Nelson Publishers, a Nashville trade publisher. Entirely new at the time and thus far never revised, the encyclopedia was prepared under the editorship of Laurence Urdang, a well-known and prolific producer of reference publications, especially dictionaries. The encyclopedia's coverage, which is highly selective and quite thin, ranges far and wide. As the publisher's introduction explains, *Nelson's* "will guide you from very early times through the present day and point you toward tomorrow. It will take you to every major country of the globe and let you explore the depths of outer space. It will tell you how machines work, why nature behaves as it does, and when the important events of history occurred." Biographical and geographical entries account for roughly 30 percent of the total coverage. Scientific and technical subjects also receive considerable attention, as do religious matters. In point of fact, religion may be overemphasized, considering the size and purpose of the encyclopedia. For example, most important names in the Judeo-Christian experience—Jesus, John, Judas Iscariot, Luke, Mark, Matthew, Peter, King David, Isaiah, Moses, Nebuchadnezzar, Noah, et al.—have individual entries, as do such topics as religion, church, Christianity, the Catholic Church, the Orthodox Church, Protestantism, Mormons, the Bible, the Psalms, hymns, Judaism, Hebrews, Jews, Jerusalem, Nazareth, Passover, Yom Kippur, etc. Conversely, the encyclopedia ignores marriage, divorce, adoption, childbirth and human sexuality, babies and infant care, suicide, and death, all subjects of great concern and curiosity to children and younger students.

Information in *Nelson's* is usually accurate and unbiased, although controversial questions are mostly avoided. The encyclopedia's contents are, generally speaking, current as of the late 1970s, but timeliness is not ordinarily a concern, due to the brevity of coverage and emphasis on historical and background information over current developments. The article *Heart,* for instance, describes how the heart works but does not attempt to cover breakthroughs like transplant surgery. The encyclopedia's writing style is commendable for its clarity and careful attention to potentially difficult or unfamiliar terms, which are italicized and defined as they occur. The text normally will be understandable to students in the upper elementary grades, and slower readers at the junior high school level will also find the set to their liking. The first half of the article *Earthquake* typifies the encyclopedia's writing style:

> An earthquake is a shaking and a breaking of the Earth's crust. It is attributed to a sudden relieving of tremendous stress built up by uneven forces exerted on and beneath the Earth's surface. The break in the crust is called a *fault.*

The Earth's crust has a number of solid pieces called *plates*. These plates are separated by cracks because the plates move and rub against each other there.

It is thought that the plates move because very slow currents are moving in the Earth's hot mantle under the crust.

Access to information in *Nelson's* is reasonably good, due in large measure to the many cross-references located throughout the text. Printed in SMALL CAPITAL LETTERS, the cross-references direct the young reader to related articles in the set. For example, the article on Paul Revere contains *See also* references to BOSTON TEA PARTY and AMERICAN REVOLUTION. Regrettably, the index, found at the end of Volume 2, is defective. The main entries in the index are almost exactly the same as the titles of the articles in the encyclopedia, thus reducing the effectiveness of the index to practically zero. The article *The Thirteen Colonies,* for instance, is duly entered in the index under "Thirteen Colonies" but not under such logical headings as "American History," "Colonial America," and "United States History."

The encyclopedia is heavily illustrated, with one and often more graphics on every text page. The illustrations, approximately half of which are in color, are all line drawings, many of them reprinted from *Black's Children's Encyclopedia,* a 12-volume British work originally published in 1961. The illustrations are not always clearly reproduced. The encyclopedia's physical format is satisfactory. The page layout is clean and attractive, the large print easy to read and appealing to children, and the binding both durable and washable. The slipcase, however, which holds the two volumes, is insubstantial and cheaply made.

To Summarize: On the surface, *Nelson's,* a two-volume work for young readers published in 1980, is a colorful, attractive, readable set of reference books. But close examination reveals a number of problems, including an ineffective index, inadequate illustrations, superficial treatment of topics covered, and very uneven coverage, with a disproportionate amount of space devoted to religious subjects. Considering these weaknesses, the encyclopedia seems overpriced at $34.95. Frances Neel Cheney, an authority on reference sources, offers another point of view in her appraisal of *Nelson's* in *American Reference Books Annual* (1981, p. 30): "The selection of entries, style of writing, large print, and low price make it worthy of consideration for home purchase, in spite of its poor illustrations."

In Comparison: *Nelson's,* published in two volumes containing approximately 350,000 words, is a small work for children and younger students. It competes with the JUNIOR ENCYCLOPEDIA OF GENERAL KNOWLEDGE (one volume; 100,000 words), JUNIOR PEARS ENCYCLOPAEDIA (one volume; 280,000 words), PURNELL'S PICTORIAL ENCYCLOPEDIA (one volume; 75,000 words), and RAND McNALLY'S CHILDREN'S

ENCYCLOPEDIA (one volume; 15,000 words). None of these titles can be enthusiastically recommended to North American consumers, although *Nelson's* (despite its many glaring limitations) and JUNIOR PEARS ENCYCLOPAEDIA (despite its heavy British bias) are the best of the lot. Macmillan, Inc., a leading North American publisher of encyclopedias (COLLIER'S ENCYCLOPEDIA; MERIT STUDENTS ENCYCLO-PEDIA) is currently preparing a small-volume encyclopedia for young children and students in the primary grades, but at this writing it is far from ready for publication. There is a real need for a substantial one- or two-volume encyclopedia for young people.

To Purchase *Nelson's Encyclopedia for Young Readers:* The encyclopedia is sold in North American retail bookstores. If it is not in stock, most bookstores will order it for you. You can also order the encyclopedia directly from the publisher, Thomas Nelson Publishers, at P.O. Box 946, 407 Seventh Avenue South, Nashville, TN 37203 or telephone 615-889-9000.

For More Information about *Nelson's Encyclopedia for Young Readers* See: *American Reference Books Annual,* 1981, p. 30 (review by Frances Neel Cheney).

New Book of Knowledge

FACTS

The New Book of Knowledge. Bernard S. Cayne, Editorial Director; Jean E. Reynolds, Editor in Chief. Danbury, CT: Grolier, Inc. 21 volumes (plus a paperbound volume entitled *Home and School Reading and Study Guides*) Former title: *Book of Knowledge* (1912–65). First published as the *New Book of Knowledge* in 1966; new printing with revisions each year. Lowest retail price: $800.00 plus shipping and handling; with discount to schools and libraries: $499.50 plus shipping and handling.

New Book of Knowledge "is uniquely related to the needs of modern children, both in school and at home. It is written for the children of today, who are standing on the threshold of a new world" (preface). The editors' preface goes on to note that the 21-volume *New Book of Knowledge* "will be useful to a wide range of readers, starting with preschool children and including students in school up to the age when they are ready for an adult encyclopedia." The encyclopedia contains 10,540 pages, 9,116 main articles, and approximately 6.8 million words. The main articles, of which more than 4,000 are of the broad-entry type, average 700 words in length (or nearly a full page). The set also includes some 5,000 very brief articles, or fact entries, in the index (called the Dictionary Index). The main articles are accompanied by 22,500 illustrations (about 75 percent in color), plus 1,046 maps. An editorial staff of 50 is listed at the front of Volume 1, and about 1,400 contributors, consultants, and reviewers (or verifiers) are identified at the back of Volume 20. Almost all of the articles are signed, except for the short entries in the Dictionary Index, which are staff written. The encyclopedia is arranged alphabetically letter by letter (*Newspapers* precedes *New York*), with access to specific information enhanced by 3,700 cross-references in the text and an analytical index (the aforementioned Dictionary Index) of 85,000 entries.

EVALUATION

The *New Book of Knowledge* appeared in 1966, replacing the popular *Book of Knowledge* (1912–65), which in turn derived from the British *Children's Encyclopaedia* edited by Arthur Mee, widely regarded as the first modern encyclopedia for young people. Intended generally for children ages seven to fourteen and particularly for students in grades three to six, the *New Book of Knowledge* is a product of Grolier, Inc., a leading North American publisher of reference materials and one of the largest publishers of encyclopedias in the world. In the Grolier family of general encyclopedias, the *New Book of Knowledge* (21 volumes; 6.8 million words) is the smallest, behind the middle-sized ACADEMIC AMERICAN ENCYCLOPEDIA (21 volumes; 9 million words), and the large ENCYCLOPEDIA AMERICANA (30 volumes; 31 million words). Reference specialists consider the *New Book of Knowledge* to be one of the five or six best general English-language encyclopedias currently published. The editors and contributors, the latter mostly North American educators, bring respectable qualifications to the work. A Spanish-language adaptation of the encyclopedia entitled *El Nuevo Tesoro de la Juventud* is published in Mexico City chiefly for the Latin American market (although the set can be acquired in the United States and Canada through Grolier).

The *New Book of Knowledge*'s coverage, which is quite well balanced, broadly reflects the North American elementary school curriculum, although out-of-school and extracurricular interests also receive considerable attention. The arts and humanities are especially well covered. Articles on literary topics, for example, frequently include selections from children's literature, such as the *Arabian Nights* stories, the *Cinderella* fairy tale, and the poem *Paul Revere's Ride*. In like fashion, the article *Folk Music* provides samples of the genre. In addition, survey articles offer a broad perspective on national and regional cultural developments, as in the case of the articles *African Art, African Literature,* and *African Music.*

Coverage of scientific and technical subjects is also impressive, as exemplified by these lengthy and informative articles in Volume 1: *Acid Rain, Aerodynamics, Aging, Agriculture, Air Conditioning, Air Pollution, Algae, Algebra, Aluminum, Anesthesia, Animals, Antibiotics, Ants, Apples, Aquariums, Arithmetic, Astronomy, Atmosphere, Atoms, Automation, Automobiles,* and *Aviation.* Articles on the study of nature and natural phenomena stand out as models of their kind. The encyclopedia also includes numerous practical projects and experiments that the young person can accomplish, such as "How to Build an Ant Observation Nest" (part of the article *Ants*), "Making Your Own Weather Observation" (part of *Weather*), and "How to Make Your Own Slide Rule" (part of *Mathematics*). Likewise, the article *Experiments and Other Science Activities* explains how to set up experiments, how to record them, how to prepare for science fairs, and the like. When the *New Book of Knowledge* first appeared, a reviewer in *Choice* (May 1967, p. 276) singled out this feature for special commendation: "A variety of activities, science projects, demonstrations, and questions provide points of departure for exploration, thus serving as a useful supplement to teachers who are seeking ways to arouse children's curiosity and to help them express themselves creatively."

This observation is as true today as it was in 1967. Recently, for example, Grolier commissioned a series of five microcomputer software programs that can be used to teach computer literacy and research skills in conjunction with the encyclopedia. The programs, entitled the *Knowledge Exploration Series,* represent yet another way in which the encyclopedia can serve as an educational tool for young students. The software is designed for use with 64K Apple computers and can be ordered from Grolier at $302.50 for the package, including ten manuals and five backup disks. (For additional information about this innovative "electronic enhancement" of the *New Book of Knowledge,* see *Booklist,* January 1, 1985, p. 658).

The *New Book of Knowledge* is a carefully edited encyclopedia. As a result, its information is normally reliable, unbiased, and up-to-date. Articles on controversial subjects ordinarily point out both sides of the issue. The brief article *Abortion,* for instance, informs the reader, "Some people believe that elective abortion is murder. Others say that it is a private matter between a woman and her doctor." Sometimes, however, sensitive questions concerning human sexuality are avoided. Several years ago, the editors wisely added a general section to the article *Reproduction* entitled "Human Reproduction," but many specific matters relating to sex—naturally of great curiosity and concern to young people—are not covered. As a reviewer in

Booklist (May 15, 1983, p. 1239) suggests, "for today's youth some consideration should have been given to such topics as homosexuality and masturbation." To their credit, the editors did add an article on menstruation in 1984. The encyclopedia's energetic annual revision program keeps the set as current as can be expected. The 1984 printing, for example, includes nearly 1,000 new or revised articles and more than 500 new illustrations and maps—all involving changes in well over a quarter of the set's 10,540 pages. Suffice it to say that the *New Book of Knowledge* can be relied upon for up-to-date information.

The encyclopedia's articles are written in a clear and easily readable manner. Efforts are made to capture the reader's attention from the start with interesting first sentences. The initial paragraphs of the article *Earthquakes* provide a good example of the set's writing style:

> The ground moves suddenly. It moves again and again, strongly and sharply. Concrete bridges fall. Buildings sway and collapse, and the falling debris traps people in the streets. This is an earthquake, one of the hundreds that occur every year. Most earthquakes do little harm, but a few kill many people and cause enormous destruction.
>
> People have had to endure earthquakes throughout history, but today there is hope that something can be done about them. Seismologists, the scientists who study earthquakes, have learned a great deal about them in recent years.
>
> People are sometimes amazed to learn that a seismologist can record an earthquake that is occurring thousands of kilometers away. The fact is, the earthquake records itself.

Note that the key words **seismology** and its derivations are printed in **bold type** and defined in a box at the beginning of the article. Likewise, other technical terms used in the article—**P wave, S wave, tsunamis,** and **magnitude**—are printed in bold letters and explained in context.

Another valuable (though perhaps less apparent) feature of the encyclopedia's writing style is its simple-to-complex, or "pyramid," approach—that is, the article begins simply and then gradually becomes more detailed and sophisticated as the text progresses. For example, at the end of *Earthquakes,* the article's content, vocabulary, and syntax (or sentence structure) are clearly more advanced than at the beginning:

> Seismographic recorders help the earth scientist to locate an earthquake and also to calculate how powerful the quake is. This information is a clue to the amount of damage the quake may do. The power, or **magnitude,** of a quake is measured on the Richter scale. It is named after Charles F. Richter, the American seismologist who developed it. Very small tremors are rated up to 2.5 on the scale. Quakes rated up to 5 can cause some minor

damage. Those of magnitude 6 and higher are major quakes that can cause widespread damage. For example, one of the greatest magnitudes ever recorded was 8.5, in an earthquake that shook Anchorage, Alaska, in 1964.

The *New Book of Knowledge* is most appropriate for users in grades three through six with average or better reading skills. Students at the junior high school level, as well as slower high school students, will also find the set a useful source of information.

The encyclopedia's contents are readily accessible, due in part to the nearly 4,000 cross-references in the text but mostly to the 85,000-entry Dictionary Index, which serves as both a finding device and a source of quick reference information not included in the regular A-to-Z section. For example, the Dictionary Index entry under "Adoption" refers the user to pages A 25–26, S 225, and O 227 where information on the subject can be found in the articles *Adoption, Social Work,* and *Orphanages and Foster-Family Care.* The preceding entry, however, provides no volume and page references but, rather, a four-line article, or fact entry, on Adonis (from Greek mythology). There are approximately 5,000 such entries in the Dictionary Index. The index is split among the set's first 20 volumes, the letters of the alphabet covered in the index corresponding to those of the volumes themselves. Volume 21, entitled "Combined Index to the New Book of Knowledge," brings together all 20 parts of the index, except for the brief articles, or fact entries, which are not reprinted but are indexed. Overall, the index provides one entry for roughly every 80 words of text in the encyclopedia, for an excellent ratio of 1:80.

Illustrations in the *New Book of Knowledge* are, in a word, outstanding. They include well-reproduced photographs, diagrams, drawings, prints, and original artwork that add immeasurably to the informational content of the work. The article *Earthquakes,* for example, contains four instructive photographs, five diagrams, and a map showing the world's major earthquake belts. New graphics are constantly added to the set. For instance, the article *Economics* was recently augmented by a two-page spread entitled "Economics in Action: How to Turn Lemons into Money," an imaginative series of captioned art that explains, in simple terms, 35 economic concepts (labor, management, inflation, profit, competitive pricing, etc.). Physically, the set is well made and pleasing to the eye. Bright and attractive, the *New Book of Knowledge* is an encyclopedia children respond to with enthusiasm.

From the start, critics have warmly endorsed the *New Book of Knowledge* as a standout encyclopedia for children and younger students. In a recent review in *American Reference Books Annual* (1984, p. 21), Janet Littlefield praises the set as "a relatively current, well-written encyclopedia that is responsive to the school and home needs of the elementary school-aged student." She is particularly impressed that "the authors have made a genuine effort to make articles as interesting to read as they are informative." William A. Katz, in his *Introduction to Reference Work* (1982, vol. 1, p. 192), notes that "among preschool and children's sets, the *New Book of Knowledge* leads in coverage, authority, recency, objectivity, and other criteria for evaluating encyclopedias." Jovian Lang, in *Reference Sources for Small and Medium-sized Libraries* (1984, p. 28), especially likes one aspect of the work: "A unique feature, unlike other, purely curriculum oriented, student encyclopedias is that more entertaining articles are written in the first person; for example, Danny Kaye reminisces about his enjoyment of Hans Christian Andersen, and the story 'The Emperor's New Clothes' immediately follows." And a reviewer in *Booklist* (December 15, 1984, p. 572) concludes that the encyclopedia is "recommended for homes and for school and public libraries serving elementary school students. It can also be used with junior and senior high school students with limited reading ability."

To Summarize: The *New Book of Knowledge* is a worthy successor to the longtime favorite *Book of Knowledge* (1912–65). Designed generally for children ages seven to fourteen and particularly for students in grades three to six, the *New Book of Knowledge* provides very good coverage of both in-school and out-of-school subjects of interest and value to young readers. Conspicuous strengths include accuracy and objectivity of information (although sensitive topics concerning human sexuality are sometimes avoided), a clear and exceptionally interesting writing style, first-class illustrations, and many articles (mainly projects and experiments in the area of science) that promote intellectual curiosity and self-education on the part of the young reader.

In Comparison: The *New Book of Knowledge,* published in 21 volumes containing approximately 6.8 million words, is intended for children and younger students in the elementary and junior high school grades. The encyclopedia competes directly with three other multivolume children's sets aimed at the same audience, namely, FINDING OUT: SILVER BURDETT'S CHILDREN'S ENCYCLOPEDIA (10 volumes; 250,000 words), the NEW KNOWLEDGE LIBRARY (35 volumes; 2 million words), and the YOUNG STUDENTS ENCYCLOPEDIA (24 volumes; 1.5 million words). In the past the *New Book of Knowledge* competed head-to-head with the BRITANNICA JUNIOR ENCYCLOPAEDIA (15 volumes; 5.4 million words) and the OXFORD JUNIOR ENCYCLO-PAEDIA (13 volumes; 3.7 million words), but these two works are now, at least temporarily, out of print. Of all of these titles, the *New Book of Knowledge* is unquestionably the best. It is also the biggest and most expensive. The encyclopedia also competes, though less directly, with other curriculum-related sets, the best known being COMPTON'S ENCYCLOPEDIA (26 volumes; 8.5 million words), MERIT STUDENTS EN-CYCLOPEDIA (20 volumes; 9 million words), and the WORLD BOOK ENCYCLOPEDIA (22 volumes; 10 million words). But these titles, though similar in approach to the *New Book of Knowledge,* are larger and are aimed at an older, more mature readership.

To Purchase the *New Book of Knowledge:* If you are an individual consumer and wish to order the encyclopedia, contact Grolier, Inc. at Sherman Turnpike, Danbury, CT 06816 or telephone toll-free 1-800-243-3356. Your name will be forwarded to a sales representative in your area who will handle the transaction. The sales representative will most likely attempt to sell you additional publications with the encyclopedia, including a yearbook entitled the *New Book of Knowledge Annual.* You need not buy any extras unless you want them. In the case of the *New Book of Knowledge Annual,* the book is a useful chronicle of the year's events but it has no real relationship to the encyclopedia (except in name).

If you are ordering the encyclopedia for a school or library, contact Grolier Educational Corporation at the address given above or telephone toll-free 1-800-243-7256. Your order will be processed immediately.

For More Information about the *New Book of Knowledge* See: *American Reference Books Annual,* 1984, pp. 18–21 (review by Janet H. Littlefield); *Booklist,* December 15, 1984, pp. 570–72 (unsigned review); *Booklist,* May 15, 1983, pp. 1239–40 (unsigned review); *Introduction to Reference Work* by William A. Katz (4th ed., New York: McGraw-Hill, 1982), vol. 1: *Basic Information Sources,* pp. 191–92; *Reference Sources for Small and Medium-sized Libraries* (4th ed., Chicago: American Library Association, 1984), p. 28 (review by Jovian P. Lang).

New Caxton Encyclopedia

FACTS

The New Caxton Encyclopedia. Graham Clarke, Editor. London, England: Caxton Publications Ltd. Distributed in North America by Pergamon Press, Inc. 20 volumes. Former title: *Purnell's New English Encyclopedia* (issued in 216 unbound weekly parts between 1966 and 1969). First published as the *New Caxton Encyclopedia* in 18 volumes in 1966; fifth edition published in 1979. Lowest retail price: $485.00.

The *New Caxton Encyclopedia* is a heavily illustrated British work intended for adults and older students. The encyclopedia aims to be "not just a compilation of facts [but] a simple scheme of universal knowledge which, taken as a whole, presents a panoramic view of the world around us—its geography, its problems, its famous people, its discoveries, its arts, and its manner of living" (introduction). The 20-volume set contains approximately 6,500 pages, 13,000 articles, and 6 million words. The articles, most of which are of the short-entry type, average 475 words in length (or about half a page). They are accompanied by 17,000 illustrations (almost all in color), plus 600 maps. Nearly 100 editors and contributors are listed at the front of Volume 1, although none of the articles is signed. The encyclopedia is arranged alphabetically word by word (*New York* precedes *Newspaper*), with access to specific information enhanced by an index of some 75,000 entries. The set has no cross-references in the text.

EVALUATION

First published in 18 volumes in 1966, the *New Caxton* was originally titled *Purnell's New English Encyclopedia,* a so-called part-work that appeared in Great Britain in weekly issues, or parts, beginning January 1, 1966. The encyclopedia actually originated in Italy as a project of the Istituto Geografico de Agostini, a firm internationally known for the excellent quality of its graphics, particularly in the cartographic field. (In fact, copyright to the *New Caxton* is held jointly by Caxton Publications and Agostini.) The idea was to produce a richly illustrated general multivolume encyclopedia that could be adapted for various national markets. Ultimately, the encyclopedia appeared in a number of versions, including the *New Caxton* in English, the French *Alpha: La grande encyclopédie universelle en couleurs,* and the Spanish *Monitor.* These titles all contain the same basic encyclopedic material (print and visual) but are edited to reflect national interests and achievements. A second edition of the *New Caxton* was issued in 1969, followed by a third (in 20 volumes) in 1973, and a fourth in 1977. In 1979, the fifth—and thus far the last—edition of the set appeared. A sixth edition, tentatively scheduled for 1982, has been delayed, and whether it will ever be published is a matter of speculation. Apparently the huge British Printing Corporation (BPC), of which Caxton Publications is a member company, has been beset by financial difficulties in recent years. Be that as it may, the current (1979) edition of the encyclopedia is a reasonably authoritative work, although none of its material is signed.

As the introduction to the set suggests (see the quote at the beginning of this review), the *New Caxton* broadly covers all areas of knowledge. The coverage is international in scope, with emphasis on Western Europe in general and the United Kingdom in particular.

This Anglo-European bias (which should come as no surprise given the encyclopedia's history) is evident in all areas, but especially so in coverage of biographical, geographical, and historical topics. For example, a review in *Booklist* (September 1, 1983, p. 52) reports, "There is, in the area of geography, an extraordinary emphasis on Europe. Names of European towns and cities account for almost 47 percent of articles on municipalities, and European regions account for 53 percent of such entries." Conversely, places in the United States and Canada receive much less attention. Moreover, articles dealing with social institutions and problems consistently reflect the British experience, as in the case of the article *Gambling, Gaming, and Betting,* which devotes most of its space to the history and legal status of wagering in Great Britain. Because of its heavy use of illustrative material, the encyclopedia also provides exceptionally strong coverage of the fine arts. As might be expected, British and European cultural history is particularly well covered. The set's weakest subject coverage comes in the area of social and political issues, such as the women's movement, race relations, suicide, adoption, and child abuse. It should also be explained that only metric measurements are given in the 1979 edition of the *New Caxton.* Omission of English (or customary) equivalents will, in the words of a review in *Booklist* (September 1, 1983, p. 56), "inhibit understanding of many facts on the part of those who do not know or use the metric system. For Americans for whose educational level this encyclopedia might be appropriate, the exclusive use of metrics will be experienced as a difficulty."

Information in the *New Caxton* is usually accurately and objectively presented, although minor errors of fact now and then intrude. A more significant factor, however, concerning the set's reliability is its age. Consumers should understand that, unlike multivolume encyclopedias produced in North America, British works such as the *New Caxton,* EVERYMAN'S ENCYCLOPAEDIA, and CHAMBERS'S ENCYCLOPAEDIA are not continuously revised with new printings each year but, rather, are updated with periodic new editions. In the case of the *New Caxton,* the last new edition appeared in 1979. Obviously, the set is now considerably out-of-date. Material on such subjects as computers, space exploration, robotics, and capital punishment is roughly a decade behind the times. Moreover, readers will look in vain for information about acquired immune deficiency syndrome (AIDS), the artificial heart, the Falkland Islands war, the demise of the D'Oyly Carte Opera Company, the new Canadian Constitution, or recent developments in Quebec province. On the latter subject, the encyclopedia's last word is that "French interests have been partially placated by the severance of nearly all the remaining official ties with Britain, the adoption of a new flag in 1964, and the succession of a French-Canadian, Pierre Trudeau, as prime minister."

The encyclopedia's writing style varies from article to article. For instance, the biographical sketch of William Gilbert (of Gilbert and Sullivan) tends to be ornate and intimate: "He was a kindly but irascible person with a brilliant gift of versification, epigram, and repartee. His collected poems form a volume called *The Bab Ballads* and contain much pungent comment on the society of his time and a good deal of delightful nonsense." In other instances, as in the case of the article *Earthquake,* the style is straightforward and erudite:

> EARTHQUAKE. A more or less violent local vibration of the Earth's crust resulting from the sudden adjustment of the rocks under stresses. The subterranean site of the adjustment is called the "focus" of the earthquake, and the point on the surface directly above it the "epicentre." The focus is very rarely more than 300 miles below the surface and usually very much less. The vibrations, which radiate from the epicentre as well as from the focus, are of two physical types: longitudinal or compression waves, and transverse or distortion waves. In the longitudinal waves the rocks vibrate to-and-fro in the direction of propagation, and may be compared with sound waves. In the transverse waves the motion is undulating and may be compared with ocean waves, each particle vibrating from side to side, or up and down, at right-angles to the direction of propagation.

The *New Caxton* is intended for adults and older students. As these examples plainly show, the encyclopedia requires high school level reading skills or better for full comprehension of the text. Note that potentially difficult or unfamiliar terms, such as *irascible, repartee, subterranean, longitudinal, propagation,* and *undulating,* are not defined or explained in context, nor is a controlled vocabulary used.

The contents of the *New Caxton* are not always as accessible as they might be. Oddly, there is not a single cross-reference in the entire text, a serious deficiency. There is, however, a general index to the set, but it is a third-rate piece of work. Located at the back of the final volume, the index lacks comprehensiveness and contains a number of errors in pagination. On the other hand, the *New Caxton*'s illustrations are of the highest quality. Indeed, as Auberon Waugh observes in his appraisal of the set in *Books and Bookmen* (July 1977, p. 21), they have no equal among English-language general encyclopedias: "It may seem frivolous to harp on about the pictures when reviewing a reference book, but excellence should always be applauded and in presentation, the pictures are far the best I have seen and compare favourably with the most expensive art books." Only the ACADEMIC AMERICAN ENCYCLOPEDIA, the WORLD BOOK ENCYCLOPEDIA, and perhaps the one-volume RANDOM HOUSE ENCYCLOPEDIA have illustrations that can begin to match those found in the *New Caxton.* Worthy of special notice are the encyclopedia's more than 3,000 handsome reproductions of paintings and other works of art. (Conveniently, these illustrations are separately indexed by architects, painters, and sculptors following the general index.) The physical format is also impressive. The page layout is inviting and the use of color eye-catching. A heavy grade of coated art paper is used to achieve the best color reproduction possible. The weight of the paper makes the volumes, which are quite thin, very heavy, each weighing around three pounds. On the negative side, the lettering on the spine is too small to be read easily at a distance.

Over the years, encyclopedia critics have given the *New Caxton* mixed reviews, most praising the set's illustrations but criticizing its Anglo-European orientation. John Farley's conclusions in his review in *American Reference Books Annual* (1981, p. 30) are typical: "The chief value of the work for an American home, school, or library would probably be as a thoroughly illustrated ready-reference encyclopedia, supplementary to an American multivolume set. Its pictorial richness will undoubtedly appeal to users of all ages, but its coverage of American topics is, for an American readership, inadequate." Another point of view is expressed in Auberon Waugh's assessment in *Books and Bookmen* (July 1977, pp. 20–21), which compares the *New Caxton* with the NEW ENCYCLOPAEDIA BRITANNICA. He concludes that "Britannica is best on the home ground [that is, for subjects the user knows something about], the *New Caxton* for expeditions to the other side."

To Summarize: The 20-volume *New Caxton,* first published in 1966 under the title *Purnell's New English Encyclopedia,* is a profusely illustrated British work for adults and older students. One critic, Nicholas Tucker, writing in the British newspaper *The Guardian* (May 29, 1979, p. 11), has called the *New Caxton* "the Concorde of the encyclopaedia world: fearfully expensive but lavish in detail and truly beautiful to look at." The problem is that the set's printed text pales in comparison with its illustrations. Specifically, the encyclopedia's coverage is heavily biased in favor of Western Europe in general and the United Kingdom in particular; its contents are now quite dated (the last revised edition appearing in 1979); and access to those contents is unsatisfactory.

In Comparison: The *New Caxton,* published in 20 volumes containing approximately 6 million words, is a medium-sized general encyclopedia for adults and students at the high school level and beyond. Aside from its superior illustrations, the encyclopedia has little to offer the large majority of North American consumers when compared head-to-head with most of the available sets in this category, namely, the ACADEMIC AMERICAN ENCYCLOPEDIA (21 volumes; 9 million words), COMPTON'S ENCYCLOPEDIA (26 volumes; 8.5 million words), FUNK & WAGNALLS NEW ENCYCLOPEDIA (29 volumes; 9 million words), MERIT STUDENTS ENCYCLOPEDIA (20 volumes; 9 million words), the NEW STANDARD ENCYCLOPEDIA (17 volumes; 6.4 million words), and the WORLD BOOK ENCYCLOPEDIA (22 volumes; 10 million words). However, anyone seeking a substantial general encyclopedia that emphasizes Anglo-European history and culture should seriously consider the *New Caxton*. Larger public and academic libraries especially may want it to provide extended reference coverage of British and European topics. It should be noted that the *New Caxton* is practically the only British-made multivolume general encyclopedia of any consequence currently on the North American market. The larger CHAMBERS'S ENCYCLOPAEDIA (15 volumes; 14.5 million words), has been out of print for years, and EVERYMAN'S ENCYCLOPAEDIA (12 volumes; 9 million words) is sold only in Canada.

To Purchase the *New Caxton Encyclopedia:* Through the years, the encyclopedia has been sold in the United States and Canada by a number of different distributors. At present, Pergamon Press lists the set as available at $485.00, although recently it was offered at the discount price of $250.00. If you wish to order the *New Caxton,* contact Pergamon Press, Inc. in the United States at Maxwell House, Fairview Park, Elmsford, NY 10523 or telephone 914-592-7700; in Canada write to Pergamon Press Canada Ltd., Suite 104, Consumers Road, Willowdale, Ontario M2J 1P9 or telephone 416-497-8337.

For More Information about the *New Caxton Encyclopedia* See: *American Reference Books Annual,* 1981, pp. 29–30 (review by John Farley); *Booklist,* September 1, 1983, pp. 52–58 (unsigned review); *Books and Bookmen,* July 1977, pp. 20–21 (review by Auberon Waugh); *The Guardian* (London and Manchester, England), May 29, 1979, p. 11 (article by Nicholas Tucker entitled "Checking the Facts"); *The Observer* (London), April 10, 1977 (article by Ken Creffield entitled "Battling Hard from A to Z"); *School Library Journal,* September 1971, pp. 98–100 (review by Sarah Law Kennerly).

New Columbia Encyclopedia

FACTS

The New Columbia Encyclopedia. William H. Harris and Judith S. Levey, Editors. New York: Columbia University Press. One volume. Former title: *Columbia Encyclopedia* (first edition, 1935; second edition, 1950; third edition, 1963). Abridged version: CONCISE COLUMBIA ENCYCLOPEDIA (1983). Illustrated version: NEW ILLUSTRATED COLUM-

BIA ENCYCLOPEDIA (24 volumes; 1978). Fourth edition published in 1975. Lowest retail price: $79.50.

The *New Columbia Encyclopedia,* a single-volume work for adults and older students, "offers authentic and accurate information in condensed form" (preface). The encyclopedia contains 3,068 pages, 50,515 articles, and approximately 6.6 million words. The articles, most of which are very brief, average 130 words in length (or about 16 articles per page). They are accompanied by 407 illustrations (all in black-and-white), plus 252 maps. Some 260 editors and consultants are identified at the front of the volume. None of the articles is signed. The encyclopedia is arranged alphabetically letter by letter (*Newspaper* precedes *New York*), with access to specific information enhanced by 66,000 cross-references in the text. The encyclopedia has no index.

EVALUATION

The *New Columbia* is actually the fourth edition of the *Columbia Encyclopedia,* a standard reference work that first appeared in 1935 and was revised in 1950 (second edition) and 1963 (third edition). The third edition spawned both an abridged and an illustrated version of the encyclopedia, namely, the *Columbia-Viking Desk Encyclopedia* (one volume; 1968) and the *Illustrated Columbia Encyclopedia* (22 volumes; 1967). In like manner, the *New Columbia,* published in 1975, has prompted an abridged (and updated) edition entitled the CONCISE COLUMBIA ENCYCLOPEDIA (one volume; 1983) as well as an illustrated edition called the NEW ILLUSTRATED COLUMBIA ENCYCLOPEDIA (24 volumes; 1978). As this publishing history implies, the name "Columbia" is well known and respected by those who buy and use encyclopedias. Certainly the *New Columbia* and its predecessors have a firmly established reputation for thorough and responsible scholarship. According to the editors' preface, "This encyclopedia is neither an official nor an unofficial publication of Columbia University, but without Columbia University this book would not have been possible." Indeed, roughly two-thirds of the encyclopedia's 91 academic consultants are identified as members of the Columbia University faculty.

Writing about the *New Columbia* when it first appeared, Israel Shenker in the *New York Times* (August 3, 1975, p. 40-L) observed, "Making a one-volume encyclopedia is like taking the broth of the universe and condensing it into a bouillon cube." Given the magnitude of the task, the *New Columbia* does a first-class job of providing broad, reasonably well balanced coverage of all major areas of knowledge. Quantitatively, biographical information predominates, accounting for nearly 45 percent of all articles. William A. Katz, in his *Introduction to Reference Work* (1982, vol. 1, p. 195), quite rightly points out that the encyclopedia's "strongest area is biography. Biographical sketches will be found here for individuals not included, or at best only mentioned, in the standard multivolume sets." Geographical topics also receive outstanding coverage, accounting for about 30 percent of the articles. Most localities in the United States with populations of 10,000 or more are covered, as are all of the republics and major cities of the Soviet Union. Coverage of the world outside North America has been greatly expanded in this edition of the encyclopedia, particularly for the nations and cultures of Asia, Africa, and South America. Scientific and technical subjects also receive more attention than heretofore: "In keeping with the increased knowledge and sophistication of readers, the science entries in this edition include more advanced and detailed technical information than those in previous editions" (preface). Continuing a policy established in the first edition in 1935, the *New Columbia* includes an article for every proper name in the Bible (King James Version). Obviously, there are inconsistencies and omissions in the coverage. The subject of adoption is accorded exactly the same amount of space devoted to the stinkbug; child abuse is accorded 13 lines whereas *Opera* receives 424 lines; the subjects of child development and human growth are apparently ignored altogether. But, on balance, both the quantity and quality of coverage found in the one-volume *New Columbia* are quite remarkable.

Information in the *New Columbia* is almost always accurate and presented in an impartial manner. The article *Apartheid,* for example, deals as objectively as possible with the controversial South African racial policy. Unfortunately, information in the encyclopedia is now very dated. When the volume initially appeared in 1975, it was current as of the early to mid-1970s, the editors having thoroughly reviewed or revised every article in the previous (1963) edition. Moreover, 7,000 new articles were added in 1975 on such subjects as the American Indian Movement (AIM), continental drift, no-fault insurance, space law, vasectomy, and Watergate. But well over a decade has passed since the *New Columbia* was published, and its contents, which have never been revised, are now dreadfully out-of-date. Readers today will look in vain for information about acquired immune deficiency syndrome (AIDS), the artificial heart, the Falkland Islands war, the new Canadian Constitution, and such contemporary political personalities as Jimmy Carter, Ronald Reagan, and Margaret Thatcher. Likewise, articles on such subjects as computer technology and capital punishment lack recent developments. A list of popes in the article *Papacy* ends with Pope Paul VI. Some of the material in the *New Columbia* has been updated in the CONCISE COLUMBIA ENCYCLOPEDIA (1983), but this abridgment is only about one-sixth the size of the parent work. When might a new (fifth) edition of the encyclopedia be expected? The editors are naturally mum on the subject, but an educated guess would be around 1990.

The encyclopedia's writing style is, in the words of a review in *Booklist* (January 1, 1979, p. 770), "lucid, concise, and expressive." Articles on complicated scientific subjects, such as genetics or nuclear energy, are written in "pyramid" style—that is, the text begins simply and becomes more detailed and complex as it progresses. Adults and older students with reading skills at the high school level should normally have little difficulty understanding most of the text. The article *Earthquake* furnishes a good example of the encyclopedia's style (the first 15 of 92 lines are quoted):

> EARTHQUAKE, trembling or shaking movement of the earth's surface. Great earthquakes usually begin with slight tremors, rapidly take the form of one or more violent shocks, and end in vibrations of gradually diminishing force. Most earthquakes are related to compressional or tensional stresses built up at the margins of the huge moving lithospheric plates that make up the earth's surface (see LITHOSPHERE). The immediate cause of most shallow earthquakes is the sudden release of stress along a FAULT, or fracture in the earth's crust, resulting in movement of the opposing blocks of rock past one another. These movements cause vibrations to pass through and around the earth in wave form, just as ripples are generated when a pebble is dropped into water.

Access to the *New Columbia*'s contents is reasonably effective, due to numerous cross-references in the text (in point of fact, there are on average 22 cross-references to the page). These references are printed in SMALL CAPITAL LETTERS and direct the user to other articles that provide additional or related information. For example, in the excerpt from the article *Earthquake* quoted above, the word FAULT is a cross-reference, indicating that the volume contains an article entitled *Fault* that might be useful for the reader to consult. As noted earlier, the encyclopedia has no index. In an introductory section called "How to Use the New Columbia Encyclopedia," the editors emphatically state, "Cross-referencing makes an index in *The New Columbia Encyclopedia* unnecessary." Ordinarily, the cross-references are sufficient to locate specific information quickly and efficiently, but in some instances the system fails. The biographical article on Anne Hutchinson, for instance, explains that some Puritan intellects viewed her "as an antinomian heretic," but there is no reference to the article *Antinomianism* (where in fact Hutchinson is discussed, but again with no reference to the article *Hutchinson, Anne*). Similarly, the article on Richard D'Oyly Carte fails to direct the reader to the article *Savoy,* which briefly describes his Savoy Theatre. Many such examples could be cited. In the final analysis, the *New Columbia* 's accessibility would be improved by the addition of a detailed index.

Illustrations in the *New Columbia* are few and far between, but those that are included add to the informational value of the work. Limited to 407 black-and-white line drawings, the illustrations mostly depict scientific and technical subjects, such as shoe and disk brakes, the human brain, a clam's anatomy, and the internal combustion engine (including the Wankel rotary engine). Note that a more heavily illustrated version of the *New Columbia* has been published in 24 volumes as the NEW ILLUSTRATED COLUMBIA ENCYCLOPEDIA. Appearing in 1978 and aimed strictly at the supermarket trade, this set, which is now out of print, added some 5,000 illustrations to the *New Columbia* 's printed text. The *New Columbia* 's physical format is satisfactory, except for the total lack of paragraphing. A review in *Booklist* (January 1, 1979, p. 771) explains: "The type is small but easy to read because of the generous leading. However, the computer-assisted composition in this edition imposes one limitation: the absence of paragraphs. This may be intimidating in articles that run over a column in length." Consumers should also know that the encyclopedia is very heavy, weighing in at over ten pounds, and will require a stand or tabletop for easy consultation. Note that the newer and smaller CONCISE COLUMBIA ENCYCLOPEDIA is desk-sized.

When it appeared in 1975, the *New Columbia* received unanimously favorable reviews. *Choice* (December 1975, p. 1292), for instance, said, "The overall judgment must be that this remains an exceptionally attractively designed, easily read yet authoritative reference work of great scope, essential for all reference collections." Eugene Sheehy, reviewing the book in *College and Research Libraries* (January 1976, p. 61), advised, "It is sure to retain favor as a useful home encyclopedia and as a source for quick reference in libraries of all sizes." Richard Gray, in *American Reference Books Annual* (1976, p. 59), came to the same conclusion: "This edition is an excellent home reference work, but it is important as a library reference tool as well. Its subject entries are discrete and precise and its brief discussions serve effectively as a first-order entree into a field of study both for the reference librarian and for the library user." Charles Bunge, in *Wilson Library Bulletin* (November 1975, p. 263), said the encyclopedia "remains a very useful source for basic facts on a very wide range of topics."

To Summarize: The *New Columbia,* a 1975 revision of the highly regarded *Columbia Encyclopedia* (third edition, 1963), is the largest and most authoritative single-volume encyclopedia available in English. Written for intelligent adults and older students, it offers outstanding coverage of basic knowledge and information, with particular emphasis on biographical, geographical, and scientific subjects. Regrettably, the encyclopedia has not been revised since it appeared in 1975, and hence is now considerably out-of-date.

In Comparison: The *New Columbia,* which contains approximately 6.6 million words, is a one-volume work for an educated adult readership. It compares directly with several other substantial small-volume encyclopedias for adults, namely, the LINCOLN LIBRARY OF ESSENTIAL INFORMATION (two volumes; 3.5 million words), the RANDOM HOUSE ENCYCLOPEDIA (one volume; 3 million words), and the VOLUME LIBRARY (two volumes; 3.5 million words). Also to be reckoned with in this category is the smaller CONCISE COLUMBIA ENCYCLOPEDIA (one volume; 1 million words), a recently published abridgment of the *New Columbia.* Among these titles, the *New Columbia,* despite its advancing age, and the RANDOM HOUSE ENCYCLOPEDIA represent the best buys, along with the CONCISE COLUMBIA ENCYCLOPEDIA if a smaller (and less expensive) work will suffice. Note that the two best single-volume encyclopedias—the *New Columbia* and the RANDOM HOUSE ENCYCLOPEDIA—are as different as can be. The *New Columbia* is a scholarly, alphabetically arranged work with comparatively few illustrations and an almost totally black-and-white look about it, whereas the RANDOM HOUSE ENCYCLOPEDIA is a popularly written, topically arranged volume with numerous illustrations and a bright, visually inviting appearance.

To Purchase the *New Columbia Encyclopedia:* In recent times, the encyclopedia has been out of stock at the publisher, Columbia University Press, but in all likelihood it will be reprinted in quantity and available again as a trade book in North American retail bookstores. If you are an individual consumer and wish to acquire the *New Columbia,* first check the bookstores in your area. If the encyclopedia is not currently in stock and no store will order it for you, you can try ordering it directly from the publisher by contacting Columbia University Press at 136 South Broadway, Irvington, NY 10533 or telephone 914-591-6471. Your order will be processed immediately if the book is in stock. If the *New Columbia* should remain out of stock for a lengthy period, contact secondhand bookstores in your area, which might have a copy or two for sale.

For More Information about the *New Columbia Encyclopedia* See: *American Reference Books Annual,* 1976, p. 59 (review by Richard A. Gray); *Booklist,* January 1, 1979, pp. 769–71 (unsigned review); *Choice,* December 1975, p. 1292 (unsigned review); *Christianity Today,* January 16, 1976, pp. 30–31 (unsigned review); *College and Research Libraries,* January 1976, p. 61 (review by Eugene P. Sheehy); *Consumers' Research Magazine,* February 1977, p. 13 (review by W.T. Johnston); *Introduction to Reference Work* by William A. Katz (4th ed., New York: McGraw-Hill, 1982), vol. 1: *Basic Information Sources,* pp. 194–95; *Library Journal,* July 1975, p. 1309 (unsigned review); *New York Times,* August 3, 1975, p. 40-L (article by Israel Shenker entitled "Columbia Encyclopedia: Instant Universe Again"); *Reference Sources for Small and Medium-sized Libraries* (4th ed., Chicago: American Library Association, 1984), pp. 28–29 (review by Jovian P. Lang); *Wilson Library Bulletin,* November 1975, p. 263 (review by Charles A. Bunge).

New Encyclopaedia Britannica

FACTS

The New Encyclopaedia Britannica in 32 Volumes. Philip W. Goetz, Editor in Chief. Chicago: Encyclopaedia Britannica, Inc. 32 volumes. Former title: *Encyclopaedia Britannica* (first to fourteenth editions, 1768–1973). Fifteenth edition published as the *New Encyclopaedia Britannica* in 30 volumes in 1974; new printing with revisions each year. Lowest retail price: $1,249.00 plus shipping and handling; with discount to schools and libraries: $999.00 plus shipping and handling.

The *New Encyclopaedia Britannica* —or simply the *Britannica,* as most people call it—is the oldest, largest, best known, and most prestigious general encyclopedia in the English language. This impressive work, which serves educated adults and serious students, intends to be a comprehensive, authoritative compendium of the world's most important knowledge and information. Published in 32 volumes since 1985, the encyclopedia contains approximately 32,000 pages, 62,000 articles, and more than 44 million words. The first volume (unnumbered), entitled the *Propaedia* (or Outline of Knowledge), is both an elaborate classification of knowledge and a subject guide to the major articles in the encyclopedia. The articles themselves appear in two different and quite distinct parts of the set: the 12-volume *Micropaedia* (or Ready Reference) section and the 17-volume *Macropaedia* (or Knowledge in Depth) section. The *Micropaedia,* which literally means "small knowledge," comprises more than 61,000 relatively short articles that average about 300 words in length (or one-fifth of a page). The *Macropaedia,* or "large knowledge," comprises 681 long, substantial articles that average 35,000 words in length (or 26 pages). The articles in the *Micropaedia* are accompanied by roughly 16,000 illustrations (about 50 percent in color), plus some 400 maps. *Macropaedia* articles are accompanied by nearly 9,000 illustrations (most in black-and-white except for 164 color insert plates), plus 900 maps. The *Propaedia* is not illustrated except for a set of overlay transparencies that show the principal parts of the human body.

Almost 5,000 editors, advisers, consultants, and contributors are noted in the *Propaedia* volume. The 681 long articles in the 17-volume *Macropaedia* are signed; the 61,000 short articles in the 12-volume *Micropaedia* are usually not. Both the *Micropaedia* and *Macropaedia* sections are arranged alphabetically word by word (*New York* precedes *Newspaper*), with access to specific information enhanced by the 485-page *Propaedia* (which functions in part as a topical index to articles in both the *Micropaedia* and *Macropaedia*), 25,000 cross-references in the *Micropaedia* to articles in the *Macropaedia,* and a two-volume, 1,700-page index of more than 411,000 entries to the contents of both the *Micropaedia* and the *Macropaedia* sections. To recap, the four major parts of the 32-volume *Britannica* are (1) the one-volume *Propaedia,* (2) the 12-volume *Micropaedia,* (3) the 17-volume *Macropaedia,* and (4) the two-volume index to the set. The encyclopedia is also available in electronic (or online) form via subscription to the NEXIS and LEXIS database services marketed by Mead Data Central of Dayton, Ohio. (For additional information about the electronic version of the *Britannica,* see the section on purchasing the encyclopedia below.)

EVALUATION

The *Britannica* first appeared in three volumes issued serially between 1768 and 1771 in Edinburgh, Scotland. Appropriately, it was inspired by the influential French *Encyclopédie,* arguably the greatest encyclopedia ever published. New and larger editions of the *Britannica* were issued periodically during the nineteenth century, including the famous ninth edition (1875–89) in 25 volumes, called the Scholars' Edition because of its long, learned articles. In 1901, ownership of the encyclopedia passed to a group of Americans who brought the set, both entrepreneurially and editorially, to the United States, where it has remained ever since. (Many casual encyclopedia consumers in the United States and Canada mistakenly believe that the *Britannica* is still edited and produced in Great Britain, a misconception fostered by the encyclopedia's continued and, some say, affected use of typical British spellings, such as *centre, favour,* and, of course, *Encyclopaedia.*) A decade later, at the end of 1910, another great edition, the eleventh, appeared. The 29-volume work was justly praised for its impeccable scholarship and elegant style. In the early 1920s, Julius Rosenwald of Sears, Roebuck and Company acquired the *Britannica* and oversaw the production of the twelfth (1922), thirteenth (1926), and fourteenth (1929) editions. In 1936, the editors wisely adopted the practice of continuous revision with updated printings issued on an annual basis, thus extending the life of the fourteenth edition to 1973, when it was replaced by the current—and controversial—fifteenth edition.

When first published in 1974 in 30 volumes, the fifteenth edition of the Britannica—now officially titled the *New Encyclopaedia Britannica*—was organized into three well-defined parts, thus giving rise to the diminutive *Britannica 3:* (1) the *Propaedia,* a one-volume outline of knowledge and topical guide to the contents of the *Macropaedia;*

(2) the *Micropaedia,* a ten-volume set of roughly 100,000 brief articles of 750 words or less; and (3) the *Macropaedia,* a 19-volume library of some 4,200 long scholarly articles reminiscent of those found in earlier editions of the encyclopedia. There was no overall index to the set, although the *Micropaedia* served double-duty as an index to the *Macropaedia.* In point of fact, *Britannica*'s editors had not only abandoned the straight alphabetical arrangement utilized in the first fourteen editions but also the principle of a separate index, which had been part of the encyclopedia as far back as the middle of the nineteenth century. A firestorm of criticism greeted the new *Britannica* and its tripartite (or three-part) arrangement, and the criticism refused to go away. Many of the encyclopedia's excellent features were obscured because users, including students and librarians, found the set's organization ineffectual, intimidating, or overly complicated, or all three.

Finally, in 1985, after living with *Britannica 3* for more than ten years, the editors corrected most of the major structural problems plaguing the set. As editor in chief Philip Goetz writes in his preface to the 1985 printing of the fifteenth edition: "The changes ... are extensive. The entire encyclopaedia has been reset and restructured. The underlying policies of the *Encyclopaedia Britannica* remain unchanged, however. The work continues to be dedicated to intelligibility, to comprehensiveness, to objectivity and neutrality. To these has been added in 1985 a renewed dedication to accessibility, to making all of the riches of this work available to the greatest number of persons. The revision has been characterized by the inclusion of thousands of cross-references, notes, and other aids to the reader as support for the new Index volumes." Broadly speaking, the 1985 printing differs from the 1974–84 versions in these ways: (1) the set has been expanded from 30 to 32 volumes, with approximately one million new words added; (2) the *Micropaedia* has been expanded from ten to twelve volumes, although the total number of articles has been reduced from about 100,000 to 61,000, and the length of the articles, though still short, is no longer limited to 750 words; (3) the *Micropaedia* no longer has an indexing function, although it does furnish some 25,000 cross-references to the *Macropaedia*; (4) the *Macropaedia* has been reduced from 19 to 17 volumes, and many of its articles, drastically reduced from 4,207 to 681, have either been consolidated or moved to the *Micropaedia*; (5) a two-volume analytical index of more than 411,000 entries has been added to the set; (6) the *Propaedia* has been simplified and made easier to use; and (7) the *Britannica Book of the Year,* an annual supplement to the set, has been retitled the *Britannica World Data Annual* and now includes current information about the countries of the world formerly found in the *Micropaedia.*

The name *Britannica* is practically synonymous with the word *encyclopedia.* At no time has the set's authority been called into question, even during the trying years of 1974–84. Editor Goetz, who is largely responsible for developing and implementing the extensive changes described in the preceding paragraph, and his editorial team are seasoned encyclopedia-makers who bring very strong credentials to their work. The present contributors maintain the *Britannica* tradition of commissioning prominent authorities to write the encyclopedia's articles. In the past, contributors have included such well-known names as Albert Einstein, Sigmund Freud, Lin Yutang, G.K. Chesterton, Henry Ford, George Bernard Shaw, and H.L. Mencken. Among the fifteenth edition's thousands of highly qualified writers are such well-known contemporary authorities as Isaac Asimov, Jacques Barzun, Anthony Burgess, René Dubos, Leon Edel, Frank Freidel, Milton Friedman, Arthur Koestler, Arthur Mizener, Howard Nemerov, Conor Cruise O'Brien, Carl Sagan, Isaac Bashevis Singer, Charles J. Sippl, Lee Strasberg, A.J.P. Taylor, Arnold Toynbee, and Alfred North Whitehead.

Beyond its imposing name and roster of editors and writers, how good is the *Britannica* today? The 1985 restructuring of the fifteenth edition, which cost the publisher an estimated $24 million, has got this great encyclopedia back on track after a decade of confusion and frustration. Not all of the problems have been solved, but the set is much improved.

As in the past, the encyclopedia's coverage is broad, deep, and reasonably well balanced. Biographical and geographical articles naturally claim a sizable share of the total text. Continents and major countries receive particularly generous coverage, with long, detailed articles in the *Macropaedia*. The arts and humanities, traditionally emphasized in the *Britannica,* continue to be covered with a thoroughness that only a very large general encyclopedia can provide. The social and behavioral sciences are also well covered. In recent times, attention to the harder sciences and technology has steadily increased, reflecting contemporary trends. In fact, scientific and technical topics now account for nearly 40 percent of the set's subject coverage. Another striking feature of the *Britannica*'s coverage is its truly international approach to knowledge. Indeed, it can be stated without fear of contradiction that the fifteenth edition of the *Britannica* accords non-Western cultural, social, and scientific developments more notice than any general English-language encyclopedia has ever done. The set's international perspective is exemplified in such articles as *Adoption; Animals, Cruelty to; Capital Punishment; Circumcision; Folk Arts; Gardens and Landscape Design; Gay Liberation Movement; Motion Pictures; Music, the Art of; Public Works; Taxation*; and *Transportation*. On the other hand, the encyclopedia provides very little by way of practical, or how-to-do-it, information. For instance, *Britannica* users will look in vain for material on how to copyright a book, how to write a business letter, how to compile a research paper, how to address government and religious leaders, how to care for pets, how to remove spots and stains, and so on—all subjects most family encyclopedias cover to one degree or another.

Information in the encyclopedia is normally accurate and impartial. Minor errors are encountered occasionally, but not often enough to cast doubt on the set's overall reliability. Controversial subjects—abortion, apartheid, capital punishment, homosexuality, the Vietnam War, etc.—are treated objectively, with both sides of an issue presented. For example, the article *Abortion* explains:

> Opponents of abortion, or of abortion for any reason other than to save the life of the mother, argue on religious or humanistic grounds that there is no rational basis for distinguishing the fetus from a newborn infant; each is totally dependent and potentially a member of society, and each possesses a degree of humanity. Proponents of liberalized regulation of abortion hold that, at least during its first three or four months, the fetus exhibits few if any human characteristics; that public opinion favours making abortion available for a range of reasons; and that the alternative to legal, medically supervised abortion is illegal and demonstrably dangerous abortion.

Information in the *Britannica* is reasonably current. By the late 1970s and early 1980s, the fifteenth edition, which had not been diligently revised since its publication in 1974, had become dated and stale. But a thoroughgoing revision in 1985 (part of the major restructuring already described) has brought the encyclopedia generally up-to-speed as far as currentness of material is concerned. Some new articles have been added, such as *Acquired Immune Deficiency Syndrome (AIDS); Health Maintenance Organization (HMO)*; and *Petroleum Exporting Countries, Organization of (OPEC)*. In addition, numerous articles have been updated. See, for example, *Afghanistan; Birth Control; Nuclear Reactor*; and *Vietnam War*. Of course, not every article in the encyclopedia is as current as it might be. The biography of Richard D'Oyly Carte, for instance, fails to note the demise of the famous D'Oyly Carte Opera Company in 1982; likewise, the article on the Sacco-Vanzetti case lacks reference to significant recent developments, such as an action several years ago by the governor of Massachusetts officially proclaiming that no stigma should be attached to the memory of the men because of prejudice in their trial. But, on balance, the *Britannica* is as current as can be expected, given the encyclopedia's size and the rapidity with which knowledge and information grow and change.

The encyclopedia's writing style sometimes varies considerably from one article to another, especially in the *Macropaedia,* where distinguished authorities have been allowed to express themselves rather freely and at some length. Anthony Burgess, for example, in the article *Literature, the Art of,* turns in a wonderfully readable, often quite personal essay on the novel that includes such lines as

"The inferior novelist tends to be preoccupied with plot" and "As the hen is unable to judge of the quality of the egg it lays, so the novelist is rarely able to explain or evaluate his work." Seldom do encyclopedias include such subjective material. More typical of the *Britannica*'s style is the article *Earthquakes* in the *Macropaedia*. Written by Charles Richter (for whom the Richter scale is named), the six-page article begins this way:

> An earthquake commonly is described as a sudden individual tremor within the Earth that creates shaking at the surface. Many earthquakes disturb the surface only to a degree observable with sensitive instruments, however, and some authorities therefore refer to earthquakes as the generation of elastic waves (seismic waves) in the Earth rather than to physical shaking.
>
> In addition to sudden events, there are gradual effects such as slow creeping of earth materials that are closely related to the production of earthquakes. Earthquakes often occur in succession, or in earthquake swarms, the effect of which is that of continuous disturbance. Other causes, largely meteorological, produce waves that are recorded on seismograms and often go on for hours or days; these are known as microseisms, but ordinarily they are not considered as earthquakes. Recently, certain extremely small individual events have been called microearthquakes. A final category includes artificial earthquakes, which are produced by man through disturbance of subsurface conditions by any of several means.

Generally speaking, articles in the *Britannica* are written in a scholarly though readable manner that normally will be comprehensible to literate adults and interested students at the college and advanced high school levels. Consumers should be aware, however, that the publisher and some of its sales representatives persist in promoting the set as useful to children and young students in the elementary and junior high school grades. Except in the case of precocious students, these claims are unfounded. In the words of Geoffrey Wolff in an article entitled "Britannica 3, History of" (in the *Atlantic,* June 1974, p. 47), "Anyone who claims—as *Britannica* salesmen have been known to claim—that the set is suitable for schoolchildren too young to drive an automobile should be had up for perjury."

Access to information in the *Britannica* has been greatly improved since 1985 due to the major restructuring of the set that occurred that year. Most significantly, a general index has been added. Published in two volumes found at the end of the set, the 1,700-page index contains approximately 411,000 analytical entries. In terms of the ratio of index entries to total words in the encyclopedia (44 million), the *Britannica* furnishes one index reference for roughly every 110 words of text, or a ratio of 1:110. Among the *Britannica*'s chief rivals, COLLIER'S ENCYCLOPEDIA has twice as good a ratio (1:50) and the ENCYCLOPEDIA AMERICANA (1:90) also beats the

Britannica. These are useful comparative figures, but how well does the *Britannica* 's new index actually perform? In a nutshell, the index is sound but not without lapses. Ordinarily, it functions quite well, as in the case of locating information about the Savoy Theatre in London where Richard D'Oyly Carte staged the comic operas of Gilbert and Sullivan. The encyclopedia does not include a separate article on the Savoy, but basic facts about it can be found by consulting the index under "Savoy Theatre," which directs the reader to the *Micropaedia* articles *Carte, Richard D'Oyly* and *Gilbert, Sir W(illiam) S(chwenk)* and the *Macropaedia* article *Theatrical Production,* all of which contain some information about the Savoy. Sometimes, however, the index does not work so well, as in the case of the D'Oyly Carte Opera Company, the group that performed Gilbert and Sullivan operettas for years until it folded in 1982. Like the Savoy Theatre, the D'Oyly Carte Opera Company does not have a separate article in the encyclopedia, but information is available in the article *Carte, Richard D'Oyly.* Unfortunately, the index has no entry for "D'Oyly Carte" (the man or company), not even a cross-reference to see "Carte, Richard D'Oyly."

In a review of the 1985 printing of the *Britannica* in *Newsweek* (May 6, 1985, p. 78), Peter Prescott observes, "Certainly the addition of a two-volume index is a signal improvement; the new Britannica is far more accessible than its predecessor." What Prescott says is true enough, but another problem concerning access to the encyclopedia's contents still remains, and that is the matter of having two separate collections of articles, both alphabetically arranged, within the same work. Surely, any thoughtful user of the *Britannica* will wonder why some articles are in the 12-volume *Micropaedia* and others are in the 17-volume *Macropaedia.* Won't some users look for, say, "abortion" in the "A" volume of the *Macropaedia* and, not finding it, assume the subject is not covered in the set? It has happened. Indeed, why aren't all articles in the encyclopedia simply in one A-to-Z sequence? Editor Goetz provides an answer in his preface to the 1985 printing: "Every edition of the *Encyclopaedia Britannica* has been characterized by many short articles and some few articles of great length. The Fifteenth Edition is unique in that it separates these two types of article in order to make clearer the different uses they serve—the short article for the seeker of information, of brief, factual data; the longer article for reading and for the more serious study of a major subject." The price of making this rather arcane distinction between short and long articles, however, is overly complicated organization of material and, ultimately, increased user difficulty and aggravation. Access to information in the *Britannica* has been greatly enhanced by the addition of the index, but it is equally true that the set's organization remains unnecessarily complex and hard to use.

Illustrations in the *Britannica* usually add to the informational content of the articles they complement, and they are almost always clearly reproduced. *Micropaedia* illustrations, which appear on nearly every page, are typically small, the size of a large postage stamp, and about half are in color. Many more, however, should be in color, not for the sake of adding dash to the page but to increase their informational value. For instance, the article on Washington Allston, said to be "the first important U.S. Romantic painter," informs the reader that "Allston is known for his experiments with dramatic subject matter and his use of light and atmospheric colour," yet the small reproduction of one of Allston's oil paintings that accompanies the article is in black-and-white. Likewise, the anemone fish is described as "bright orange, with three wide, blue-white bands circling the body," but the accompanying illustration is in black-and-white. Numerous similar examples could be cited. *Macropaedia* illustrations, usually larger than those found in the *Micropaedia,* are mostly in black-and-white, except for 164 color plates. The plates, printed on enameled stock, are excellent. By way of example, see the articles *Birds; Coloration; Exploration; Mimicry* ; and *Southeast Asian Arts.* The *Britannica* provides adequate map coverage (courtesy of Rand McNally) for the continents and major countries of the world, but strangely, there are no maps in the set for individual U.S. states or Canadian provinces. This omission is serious, especially for consumers using the encyclopedia at home who might not have a North American atlas readily at hand. The *Britannica*'s physical format is satisfactory in every respect. The impression is of a handsome, dignified, solid set of reference books bound to serve the user for many years.

To Summarize: Currently published in 32 volumes, the *Britannica* (1768–) is the oldest, largest, and most prominent general encyclopedia in the English language. It is not, however, without its problems. The fifteenth edition, which first appeared in 1974 in 30 volumes, has been criticized, sometimes harshly, for its overly complex organization and lack of easy access to the set's contents. In 1985, a major restructuring, highlighted by the addition of a two-volume index, corrected many, but not all, of the problems. Today, the encyclopedia's conspicuous strengths are authoritative, accurate, impartial, reasonably current, and intelligently written articles that provide broad, deep, and well-balanced coverage of the world's essential knowledge and information. In addition, accessibility of material has been greatly improved due to the extensive 1985 revision. On the negative side, the *Britannica*'s new index is not always as effective as it might be; the set's complicated arrangement will continue to disconcert some users; and its illustrations frequently lack color where color is clearly required. When all is said and done, however, this great encyclopedia is now back on track after a decade of confusion and frustration.

In Comparison: The *Britannica,* published in 32 volumes containing 44 million words, is a large encyclopedia for adults and college and advanced high school students with serious informational needs. It compares quite favorably with the other two large general adult encyclopedias currently available, namely, COLLIER'S ENCYCLOPEDIA (24 volumes; 21 million words) and the ENCYCLOPEDIA AMERICANA (30 volumes; 31 million words). Of these three large sets, the *Britannica* is the largest, most thorough, most scholarly, and most prestigious of the three. It is also the least accessible and most expensive. On the other hand, COLLIER'S ENCYCLOPEDIA is the smallest, but also the most current, best indexed, easiest to read, and least expensive, and the ENCYCLOPEDIA AMERICANA, which runs second in just about every evaluative category (size, readability, accessibility, up-to-dateness, prestige, price, etc.), offers especially good coverage of North American people, places, and events. Each of these large sets is, on balance, an excellent work that can be recommended without hesitation to those who truly require a large, costly adult encyclopedia. Because of the expense involved (each of these encyclopedias costs more than $1,000 at retail), consumers are urged to examine all three sets closely prior to making a final purchase decision.

To Purchase the *New Encyclopaedia Britannica:* If you are an individual consumer and wish to order the encyclopedia, consult the white pages of the local telephone directory under "Encyclopaedia Britannica, Inc." for the sales representative in your area. If the company is not listed in the directory, contact Encyclopaedia Britannica, Inc. at Britannica Centre, Customer Service Department, 310 South Michigan Avenue, Chicago, IL 60604 or telephone collect 312-347-7298. Your name will be forwarded to a sales representative in your area who will handle the transaction. Note that educators receive a $150 discount off the retail price. The sales representative will most likely attempt to sell you additional publications along with the encyclopedia, including three yearbooks entitled the *Britannica World Data Annual* (which also includes the *Britannica Book of the Year*), the *Britannica Yearbook of Science and the Future,* and the *Medical and Health Annual.* You need not buy any extras, of course, unless you want them. In the case of the yearbooks, the *Britannica World Data Annual,* which began in 1985 and is free to purchasers of the encyclopedia for the first year and $25.95 each year thereafter, should be carefully considered as an updating service to the encyclopedia for current information about the nations of the world.

Retail customers who wish to trade in an old set of the *Britannica* for the current printing will receive a $100 allowance on the old set, no matter when it was published or purchased. The company also offers a flat $50 trade-in allowance on major encyclopedias from other publishers.

If you are ordering the *Britannica* for a school or library, contact Encyclopaedia Britannica Educational Corporation at the address above or call toll-free 1-800-554-9862. Your order will be processed immediately. Note that the trade-in offers described in the preceding paragraph do not apply to schools and libraries.

As pointed out earlier, the *Britannica* is now also published in electronic (or online) form. The electronic version, which provides full-text searching capability, is available to subscribers of both the NEXIS and LEXIS database services offered by Mead Data Central of Dayton, Ohio. Consumers should be aware, however, that the NEXIS and LEXIS services are not currently available to individuals, schools, or libraries (they are principally marketed to law firms, news services, businesses, and research companies). Moreover, the encyclopedia's use in electronic form is restricted, at least at present, to being read at the computer terminal, as the text will not print out. For access and price information, contact Mead Data Central at 9393 Springboro Pike, P.O. Box 933, Dayton OH 45401 or telephone 513-865-6800.

For More Information about the *New Encyclopaedia Britannica* See: Critical reaction to the 1985 restructuring of the fifteenth edition of the encyclopedia just began to appear as *Best Encyclopedias* went to press. Interested consumers should see Peter Prescott's early review in *Newsweek* (May 6, 1985, pp. 78–79), while bearing in mind that some of his criticisms are incorrect or exaggerated (check them for yourself). In addition, Edwin McDowell furnishes an informative background piece entitled "Encyclopaedia Britannica Revised" in the *New York Times* (March 25, 1985, p. 13-C), and there is a lengthy and informative review in *Booklist* (November 15, 1985, pp. 472-74). For consumers who might want to know more about the controversy surrounding the fifteenth edition when it first appeared in 1974, the following list of selected articles and reviews will be helpful:

"Britannica 3 as a Reference Tool: A Review" by Dorothy Ethlyn Cole in the *Wilson Library Bulletin,* June 1974, pp. 821–25.

"Britannica 3, History of" by Geoffrey Wolff in the *Atlantic,* June 1974, pp. 37–47; see also Wolff's follow-up article entitled "Britannica 3, Failures of" in the *Atlantic,* November 1976, pp. 107–10.

"Encyclopaedia Britannica: EB 3, Two Years Later" by Dennis V. Waite in *Publishers Weekly,* June 21, 1976, pp. 44–45.

"The Guest Word" by Robert G. Hazo in the *New York Times Book Review,* March 9, 1975, p. 31.

"A New Britannica Is Born" by John F. Baker in *Publishers Weekly,* January 14, 1974, pp. 64–65.

"The Scandal of 'Britannica 3,'" by Samuel McCracken in *Commentary,* February 1976, pp. 63–68.

"Subject: The Universe" by Robert Gorham Davis in the *New York Times Book Review,* December 1, 1974, pp. 98–100.

New Hutchinson 20th Century Encyclopedia

FACTS

The *New Hutchinson 20th Century Encyclopedia*. E.M. Horsley, Editor. London, England: Hutchinson & Company Ltd. One volume. Former titles: *Hutchinson's Twentieth Century Encyclopedia* (first to third editions, 1948–56); *Hutchinson's New 20th Century Encyclopedia* (fourth and fifth editions, 1964–70). Sixth revised edition published in 1977; out of print in North America since 1980 (last priced at $29.95).

The *New Hutchinson 20th Century Encyclopedia* is a single-volume, desk-sized British work for adults and older students that periodically appears on the North American market, most recently in the late 1970s. Although not available at this time in the United States or Canada, the encyclopedia has been revised a number of times since its original publication in 1948, and a new revision might occur at any time. When last published in 1977 (sixth edition), the *New Hutchinson* contained 1,326 pages, approximately 15,000 articles, and 1.5 million words. The articles, almost all of which are very brief, average about 100 words in length (or 12 articles per page). They are accompanied by some 1,300 illustrations (all in black-and-white), plus 300 maps, including a 32-page color atlas found in the center of the volume. Aside from the editor, E.M. Horsley, no staff or contributors are identified, nor are any of the articles signed. The encyclopedia is arranged alphabetically letter by letter (*Newspaper* precedes *New York*), with access to specific information enhanced by roughly 1,500 cross-references in the text. The set has no index.

EVALUATION

The *New Hutchinson* has been a standard reference item in Great Britain for nearly 40 years. First published in 1948 as *Hutchinson's Twentieth Century Encyclopedia* with revisions in 1951 and 1956, the one-volume work was again revised in 1964 and 1970 under the slightly altered title *Hutchinson's 20th Century Encyclopedia*. In 1977, the most recent revision was issued under the title *New Hutchinson 20th Century Encyclopedia*. The 1970 (fifth) edition appeared in North America as the *McKay One-Volume International Encyclopedia*.

Long since discontinued, the *McKay* title found relatively little favor in the United States and Canada because, in the words of a review in *Booklist* (June 15, 1972, p. 868), "its British emphasis, use of British spelling and terminology, and lack of adequate coverage of American geography, biography, social, and political events limit its usefulness to the average American home, office, or library." The 1977 edition was also distributed for a time in North America (by the Merrimack Book Service of Salem, New Hampshire), but it was withdrawn from the market in 1980.

As the *Booklist* review of an earlier edition of the *New Hutchinson* notes, the encyclopedia has a heavily British orientation, especially in its coverage of people and places, which together account for something like 65 percent of all of the articles. The volume's British accent can be viewed as a mixed blessing, as Charles Bunge points out in his review of the 1977 edition in *Wilson Library Bulletin* (January 1979, p. 408): "The book's British bias can be a strength, since it thus contains entries and emphases missing from American one-volume encyclopedias. American readers, however, especially younger ones, may be confused by having our corn called 'maize' and having products 'tinned' rather than canned." Scientific and technical subjects, particularly flora and fauna, also receive fairly generous coverage. Articles in the encyclopedia, however, normally provide only very basic information. Readers seeking any sort of depth of treatment must look elsewhere. Other limitations include poor accessibility (the cross-references are helpful but do not entirely compensate for the lack of a general index), indifferent illustrations that are sometimes poorly placed, a dull format and weak binding, and, of course, lack of up-to-dateness of material (a problem that a new edition might cure quite readily). On the positive side, the articles are clearly and objectively presented.

To Summarize: The *New Hutchinson,* last published in 1977, is a one-volume work produced in Great Britain with a strong British flavor. No longer available in North America (at least for the present), the encyclopedia has little to tempt the discriminating consumer in the United States or Canada.

In Comparison: It is easy to understand why the *New Hutchinson* has not fared well on the North American market in the past, with such formidable small-volume competitors as the LINCOLN LIBRARY OF ESSENTIAL INFORMATION, the NEW COLUMBIA ENCYCLOPEDIA, the RANDOM HOUSE ENCYCLOPEDIA, and the VOLUME LIBRARY available, not to mention the more recent CONCISE COLUMBIA ENCYCLOPEDIA. In addition, consumers who want a British slant to their information can choose among COLLINS GEM ENCYCLOPEDIA, the KNOWLEDGE ENCYCLOPEDIA, and PEARS CYCLOPAEDIA, all small, inexpensive works produced in Great Britain.

For More Information about the *New Hutchinson 20th Century Encyclopedia* See: *American Reference Books Annual,* 1979, p. 34

(review by Frances Neel Cheney); *Booklist,* April 1, 1979, pp. 1233–34 (unsigned review); *Wilson Library Bulletin,* January 1979, p. 408 (review by Charles Bunge).

New Illustrated Columbia Encyclopedia

FACTS

The New Illustrated Columbia Encyclopedia. William H. Harris and Judith S. Levey, Editors. Garden City, NY: Rockville House Publishers, Inc. 24 volumes. Based on the NEW COLUMBIA ENCYCLOPEDIA (1975). Second edition published in 1980; out of print since 1984 (last priced at $69.75).

The 24-volume *New Illustrated Columbia Encyclopedia,* published in 1978 and again in 1980 for the supermarket and mail-order trade, is an expanded version of the one-volume NEW COLUMBIA ENCYCLOPEDIA (1975). The essential difference between the two encyclopedias, aside from their titles and number of volumes, is that the *New Illustrated Columbia* includes some 5,000 illustrations, many in color, whereas the NEW COLUMBIA has only 659 illustrations, all in black-and-white. Otherwise the text of the two works is practically the same. The encyclopedias also differ physically, in that the *New Illustrated Columbia* has a somewhat larger type size than the NEW COLUMBIA but a considerably smaller page size: 7 by 9¼ in. (16 by 24 cm.) as opposed to the NEW COLUMBIA's 9 by 12 in. (23 by 30 cm.). Actually, the printed text of the *New Illustrated Columbia* is a slightly enlarged photographic reproduction of the NEW COLUMBIA's text.

The *New Illustrated Columbia* contains 7,522 pages, 50,515 articles, and approximately 6.6 million words. The articles, most of which are very brief, average 130 words in length (or about seven articles per page). They are accompanied by almost 5,000 illustrations (60 percent in color), plus 252 maps. Some 260 editors and contributors are identified at the front of Volume 1. None of the articles is signed, although picture credits are listed in the front matter. The encyclopedia is arranged alphabetically letter by letter (*Newspaper* precedes *New York*), with access to specific information enhanced by 66,000 cross-references in the text. The set has no index.

EVALUATION

Soon after the appearance of the highly regarded one-volume NEW COLUMBIA ENCYCLOPEDIA in 1975, the publisher, Columbia University Press, granted Rockville House Publishers, Inc. of Garden City, New York, the rights to produce an inexpensive illustrated version of the work in a multivolume format for sale in supermarkets and via mail order. The 24-volume *New Illustrated Columbia Encyclopedia* duly appeared in 1978 under the imprint of Rockville House "by arrangement with Columbia University Press." Time-Life Books distributed the set, which was modestly updated in 1980. In 1984, the encyclopedia went out of print, at least for the time being. A direct forebear of the *New Illustrated Columbia* is the *Illustrated Columbia Encyclopedia,* a 22-volume set published in 1970 by Rockville House. The *Illustrated Columbia,* also aimed at the supermarket customer, was an expanded version of the one-volume *Columbia Encyclopedia* (1963), an earlier edition of the NEW COLUMBIA ENCYCLOPEDIA. Now long out of print, the *Illustrated Columbia* apparently sold well but critics were unhappy with the quality of the set's illustrations. Louis Barron, for instance, in his review in *Library Journal* (March 1, 1971, p. 820), characterized the illustrations as "extravagant rather than necessary, and many of them are atrociously reproduced. Some of them pretty up the page; some are fun to look at; but that they significantly aid understanding is doubtful."

As indicated at the outset of this review, the *New Illustrated Columbia Encyclopedia* differs from the NEW COLUMBIA ENCYCLOPEDIA in terms of number of volumes (24 versus one), number of illustrations (5,000 versus 659), and type and page size (the *New Illustrated Columbia* having larger type but a smaller page). Aside from these differences, the two encyclopedias are virtually the same work, except for a few minor alterations in the text and, of course, the addition of many picture captions in the *New Illustrated Columbia.* Like the NEW COLUMBIA, the *New Illustrated Columbia* offers broad, well-balanced coverage of all major areas of knowledge, with emphasis on biographical, geographical, and scientific subjects. Information in the set is almost always accurate and presented in an objective manner. Unfortunately, that information is now over a decade old and therefore often quite dated. Access to the information is reasonably good, due to numerous cross-references in the text, but the lack of a general index does sometimes hamper effective retrieval.

The encyclopedia's writing style is clear and concise. Comprehension requires reading skills at the high school level and beyond. (For an example of the encyclopedia's prose, see the excerpt from the article *Earthquake* in the NEW COLUMBIA ENCYCLOPEDIA review in this book.) Consumers should be aware, however, that advertising for the *New Illustrated Columbia* has suggested—inaccurately—that the set is for children and younger students. For example, one promotional brochure claims that the encyclopedia is "specially designed not just to help your children complete homework assignments, but as a study aid for tests, reports and projects ... term papers and lab assignments ... as a constant source for answers to all their questions." Elsewhere the brochure says "the New Illustrated Columbia Encyclopedia is designed for everyone in your family. For your children as well as yourself." Such statements are false and misleading. Articles in the *New Illustrated Columbia* are normally much too difficult for youngsters. Moreover, not only is the level of writing well beyond a child's understanding, the printed text consists of long, unbroken paragraphs that will defeat even the most diligent of young readers.

What most emphatically distinguishes the *New Illustrated Columbia* from the NEW COLUMBIA, as their titles suggest, is the former's many illustrations. Numbering around 5,000, with 3,000 in color, the illustrations were selected and added to the text by the Italian firm of Fratelli Fabbri Editori, which relied on its own large illustration bank for most of the pictures (mainly photographs and art reproductions). Regrettably, like the illustrations in the earlier *Illustrated Columbia Encyclopedia,* those in the *New Illustrated Columbia* are mediocre at best. Some are very poorly reproduced, being either muddy (if in color) or inordinately dark (if in black-and-white). Too often, the illustrations add little or nothing to the informational content of the encyclopedia, serving only as bright or splashy space-fillers. Likewise, the illustrations are sometimes much larger than they need to be, as in the case of an Andy Warhol silkscreen of Marilyn Monroe that inexplicably takes up two-thirds of a page. In yet other instances, the illustrations are poorly placed in relation to the articles they represent. For another view of the set's illustrations, see *Booklist* (May 15, 1981, p. 1270), which finds that "the illustrations appear to have been carefully selected and they are, on the whole, a good addition to an excellent one-volume encyclopedia."

To Summarize: the 24-volume *New Illustrated Columbia,* an inexpensive set published specifically for the supermarket and mail-order trade, combines the rather erudite text of the highly regarded NEW COLUMBIA ENCYCLOPEDIA with 5,000 mediocre, sometimes showy, illustrations supplied by Fratelli Fabbri Editori. The union is not an especially happy one, as the printed text is far too demanding for the intended audience; despite claims to the contrary, the *New Illustrated Columbia* is not appropriate for children and younger students. The encyclopedia was recently declared out of print, at least for the present.

In Comparison: The *New Illustrated Columbia,* published in 24 volumes containing approximately 6.6 million words, is a medium-sized general encyclopedia for adults and older students. Produced strictly for sale in supermarkets and by mail order, the encyclopedia, when it is available, competes directly with FUNK & WAGNALLS NEW ENCYCLOPEDIA (29 volumes; 9 million words), the leading supermarket set. When compared head-to-head, FUNK & WAGNALLS NEW ENCYCLOPEDIA is overall the better work. For example, its illustrations are an integral part of the editorial process from the beginning, whereas those in the *New Illustrated Columbia* have been tacked on as an afterthought. In competition with other available middle-sized multivolume encyclopedias for adults and older students (such as the ACADEMIC AMERICAN ENCYCLOPEDIA, COMPTON'S ENCYCLOPEDIA, MERIT STUDENTS ENCYCLOPEDIA, the NEW STANDARD ENCYCLOPEDIA, and the WORLD BOOK ENCYCLOPEDIA), the only edge the *New Illustrated Columbia* has is its very low price.

For More Information about the *New Illustrated Columbia Encyclopedia* See: *Booklist,* May 15, 1981, p. 1270 (unsigned review).

New Knowledge Library

FACTS

New Knowledge Library: Universal Reference Encyclopedia. George Barber, Publisher; Christine Herbert, Managing Editor. London, England, and Sydney, Australia: Bay Books Pty. Ltd. Distributed in North America by Farwell Promotional Books, a division of Gareth Stevens, Inc. 35 volumes. First edition published in 1981. School and library price: $299.95 (encyclopedia is not available to individual retail consumers).

The *New Knowledge Library,* subtitled "Universal Reference Encyclopedia," is a set of 35 thin volumes (96 pages each) intended mainly for younger students and children ages seven to fourteen. Produced in Australia, the heavily illustrated encyclopedia "is a concise and comprehensive guide to the many aspects of human learning, belief and achievement, ranging from ancient times to the present day. Its wide scope will make it equally attractive to both the serious student and the casual, inquisitive reader; its conciseness will facilitate usage" (introduction). The set contains 3,361 pages, approximately 3,000 articles, and 2 million words. The articles, most of which are of the specific-entry type, average 700 words in length (or roughly one full page). They are accompanied by some 6,000 illustrations (almost all in color), plus 160 maps, including a 21-page color atlas in the final volume. An editorial staff of 61, including 22 writers, and a 13-member advisory board are listed at the front of the initial volume. None of the articles is signed. The encyclopedia is arranged alphabetically letter by letter (*Newspaper* precedes *New York City*), with access to specific information enhanced by about 1,000 cross-references in the text and an index of 8,500 entries.

EVALUATION

A product of Bay Books Pty. (Proprietary) Ltd. of Sydney, Australia (part of the Rupert Murdoch publishing empire), the 35-volume *New Knowledge Library* first appeared in 1981 and has not been revised since that time. The set is distributed in the United States and Canada by Farwell Promotional Books (a division of Gareth Stevens, Inc.), a relatively new company located in Milwaukee that limits its business to the school and library market.

The encyclopedia's coverage is heavily slanted toward subjects of particular interest to Australian and New Zealand readers. For example, the article on kangaroos and wallabies is four pages long, whereas cats are covered in one page and buffalo in less than a page. The article *Aborigines, Australian* is seven pages long, whereas *American Indians* is less than two pages in length. Such articles as *Bird* and *Sheep* tend to emphasize Australian varieties. In the area of geography, the various Australian states (New South Wales, Queensland, etc.) are accorded extensive coverage, while the U.S. states (except for Alaska and Hawaii) and Canadian provinces are completely ignored. Likewise, such Australian place-names as the Latrobe Valley, Mount Kosciusko, the Murray-Darling river system, and Siding Spring Mountain are covered but such major North American cities as Atlanta, New Orleans, and Toronto are not. Sports coverage is similarly biased: cricket has an article, baseball does not; the article *Football* is, from the North American perspective, not about football at all but rather soccer and rugby. British-Australian spelling (for example, *behaviour*) and vocabulary (lift for elevator) are used throughout, and measurements are given only in metric form, which will pose problems for some North American readers. In addition to its Australian-New Zealand-Commonwealth orientation, the *New Knowledge Library* also emphasizes scientific and technical subjects. See, for instance, such substantial articles as *Acupuncture, Algae, Animal Kingdom, Astronomy, Balloon and Airship, Cable Car and Tram, Conservation, Embryo, Evolution, Hair, Heat, Heredity, Light, Moth and Butterfly, Radar, Radio, Radioactive Fall-Out, Railways, Storm, Surgery, X-rays,* and *Zoological Garden.*

Information in the *New Knowledge Library* is usually reliable. Minor inaccuracies are encountered now and then, but not often enough to call the set's authority into question. Information is also usually presented in an objective manner. The article *Sexual Behaviour, Human,* for example, is straightforward and factual without being moralistic or patronizing. In some instances, however, the encyclopedia avoids controversial issues, as in the case of the article *Abortion,* which merely notes that "while Roman Catholics continue to oppose it, a more lenient attitude is taken by Protestants and Jews," but never explains why the issue arouses such strong feelings and what the arguments are on both sides. In the area of up-to-dateness, the encyclopedia is consistently current as of the late 1970s. The article *Nicaragua,* for instance, concludes with the overthrow of the Somoza government and the coming to power of the Sandinistas in 1979.

The encyclopedia's writing style is clear and direct. Most of the text will be understandable to serious elementary school students in grades three to six, although some science articles may be beyond their comprehension. Average readers at the secondary school level should ordinarily have no difficulty with the text. Consider, for example, the first two paragraphs of the article *Earthquake:*

> Most earthquakes occur in narrow bands along the major fractures, or faults, in the earth's crust and upper mantle which mark the edges of the crust plates, and the basic causes of earthquakes are strains induced by movements of these plates. Seismologists analyse the location and nature of earthquakes and are consequently able accurately to map the location of plate boundaries.
>
> The plates are constantly moving very slowly and are locked together by frictional forces caused by the downward pressures of rock formations overlying them. If two adjoining plates are moving in opposite directions, the frictional force prevents them from easily sliding past each other, and a strain builds up until the frictional bond is broken and the plates very suddenly slip past each other. This sudden movement is the earthquake, and the point at which the two plates break is called the focus. Once the break occurs, it can travel at 3.5 km/s for as far as 1000 km, and in major earthquakes the slip, or distance that the plates move, can be as great as 15 m.

Access to the contents of the *New Knowledge Library* is poor. First, there are too few cross-references in the text. For example, there is no *See* reference from "Civil War" to the article *American Civil War* or *English Civil War.* There is no reference from "Elevator" to the article *Lift and Elevator.* The article *South Africa,* which mentions but does not explain apartheid, fails to provide a *See also* reference to the article *Apartheid,* which does briefly explain the subject. Many similar examples could be cited. And second, the encyclopedia's index, found at the end of Volume 35, is practically worthless. All it does is repeat the titles of the articles themselves and their subheadings. No other effort is made to index the subject content of the set. Hence, information on the Somoza family in the article on Nicaragua is not indexed and therefore not readily accessible. The same is true of information about the metronome, which is described and pictured in the article *Music, Contemporary* but is inaccessible through the index. Likewise the Beatles, who are discussed at some length and also pictured in *Music, Contemporary* but not indexed. Soccer and rugby, covered in *Football,* also are not found in the index. The article *Silent Film,* indexed only under "Silent Film," is not accessible under "Film," "Movies," "Motion Pictures," or "Cinema," all places a user might logically look for information about early films. Again, many more examples could be given.

On the other hand, the set's illustrations, which account for roughly 50 percent of the total text, are very good indeed. Almost all in color, they include photographs, prints, art reproductions, diagrams, and cutaway drawings. The latter are particularly effective. See, for example, the aforementioned article *Earthquake,* which includes a cutaway showing a fault in the earth and how it occurs. The abundance and high quality of the illustrations make the *New Knowledge Library* an attractive browsing set for young students, including reluctant readers. The encyclopedia's physical format is both well made and appealing to the eye.

To Summarize: The 35-volume *New Knowledge Library* —subtitled "Universal Reference Encyclopedia"—is a heavily illustrated, Australian-made reference work chiefly for younger students and children ages seven to fourteen. It may also serve the needs of students at the secondary level. Published in 1981, the encyclopedia is reasonably current, clearly written, and very well illustrated. On the negative side, the coverage is strongly slanted toward the subject matter of particular interest to Australian and New Zealand readers, and access to the set's contents is inadequate.

In Comparison: The *New Knowledge Library,* published in 35 slender volumes (only 96 pages each) containing approximately 2 million words, is intended mainly for children and younger students in the elementary and junior high school grades. The encyclopedia competes directly with three other multivolume children's sets aimed at the same general audience, namely, FINDING OUT: SILVER BURDETT'S CHILDREN'S ENCYCLOPEDIA (10 volumes; 250,000 words), the NEW BOOK OF KNOWLEDGE (21 volumes; 6.8 million words), and the YOUNG STUDENTS ENCYCLOPEDIA (24 volumes; 1.5 million words). Among these titles, the NEW BOOK OF KNOWLEDGE is clearly the best, but it is also the most expensive. The *New Knowledge Library,* though handsomely illustrated and fairly priced, has limited appeal to a North American readership because of its heavy "Down Under" bias.

To Purchase the *New Knowledge Library:* As previously noted, the *New Knowledge Library* is available in North America only to schools and libraries. To order the encyclopedia, contact Farwell Promotional

Books (a division of Gareth Stevens, Inc.) at 7221 West Greentree Road, Milwaukee, WI 53223 or telephone 414-466-7550. Your name will be forwarded to the Farwell sales representative covering your area.

No other reviews of the *New Knowledge Library* are available at this time.

New Standard Encyclopedia

FACTS

New Standard Encyclopedia. Douglas W. Downey, Editor in Chief. Chicago: Standard Educational Corporation. 17 volumes. Former titles: *Aiton's Encyclopedia* (1910–11); *National Encyclopedia for the Home, School and Library* (1923–26); *Standard Reference Work for the Home, School and Library* (1912–22, 1927–29). First published as the *New Standard Encyclopedia* in 1930; new printing with revisions each year. Suggested retail price: $649.50 delivered; with discount to schools and libraries: $380.70 plus shipping and handling.

The 17-volume *New Standard Encyclopedia* aims "to provide as much information of interest to the general reader as is possible within an illustrated set selling for a moderate price. Although children as young as nine or ten can understand much of the material, the content is not juvenile and the level of detail is sufficient for basic reference use by persons of any age" (foreword). The encyclopedia contains approximately 10,000 pages, 17,500 articles, and 6.4 million words. The articles, most of which are of the specific-entry type, average 375 words in length (or somewhat more than half a page). They are accompanied by 12,000 illustrations (nearly 5,000 in color), plus 650 maps. An editorial staff of 90, plus some 700 contributors, consultants, advisers, and authenticators (or article reviewers) are identified at the beginning of Volume 1. None of the articles is signed. The encyclopedia is arranged alphabetically word by word (*New York* precedes *Newspaper*), with access to specific information enhanced by 53,500 cross-references in the text. The set has no index.

EVALUATION

The *New Standard,* first published in 1930 in ten volumes, derives from the six-volume *Standard Reference Work for the Home, School and Library* (1912–22, 1927–29), which also appeared for a time as the *National Encyclopedia for the Home, School and Library* (1923–26). The sire of all of these titles was *Aiton's Encyclopedia* (1910–11), a five-volume work edited by and named for George Briggs Aiton, a Minnesota educator. Over the years, the *New Standard* has grown slowly but steadily in size, expanding most recently in 1983 from 14 to 17 volumes. Although not as well known as some of its competitors, the encyclopedia is a solid, respectable set for older students and the whole family. The publication has been most fortunate to have had a dedicated and experienced editor, Douglas Downey, for more than 20 years.

The *New Standard* provides reasonably well balanced coverage of the major areas of knowledge. Scientific and technical subjects are covered in the most depth, as such substantial articles as *Animal, Atomic Energy, Automobile, Biology, Bird, Desert, Earth, Heart, Heat, Iron and Steel, Medicine, Mining, Petroleum, Plastics, Printing, Radiation, Space Exploration, Stem, Teeth, Telegraphy, Telephone, Telescope, Turbine, Vitamins,* and *Weather* attest. The encyclopedia also includes a great amount of practical information on such down-to-earth subjects as nutrition, consumer protection, lawn care, first aid, vaccination, fire protection and prevention, photography, sewing, canning, veterans' benefits, grafting and pruning plants, raising dogs, rules for playing various games, and how bank checks work. Indeed, the *New Standard* probably provides more of this sort of utilitarian material than any other general encyclopedia currently available. Biographical and geographical coverage tends to emphasize North American people and places. As Frances Neel Cheney observes in her review of the *New Standard* in *American Reference Books Annual* (1984, pp. 21–22), "Geographical entries give more space to U.S. states than to some foreign countries, e.g., 10 columns for Denmark and 16 columns for Delaware—not unusual in U.S. encyclopedias." In any event, efforts are currently under way to improve the set's international coverage. Occasionally, the *New Standard*'s treatment is disappointingly brief or superficial, as in the case of the articles *Adoption* (limited to 14 lines) and *Apartheid* (11 lines). Overall, however, the encyclopedia's coverage of essential knowledge and information is quite good.

Information in the *New Standard* is normally accurate and impartial. The article *Capital Punishment,* for example, informs the reader, "Capital punishment has been a controversial issue since the 18th century. Opponents of the death penalty have argued that it is a throwback to the barbarism of the past and also that is [sic] has no effect on reducing violent crime. They have called for its abolition. Supporters of capital punishment have held that it serves as a deterrent to serious criminality and that it is essential to public safety." In some instances, however, sensitive or polemical issues are simply ignored, as in the case of the articles *Abortion* and *Scientology*, neither of which contains a hint of the controversy surrounding the subject. In the case of circumcision, the subject is not even mentioned in the encyclopedia. Information in the *New Standard* is, on the other hand, admirably current. In 1985, for instance, more than 2,000 of the set's 17,500 articles were revised, and some 50 new articles and 175 illustrations (most in color) were added—all involving changes in approximately 2,500 of the encyclopedia's 10,000 pages. These are impressive statistics, and use bears out their validity. Among the new or recently revised articles are *AIDS (Acquired Immune Deficiency Syndrome), Amyothrophic Lateral Sclerosis (ALS), Compact Disc Player, Computer, Dioxin, Hare Krishna, Holistic Medicine, Options Trading, Radio Free Europe, Robot, Space Shuttle, Sports Medicine,* and *Toxic Shock Syndrome.* New biographees include Mikhail Baryshnikov, Geraldine Ferraro, Milton Friedman, William Gass, Zubin Mehta, Harold Pinter, Sally Ride, Gloria Steinem, Lech Walesa, and Tom Wolfe. In a word, the *New Standard* is up-to-date.

The set's writing style is usually clear, direct, and unpretentious. The goal is clarity rather than fine writing. A note at the front of Volume 1 explains, "Most of the writing is done by the editorial staff. These writers are specialists both in the fields they cover and in the techniques of encyclopedia writing." Ordinarily, the text will be comprehensible to users reading at the seventh or eighth grade level and beyond. The article *Earthquake* typifies the encyclopedia's style (the first two paragraphs are quoted):

EARTHQUAKE, or TEMBLOR, a shaking of the earth's surface. Earthquakes have toppled entire cities, killed thousands of persons, and caused disastrous fires and oceanic waves (tsunamis). However, most earthquakes, of which there are thousands each year, are relatively weak and cause little or no damage. No part of the world is entirely free of earthquakes, but they occur most frequently in areas in which the earth's crust is still changing. These areas, called earthquake belts, include the shores of the Pacific Ocean and an area extending from south-central Asia to the Mediterranean Sea.

Major earthquakes often leave visible signs of their power, altering features on the earth's surface. Reelfoot Lake in northwestern Tennessee was created by a series of earthquakes centered around New Madrid, Missouri, in 1811–12. The San Francisco earthquake of 1906 was associated with the great San Andreas Fault in California, a fracture in the earth's surface that can be traced for more than 500 miles (800 km).

The contents of the *New Standard* are reasonably accessible. As already noted, the set lacks an index, but its extensive system of cross-references usually points the reader in the right direction. For example, there is a *See* reference under "Polygraph" directing the user to the article *Lie Detector.* In similar fashion, a *See* reference under "Health Maintenance Organization (HMO)" leads the user to the article *Cooperative,* where information about HMOs can be found. Numerous *See* and *See also* references also appear within the text or at the end of articles. The article *Animal,* for instance, includes more than 60 references to other articles in the set, such as *Zoology, Fossil, Extinct Animals, Taxonomy, Mammals, Vertebrates, Adaptation, Hibernation, Bird, Cave Animals,* and *Evolution.* But in some instances the elaborate cross-reference system breaks down. For example, the article *Novel* contains a short discussion of the stream-of-consciousness style utilized by James Joyce and various other twentieth-century writers, but fails to alert the reader to the article *Stream of Consciousness,* where a much fuller exposition of the subject can be found. In another type of situation, the user seeking information about how animals change color or camouflage themselves for either protection or food gathering will find nothing useful in the article *Camouflage,* only a brief mention in the article *Color* ("Color is also used in the opposite way—to make objects blend with their surroundings, as in camouflage or protective coloration of animals"), and nothing under the heading "Coloration." Only by going through the lengthy (13-page) article *Animal* can the user find information on the subject and, in the process, discover a cross-reference to the article *Adaptation,* which discusses the phenomena of protective and warning colorations. In such cases, an index would make the encyclopedia's contents more readily and efficiently accessible.

Illustrations in the *New Standard* have been steadily upgraded in recent years, but room for improvement still exists. The illustrations, the majority of which are in black-and-white, normally add to the informational value of the articles they accompany. The aforementioned *Animal,* for instance, includes drawings showing how various animals are used by humans and how animals adapt to their environment, as well as an illustrated chart depicting maximum speeds of certain animals (an elephant can travel as fast as 25 miles per hour, a cheetah at 70 miles per hour, etc.). Many new color illustrations have been added during the past decade, but more are needed. For example, the article *Forget-me-not* informs the reader that the plant has "small blue flowers with yellow, white, or pink centers," but the accompanying illustration is in black-and-white. The editors are aware of the problem and, as indicated, are moving as rapidly as possible to increase the amount of color in the set. The encyclopedia's physical format is satisfactory, the binding being very sturdy and the page layout, typeface, etc. serviceable.

Over the years, the *New Standard* has not received much critical attention, and those reviews that have appeared have not been entirely favorable, largely because of the set's lack of an index and its sometimes overly concise or superficial coverage. In a recent review in *American Reference Books Annual* (1984, p. 22), Frances Neel Cheney, a highly respected reference book critic, writes disparagingly of the *New Standard* that "libraries will continue to prefer encyclopedias that treat their subjects more fully or that are aimed more directly at the school curriculum, while the increased price may make the set less attractive for home purchase." The most recent review in *Booklist* (December 15, 1984, p. 574) says much the same, finding that the encyclopedia "continues to do acceptably what it has done in the past: provide basic, up-to-date information about a variety of topics. Although it is accurate, *New Standard* is not always comprehensive in its treatment of topics, and its coverage of more difficult subjects is generally less satisfactory than that provided by the other encyclopedias analyzed in this survey." Interestingly, this review does not mention the set's lack of an index. In earlier reviews, the *Booklist* critics apparently could not decide whether an index was needed or not. In its November 1, 1977, review (p. 497), *Booklist* stated unequivocally that " *New Standard* 's cross-reference structure is inconsistent and does not take the place of a good index." But a year later, *Booklist* (December 15, 1978, p. 712) "found the many cross-references to be almost an adequate substitute" for an index. And, as noted, the most recent *Booklist* review simply avoids the index question.

To Summarize: The *New Standard,* now published in 17 volumes (up from 14 in 1983), is a well-maintained, carefully edited set for the whole family. It emphasizes scientific and technical topics, practical information, and North American biography and geography. Up-to-dateness of material and a clear, unpretentious writing style are conspicuous strengths, whereas the lack of an index sometimes hampers easy and effective access to the set's contents.

In Comparison: The *New Standard,* published in 17 volumes containing 6.4 million words, is a middle-sized encyclopedia for adults and older students from the seventh grade on. It competes with other in-print encyclopedias in that category, namely the ACADEMIC AMERICAN ENCYCLOPEDIA (21 volumes; 9 million words), COMPTON'S ENCYCLOPEDIA (26 volumes; 8.5 million words), FUNK & WAGNALLS NEW ENCYCLOPEDIA (29 volumes; 9 million words), MERIT STUDENTS ENCYCLOPEDIA (20 volumes; 9 million words), the NEW CAXTON ENCYCLOPEDIA (20 volumes; 6 million words), and the WORLD BOOK ENCYCLOPEDIA (22 volumes; 10 million words). Without question, the ACADEMIC AMERICAN ENCYCLOPEDIA and the WORLD BOOK ENCYCLOPEDIA are the best of this group, although each encyclopedia has its own particular appeal. In the case of the *New Standard,* the set's large amount of practical information and its outstanding continuous revision program make the encyclopedia an attractive purchase for families. But, overall, the *New Standard* cannot match the consistent superiority of the ACADEMIC AMERICAN ENCYCLOPEDIA and the WORLD BOOK ENCYCLOPEDIA.

To Purchase the *New Standard Encyclopedia:* If you are an individual consumer and wish to order the encyclopedia, contact the Standard Educational Corporation at 200 West Monroe Street, Chicago, IL 60606 or telephone 312-346-7440. Your name will be forwarded to an independent distributor in your area who will handle the transaction. The distributor will most likely attempt to sell you additional publications along with the encyclopedia, including *Child Horizons,* a ten-volume set of books for young people also published by Standard Educational Corporation, and an updating supplement entitled *World Progress: The Standard Quarterly Review.* You need not buy any extras unless you want them. In the case of *World Progress,* a loose-leaf publication that comes with its own binder, the work has no direct connection with the encyclopedia and should be avoided unless you are sure it will be used.

If you are ordering the *New Standard* for a school or library, contact Standard Educational Corporation at the address or telephone number given above. Your order will be processed immediately.

For More Information about the *New Standard Encyclopedia* See: *American Reference Books Annual,* 1984, pp. 21–22 (review by Frances Neel Cheney); *Booklist,* December 15, 1984, pp. 572–74 (unsigned review).

New Talking Cassette Encyclopedia

FACTS

The New Talking Cassette Encyclopedia. Mahwah, NJ: Troll Associates. Ten volumes (or albums). Former title: *Talking Cassette Encyclopedia.* Second edition published in 1984. Lowest retail price: $695.00 plus shipping and handling.

The *New Talking Cassette Encyclopedia,* as its title suggests, is published in audio rather than print form. Intended chiefly for classroom use at the kindergarten and elementary school levels, the encyclopedia consists of 100 cassette tapes, each covering a different subject (Africa, agriculture, air, the American Revolution, etc.). The set contains approximately 100,000 words, each tape averaging roughly 1,000 words, or ten to twelve minutes of listening time. No editors, writers, or narrators are identified, nor is attribution given for any of the material. The tapes are arranged alphabetically by title in ten "volumes" (or albums), with access to specific information enhanced by a printed index, called the "Cross-Referenced Subject Guide," containing 162 entries. The ten albums are housed in a pasteboard slipcase. A cassette player and a set of test questions (one for each of the 100 tapes) come with the encyclopedia.

EVALUATION

Troll Associates, well known to librarians and teachers as a publisher of quality educational products, including audiovisual and read-along materials, first issued the encyclopedia in 1971 under the title *Talking Cassette Encyclopedia.* In 1984, the set was completely revised and reissued as the *New Talking Cassette Encyclopedia.* Not unexpectedly, the encyclopedia's coverage emphasizes subjects frequently studied in North American elementary schools. Included among the 100 topics covered are these tapes: *Africa, Agriculture, Air, American Revolution, Ancient China, Ancient Egypt, Ancient Greece, Ancient Rome, Babe Ruth, Birds, Colonial Life in America, Computers, Congressperson, Conservation and Pollution, Earth, Earthquakes and Volcanoes, Ecosystems and Food Chains, Energy and Fuels, Fossils, Freedom Documents, George Washington, Harriet Tubman, Helen Keller, Human Body, Indian Crafts, Indian Festivals, Jackie Robinson, Mexico and Central America, Mountains, Oregon Trail, Pioneers, President, Reptiles and Amphibians, Rivers, Space Exploration and Travel, Stars, Supreme Court, Using the Library,* and *Whales and Dolphins.*

Obviously, being limited to 100 such topics, the encyclopedia's coverage is highly selective. For example, only 16 of the tapes cover people, and two of these are mythical characters (Johnny Appleseed and Paul Bunyan). Moreover, the treatment of those topics that are included is necessarily brief, although much basic information is provided. A review in *Booklist* (July 1985, p. 1586) rightly notes, "Ten minutes does not seem to be much time to cover such broad topics as agriculture and the Renaissance, but on these and all the other tapes the producers have managed to cover the most important concepts and facts in a logical and interesting way." Nevertheless, by no stretch of the imagination can the *New Talking Cassette Encyclopedia* be considered a full-fledged encyclopedia for children. Rather, it is an introductory work designed to acquaint young students with the idea of an encyclopedia while at the same time presenting new facts in an attention-getting manner. In purpose and scope (but not format), the *New Talking Cassette Encyclopedia* is similar to such sets as CHARLIE BROWN'S 'CYCLOPEDIA, CHILDCRAFT, and COMPTON'S PRECYCLOPEDIA.

Information in the *New Talking Cassette Encyclopedia* is accurately and objectively presented. The encyclopedia's contents are also quite current. Topics that were becoming stale in the original 1971 edition have been either dropped or revised. Only 42 of the original 100 topics have been carried over into the 1984 version (for example, the tapes *Birds, Caves, Christopher Columbus, George Washington, Helen Keller, Martin Luther King, Sun, Rivers,* and *Thomas Jefferson*). Among the new tapes added to the 1984 edition are *Abraham Lincoln, American Revolution, Babe Ruth, Colonial Life in America, Forests and Jungles, Middle Ages, Pilgrims and Thanksgiving, Pioneers, Rockets and Satellites,* and *Space Exploration and Travel*.

Ordinarily, the encyclopedia's spoken text will be comprehensible to children from the preschool level to the upper elementary grades. Potentially difficult or unfamiliar vocabulary is defined or explained in context. For example, the tape *Earthquakes and Volcanoes* gives the meaning of such technical terms as *mantle, crust, plate, fault, Richter scale, seismography,* and *tsunami*. The text is consistently clear and interesting. Likewise, the narration, normally accompanied by appropriate sound effects and background music, is skillfully delivered. Almost without exception, the tapes will arouse and maintain the young person's interest. By way of example, here are the first few sentences (sans music and sound effects) of *Earthquakes and Volcanoes:*

There is a rumbling in the earth. The ground trembles. A loud bang echoes across the hills. Suddenly, a jagged crack appears and rips across the ground like a bolt of lightning. On one side of the crack the ground pushes up, while the other side drops down. Trees snap in two and huge boulders roll into the widening gap of land. At last the quaking of the earth stops, but the earthquake has changed the landscape forever.

Access to specific information in the *New Talking Cassette Encyclopedia* is poor. The spoken text lacks cross-references, and the printed index, called the "Cross-Referenced Subject Guide," is of little use. Limited to a single page and only 162 entries, all the index does is list titles of the tapes under broad headings. Under the heading "History," for instance, the user will find *American Revolution, Ancient China, Ancient Egypt, Ancient Greece, Ancient Rome, Colonial Life in America,* and so forth. No effort is made to index the contents of the tapes themselves; for example, Mount St. Helens is discussed at some length in *Earthquakes and Volcanoes,* but the user will not learn this from the index. The encyclopedia's physical format is satisfactory, although the albums (which hold the tapes) are not sturdy and probably will not fare well under heavy use. An attractive feature of the tapes is that the text is recorded in its entirety on both sides, thus eliminating the need for rewinding at the end. Another feature that will be useful to teachers is the provision of duplicating masters of tests covering each of the 100 tapes. The test for *Earthquakes and Volcanoes,* for example, poses 11 questions, such as, true or false, "The cities of Los Angeles and San Francisco are on plates that are slowly sliding past each other." An answer sheet is provided.

To Summarize: The *New Talking Cassette Encyclopedia,* a 1984 revision of the earlier *Talking Cassette Encyclopedia* (1971), is a unique reference work for use in the classroom with young students from preschool to the upper elementary grades. Produced in audio rather than print form, the set consists of 100 cassette tapes, each covering a subject likely to be part of the North American elementary school curriculum. Obviously, coverage is selective (as opposed to systematic) and the *New Talking Cassette Encyclopedia* should not, despite its title, be considered a comprehensive encyclopedia for children.

In Comparison: The *New Talking Cassette Encyclopedia,* published in 100 cassette tapes in ten "volumes" (or albums) containing approximately 100,000 words, is intended for children and younger students. Although unique in terms of its physical format, the encyclopedia is similar in purpose and scope to four print titles currently on the market, namely CHARLIE BROWN'S 'CYCLOPEDIA (15 volumes; 180,000 words), CHILDCRAFT (15 volumes; 750,000 words), COMPTON'S PRECYCLOPEDIA (16 volumes; 325,000 words), and DISNEY'S WONDERFUL WORLD OF KNOWLEDGE (20 volumes; 750,000 words). Consumers interested in a multivolume encyclopedia for beginning readers would do well to acquire either CHILDCRAFT or COMPTON'S PRECYCLOPEDIA. Both are fine works of their kind, though neither pretends to completeness. The *New Talking Cassette Encyclopedia,* on the other hand, is much too expensive ($695.00) and specialized (in terms of format) to be used effectively anywhere except the classroom. In addition, the encyclopedia can be useful in work with visually handicapped young people. The only other general encyclopedia currently available in audio form is the *Talking World Book,* a version of the WORLD BOOK ENCYCLOPEDIA, published in 219 cassette tapes (six playing hours each) in 19 volumes (or albums) at an estimated cost of $1,175.00.

To Purchase the *New Talking Cassette Encyclopedia:* Anyone wishing to order the encyclopedia should contact the publisher, Troll Associates, at 320 Route 17, Mahwah, NJ 07430 or telephone toll-free 1-800-526-5289. Your on-approval order will be processed immediately.

For More Information about the *New Talking Cassette Encyclopedia* See: *Booklist,* July 1985, p. 1586 (unsigned review).

New Universal Family Encyclopedia

FACTS

The New Universal Family Encyclopedia. Published abroad as the *Macmillan Encyclopedia.* Stephen Elliott, North American Editor in Chief. New York: Random House, Inc. Copyright by Lawrence Urdang Associates and Ottenheimer Publishers, Inc. One volume. Revised edition published in 1985. Lowest retail price: $39.95.

The *New Universal Family Encyclopedia* is a single-volume, desk-sized work for adults and older students from junior high school through college. The encyclopedia, first published in 1981 and revised in 1985, contains approximately 1,110 pages, 25,000 articles, and 1.5 million words. The articles, which are of the specific-entry type, average 60 words in length (or roughly 23 articles per page). They are accompanied by some 1,200 illustrations (all in black-and-white), plus a 16-page color world atlas. An editorial staff of about 60 is noted at the front of the volume. The encyclopedia is arranged letter by letter (*Newspaper* precedes *New York*), with access to specific information enhanced by more than 10,000 cross-references in the text. There is no index.

COMMENTS

At this writing, the author of *Best Encyclopedias* has not seen the *New Universal Family Encyclopedia* ; it was published for the first time in North America just as the guide was going to press. According to prepublication information furnished by Random House, the encyclopedia "covers history, science, the arts, geography, biography, ideas and beliefs, sports, hobbies and pastimes, etc. To cover all aspects of the world, past and present, in one easy-to-use volume, the editors, specialists, and consultants have kept it *factual, concise, and in words the average reader can understand.* It is packed full of necessary, useful, interesting information for everyone, including all levels of students—and the extensive cross-references make it self-indexing." The publisher also points out that, although it first appeared in Great Britain in 1981 (as the *Macmillan Encyclopedia*), the *New Universal Family Encyclopedia* has been thoroughly "Americanized." Specifically, Random House rewrote many articles and added nearly 5,000 new ones to accommodate North American readers.

The one-volume encyclopedia, which contains 1.5 million words, will compete directly with the smaller one- and two-volume encyclopedias for adults and older students, namely COLLINS GEM ENCYCLOPEDIA (two volumes; 450,000 words), the CONCISE COLUMBIA ENCYCLOPEDIA (one volume; one million words), the KNOWLEDGE ENCYCLOPEDIA (one volume; 300,000 words), PEARS CYCLOPAEDIA (one volume; 1.2 million words), and the QUICK REFERENCE HANDBOOK OF BASIC KNOWLEDGE (one volume; 750,000 words).

The *New Universal Family Encyclopedia* will be fully evaluated in the next edition of *Best Encyclopedias.*

Oxford Illustrated Encyclopedia

FACTS

Oxford Illustrated Encyclopedia. Harry Judge, General Editor. London, England, and New York: Oxford University Press. 8 volumes (in progress). First two volumes published in 1985, with two new volumes scheduled for publication each year through 1988. Lowest retail price: $35 per volume.

The *Oxford Illustrated Encyclopedia* is a new multivolume encyclopedia "designed for the student, general reader, and interested nonspecialist" (advertisement in *Booklist,* December 1, 1985, p. 551). The first two volumes of *Oxford Illustrated,* projected to be an eight-volume set, appeared in 1985. Two additional volumes are scheduled to be published each year between 1986 and 1988, when the set will be completed. The encyclopedia is thematically arranged, with each volume covering a broad area of knowledge: Volume 1 is entitled *The Physical World* and Volume 2 *The Natural World.* Eventually, all major fields of human knowledge will be covered. Each volume consists of 384 pages, some 2,500 alphabetical entries, and roughly 400 illustrations (about half in color). When completed, the eight-volume set will contain more than 3,000 pages, 20,000 entries, and approximately 3,500 illustrations. Access to specific information is enhanced by cross-references in each volume, and a general index to the set is planned.

COMMENTS

At this writing, the author of *Best Encyclopedias* has not seen the *Oxford Illustrated Encyclopedia*; a request for review copies of the initial volumes has gone unanswered. According to the aforementioned advertisement for the set in *Booklist* (December 1, 1985, p. 551), "Individually each volume stands alone as an authoritative, handsome, and accessible reference to its field. Together the eight volumes will comprise a comprehensive encyclopedia of human knowledge and achievement." The advertisement goes on to characterize the volumes as having a "succinct, engaging writing style—accessible to the student and general reader" and being an "up-to-date, authoritative treatment of every subject." Dr Harry Judge, general editor of the set, is identified as Director of the University of Oxford Department of Educational Studies.

To date, reviews of the first two volumes of *Oxford Illustrated* have appeared in *Choice* (February 1986, p. 852) and *Library Journal* (March 1, 1986, p. 88). Reviewing Volume 1 (*The Physical World*) in *Choice*, N.F. George writes:

> This first volume of a projected eight-volume series bears eloquent testimony to the ingenuity, if not the duplicity, of publishers. Touted as 'independent' of its successors-to-be, the work is a brief-entry compilation of definitions and biographical sketches relevant to the disciplines of mathematics, physics, chemistry, geology, oceanography, and meteorology. Some exclusions are paleontology, all applied science, and all living persons regardless of the field of expertise (living persons are to be noted in Volume 7). Results are mixed.... Not essential for academic or public libraries, but could be useful in schools.

And T. Kirk, reviewing Volume 2 (*The Natural World*) in *Choice*, observes that the book "can best be characterized in level and content as the equivalent of a college-level general biology text that has been reorganized, shortened, and dressed up with color illustrations." Joseph Hannibal, in his review of both Volumes 1 and 2 in *Library Journal*, concludes: "These books can be recommended to students, informed laypersons, and the general public. However, comparable, or more extensive treatment of a large proportion of the entries in these volumes can be found in the better general encyclopedias."

It would appear that *Oxford Illustrated* is intended to either replace or complement the publisher's OXFORD JUNIOR ENCYCLOPAEDIA, a thematically arranged 13-volume set recently withdrawn from the market, principally due to its age.

The *Oxford Illustrated Encyclopedia* will be fully evaluated in the next edition of *Best Encyclopedias*.

Oxford Junior Encyclopaedia

FACTS

Oxford Junior Encyclopaedia. Laura E. Salt, Geoffrey Boumphrey, and Robert Sinclair, Editors. London, England, and New York: Oxford University Press. 13 volumes. Second edition published in 1964, with corrected reprints issued between 1974 and 1976; out of print in North America since 1982 (last priced at $189).

The *Oxford Junior Encyclopaedia* is a British-made reference work "suitable for the young reader" (preface). The 13-volume encyclopedia contains approximately 6,500 pages, 3,600 articles, and 3.7 million words. The articles, many of which are of the broad-entry type, average slightly more than 1,000 words in length (or roughly two pages). They are accompanied by 6,100 illustrations (the large majority in black-and-white), plus 150 maps. More than 1,000 editors and contributors are noted, but none of the articles is signed. The encyclopedia is arranged topically, each of the first 12 volumes dealing with a broad subject or theme: *Mankind* (Volume 1); *Natural History* (Volume 2); *The Universe* (Volume 3); *Communications* (Volume 4); *Great Lives* (Volume 5); *Farming and Fisheries* (Volume 6); *Industry and Commerce* (Volume 7); *Engineering* (Volume 8); *Recreations* (Volume 9); *Law and Society* (Volume 10); *Home and Health* (Volume 11); and *The Arts* (Volume 12). Articles within each volume are arranged alphabetically letter by letter (*Newspaper* precedes *New York*). Access to specific information is enhanced by about 2,000 cross-references in the text and a general index (Volume 13) of some 35,000 entries.

EVALUATION

Oxford Junior, widely regarded as one of the best British encyclopedias for children and younger students, was originally published in 13 volumes between 1948 and 1954. A second revised edition appeared in the early 1960s, and in the 1970s all volumes in the set were modestly updated and reissued in "corrected reprints." Each of the first 12 volumes has its own editors and contributors, many of whom are noted scholars. Volume 9 (*Recreations*), for example, is edited by C. Day Lewis, a well-known writer and former Oxford don. Contributors to the encyclopedia include such prominent British academicians as A.J.P. Taylor, E.O. James, Jacquetta Hawkes, and Asa Briggs. But despite its fine reputation and impressive authority, *Oxford Junior* has never sold well in the United States and Canada, doubtless due to its strong British orientation. Not unexpectedly, distribution of the set in North America was discontinued in the early 1980s. However, should a new revised edition be issued in the future, as well it might, *Oxford Junior* will surely become available in North America again. Note that the publisher is currently issuing a similar set in eight volumes entitled the OXFORD ILLUSTRATED ENCYCLOPEDIA.

As already indicated, the encyclopedia's principal weakness, as far as North American users are concerned, is its heavy emphasis on British customs and institutions. For instance, Santa Claus is found in an article entitled *Father Christmas*; the U.S. Congress is described as "a national parliament"; sports and games are covered almost exclusively from the British perspective, as exemplified by such articles as *Association Football, Eton football, Hare Hunting,* and *Pub Games.* Similarly, many people and places of potential interest to U.S. and Canadian students lack coverage. For instance, a review of *Oxford Junior* in *Booklist* (May 1, 1979, p. 1396) points out, "The American child will not find many familiar names in the fields of music, sports, government, and history. There is nothing on Louis Armstrong or Leonard Bernstein, Babe Ruth or Howard Cosell, Harry S. Truman or Richard Nixon, Betsy Ross or Paul Revere. In fact, volume V, *Great Lives,* excludes living persons." In addition, the text provides only metric measurements. Such statements as "Jute is an annual plant, growing to a height of from 2 to 3 metres" will puzzle some North American readers. Other limitations in the set include lack of current information, avoidance of sensitive material of concern to young people (such as sex and drugs), dated and sometimes poorly placed illustrations, and a topical arrangement that will be strange and possibly confusing to some users.

On the plus side, *Oxford Junior* is a well-edited, attractively produced encyclopedia that offers accurate and impartial treatment of the topics that it does cover. The set's writing style, while it tends to vary from volume to volume, is customarily clear and free from condescending, or babyish, remarks (although the use of British terminology and spelling might occasionally cause problems for some readers). Generally speaking, the text will be comprehensible to serious students at the sixth grade level and up.

To Summarize: The 13-volume *Oxford Junior,* first published in 1948–54 and revised in the 1960s and 1970s, is a highly regarded British encyclopedia for young people. Its usefulness in the United States and Canada, however, is limited due to its strong British emphasis. Not unexpectedly, the set has recently been discontinued in North America, at least for the time being.

In Comparison: When it was available in North America, *Oxford Junior* competed directly with the BRITANNICA JUNIOR ENCYCLOPAE-

DIA (now also discontinued), the NEW BOOK OF KNOWLEDGE, and the YOUNG STUDENTS ENCYCLOPEDIA, all substantial multivolume sets intended for children and younger students. Also competitive in this age group are the larger and more sophisticated COMPTON'S ENCYCLO-PEDIA, MERIT STUDENTS ENCYCLOPEDIA, and the WORLD BOOK ENCY-CLOPEDIA. Given this sort of competition, *Oxford Junior* made little impression on the market. As a reviewer in *Booklist* (May 1, 1979, p. 1396) nicely put it, "While of value to children in the United Kingdom, the set offers little to children in the U.S. who have access to excellent encyclopedias published in this country."

For More Information about the *Oxford Junior Encyclopaedia* See: *Booklist,* May 1, 1979, pp. 1395–96 (unsigned review).

Pears Cyclopaedia

FACTS

Pears Cyclopaedia: A Book of Background Information and Reference for Everyday Use. Christopher Cook, Editor; L. Mary Barker, Consultant Editor. London, England: Pelham Books Ltd. Distributed in North America by Merrimack Publishers' Circle. One volume. Original title: *Pears' Shilling Cyclopaedia.* First edition published in 1897; new revised edition each year. Lowest retail price: $14.95.

The one-volume *Pears Cyclopaedia* is a venerable desk-sized compendium of basic reference information and miscellaneous facts for adults and older students that has been produced every year in Great Britain since Queen Victoria's diamond jubilee in 1897. The encyclopedia contains more than 1,050 pages, approximately 15,000 articles, and 1.3 million words. The articles, which include lists, chronologies, glossaries, etc., are usually brief, averaging under 100 words in length (or about 15 entries per page). They are accompanied by about 25 illustrations (all in black-and-white), plus 25 maps, including a 36-plate color atlas in the center of the book. None of the material is signed. The encyclopedia is arranged topically, the contents grouped by subject under 20 broad headings ("Events—Historical and Contemporary," "Prominent People," "Background to Public Affairs," "Political Compendium," "The World of Music," "The World of Science," "Background to Economic Events," "Money Matters," "Classical Mythology," "Ideas and Beliefs," "Gazetteer of the World," "General Information," "Literary Companion," "General Compendium," "Medical Matters," "Introduction to Psychology," "Sporting Records," "Biblical Glossary," "Introduction to Computing," and "The Cinema"), with access to specific information enhanced by detailed tables of contents for most of the chapters, some 1,200 cross-references in the text, and a general index of 1,100 entries.

EVALUATION

Pears, which first appeared in 1897 as *Pears' Shilling Cyclopaedia,* is named for its patron and original publisher, Pears soap. An immediate success with the Victorian reading public, *Pears' Shilling Cyclopaedia* provided a m6elange of practical and exotic information, ranging from a "Dictionary of Synonyms and Antonyms" to a physical description of Heaven. In 1977, Pelham Books, *Pears'* publisher since the early 1960s, brought out a facsimile edition of the first *Shilling Cyclopaedia* (priced at $5.00, or $11.95, the reprint costing 100 times what it did in 1897). This interesting historical document is the subject of an informative piece entitled "Onward and Upward with the Arts: Next to Godliness" by Mary-Kay Wilmers in the *New Yorker* (October 8, 1979, pp. 145–63). Today, *Pears* is 90 years old and, as Wilmers reports, "still flourishing." Also, since 1961, a young people's version of *Pears* has been published under the title JUNIOR PEARS ENCYCLOPAEDIA.

Coverage in *Pears* is selective rather than comprehensive. Some subjects are covered in surprising depth for a single volume work, as in the case of Scientology, which receives substantial treatment in the chapter "Ideas and Beliefs," as do such topics as acupuncture, antiSemitism, capitalism, faith healing, fascism, humanism, Marxism, nihilism, pragmatism, the Reformation, Sikhism, socialism, Taoism, Unitarianism, and Zen Buddhism. But many subjects users would expect to find in a small adult encyclopedia are not even mentioned, such as gambling, mass transportation, robots, American Indians, homosexuality, abortion, adoption, suicide, and the D'Oyly Carte Opera Company. Likewise, numerous important people are not covered in *Pears,* including Yasir Arafat, Paul Gauguin, James Madison, and John Updike. In other instances, the book's coverage is so abbreviated as to be of minimal value. For example, the entry on the German city of Dresden in the "Gazetteer of the World" section fails to note the horrific bombing that occurred there during World War II.

Actually, *Pears* is a cross between an encyclopedia and an almanac, or yearbook. Emphasis is on current as opposed to retrospective information. Sometimes new chapters are added from year to year covering subjects much in the public mind, such as computers. The book is not only edited and published in Great Britain but it has a pronounced British accent, especially in social and cultural areas. The chapter "Political Compendium," for instance, deals entirely with the British political system; "Background to Economic Events" is likewise devoted to the British situation; "Sporting Records" emphasizes British sports and winners; an article on newspapers in "General Information" discusses only British publications. On the other hand, *Pears* does include much general material of potential interest to North Americans in such chapters as "The World of Music," "The World of Science," "Classical Mythology," "Ideas and Beliefs," "Introduction to Psychology" and "The Cinema." Like the first edition back in 1897, the current *Pears* is a mine of all sorts of intriguing information, both practical and arcane. The chapter "Medical Matters," for example, offers an extensive and explicit discussion of birth control methods, while "Literary Companion" provides instruction in how to enjoy a poem.

Information in *Pears* is normally accurate, unbiased, and current. For instance, the aforementioned material on birth control is up-to-date and presented in a reliable, disinterested manner. The encyclopedia's writing style is equally impressive, being clear, direct, concise, and uncompromisingly adult. The first several sentences of the article *Earthquake* (in "General Information") are fairly typical of *Pears* ' style and readability:

> EARTHQUAKE, a sudden violent disturbance of the earth's crust; the region of the surface immediately above the "focus", or source where the earthquake originates, is termed the "epicentre." On account of their destructive power earthquakes have attracted attention from the earliest times, but accurate study dates only from the last century and the development of a world-wide network of recording stations from the present one. The majority of severe earthquakes result from fractures, usually along existing faults, in underlying rock strata subjected to great strains, the shearing movement sometimes extending to the surface. These dislocations set up vibrations which are propagated as waves throughout the bulk of the earth or round the crust.

Access to information in *Pears* is poor. Not only are cross-references in the text in short supply, but the index at the end of the volume is grossly inadequate. For example, the index furnishes an entry under "Newspapers" that refers the reader to a list of major British dailies in the "Political Compendium" section, but it fails to include a reference to the substantial article on newspapers in "General Information." Numerous similar examples of index failure could be cited. In short, finding specific information in *Pears* is very much a hit-or-miss business. The encyclopedia's illustrations and physical format also leave much to be desired. Aside from the

36-plate color world atlas (maps by George Philip & Son Ltd.) in the center of the book and some 25 black-and-white line drawings in "Introduction to Computers," the volume is almost solid print—very, very small print with very, very narrow margins. Only the most dedicated seekers of information will read *Pears* without lamenting the type size.

To Summarize: *Pears,* a one-volume work that dates from 1897, is a British institution, like double-decker buses and pubs. Part encyclopedia and part almanac, its coverage is selective rather than comprehensive, with emphasis on current developments in Great Britain and the Commonwealth. From the North American point of view, *Pears* is too eccentric and too British to be a reference source of first choice, but it is jolly good fun to browse in. Note that JUNIOR PEARS ENCYCLOPAEDIA is a young people's version of *Pears.*

In Comparison: *Pears,* published in a single volume containing approximately 1.3 million words, is an annually revised reference work for adults and older students. It cannot compare with the leading one- and two-volume general adult encyclopedias currently on the North American market, namely the LINCOLN LIBRARY OF ESSENTIAL INFORMATION (two volumes; 3.5 million words), the NEW COLUMBIA ENCYCLOPEDIA (one volume; 6.6 million words), the RANDOM HOUSE ENCYCLOPEDIA (one volume; 3 million words), and the VOLUME LIBRARY (two volumes; 3.5 million words). All of these encyclopedias, as the figures indicate, offer much more information than *Pears.* Also, they are much more expensive. More in *Pears'* league are COLLINS GEM ENCYCLOPEDIA (two volumes; 450,000 words), the CONCISE COLUMBIA ENCYCLOPEDIA (one volume; one million words), the KNOWLEDGE ENCYCLOPEDIA (one volume; 300,000 words), and the QUICK REFERENCE HANDBOOK OF BASIC KNOWLEDGE (one volume; 750,000 words). Among these small desk-sized general encyclopedias for adults, the CONCISE COLUMBIA ENCYCLOPEDIA is the standout choice for U.S. and Canadian consumers. In the last analysis, the only things *Pears* has going for it, comparatively speaking, are its timeliness, low price, and British charm.

To Purchase *Pears Cyclopaedia:* *Pears* is sold in North American retail bookstores. If it is not in stock (and it might not be), most bookstores will order it for you. You can also order the book directly from the distributor, Merrimack Publishers' Circle, at 99 Main Street, Salem, NH 03079 or telephone 617-887-2440.

For More Information about *Pears Cyclopaedia* See: *American Reference Books Annual,* 1979, p. 39 (review by Frances Neel Cheney); *Booklist,* November 15, 1980, p. 479 (unsigned review); *Booklist,* July 15, 1977, pp. 1750–51 (unsigned review).

Purnell's Pictorial Encyclopedia

FACTS

Purnell's Pictorial Encyclopedia. Theodore Rowland-Entwistle and Jean Cooke, Editors. Maidenhead, Berkshire, England: Purnell & Sons Ltd. Distributed in North America by Pergamon Press. One volume. First edition published in 1979. Lowest retail price: $19.95.

Purnell's Pictorial Encyclopedia, a single-volume work for children ages seven to fourteen produced in Great Britain, is "specially written and designed to fire enthusiasm and interest in the fascinating world around us" (dust jacket). The encyclopedia contains 192 pages, 88 articles, and approximately 75,000 words. The articles, which are of the broad-entry type, are all two-page spreads averaging 850 words in length. The articles are accompanied by 550 illustrations (most in black-and-white). There are no maps in the book. An editorial staff of 17 is listed on the back of the title page. None of the articles is signed. The encyclopedia is arranged topically, the articles grouped by subject under six broad headings ("Earth and the Universe," "The Living World," "The World of Ideas," "Sounds and Pictures," "People and Places," and "Science and Technology"), with access to specific information enhanced by an index of 975 entries. The encyclopedia has no cross-references in the text.

EVALUATION

This small item for young readers appeared in 1979 as a new work and has never been revised. The publisher, Purnell & Sons Ltd., is well known in the United Kingdom for its reference publications, such as *Purnell's First Encyclopedia in Colour* and the companion *Purnell's First Encyclopedia of Animals* (both issued in 1974 and now out of print). Editors Theodore Rowland-Entwistle and Jean Cooke, a husband-and-wife team, have produced a number of reference books for children, including the JUNIOR ENCYCLOPEDIA OF GENERAL KNOWLEDGE, (one volume; 100,000 words), which is similar in size, purpose, style, and organization to *Purnell's Pictorial Encyclopedia.*

Obviously, *Purnell's Pictorial Encyclopedia,* with just 88 two-page articles, can provide only very selective coverage of those subjects of potential interest to children and younger students. A seven-line paragraph on Christianity in the article *The Great Religions,* for example, is hardly sufficient for readers at any age. Likewise, sharks are mentioned in *Plants and Animals of the Oceans,* but the reader learns little more than "sharks are big fish." Such topics as adoption, Thomas Jefferson, and sports are completely ignored. On the other hand, some scientific and technical subjects—energy, water, the solar system, lasers, the microscope, plastics, various means of transportation—are covered in reasonable depth, relatively speaking. Information in the encyclopedia is usually reliable, unbiased, and as current as a small children's reference work need be. The writing style is admirably clear, and will be comprehensible to most young people reading at the third grade level and beyond. The following excerpt from the article *Earth's Surface: The Land* is typical of the encyclopedia's style:

> The most violent changes to the Earth's surface are the result of forces inside the Earth, some of which we can see as volcanoes and earthquakes, as described on pages 12–13. Some changes happen comparatively quickly. For example, the southern part of England is slowly sinking, but it will be many thousands of years before it is under the sea.

The contents of *Purnell's Pictorial Encyclopedia* are not easily accessible. Because the text includes no cross-references, access to specific information must be obtained through the index at the back of the book. Unfortunately, the index, which contains only 975 entries, is sadly deficient. For example, Zeus is discussed at some length in the article *Myths and Legends,* but the index has no entry under "Zeus." The subject of television is covered in *Radio and Television* (on pages 80–81) and also in *Sharing Ideas* (on page 73), but the index entry "Television" refers the reader only to page 71, which contains information about myths but not television. Many similar indexing lapses could be cited. Moreover, the illustrations, which make up approximately half of the book's total text, are not indexed at all. The illustrations themselves are mainly black-and-white photographs, although some drawings, diagrams, and reproductions of artwork are also included. Ordinarily, the illustrations add to the informational content of the encyclopedia, but in some instances they are unnecessarily large, as in the case of a full-page photograph of a child playing with clay that is captioned, "Wedging clay is an important preliminary to successful pottery—and it's also great fun." This sort of utilization of space in a 192-page encyclopedia seems both wasteful and capricious. Overall, the illustrations are disappointing.

To Summarize: The one-volume *Purnell's Pictorial Encyclopedia* is a small, inconsequential work for young readers ages seven to fourteen. Produced in Great Britain, the encyclopedia consists of 88 two-page articles that only very selectively cover knowledge and information of potential interest to young people. Other limitations include a dreadfully bad index and, despite the book's title, indifferent illustrations.

In Comparison: *Purnell's Pictorial Encyclopedia,* published in a single volume containing approximately 75,000 words, is a small work for children and younger students. It competes with the JUNIOR ENCYCLOPEDIA OF GENERAL KNOWLEDGE (one volume; 100,000 words), the JUNIOR PEARS ENCYCLOPAEDIA (one volume; 280,000 words), NELSON'S ENCYCLOPEDIA FOR YOUNG READERS (two volumes; 350,000 words), and RAND McNALLY'S CHILDREN'S ENCYCLOPEDIA (one volume; 15,000 words). None of these titles can be enthusiastically recommended, although NELSON'S ENCYCLOPEDIA FOR YOUNG READERS and the JUNIOR PEARS ENCYCLOPAEDIA are the best of the lot. Macmillan, Inc., a leading North American publisher of encyclopedias (COLLIER'S ENCYCLOPEDIA; MERIT STUDENTS ENCYCLOPEDIA), is currently preparing a small-volume encyclopedia for young children and students in the primary grades, but at this time it is far from ready for publication. There is a real need for a substantial one- or two-volume encyclopedia for young people.

To Purchase *Purnell's Pictorial Encyclopedia:* The encyclopedia is sold in North American retail bookstores. If it is not in stock (and it most likely will not be), most bookstores will order it for you. You can also order the book directly from the distributor, Pergamon Press, Inc. In the United States, contact Pergamon at Maxwell House, Fairview Park, Elmsford, NY, 10523 or telephone 914-592-7700; in Canada write to Pergamon Press Canada Ltd., Suite 104, Consumers Road, Willowdale, Ontario M2J 1P9 or telephone 416-497-8337.

No other reviews of *Purnell's Pictorial Encyclopedia* are available at this time.

Quick Reference Handbook of Basic Knowledge

FACTS

The Quick Reference Handbook of Basic Knowledge. Calvin D. Linton and Edward H. Litchfield, Consulting Editors; Elvin Abeles and Robert M. Segal, Updating Editors. Nashville, TN: Royal Publishers, a division of Thomas Nelson, Inc. One volume. Former titles: *Complete Reference Handbook* (1964); *Quick Reference Encyclopedia* (1976). First published as the *Quick Reference Handbook of Basic Knowledge* in 1979; revised encyclopedic edition in 1982. Lowest retail price: $25.40; with discount to schools and libraries: $20.00.

The *Quick Reference Handbook of Basic Knowledge* aims to provide "the kind of information that high-school and college students and the assistants to business executives generally need" (preface). Encyclopedic in scope, the handbook contains 895 pages, approximately 5,000 articles, and 750,000 words. The articles, which include lists, glossaries, sections of long narratives, etc., average 150 words in length (or five articles per page). They are accompanied by about 600 illustrations (almost all in black-and-white), plus nine maps, including an eight-page color world atlas in the center of the book. Some 40 editors and contributors are noted following the title page, although none of the material is signed. The handbook is arranged topically, the contents grouped by subject in 22 sections, or chapters ("The English Language," "Useful Aids for Writing," "Reading Skills," "Authors and Their Works," "World History," "American History," "States and Countries," "Physics," "Chemistry," "Astronomy," "Geology," "Biology," "The New Math," "Algebra," "Geometry," "Trigonometry," "Philosophy and Religion," "Western Art," "Sports," "Four Hundred Famous Americans," "The Business World," and "Colleges and Universities"), with access to specific information enhanced by a detailed table of contents and an index of roughly 1,500 entries. There are no cross-references in the text.

EVALUATION

The 895-page *Quick Reference Handbook,* last published in 1982, is a revised and updated version of the 880-page *Quick Reference Encyclopedia* (1976), which in turn derived from the 720-page *Complete Reference Handbook* (1964). Essentially, all of these titles have similar contents, except that each revision has added some new material. Neither the *Quick Reference Encyclopedia* nor the *Complete Reference Handbook* was well received by the critics. Donald G. Davis, Jr., who reviewed the *Quick Reference Encyclopedia* in *American Reference Books Annual* (1978, p. 54), pointed out that the book "contains little that is not readily available, in both easier-to-use format and more extensive treatments, within commonly found reference works." And *Booklist* (July 1, 1965, p. 1002) found the *Complete Reference Handbook* to be "too brief and too highly selective to be of practical application."

Like its predecessors, the *Quick Reference Handbook* emphasizes detailed information on English language usage, particularly in business writing. In addition, historical and geographical topics receive a fair amount of attention. Unlike the earlier titles, however, the *Quick Reference Handbook* provides extensive coverage of the physical sciences. Long survey articles have been added that cover the rudiments of physics, chemistry, astronomy, geology, biology, and mathematics. As the editors note in their preface, "This edition contains more detailed sections on mathematics and science to enhance the handbook's usefulness and bring it closer to the goal of being a comprehensive study aid." While this statement is true, the book's coverage of basic knowledge and information remains highly selective and badly out-of-balance. For example, the handbook completely neglects whole areas of knowledge, such as health and medicine, economics, sociology and anthropology, the performing arts, and the electronic and computer sciences. The user of the *Quick Reference Handbook* will find nothing, for instance, on abortion, adoption, asbestos, capital punishment, drugs, gambling, robots, and Scientology. Moreover, the coverage that is provided is sometimes questionable, as in the case of the chapter "Four Hundred Famous Americans," which is overloaded with obscure religious leaders. Do such names as Lyman Abbott, Francis Asbury, James Gibbons, Washington Gladden, Carl F.H. Henry, E. Stanley Jones, Adoniram Judson, J. Gresham Machen, and Samuel Seabury really belong in such select company? And why are people like Samuel Barber, Louis Brandeis, Charles Beard, Aaron Copland, Oliver Wendell Holmes, Francis Scott Key, Georgia O'Keefe, Paul Revere, and Earl Warren not included?

Information in the *Quick Reference Handbook* is not always accurate. The article *Detente* in the "World History" section, for example, states that the country of Vietnam was unified in 1973, when actually unification did not occur until 1975. In *Profile of a Superpower Since 1955* in the "American History" section, the 1979–80 Iranian hostage crisis is erroneously described in these terms: "The students held 50 hostages for several months, ignoring the pleas of the United Nations and the new Islamic government of Iran." In *Florida* in the "States and Countries" chapter, the reader learns, again incorrectly, that Florida "has no lieutenant-governor." Many similar examples of factual errors could be cited. Information in the handbook is usually presented in an impartial manner, although most controversial material is ignored, such as abortion and homosexuality. The book's contents are usually current as of the late 1970s or early 1980s. For instance, the latest edition (1982) includes a new article entitled *Assassins and the Presidency* in the "American History" chapter that mentions the attempt on Ronald Reagan's life in 1981.

The handbook's writing style varies considerably from chapter to chapter, the science sections being more advanced than those in other areas. Ordinarily, the text is clearly written and will be comprehensible to adults and older students reading at the junior high school level and beyond. Technical terms are usually printed in **bold type** and defined in context. The initial paragraph of the article *Tectonism* in the "Geology" chapter provides a fair example of the book's style:

> As usually considered, tectonism includes those processes which have resulted in deformation of the earth's crust. Tectonic movements normally occur slowly and imperceptibly over long periods of time. But some—for example, an earthquake—may take place suddenly and violently. In some instances the rocks will move vertically, resulting in uplift or subsidence of the land. They may also move horizontally, or laterally (sidewise), as a result of compression or tension. The two major types of tectonic movements, **epeirogeny** (vertical movements) and **orogeny** (essentially lateral movements) are discussed below.

Access to information in the *Quick Reference Handbook* leaves much to be desired. The handbook lacks cross-references in the text, and the small, 1,500-entry index at the back of the book is not comprehensive. For instance, the material about earthquakes quoted in the preceding paragraph cannot be found through the index under "Earthquakes" because there is no entry under that subject. Likewise, the subject of apartheid is defined and discussed in the article *South Africa* in the "States and Countries" chapter, but there is no index entry under "Apartheid." Illustrations in the handbook are also less than satisfactory. All are in black-and-white, except for handsome color portraits of all the U.S. presidents in the "American History" chapter and a small, eight-plate color atlas of the world in the center of the book (maps by the George F. Cram Company). The black-and-white illustrations tend to be excessively dark and poorly reproduced. In some instances, color is clearly needed, especially in the "Western Art" chapter where, for example, a black-and-white reproduction of Degas' *The Rehearsal* accompanies the article on the Impressionists ("Their main concentration was on the small patches of color that actually made up the painting and on how light and shadow affect color and the reflection of light"). In other instances, the illustrations are poorly placed and captioned.

To Summarize: The desk-sized *Quick Reference Handbook,* an adult work of encyclopedic scope last published in 1982, has little to recommend it to discerning consumers. Specifically, the book's coverage is highly selective and badly out of balance, its contents are not always accurate nor readily accessible, and its illustrations are deficient.

In Comparison: The *Quick Reference Handbook,* published in a single volume containing approximately 750,000 words, is an encyclopedic work for adults and older students. It cannot compare with the leading one- and two-volume general adult encyclopedias currently available, namely the LINCOLN LIBRARY OF ESSENTIAL INFORMATION (two volumes; 3.5 million words), the NEW COLUMBIA ENCYCLOPEDIA (one volume; 6.6 million words), the RANDOM HOUSE ENCY-

CLOPEDIA (one volume; 3 million words), and the VOLUME LIBRARY (two volumes; 3.5 million words). All of these encyclopedias, as the figures indicate, offer much more information than the *Quick Reference Handbook*. Also, they are much more expensive. More in the handbook's league are COLLINS GEM ENCYCLOPEDIA (two volumes; 450,000 words), the CONCISE COLUMBIA ENCYCLOPEDIA (one volume; one million words), the KNOWLEDGE ENCYCLOPEDIA (one volume; 300,000 words), and PEARS CYCLOPAEDIA (one volume; 1.3 million words). Among these small desk-sized general encyclopedias for adults, the CONCISE COLUMBIA ENCYCLOPEDIA is the standout choice for U.S. and Canadian consumers. In the final analysis, the *Quick Reference Handbook* is an inferior work that should be avoided.

To Purchase the *Quick Reference Handbook of Basic Knowledge:* The handbook is sold in North American retail bookstores. If it is not in stock, most bookstores will order it for you. You can also order the book directly from the publisher, Thomas Nelson Publishers, at P.O. Box 946, 407 Seventh Avenue South, Nashville, TN 37203 or telephone 615-889-9000.

No other reviews of the *Quick Reference Handbook of Basic Knowledge* are available at this time. Interested consumers might, however, want to consult these reviews of earlier versions of the handbook: *American Reference Books Annual,* 1978, p. 54 (review by Donald G. Davis, Jr., of the *Quick Reference Encyclopedia*); *Booklist* July 1, 1965, pp. 1001–03 (unsigned review of the *Complete Reference Handbook*).

Rand McNally's Children's Encyclopedia

FACTS

Rand McNally's Children's Encyclopedia. Published abroad as *Ward Lock's Children's Encyclopedia.* John Paton, Editor. Chicago: Rand McNally & Company. Copyright by Grisewood & Dempsey Ltd. of London, England. One volume. First edition published in 1976. Lowest retail price: $4.95.

Rand McNally's Children's Encyclopedia is a small, one-volume item for children ages seven to twelve. The encyclopedia contains 61 pages, 27 articles, and approximately 15,000 words. The articles, which are of the broad-entry type, average 500 words in length (or two full pages). They are accompanied by 300 illustrations (all in color). There are no maps in the book. Aside from the editor, no editorial staff or contributors are identified, nor are the articles signed. The encyclopedia is arranged topically, the articles grouped by subject under five broad headings ("Our Wonderful World," "Wonders of Life," "Around the World," "The Story of Man," and "Here, There and Everywhere"), with access to specific information enhanced by an index of 350 entries. There are no cross-references in the text.

EVALUATION

Rand McNally's Children's Encyclopedia first appeared in Great Britain in 1976 as *Ward Lock's Children's Encyclopedia,* and the following year Rand McNally & Company brought out a North American edition (the only change being the title). The encyclopedia's editor, John Paton, has produced other reference works for young people, including the ten-volume FINDING OUT: SILVER BURDETT'S CHILDREN'S ENCYCLOPEDIA and the one-volume KNOWLEDGE ENCYCLOPEDIA, both of which were also originally published in Great Britain by Grisewood & Dempsey Ltd. The 61-page *Rand McNally's Children's Encyclopedia* obviously offers very limited coverage of knowledge and information of potential interest to children and younger students. Most of the book's 27 two-page articles deal with scientific and technical topics, such as plant and animal life, the human body, food and agriculture, mountains and forests, and the solar system. On the other hand, such large subjects as the countries of the world, famous people living or dead, sports and games, music, religion, and the visual and performing arts are not covered at all. Moreover, some topics that are covered receive very superficial treatment, a criticism noted in Marion Amdursky's review of the book in *American Reference Books Annual* (1978, p. 40): "Occasionally the material is oversimplified. For example, cacti are described and included in a picture, but are never identified further than as 'desert plants.'" As an encyclopedia, this little work is of negligible value, but it can be useful as a browsing item for inquisitive young readers, especially those with a penchant for science.

Information in *Rand McNally's Children's Encyclopedia* is factually reliable and impartially presented, although controversial or sensitive subject matter is rarely encountered. The encyclopedia's contents are as current as they need to be, given the book's size and intended readership. The writing style is clear and simple enough that most elementary school students will have little difficulty comprehending the text. Access to the encyclopedia's contents is reasonably good, due to the index at the back of the book and a table of contents at the front that lists all 27 articles. Illustrations in the encyclopedia account for roughly half of the total text. All in color and usually informative, the illustrations are quite similar to those found in several other British-made encyclopedias for children, namely FINDING OUT: SILVER BURDETT'S CHILDREN'S ENCYCLOPEDIA, HARVER JUNIOR WORLD ENCYCLOPEDIA, the JUNIOR ENCYCLOPEDIA OF GENERAL KNOWLEDGE, and PURNELL'S PICTORIAL ENCYCLOPEDIA .

To Summarize: The very small, 61-page *Rand McNally's Children's Encyclopedia* first appeared in Great Britain in 1976 under the title *Ward Lock's Children's Encyclopedia,* and a year later Rand McNally & Company issued it in North America. The book's contents, which emphasize scientific and technical subjects, are much too limited in scope to be considered truly encyclopedic, and what coverage there is tends to be superficial. In short, the book has little real reference value.

In Comparison: *Rand McNally's Children's Encyclopedia,* published in a single volume containing approximately 15,000 words, is a small item for children ages seven to twelve. It competes with the JUNIOR ENCYCLOPEDIA OF GENERAL KNOWLEDGE (one volume; 100,000 words), the JUNIOR PEARS ENCYCLOPAEDIA (one volume; 280,000 words), NELSON'S ENCYCLOPEDIA FOR YOUNG READERS (two volumes; 350,000 words), and PURNELL'S PICTORIAL ENCYCLOPEDIA (one volume; 75,000 words). None of these titles can be enthusiastically recommended, although NELSON'S ENCYCLOPEDIA FOR YOUNG READERS and the JUNIOR PEARS ENCYCLOPAEDIA are the best of the lot. Macmillan, Inc., a leading North American publisher of encyclopedias (COLLIER'S ENCYCLOPEDIA; MERIT STUDENTS ENCYCLOPEDIA), is currently preparing a small-volume encyclopedia for young children and students in the primary grades, but at this time it is far from ready for publication. There is a real need for a substantial one- or two-volume encyclopedia for young people.

To Purchase *Rand McNally's Children's Encyclopedia:* The book is sold in North American retail bookstores. If it is not in stock (and it may well not be), most bookstores will order it for you. You can also order the book directly from the publisher, Rand McNally & Company, at P.O. Box 7600, Chicago, IL 60680 or telephone 312-673-9100.

For More Information about *Rand McNally's Children's Encyclopedia* See: *American Reference Books Annual,* 1978, p. 40 (review by Marion Amdursky).

Random House Encyclopedia

FACTS

The Random House Encyclopedia. Published abroad as the *Joy of Knowledge* (ten volumes). Jess Stein and Stuart B. Flexner, Editorial Directors; James Mitchell, Editor in Chief. New York: Random House, Inc. One volume. New revised (second) edition published in 1983. Lowest retail price: $99.95; standard discount to schools and libraries.

The *Random House Encyclopedia,* a single-volume reference work "primarily for teenagers and adults," intends to be "a 'family bible' of knowledge for our times" (preface). The encyclopedia contains 2,918 pages, approximately 26,000 articles, and 3 million words. The articles appear in two different and quite distinct parts of the encyclopedia: the 1,792-page *Colorpedia,* which comprises 875 copiously illustrated two-page articles, and the 884-page *Alphapedia,* which includes more than 25,000 short-entry articles (about 30 per page). Between the *Colorpedia* and *Alphapedia* is a 48-page time chart showing major historical events from 4000 B.C. through 1982. The articles in the *Colorpedia* are accompanied by some 11,000 illustrations (almost all in color), plus 250 thematic maps; the *Alphapedia* has 1,150 illustrations (all in black-and-white), plus 150 locator maps. In addition, the *Alphapedia* is followed by a nine-page section on flags of the world and an 80-page color world atlas.

Nearly 600 editors, designers, and contributors are noted at the front of the volume. However, except for introductory essays in the *Colorpedia,* none of the material is signed. The *Colorpedia* is arranged topically, the two-page articles grouped by subject under seven broad headings ("The Universe," "The Earth," "Life on Earth," "Man," "History and Culture," "Man and Science," and "Man and Machines"), with access to specific information enhanced by (1) a detailed table of contents that lists all 875 articles in the *Colorpedia,* (2) numerous cross-references—called "connections"—at the beginning of articles in the *Colorpedia,* and (3) roughly 35,000 cross-references and index entries in the *Alphapedia* that refer to articles in the *Colorpedia.* The *Alphapedia,* which consists of both short factual articles and references to the *Colorpedia,* is arranged alphabetically letter by letter (*Newspapers* precedes *New York*), with access to specific information enhanced by 10,000 *See also* references in the text. There are no references from the *Colorpedia* to the *Alphapedia.* Finally, the world atlas at the back of the book has an index of more than 21,000 place-names.

EVALUATION

The *Random House Encyclopedia,* first published in 1977 and revised in 1983, was conceived in Great Britain by James Mitchell and the late John Beazley, both experienced makers of reference books and cofounders of Mitchell Beazley Publishers Ltd., which developed and produced the encyclopedia at an estimated cost of $7 million. The encyclopedia has appeared in a number of national editions around the world, including the ten-volume *Joy of Knowledge* in Great Britain and the single-volume *Random House Encyclopedia* in North America. James Mitchell elaborates on this coproduction activity in his preface to the revised (1983) edition: "Six years have passed since the first publication of *The Random House Encyclopedia* in North America and during those years the work has been published (or arrangements for publication have been concluded) in no less than 27 editions in 22 languages around the world. No other popular family encyclopedia has ever achieved such universal acceptance. One day the Encyclopedia is to appear in the People's Republic of China, and certain volumes are being published in the Soviet Union." Many prominent people have been involved in the production of the *Random House Encyclopedia.* In addition to Mitchell, who continues as editor in chief, and Beazley, the late Jess Stein served as editorial director for the first (1977) edition. Stein was for many years head of Random House's reference department, which publishes, among other works, an excellent line of dictionaries. Editorial director for the revised edition is Stuart Flexner, Stein's successor at Random House and a distinguished lexicographer. Philip Goetz, editor in chief of the NEW ENCYCLOPAEDIA BRITANNICA, has acted as a consulting editor. Among the nearly 500 contributors are many academicians, mostly British, including such well-known figures as H.J. Eysenck, Kenneth Katzner, Patrick Moore, and Geoffrey Parrinder.

The encyclopedia's coverage is quite broad, though, as might be expected in a single-volume work, not especially deep. Edmund SantaVicca, reviewing the revised edition in *American Reference Books Annual* (1984, p. 22), puts it well: "The basic strength of *The Random House Encyclopedia* continues to be the breadth of information presented. The editors have tapped some of the great intellects of our times to present the reader with succinct, adequate, and—in most cases—reliable information." Coverage in the larger *Colorpedia* tends to be most expansive in those areas that lend themselves to visual treatment, such as the fine arts and the natural, technical, and medical sciences. On the other hand, coverage is less impressive in those areas not customarily enhanced by pictorial illustration, such as literature, philosophy, religion, political science, and sociology. For example, computers, earthquakes, and the human body are subjects best described using both words and pictures, whereas explanations of, say, capital punishment, poetry, socialism, or existentialism are not particularly improved or clarified by visual representation. Hence, the encyclopedia includes no less than four two-page spreads in the *Colorpedia* on amphibians and reptiles, replete with informative drawings showing various species, whereas the subject of adoption is relegated to a cursory, eight-line article in the *Alphapedia*. The *Alphapedia* itself briefly covers important people, places, things, and events. For instance, there is a seven-line article on the Falkland Islands, as well as a longer, 20-line article entitled *Falklands War*.

Information in the *Random House Encyclopedia* is normally accurate, although in the first printing of the revised edition all 21,000 page references in the index to the world atlas in the back of the book were incorrect, each off by 62 pages. However, this editorial gaffe has been corrected in subsequent printings. Ordinarily, information in the encyclopedia is presented in an objective matter. In his preface to the first edition, James Mitchell states, "We have done our best to be as balanced as we can; where there is controversy we have tried to present both sides of a case; where there is uncertainty our contributors have been encouraged to say so; where there are questions we have asked them." The article *Abortion* in the *Alphapedia,* for instance, provides impartial treatment of this sensitive issue: "Many religions have condemned induced abortion but it became illegal in practice only in the 19th century. Efforts to legalize abortion have increased in response to the rapid expansion of world population, pressure from women's rights movements, and a high maternal death rate from illegal abortions. Many states of the United States liberalized their laws, but opponents continue to press for prohibition by constitutional amendment." In addition, at the end of the article there are two cross-references to *Colorpedia* articles—*Birth Control* and *Questions of Life and Death*—that place the subject of abortion in a larger context. As already noted, the encyclopedia, originally published in 1977, appeared in a revised and updated second edition in 1983. As a result, its contents are usually current through the early 1980s, as the aforementioned article on the war over the Falkland Islands indicates.

The encyclopedia's writing style is typically clear, direct, and simple enough for adults and older students who are reading at the junior high school level and up. James Mitchell notes in his preface to the first edition, "The ability to make even complicated subjects clear, to distill, to extract the principles from behind the complicated formulas, the gift of getting to the heart of things: these are the elements that make popular encyclopedias really useful to the people who read them. We have done our best to follow these principles."

The article *Earthquakes* in the *Colorpedia,* for example, begins this way:

> An earthquake at the Earth's surface is the sudden release of energy in the form of vibrations and tremors caused by compressed or stretched rock snapping along a fault in the Earth's surface. Rising lava under a volcano can also produce small tremors. It has been estimated that about a million earthquakes occur each year, but most of these are so minor that they pass unnoticed. The cause of deep earthquakes—those as much as 450 miles (700km) below the surface—is not known.
>
> Slippage along a fault is initially prevented by friction along the fault plane. This causes energy, which generates movement, to be stored up as elastic strain; a similar effect is created when a bow is drawn. Eventually the strain reaches a critical point, the friction is overcome, and the rocks snap past each other, releasing the stored energy in the form of earthquakes by vibrating back and forth. Earthquakes can also occur when rock folds that can no longer support the elastic strain break to form a fault. The point on the Earth's surface immediately above the source of the original disturbance is known as the epicenter [5], while the actual point of fracture within the Earth is known as the focus.

Note that the word *epicenter* in the final sentence above is followed by the number [5] in brackets. This reference alerts the reader to see illustration number 5 in the two-page layout, which visually depicts and further explains the epicenter.

The contents of the *Random House Encyclopedia* are reasonably accessible. As previously pointed out, the *Alphapedia* furnishes some 35,000 cross-references and index entries to the larger *Colorpedia,* as well as the time chart that follows it. For example, the brief article *Earthquake* in the *Alphapedia* concludes with five references to the *Colorpedia* that lead the reader to such two-page articles as *Earthquakes* (quoted from in the preceding paragraph), *Global Tectonics, Folds and Faults,* and *Early Oriental and Western Science,* and one reference to the time chart (where the reader learns that Lisbon was destroyed by an earthquake in 1755). In addition, cross-references (called "connections") at the beginning of each article in the *Colorpedia* guide the reader to related articles in the *Colorpedia.* In the case of the article *Earthquakes,* the connections are to *Anatomy of the Earth, Folds and Faults,* and *Volcanoes.* There are no cross-references from the *Colorpedia* to the *Alphapedia,* but the *Alphapedia* does include approximately 10,000 *See also* references within its text. For example, the *Alphapedia* article *Earthquake* provides a *See also* reference to the article *Seismology* (also in the *Alphapedia*). If all of this sounds complicated, it is. In the final analysis, the *Random House Encyclopedia* is not as simple to use or understand as an encyclopedia arranged in straight A-to-Z fashion. But the encyclopedia's elaborate system of cross-references and other finding devices does get the reader to the desired article or information most of the time.

The illustrations, which constitute about 40 percent of the total text, add enormously to the encyclopedia's informational content, especially in the *Colorpedia*. In his preface to the first edition, James Mitchell explains the editorial philosophy behind the illustrations in the *Random House Encyclopedia:* "The diagrams and pictures in this encyclopedia—there are more than 13,800 of them—took six years to research and make, and the information that they provide is intended to be more concise, simpler, and easier to learn from than that contained in traditional works. For a new generation brought up with television, words alone are no longer enough, and so in our *Colorpedia* section we have tried to make a new type of compact pictorial encyclopedia for a visually oriented age." Indeed, this is the first encyclopedia in which illustrations are as vital informationally as the written text. And, as seen in the excerpt from the article *Earthquakes* above, pictorial matter in the *Colorpedia* is directly related to the printed word by means of numbered references in brackets. The *Colorpedia* portion of the *Random House Encyclopedia* is simply stunning in terms of both visual quality and informational content. Also noteworthy is the great amount of hard factual information that is conveyed in picture captions. The encyclopedia is also very well mapped, including an 80-page color world atlas at the back of the book (maps by Rand McNally) and outstanding historical and thematic maps throughout the *Colorpedia*. Overall, the *Random House Encyclopedia* ranks with the best illustrated general encyclopedias currently on the market, such as the ACADEMIC AMERICAN ENCYCLOPEDIA, the NEW CAXTON ENCYCLOPEDIA, and the WORLD BOOK ENCYCLOPEDIA.

As far as its physical format goes, the encyclopedia is both well made and aesthetically appealing, although Harry Whitmore, in his review of the revised edition in *Library Journal* (April 1, 1984, p. 714), makes two important criticisms: "Type may be uncomfortably small for some readers, as will many of the color prints. The size of the volume makes it difficult to handle." Concerning the last point, consumers should be aware that the volume is quite heavy (nearly 12 pounds) and bulky (4 inches thick), and that it will require a stand or tabletop for easy consultation.

Critical reaction to the first edition of the *Random House Encyclopedia* (1977) was plentiful and mixed. Because Random House is a major North American trade publisher, the encyclopedia received reviews in publications that normally ignore reference works, such as *Time* and *Newsweek.* Comments on the colorful and innovative encyclopedia ran the gamut from unreserved praise ("a splendid attempt to summarize modern knowledge in one convenient volume," enthused *Business Week,* October 3, 1977, p. 13) to unbridled hostility ("a sad, gaudy book," lamented Walter Clemons in *Newsweek,* October 10, 1977, p. 105). *Harper's* magazine (December 1977, pp. 102–07) ran a long, vituperative attack on the encyclopedia by Hugh Kenner entitled "Images at Random," but *Time* magazine (October 10, 1977, p. 106) reported that "the book changes browsers into learners. Whatever its flaws, the *R.H.E.* is a welcome invitation not only to the mind's eye but also to the eye's mind." Criticism of the 1983 revision has been less abundant, more temperate, and mostly limited to the professional reference book review literature. For example, the aforementioned review by Harry Whitmore in *Library Journal* (April 1, 1984, p. 714) concludes, "Like its predecessor, this can be recommended with the caveat that some readers will be better served by more traditional encyclopedias." James Rettig, in *Wilson Library Bulletin* (March 1984, p. 518), notes that when first published, "no other encyclopedia offered comparable color illustration. Since then the *Academic American* ... has deprived *Random House* of that exclusive claim. This, plus the fact that libraries have a variety of other ready-reference fact sources, diminishes libraries' need for the *Random House Encyclopedia*." And Edmund SantaVicca, in *American Reference Books Annual* (1984, p. 23), points out, "Of the one-volume encyclopedias on the market, *The Random House Encyclopedia* continues to have greater pictorial appeal than many of its competitors."

To Summarize: First published in 1977 and revised in 1983, the *Random House Encyclopedia* is a large (nearly 12 pounds), single-volume work for adults and older students. Heavily illustrated, it aims to serve "a new generation brought up with television" (preface). Indeed, the *Colorpedia,* the encyclopedia's largest section, succeeds in integrating words and pictures in a way that has never been attempted before. In addition, the encyclopedia is authoritative, objective, reasonably current, and easy to comprehend. On the minus side, the encyclopedia's complex organization and elaborate system of cross-references might be confusing or forbidding to some readers.

In Comparison: The *Random House Encyclopedia,* published in one volume containing approximately 3 million words, competes directly with several other substantial small-volume encyclopedias in the adult and older student category, namely, the LINCOLN LIBRARY OF ESSENTIAL INFORMATION (two volumes; 3.5 million words), the NEW COLUMBIA ENCYCLOPEDIA (one volume; 6.6 million words), and the VOLUME LIBRARY (two volumes; 3.5 million words). Also to be reckoned with in this category is the smaller CONCISE COLUMBIA ENCYCLOPEDIA (one volume; one million words), a recently published abridgment of the NEW COLUMBIA ENCYCLOPEDIA. Among these titles, the *Random House Encyclopedia* and the NEW COLUMBIA ENCYCLOPEDIA represent the best buys, along with the CONCISE COLUMBIA ENCYCLOPEDIA if a smaller (and less expensive) work will suffice. Note that the two best single-volume general encyclopedias—the NEW COLUMBIA ENCYCLOPEDIA and the *Random House Encyclopedia*—are as different as can be. The NEW COLUMBIA is a scholarly, alphabetically arranged work with comparatively few illustrations and an almost totally black-and-white look about it, whereas the *Random House* is a popularly written, topically arranged volume with numerous illustrations and a bright, visually inviting appearance.

To Purchase the *Random House Encyclopedia:* If you are an individual consumer and wish to buy the encyclopedia, first check with the retail bookstores in your area. If the encyclopedia is not in stock and no store will order it for you, you can acquire the encyclopedia directly from the publisher by contacting Random House, Inc. at 201 East 50th Street, New York, NY 10022 or telephone 212-751-2600. If you are ordering the encyclopedia for a school or library, place the order with your local book wholesaler. Note that the special two-volume school and library edition of the encyclopedia published by Encyclopaedia Britannica Educational Corporation in 1977 has been discontinued.

For More Information about the *Random House Encyclopedia* See: *American Reference Books Annual,* 1984, pp. 22–23 (review by Edmund F. SantaVicca); *Booklist,* July 1984, p. 1536 (unsigned review); *Introduction to Reference Work* by William A. Katz (4th ed., New York: McGraw-Hill, 1982), vol. 1: *Basic Information Sources,* pp. 194–96; *Library Journal,* April 1, 1984, p. 714 (review by Harry E. Whitmore); *Wilson Library Bulletin,* March 1984, p. 518 (review by James Rettig).

University Desk Encyclopedia

FACTS

The University Desk Encyclopedia. Also published in North America as the *Concord Desk Encyclopedia* (three volumes; 1981). Herman Friedhoff and Ben Lenthall, Editors in Chief. New York: E.P. Dutton, Inc. Copyright by Elsevier Publishing Projects. One volume. First edition published in 1977; out of print since 1981 (last priced at $69.95).

The *University Desk Encyclopedia,* a single-volume work for adults and older students, created abroad for North American consumption, "has condensed for you the vital facts from every field of knowledge with special emphasis on relevance for today and therefore a lot of space on science and technology" (editors' introduction). Now out of print, *University Desk* will be found in many libraries and may also be encountered on the secondhand and remainder book markets. The encyclopedia contains 1,055 pages, approximately 25,000 articles, and 2 million words. The articles, all but 46 of which are very brief, average 80 words in length (or about 25 articles per page). They are accompanied by some 3,000 illustrations (all in color), plus 350 maps. More than 250 editors, advisers, consultants, and contributors are listed at the front of the volume. None of the material is signed, although author credits for 46 feature articles are given. The encyclopedia is arranged alphabetically letter by letter (*Newspaper* precedes *New York*), with access to specific information enhanced by nearly 35,000 cross-references in the text. There is no index.

EVALUATION

University Desk, published in early 1977, has never been revised and, as already noted, is currently out of print. The encyclopedia was produced abroad by the Elsevier Publishing Company, a major publisher in the Netherlands. Actually, much of the encyclopedia's text and illustrative matter derives from Elsevier's heavily illustrated *Grote Winkler Prins,* (see Appendix C) a standard Dutch general encyclopedia in 20 volumes. *University Desk* was published in North America by E.P. Dutton, Inc., then owned by Elsevier. In 1981, Time, Inc. published a modified version of the encyclopedia under the title *Concord Desk Encyclopedia.* Marketed exclusively as a premium for new subscribers to *Time* magazine, the *Concord Desk Encyclopedia* appeared in a three-volume paperbound boxed set that added some material to the original work, including a world atlas section.

Coverage in *University Desk* is fairly well balanced, although biographical, geographical, and scientific topics predominate. Plant and animal life, chemical elements and compounds, and natural phenomena are particularly well covered. But while the coverage is broad it usually lacks depth. With the exception of 46 long essays (which average 1,000–2,000 words, or a page or more), articles in the encyclopedia tend to be little more than dictionary-style definitions. For example, the 250-word article *Supreme Court* neither explains how the court operates nor lists prominent justices, past or present. The encyclopedia can also be faulted for occasional factual and typographical errors, lack of bibliographies, and an uneven writing style. On this last point, the encyclopedia's text is usually clear, concise, and dry, but articles on scientific subjects are often too difficult for the average adult reader. A reviewer in *Booklist* (September 15, 1978, p. 250) put it this way: "Technical entries are written for the expert and are incomprehensible even to the educated layperson." Other weaknesses include some poorly placed illustrations, out-of-date information, and the fact that 46 feature articles (on such subjects as American Indians, contemporary China, consumer protection, pollution, and heart surgery) are not accessible via the encyclopedia's cross-reference system. On the positive side, the illustrations, which include colorful photographs, reproductions of artwork, diagrams, line drawings, and the like, are normally informative and appealing, though they are not on par with those found in the RANDOM HOUSE ENCYCLOPEDIA.

To Summarize: *University Desk,* first published in 1977 and now out of print (at least for the time being), is a mediocre single-volume encyclopedia for adults and older students. Its most glaring limitation is superficial treatment of most subjects covered, but it can also be faulted for lapses in accuracy, an uneven writing style, lack of current information, lack of bibliographies, and poor accessibility of certain material. Only the encyclopedia's illustrations are a plus. *University Desk* has also appeared in a modified version entitled the *Concord Desk Encyclopedia,* a three-volume set published in 1981 by Time, Inc., as a premium for new subscribers to *Time* magazine.

In Comparison: During the relatively few years that it was on the market, *University Desk* competed directly with the leading small-volume adult general encyclopedias, namely, the LINCOLN LIBRARY OF ESSENTIAL INFORMATION, the NEW COLUMBIA ENCYCLOPEDIA, the RANDOM HOUSE ENCYCLOPEDIA, and the VOLUME LIBRARY. Today, these works are still available, along with an attractive newcomer, the CONCISE COLUMBIA ENCYCLOPEDIA, whereas *University Desk,* a badly flawed work, is out of print.

For More Information about the *University Desk Encyclopedia* See: *American Reference Books Annual,* 1978, pp. 42–43 (review by Frances Neel Cheney); *Booklist,* September 15, 1978, pp. 249–51 (unsigned review); *Choice,* April 1979, p. 208 (unsigned review), *Library Journal,* June 1, 1977, p. 1267 (review by John D. Campbell); *New York Times Book Review,* October 2, 1977, p. 18 (review by Raymond A. Sokolov); *Wilson Library Bulletin,* September 1977, p. 93 (review by Charles A. Bunge).

Volume Library

FACTS

The Volume Library: A Modern, Authoritative Reference for Home and School Use. Nashville, TN: The Southwestern Company. Two volumes. Former titles: *Cowles Comprehensive Encyclopedia: the Volume Library* (1963–67); *Cowles Volume Library* (1968–69). Published as the *Volume Library* between 1911 and 1962 and since 1970; new printing with revisions every two or three years (most recently in 1985). Lowest retail price: $109.95 delivered.

The *Volume Library* is intended for "the average well-informed person—the student, the businessman or woman whose job requires instant access to information, the adult who needs a convenient reference book on his home bookshelf, the parents who want to keep up with the developments and subjects their children are studying in school" (preface). The two-volume encyclopedia contains approximately 2,650 pages, 8,500 articles, and 3.5 million words. The articles, many of which are of the broad-entry type, average roughly 400 words in length (or one-third of a page). They are accompanied by some 2,000 illustrations (most in black-and-white), plus 200 maps, including a 64-page color world atlas at the end of Volume 2. Nearly 300 editors, advisers, and contributors are noted at the beginning of Volume 1. About 75 percent of the articles are signed. The encyclopedia is arranged topically, the contents grouped by subject in 25 alphabetical sections, or "volumes" ("Animals," "Arts," "Biography," "Careers," "Child Development," "Earth Sciences," "Economics and Business," "Education," "Food and Agriculture," "Geography," "Government and Law," "Health," "History," "Industry and Technology," "Language and Grammar," "Literature," "Mathematics," "Philosophy and Religion," "Plants," "Recreation," "Science," "Social Science," "United States," "World," and "Atlas"), with access to specific information enhanced by (1) a detailed table of contents, (2) some 500 cross-references in the text, and (3) an index of almost 50,000 entries.

EVALUATION

The *Volume Library,* the oldest small-volume encyclopedia of North American origin still on the market, has been continuously published for three-quarters of a century. It first appeared in 1911 under the imprint of the W.E. Richardson Company of Chicago. In the early 1960s, Cowles Communications, Inc. acquired the work, revising and retitling it *Cowles Comprehensive Encyclopedia: the Volume Library* (1963–67). Later the title was shortened to *Cowles Volume Library* (1968–69), and when the Southwestern Company of Nashville obtained the rights to the work in 1970, it reverted to its original title. Interestingly, the *Volume Library*'s first editor, Henry Woldmar Ruoff, also produced a single-volume reference publication entitled the *Standard Dictionary of Facts* (1908–27), which eventually served as the basis for the LINCOLN LIBRARY OF ESSENTIAL INFORMATION, a two-volume encyclopedia that closely resembles the *Volume Library* in purpose, scope, arrangement, format, and intended usership. Despite its longevity, the *Volume Library* has never been considered a first-class encyclopedia by critics, librarians, and others who seriously know and use reference materials. Nevertheless, the *Volume Library* continues to do well in the marketplace, particularly with the door-to-door trade, and in 1985 it expanded from one to two volumes.

The encyclopedia's coverage is broad but uneven and often superficial. Biographical, geographical, and scientific and technical subjects are covered most fully, while social issues and the arts and humanities receive comparatively less attention. For example, the *Volume Library* provides little or no information on such topics as abortion, acquired immune deficiency syndrome (AIDS), adoption, apartheid, birth control, capital punishment, circumcision, drug abuse, health insurance and health maintenance organizations (HMOs), homosexuality, American Indians, and Scientology. Moreover, the encyclopedia's scope is frequently limited to developments in the United States, as in the case of the "Education" section. Even "Geography" lacks information about the Canadian provinces, which, incredibly, are not described anywhere in the set. On the other hand, one of the best features of the *Volume Library* is its numerous charts and tables. The chapter "Economics and Business," for instance, furnishes much useful information in tabular form. In addition, many chapters include glossaries of specialized terminology.

Information in the *Volume Library* unfortunately is not always accurate, although some of the worst errors have been corrected in recent printings. There is also considerable evidence of careless editing. A reviewer in *Booklist* (January 1, 1979, p. 771) bluntly observes, "Numerous errors have been found in this encyclopedia. For example, geological era dates are not consistent with periods cited elsewhere. Mesons, contrary to the text, do not always have a mass that 'lies between that of the electron and that of the proton,' and the valences given for molybdenum, neodymium, and nobelium are incomplete.... While the error rate seemed lowest in mathematics, biographies, agriculture, and geography, the number of inaccurate statements found elsewhere is beyond an acceptable level." The encyclopedia usually presents its material in an impartial manner, although as already noted most controversial subjects are superficially treated or ignored altogether. Sometimes, however, political and business coverage reflects a conservative bias. For example, the definition of communism in the glossary of the "Government and Law" section states, "Communism, of which Soviet Russia is a present-day exponent, aims at world-wide revolution ... Today ideological [sic] differences have produced a serious rift between these two totalitarian regimes, and the monolithic character of international communism has been disrupted for the time being at least." In addition, the *Volume Library* continues to use sexist language, the article *Sociology* in the "Social Science" chapter, for instance, informing the reader that "every man is born into a group of men and throughout his life will belong to many groups." Likewise, illustrations in the encyclopedia tend to perpetuate sex stereotypes (physicians are always male, nurses female, etc.).

Over the years, the *Volume Library* has been justifiably criticized for being out-of-date in many areas. Efforts have been made recently, however, to improve the situation. Specifically, the 1985 revision was undertaken on a contractual basis by the Hudson Group, Inc., a Pleasantville, New York, firm that specializes in editorial consulting, designing, and production. Under the direction of Gorton Carruth, an experienced reference book editor, the Hudson Group thoroughly overhauled the encyclopedia, so that today it is reasonably current, although there are still areas that need work. Moreover, the contents of the set, which were expanded to two volumes in 1985, are now on computer tape, meaning that future revisions should be easier and more efficient.

The encyclopedia's writing style varies considerably from section to section. Ordinarily, the text will be comprehensible to adults and students reading at the high school level, but in some instances articles may be too difficult for average readers. A review in *Booklist* (January 1, 1979, p. 772) correctly points out, "There are plentiful instances where the language roams beyond that which is understandable to the typical high school student. While the writing in science and mathematics is uncompromisingly adult, other sections employ expository techniques, such as rhetorical questions, that are more appropriate for the textbook than for an encyclopedia." The contents of the *Volume Library* are fairly accessible, due in large part to the substantial index at the back of Volume 1. Regrettably, there are relatively few cross-references in the text.

Illustrations in the encyclopedia, which are 95 percent black-and-white, tend to be dull, drab, and poorly reproduced. Also, many of the photographs bespeak another era. Color plates appear occasionally, but they add little to the informational value of the set. For example, "Recreation" includes eight pages of glossy but fuzzy color photographs of the postcard variety, courtesy of various tourist bureaus. The physical format is satisfactory, although there is a decidedly antique look about the type and page layout. As previously indicated, the work is now in two volumes, a move made, according to a spokesperson for the publisher, "so the book won't split down the spine anymore."

To Summarize: The *Volume Library,* recently expanded from one to two volumes, is the oldest continuously published small-volume general encyclopedia on the North American market, first appearing in 1911 and still going strong. Intended for adults and older students, the set's quality is not as impressive as its age. Specifically, the *Volume Library* provides uneven and superficial coverage in many areas and its text is sometimes inaccurate and carelessly edited, biased in favor of conservative views, and unevenly written. In addition, its illustrations are poor and the format is old-fashioned in appearance.

In Comparison: The *Volume Library,* published in two volumes containing approximately 3.5 million words, is a small encyclopedia for adults and students at the secondary school and college levels. It compares directly with three other substantial small-volume adult encyclopedias, namely, the LINCOLN LIBRARY OF ESSENTIAL INFORMATION (two volumes; 3.5 million words), the NEW COLUMBIA ENCYCLOPEDIA (one volume; 6.6 million words), and the RANDOM HOUSE ENCYCLOPEDIA (one volume; 3 million words). Also to be reckoned with in this category is the smaller CONCISE COLUMBIA ENCYCLOPEDIA (one volume; 1 million words), a recently published abridgment of the NEW COLUMBIA ENCYCLOPEDIA. Among these titles, the NEW COLUMBIA ENCYCLOPEDIA and the RANDOM HOUSE ENCYCLOPEDIA represent the best buys, along with the CONCISE COLUMBIA ENCYCLOPEDIA if a smaller (and less expensive) work will suffice. The *Volume Library,* on the other hand, has very little to offer the wise consumer, comparatively speaking. Note also that the *Volume Library* costs more than the NEW COLUMBIA ENCYCLOPEDIA or the RANDOM HOUSE ENCYCLOPEDIA .

To Purchase the *Volume Library:* If you are an individual consumer and wish to buy the encyclopedia, first check with the retail bookstores in your area. If the encyclopedia is not in stock and no store will order it for you, you can purchase the set directly from the publisher by contacting the Southwestern Company at Box 810, Nashville, TN 37202 or telephone 615-790-4000. If you are ordering the encyclopedia for a school or library, place the order with your local book wholesaler. Note that the publisher does not extend a discount to schools and libraries.

For More Information about the *Volume Library* **See:** *Booklist,* January 1, 1979, pp. 771–72 (unsigned review).

World Book Encyclopedia

FACTS

The World Book Encyclopedia. William H. Nault, Publisher; Robert O. Zeleny, Editor in Chief; A. Richard Harmet, Executive Editor. Chicago: World Book, Inc. 22 volumes. First edition published in 1917; new printing with revisions each year. Lowest retail price: $499.00 plus $29.00 shipping and handling; with discount to schools and libraries: $462.00 delivered.

The *World Book Encyclopedia,* the best-selling encyclopedia in North America, is designed "especially to meet the reference and study needs of students in elementary school, junior high school, and high school. *World Book* also serves as a general family reference tool" (preface). The 22-volume encyclopedia contains approximately 14,000 pages, 18,300 articles, and 10 million words. The articles, most of which are of the specific-entry type, average 550 words in length (or about three-quarters of a page). They are accompanied by some 29,500 illustrations (50 percent in color), plus 2,350 maps. Well over 3,000 editors, contributors, advisers, and consultants are identified at the front of Volume 1. All but a few of the articles are signed. The encyclopedia is arranged alphabetically word by word (*New York* precedes *Newspaper*), with access to specific information enhanced by 100,000 cross-references in the text and an analytical index of more than 150,000 entries.

EVALUATION

World Book first appeared in 1917 in eight volumes. An immediate success, the set grew to ten volumes the following year, 13 volumes in 1929, 19 volumes in 1933, 20 volumes in 1960, and its present 22 volumes in 1971. Over the years, the encyclopedia has benefited from enlightened ownership and dedicated editorship. The Hanson-

Roach-Fowler Company and its successor, W.F. Quarrie & Company, both of Chicago, published *World Book* into the 1940s. During this time, the set's now traditional high standards were established by its founding editor, Michael Vincent O'Shea, a professor of education at the University of Wisconsin at Madison prior to joining the encyclopedia. In 1945, *World Book* was acquired by Field Enterprises, Inc., a subsidiary of the Marshall Field organization, a giant Chicago-based corporation. Around the same time, John Morris Jones, a Welsh-born educator, became the set's editor. Jones, like O'Shea before him, provided strong and innovative editorial leadership. In 1947, for instance, the entire encyclopedia was revised and restructured, with many new articles and illustrations added to keep the set abreast of postwar developments. Soon after the death of Jones in 1962, William H. Nault, another educator with impressive credentials, became *World Book*'s guiding editorial force, a position he has held now for more than two decades. In 1978, the encyclopedia was acquired by the Scott Fetzer Company of Lakewood, Ohio, a firm that manufactures and sells Kirby vacuum cleaners and related products.

Under William Nault's progressive management, *World Book* has gained a reputation as one of the best—if not the best—general English-language encyclopedias in the world. In 1975, for example, *World Book* added metric equivalents throughout the set, thus becoming the first major encyclopedia to include both customary and metric measurements. In 1977, the publisher installed a sophisticated electronic composition system, then the most advanced in the encyclopedia industry. The computerized system, which permits editors, writers, and illustrators to work on page revision directly at video display terminals, improves both updating and design capabilities. In 1980, a Portuguese-language version of *World Book* entitled *Enciclopedia Delta Universal* was published in 15 volumes in Brazil by Editora Delta of Rio de Janeiro. In 1982, *World Book* became available on tape for the visually handicapped. Called the *Talking World Book,* the recorded edition of the encyclopedia consists of 19 volumes, or albums, that hold 219 four-track tape cassettes, each containing six hours of spoken material. An index in both Braille and large type and a fast-forward, quick-access cassette player allow users to locate and listen to specific articles or information. The *Talking World Book* is published in cooperation with the American Printing House for the Blind, a nonprofit organization that distributes the set. (See the section on purchasing *World Book* below for additional information.) Earlier, in the 1960s, the encyclopedia was published in a massive 145-volume Braille edition and in large type in 30 volumes. These and similar developments have made the name *World Book* a symbol of encyclopedic excellence the world over.

World Book's coverage is quite well balanced among the major areas of knowledge. Biographical and geographical topics are especially well covered. For instance, considerable attention is given to the continents and countries of the world, the U.S. states and Canadian provinces, and other important place-names in North America and abroad, as well as prominent historical figures such as Alexander Graham Bell, Leonardo da Vinci, Alexander Hamilton, Lenin, Martin Luther, Napoleon, Shakespeare, and Daniel Webster, along with all of the U.S. presidents and Canadian prime ministers. Most of the encyclopedia's more than 18,000 articles are relatively short, averaging under 500 words in length, but some are much longer, running to 30 or more pages. In Volume 13 (M), for example, the article *Madison, James* covers five pages, *Magazine* four pages, *Magnet and Magnetism* five pages, *Maine* (the U.S. state) 25 pages, *Malaysia* five pages, *Mammal* 14 pages, *Manitoba* 20 pages, *Map* ten pages, *Medicine* 17 pages, *Money* 15 pages, *Montreal* 12 pages, *Moon* 14 pages, *Motion Picture* 28 pages, and *Music* 13 pages. Coverage naturally emphasizes material of interest to North American readers, but, when appropriate, international developments are included, as in the case of the article *Motion Picture,* which provides extensive commentary on films and filmmakers in postwar Europe and Asia.

The breadth and depth of the encyclopedia's coverage is determined to some extent by an ongoing study of what is currently taught in elementary and secondary schools in the United States and Canada. Called the *Nault-Caswell-Brain Curriculum Analysis* (in 61 loose-leaf volumes), the study not only informs *World Book* editors about what subjects are being taught at what grade levels but it also identifies curricular changes and trends. In the same vein, the encyclopedia is continuously monitored for effectiveness as a reference source in some 400 selected classrooms in North America. Students doing research fill out cards each time they used the encyclopedia, indicating what information they sought, what subject headings they looked under, and whether they found what they were looking for. This system of structured feedback from readers helps the editors make the encyclopedia as user-oriented as possible. No other encyclopedia on the market today is so closely in touch with the school curriculum and informational needs of students. Do not, however, make the mistake (as some do) of assuming that *World Book* covers only subjects studied in school. In point of fact, the encyclopedia includes an enormous amount of extracurricular or noncurricular material of potential interest to both adults and young people, such as how air conditioning works, how an automobile runs, how helicopters fly, bicycle safety rules, boats and boating, canning, camping, cooking, fishing, first aid, fire prevention and safety, furniture, gardening, lawn care, types of insurance and pensions, parliamentary procedure, safety in the home, sewing, skiing, skin diving, and all sorts of other sports and games.

Information in *World Book* is accurately and objectively presented. Articles dealing with controversial issues almost always discuss the pros and cons in an evenhanded manner. The article *Abortion,* for instance, provides two paragraphs subtitled "Arguments Against Abortion" and two paragraphs offering "Arguments for Abortion." Also, in recent years the editors have systematically eliminated sexist language and sex stereotyping from the encyclopedia. Occasionally, however, polemical or sensitive subjects are ignored. Carol Rasmussen, in a long and informative review of *World Book* in *American Reference Books Annual* (1984, p. 24), points out, "Perhaps in an effort to maintain objectivity, the entries also sometimes avoid mentioning controversial aspects of a subject. This can result in excellent, reasoned entries, such as that for rape; but it can also result in vital facets being omitted, as in the entry for El Salvador, which is up to date as to events but does not mention the bloody fighting that has been going on there for years. The entry for Richard Wagner ignores his anti-Semitism (and, in fact, all of his extramusical ideas). In these and other cases, the missing information is essential to a real understanding of a difficult issue."

Information in the encyclopedia is normally as current as can be expected in an annually revised reference work. The preface notes the editors' commitment to up-to-dateness and the need for vigorous continuous revision: "An encyclopedia must be up to date if it is to serve the best interests of its users. A revised edition of *World Book* is published each year. Each edition reflects up-to-date information and the latest changes in educational viewpoints. Every subject area is under continuing surveillance." These are not empty words. In 1985, for example, the publisher spent some $2 million updating the set. More than 1,500 articles were partially revised, another 500 were either new or completely revised, and many illustrations and maps were replaced or updated—all involving changes in over 5,000 of the encyclopedia's nearly 14,000 pages. The 1984 printing had similar revision statistics, with more than 1,700 partially revised and 550 new or entirely revised articles, entailing changes in roughly 6,000 pages. A review in *Booklist* (February 1, 1984, p. 794) says that *World Book* "deserves high marks for its overall currentness of information." The author of *Best Encyclopedias* agrees.

World Book's writing style is another outstanding feature of this outstanding encyclopedia. Invariably, articles are clearly and interestingly written. Some 20 years ago a critic in *Choice* (December 1968, p. 1280) remarked that "*World Book* has a knack for clarity on complicated subjects," and that observation remains true today. When appropriate, the material is written at the grade level where it is likely to be read or studied. For example, the article *Animal* is written for a younger reader than, say, *Environmental Pollution* or *Radiation.* New articles are carefully examined by the encyclopedia's readability specialist, Dr. Edgar Dale, who ensures that the vocabulary is geared to the intended grade level. Technical terms are used when required, but they are italicized and defined or explained in context. The initial paragraphs of the article *Earthquake* typify the encyclopedia's style:

> EARTHQUAKE is a shaking, rolling, or sudden shock of the earth's surface. There may be as many as a million earthquakes in a single year. Most of them take place beneath the surface of the sea. Few of these cause any damage. But earthquakes that occur near large cities cause much damage and loss of life, especially if the cities rest on soft ground. The energy released by a large earthquake may equal that of about 200 million short tons (180 million metric tons) of TNT. In other words, its energy may be 10,000 times as great as that of the first atomic bomb. The strength of an earthquake is measured on a scale of numbers called the *Richter Scale* (see RICHTER MAGNITUDE).
>
> Large earthquakes cause violent motions of the earth's surface. Sometimes they cause huge sea waves that sweep up on land and add to the general destruction. Such waves often occur in the Pacific Ocean because of many earthquakes there. Geologists use a Japanese word, *tsunami,* for these destructive waves.

Another useful (though less apparent) technique employed by *World Book* is its "pyramid" writing style—that is, the article begins with the simplest or most elementary material and then gradually becomes more detailed or complex as the text progresses. For example, toward the middle of *Earthquake,* the article's content and vocabulary are clearly more sophisticated than at the beginning:

> Seismic waves consist of compressional waves, shear waves, and surface waves. *Compressional* (longitudinal) *waves* are really sound waves, and travel at a speed of 5 miles (8 kilometers) a second. The rocks vibrate in the direction traveled by the wave. This causes the rocks to change volume. *Shear* (transverse) *waves* travel about half as fast as compressional waves. The rocks vibrate at right angles to the direction traveled by the waves. This causes the rocks to change shape. *Surface waves* travel slightly slower than shear waves. They are confined to the earth's surface in much the same way that ocean waves are limited to the surface of the sea.

Like its chief competitors (COMPTON'S ENCYCLOPEDIA and MERIT STUDENTS ENCYCLOPEDIA), *World Book* is most appropriate for users with reading skills from the seventh to the twelfth grade levels. In addition, much of the text can be comprehended by readers in the upper elementary grades.

The contents of *World Book* are easily retrievable. Numerous cross-references in the text help point the user in the right direction. For example, in the excerpt from the article *Earthquake* quoted above, there is a *See* reference to the article *Richter Magnitude* where additional information can be found. In addition, *See also* references appear in great abundance at the end of many articles, as in the case of *Earthquake,* which refers the reader to such related articles as

Continental Drift, Earth, San Andreas Fault, Seismograph, and *Tectonics.* But the set's principal finding device is a large, 990-page analytical index of more than 150,000 entries. Found in Volume 22, the index is excellent. In terms of the ratio of index entries to total words in the encyclopedia (10 million), *World Book* provides one index entry for every 70 words of text, or a ratio of 1:70. Only the ACADEMIC AMERICAN ENCYCLOPEDIA (1:45), COLLIER'S ENCYCLOPEDIA (1:50), and MERIT STUDENTS ENCYCLOPEDIA (1:65) have better ratios.

The illustrations, about half of which are in color, add much to the encyclopedia's informational content. The aforementioned article *Earthquake,* for instance, includes a black-and-white photograph depicting the damage an earthquake can cause in a modern city, several color drawings that help explain how earthquakes occur, and a color map showing the world's major earthquake belts. Jovian Lang, in *Reference Sources for Small and Medium-sized Libraries* (1984, p. 30), comments that the encyclopedia's illustrations "are varied, effectively related to the text, and add meaning and aesthetic value. The excellent maps are designed by the publisher's cartographic staff and placed near related text." Overall, illustrations found in *World Book* compare favorably with those in the best illustrated general encyclopedias on the market today, namely, the ACADEMIC AMERICAN ENCYCLOPEDIA, the NEW CAXTON ENCYCLOPEDIA, and the RANDOM HOUSE ENCYCLOPEDIA. Another important feature of the encyclopedia is its bibliographies, or lists of materials for further study. Recently expanded and updated, the bibliographies are well selected and reasonably current. In addition, some of the lists are now divided into two levels based on reading difficulty. The encyclopedia's physical format is both well made and attractive.

Over the years, encyclopedia users and reviewers alike have generally praised *World Book* as a first-class source of knowledge and information. A recent survey named *World Book* as the overwhelming first choice of U.S. public reference librarians, professionals who use encyclopedias practically every day (see "Encyclopedias and the Public Library: A National Survey" by Kenneth Kister in *Library Journal,* April 15, 1979, pp. 890–93). William A. Katz, a well-known authority on reference materials, observes in his *Introduction to Reference Work* (1983, vol. 1, p. 189), "The triumph of the *World Book* is not an accident but a careful combination of many elements, not the least of which is a nice balance between timely illustrations and text." A recent review of the encyclopedia in *Booklist* (December 15, 1984, p. 576) concludes that *World Book* "continues to be a superior encyclopedia well suited to meet the reference and study needs of students in grades 4–12 and to serve as a general reference source for adults." And James Rettig, in *Wilson Library Bulletin* (June 1985, p. 719), finds that " *World Book,* as intelligent as it is intelligible, is a solid selection for home or library. It will meet the general information needs of children and young adults and satisfy many of their parents as well."

To Summarize: *World Book,* the best-selling encyclopedia in North America, is a reference work of preeminently high quality. The set is noteworthy for its readability, ease of use, broad and balanced coverage, accurate and up-to-date articles, and appealing illustrations and layout. The encyclopedia has been a favorite with the U.S. and Canadian public for 70 years, and professionals who work with information find that it consistently outperforms the competition. *World Book* remains, in this reviewer's judgment, page for page the best general encyclopedia currently available.

In Comparison: *World Book,* published in 22 volumes containing 10 million words, falls mainly into the category of encyclopedias for adults and older students, although in many instances it will also be appropriate for younger readers (the set's editors claim its readability begins at the elementary school level). Generally speaking, *World Book* competes directly with the ACADEMIC AMERICAN ENCYCLOPEDIA (21 volumes, 9 million words), COMPTON'S ENCYCLOPEDIA (26 volumes, 8.5 million words), FUNK & WAGNALLS NEW ENCYCLOPEDIA (29 volumes, 9 million words), MERIT STUDENTS ENCYCLOPEDIA (20 volumes; 9 million words), and the NEW STANDARD ENCYCLOPEDIA (17 volumes; 6.4 million words). Overall, *World Book* is the best encyclopedia in its class, although the new and innovative ACADEMIC AMERICAN ENCYCLOPEDIA, which is aimed at a somewhat more advanced readership, provides strong competition. In addition, MERIT STUDENTS ENCYCLOPEDIA is capable of holding its own against *World Book* in most areas, and *World Book*'s traditional rival, COMPTON'S ENCYCLOPEDIA, is currently undergoing a complete overhaul that should make it competitive once again. Dollar-conscious consumers should also note that, with the exception of FUNK & WAGNALLS NEW ENCYCLOPEDIA, *World Book* is the least expensive encyclopedia in its class.

To Purchase the *World Book Encyclopedia:* If you are either an individual consumer or representing an educational institution and wish to order the set, consult the yellow pages of the local telephone directory under "Encyclopedias" for the World Book, Inc. sales representative in your area. If the company is not listed in the directory, contact World Book, Inc. at Merchandise Mart Plaza, Chicago, IL 60654 or telephone toll-free 1-800-621-8202. Your name will be forwarded to the sales representative nearest you who will handle the transaction. The sales representative will most likely attempt to sell you additional publications along with the encyclopedia, including CHILDCRAFT: THE HOW AND WHY LIBRARY (a 15-volume set for beginning readers), the *World Book Year Book, Science Year,* and *Medical Update* (the latter three titles being annual supplements to *World Book*). You need not buy any extras unless you want them. Purchasers of the encyclopedia, however, should seriously consider taking the *World Book Year Book,* which is an excellent review of the year's events as well as an updating source that directly connects the encyclopedia with the yearbook by means of cross-reference tabs.

Consumers should also be aware of the publisher's trade-in policies for individuals (but not schools and libraries). Consumers who already own a set of *World Book* that is between five and ten years old can trade it in and receive $80.00 off the price of a new set. Those trading in both *World Book* and CHILDCRAFT can acquire a new *World Book* at half price. In addition, the publisher allows up to $130.00 off the price of a new *World Book* to those who own up to ten volumes of the *World Book Year Book* (the allowance is $13 per volume).

Consumers interested in the 219-tape recorded edition of the encyclopedia called the *Talking World Book* (described near the beginning of this review) should contact the distributor, the American Printing House for the Blind, Inc. at 1839 Frankfort Avenue, Box 6349, Louisville, KY 40206 or telephone 502-895-2405. The *Talking World Book,* a boon for the blind and partially sighted, sells for $1,176.00 (a not-for-profit price), which includes the tapes and a special cassette player.

For More Information about the *World Book Encyclopedia* See: *American Reference Books Annual,* 1984, pp. 23–26 (review by Carol Rasmussen); *Booklist,* December 15, 1984, pp. 574–76 (unsigned review); *Booklist,* February 1, 1984, pp. 791–94 (unsigned review); *Introduction to Reference Work* by William A. Katz (4th ed., New York: McGraw-Hill, 1982), vol. 1: *Basic Information Sources,* pp. 189–91; *Reference Sources for Small and Medium-sized Libraries* (4th ed., Chicago: American Library Association, 1984), p. 30 (review by Jovian P. Lang); *Wilson Library Bulletin,* June 1985, pp. 707, 719 (review by James Rettig).

Young Children's Encyclopedia

FACTS

The Young Children's Encyclopedia. Also published as COMPTON'S PRECYCLOPEDIA. Howard L. Goodkind, Editor in Chief; Margaret Sutton, Managing Editor. Chicago: Encyclopaedia Britannica, Inc. 16

volumes. First edition published in 1970; revised periodically, most recently in 1985. Lowest retail price: $149.50.

The *Young Children's Encyclopedia* is a collection of stories, poems, games, and factual descriptions intended for the beginning reader. The 16-volume encyclopedia contains 2,560 pages, 650 articles, and approximately 315,000 words. The articles, which are normally quite long, average 500 words in length (or about five full pages). They are accompanied by 2,400 illustrations (all in color), plus 20 maps. Some 200 editors, writers, artists, advisers, and consultants are listed at the front of Volume 1. None of the material is signed, but the last page of each volume does identify those responsible for the text in that volume. The set is arranged alphabetically letter by letter (*Newspapers* precedes *New York*), with access to specific information enhanced by roughly 500 cross-references in the text. The set has no index.

EVALUATION

Young Children's first appeared in 1970 and was modestly revised in 1977 and again in 1985. Initially, the set was merchandised in supermarkets and via mail order, but it is now sold in-home in combination with the NEW ENCYCLOPAEDIA BRITANNICA. A very similar version of the encyclopedia is published under the title COMPTON'S PRECYCLOPEDIA. The two sets are exactly the same except for these minor differences: (1) COMPTON'S PRECYCLOPEDIA includes a 24-page activity, or "Things to Do," section at the beginning of each volume, whereas *Young Children's* does not; (2) COMPTON'S PRECYCLOPEDIA comes with a 110-page paperbound *Teaching Guide and Index* volume, whereas *Young Children's* does not; and (3) COMPTON'S PRECYCLOPEDIA is usually sold in conjunction with COMPTON'S ENCYCLOPEDIA, whereas *Young Children's* is sold with the NEW ENCYCLOPAEDIA BRITANNICA. Both *Young Children's* and COMPTON'S PRECYCLOPEDIA are considered among the best beginning encyclopedias available for children between the ages of four and ten.

Like its chief competitor, CHILDCRAFT, *Young Children's* consists of stories, folktales, games, riddles, jingles, jokes, poems, and factual articles on subjects likely to be of interest to young readers. For example, Volume 1 includes a story set in Africa (*Amos Wins the Big Race*), biographical information about Louisa May Alcott (*Tales of Happy Families*), an adventure piece about the Amazon (*Exploring the Amazon River*), and three articles about astronauts (*Doing the Job, A Walk in Space,* and *More about Astronauts*). Users and prospective purchasers of *Young Children's* should understand that no effort has been made to provide comprehensive coverage of the world's knowledge, and that in the strictest sense *Young Children's* is not really an encyclopedia but a browsing set designed to stimulate the child's desire to know. Information in *Young Children's* is accurately and objectively presented. Likewise, the material is reasonably current, although timeliness is not as crucial in a work of this type as it is in a true encyclopedia. Occasionally, however, the addition of new information would improve an article. The two-page entry on the Panama Canal, for instance, lacks any mention of the recently negotiated treaties involving the Canal Zone. In the set's latest revision (1985), five new articles have been added, all dealing with famous women (including Louisa May Alcott, Susan B. Anthony, and Emily Dickinson), six articles have been dropped, and 25 articles have been rewritten or updated and, in some cases, reillustrated (among them, the articles on computers, space, and the ocean).

The encyclopedia's writing style is normally clear, interesting, and informal. Reading levels vary from article to article, but in most instances the text will be comprehensible to beginning readers in the primary grades. Consider, for example, the last portion of the article *Inside the Earth,* which deals with earthquakes:

> Sometimes a big layer of rock that is deep, deep down slips and rubs against another layer of rock. This causes a shaking and rumbling called an *earthquake*.
>
> Scientists learn something about what's inside the Earth by using special earthquake instruments. What's inside the Earth is a riddle. Nature gives us some hints when volcanoes shoot out melted rock and there are earthquakes. It lets us know that in some places there is solid rock, and in other places hot melted rock, and in still other places hot melted iron. But we still need to know a lot more than we do.

Access to specific information in *Young Children's* is quite limited due to the lack of an index. The reader seeking information on, say, the Panama Canal or earthquakes must rely on the table of contents at the beginning of each volume, an approach that is certainly less effective than consulting an index. (Note that COMPTON'S PRECYCLOPEDIA does come with an index.) Nonetheless, providing hard information is not the primary function of *Young Children's* (or COMPTON'S PRECYCLOPEDIA), and the lack of an index is not a major deficiency. In addition, *Young Children's* does include cross-references at the end of many articles. For instance, at the end of *More About Canals* (which discusses the Panama Canal) there is this notation: " *If you want to learn about* Mosquitoes, *you may read about them in Volume 10.*" Illustrations, all in color, make up about half the set's total text. Mostly drawings, the illustrations add much to both the instructional and visual appeal of *Young Children's.* The set's physical format is satisfactory, except for these problems: Guide words (or running heads) are not included at the top of each page, thus making it difficult to locate an article by browsing; some pages lack numbers, which may confuse or frustrate young users; and, most seriously, the volumes do not always lie flat when open, thus rendering the set physically awkward to use for reference purposes.

To Summarize: *Young Children's,* a 16-volume set for beginning readers first published in 1970 and revised periodically since that time, is more a collection of stories than a real encyclopedia, although it is arranged alphabetically and does include cross-references. The set offers an interesting writing style and imaginative illustrations, but the coverage is highly eclectic, there is no index, the physical format leaves much to be desired, and the volumes will be quickly outgrown. Note that *Young Children's* has practically the same text as COMPTON'S PRECYCLOPEDIA.

In Comparison: *Young Children's,* published in 16 volumes containing approximately 315,000 words, is an attractive work for children ages four to ten. The encyclopedia's main competition is CHILDCRAFT (15 volumes; 750,000 words). Arranged topically (whereas *Young Children's* is alphabetical), CHILDCRAFT is the outstanding encyclopedic set for beginning readers. Although *Young Children's* possesses a number of appealing featues, it lacks CHILDCRAFT's superior design and vitality. Also aimed at roughly the same age group are CHARLIE BROWN'S 'CYCLOPEDIA (15 volumes; 180,000 words), DISNEY'S WONDERFUL WORLD OF KNOWLEDGE (20 volumes; 750,000 words), and the NEW TALKING CASSETTE ENCYCLOPEDIA (10 volumes; 100,000 words). In terms of quality, however, none of these titles comes close to CHILDCRAFT or, for that matter, *Young Children's* (also published as COMPTON'S PRECYCLOPEDIA).

To Purchase the *Young Children's Encyclopedia:* If you are an individual consumer and wish to order the encyclopedia, consult the white pages of the local telephone directory under "Encyclopaedia Britannica, Inc." for the sales representative in your area. If the company is not listed in the directory, contact Encyclopaedia Britannica, Inc. at Britannica Centre, Customer Service Department, 310 South Michigan Avenue, Chicago, IL 60604 or telephone collect 312-347-7298. Your name will be forwarded to a sales representative in your area who will handle the transaction. *Young Children's* is normally sold in the home as part of a package deal involving the NEW ENCYCLOPAEDIA BRITANNICA, a much larger work for adults and advanced students. (Note that COMPTON'S PRECYCLOPEDIA, which is practically the same work as *Young Children's,* is usually sold in combination with COMPTON'S ENCYCLOPEDIA.) Of course, you need not buy the NEW ENCYCLOPAEDIA BRITANNICA or any other Britannica products in order to purchase *Young Children's.*

Young Children's is not sold to schools and libraries. Instead, educational institutions are sold COMPTON'S PRECYCLOPEDIA, which comes with an extra volume entitled *Teaching Guide and Index.*

For More Information about the *Young Children's Encyclopedia* See: No recent reviews of *Young Children's* have been published, but interested consumers will want to consult the following reviews of COMPTON'S PRECYCLOPEDIA, which has the same basic text as *Young Children's: American Reference Books Annual,* 1975, pp. 33–34 (review by Sally Wynkoop); *Booklist,* November 1, 1979, pp. 453–56 (unsigned review); *Introduction to Reference Work* by William A. Katz (4th ed., New York: McGraw-Hill, 1982), vol. 1: *Basic Information Sources,* pp. 192–93; *Reference Sources for Small and Medium-sized Libraries* (4th ed., Chicago: American Library Association, 1984), p. 27 (review by Jovian P. Lang).

Young Students Encyclopedia

FACTS

Young Students Encyclopedia: Specially Prepared with the Staff of My Weekly Reader. George H. Wolfson, Editorial Director; Richard Harkins, Managing Editor; George C. Kohn, 1982 Revision Editor. Middletown, CT: Weekly Reader Books (a Xerox company). 24 volumes (including a one-volume world atlas and two-volume dictionary). First edition published in 1972; revised periodically, most recently in 1982. Lowest retail price: $230.00 delivered; to schools and libraries: $199.00 delivered.

The *Young Students Encyclopedia* is "designed for young people, for use as an early reference and activities source at home or at school" (introduction). The 24-volume encyclopedia contains approximately 3,500 pages, 2,500 articles, and 1.5 million words. The articles, confined to the first 21 volumes, are of the specific-entry type, averaging just under 500 words in length (or one full page). They are accompanied by 4,500 illustrations (60 percent in color), plus 350 maps, including those in a 96-page color world atlas volume at the back of the set. In addition, the encyclopedia includes a two-volume, 800-page general dictionary entitled the *Xerox Intermediate Dictionary,* which contains 34,000 entries and some 1,400 illustrations. Nearly 100 editors, consultants, and contributors are noted in Volume 1, although none of the material is signed. The encyclopedia is arranged alphabetically letter by letter (*Newspaper* precedes *New York*), with access to specific information enhanced by roughly 10,000 cross-references in the text and an index of 17,000 entries in Volume 21.

EVALUATION

Young Students first appeared in 1972, a cooperative publishing venture between Funk & Wagnalls, Inc. and Xerox Education Publications (which drew upon the editorial resources of *My Weekly Reader,* a Xerox publication). At that time, Funk & Wagnalls sold the set in supermarkets, whereas Xerox marketed it to schools and libraries as well as the mail-order trade. In 1977, Xerox published a revision prepared by Laurence Urdang, Inc., a Connecticut firm that specializes in producing dictionaries and other reference materials. Meanwhile, Funk & Wagnalls sold off its original 1972 printing and presumably no longer has an interest in the set. The encyclopedia was most recently revised in 1982, with George C. Kohn of Laurence Urdang, Inc. serving as revision editor. During its 15 years on the market, *Young Students* has achieved a reputation as an attractive but superficial encyclopedia for children ages seven to fourteen. Unfortunately for *Young Students,* it must compete directly with the NEW BOOK OF KNOWLEDGE, which is generally acknowledged to be the best encyclopedia for that age group ever produced.

To a large extent, the encyclopedia's coverage is determined by those subjects studied in U.S. elementary schools. The introduction to the set explains the intention to cover "those ideas most often included in school curriculums.... Approximately a hundred categories were chosen for particular emphasis, from ancient history to physics to personal relationships. They represent the prime concepts underlying current elementary school programs of study as well as children's outside interests." As might be expected, the encyclopedia devotes considerable attention to biographical and geographical subjects, including prominent historical figures (such as the U.S. presidents), the countries of the world, the U.S. states and Canadian provinces, and other major place-names here and abroad. Children's games are also emphasized. An interesting feature is the inclusion of numerous educational activities, or "learning by doing" exercises, throughout the set. Printed in blue type, these exercises are intended to make the encyclopedia an interactive learning tool. The article *Poetry,* for example, discusses haiku, a popular form of Japanese poetry, and then (in blue type) invites the reader to try writing haiku.

Articles in *Young Students* are normally quite brief and, as suggested earlier, tend to lack substance. For instance, the overly brief article *Adoption* is short on facts and long on such sentiments as "Many people who adopt these children find special happiness in making the children part of their family." The article *Argentina* covers the history of the country in 65 words, concluding that "Argentina is now an independent republic. The military has taken control of the government at various times." The article *Canada* is filled with generalizations like "Canadians are used to tackling problems; they believe that hard work will keep the country one of the leaders of the world." *Quebec* includes one brief paragraph on the separatist question, failing even to note the historic 1980 referendum that clearly rejected the notion of secession. Many similar examples of superficial treatment could be cited. Essentially, the encyclopedia appears to be more concerned with stimulating the reader's imagination than it is with providing a reasonably full summary of basic knowledge and information.

Information in *Young Students* is usually accurate and objective, although occasional errors of fact do occur. For example, the number of U.S. casualties in the Vietnam War is incorrectly reported. Sometimes, also, controversial issues are entirely ignored. This practice is especially true in the area of human sexuality. Children ages seven to fourteen naturally have a great interest in and concern about such questions as abortion, birth control, menstruation, masturbation, homosexuality, and circumcision, but they will not find answers in this encyclopedia. Information in *Young Students* is usually current as of the early 1980s, although many important recent developments are not covered, as in the case of Canada's new constitution (1982). Often it is difficult to know if significant events are missing due to lack of diligent revision or due to shallow treatment of the subject.

The encyclopedia's writing style is, in the words of a review in *Booklist* (July 15, 1980, p. 1690), "conversational, with facts presented in a clear, noncondescending manner." Potentially difficult or unfamiliar terms are italicized and defined or explained in context. When appropriate, articles are written at the grade level where they are most likely to be read or studied. Likewise, the "pyramid" style of writing is sometimes employed—that is, the article begins with the simplest or most elementary material and then gradually becomes more detailed or complex as the text progresses. Ordinarily, the text will be comprehensible to students in grades three through eight. The first two paragraphs of the article *Earthquake* provide a typical example of the encyclopedia's style:

The people of Charleston, South Carolina, felt the ground shake several times on August 31, 1886. Each tremor was a little stronger than the one before. A rumbling sound seemed to approach the city. The rumble increased to a roar, as if a huge train were rushing through a tunnel under the town. The ground rose and fell in waves. All these events lasted a little more than a minute. Eight minutes later the ground shook and rumbled again in an aftershock.

People were thrown off their feet by the shaking of the earth. Chimneys and walls fell into crumbled heaps of rubbish. Every building in Charleston was damaged. Many persons were injured or killed by falling buildings. Cracks, called *fissures,* opened in the ground. Railway tracks were twisted.

The encyclopedia's contents are easily accessible, thanks to a reasonably detailed index (located in Volume 21) and an abundance of cross-references found at the end of most articles. For instance, the article on earthquakes quoted from in the preceding paragraph concludes with *See also* references to *Earth, Earth History, Geology,* and *Mountain.* Generally speaking, *Young Students* is well organized and easy to use. Finding specific information in the set should present no problems for even the youngest users.

Young Students is heavily illustrated, with approximately 40 percent of the total text given over to photographs, drawings, diagrams, reproductions of artwork, maps, and the like. The illustrations, most of which are in color, usually add to the informational value of the set, but in some cases the quality of reproduction is poor. In other instances, photographs are blurry or excessively dark or simply too small to be of much value from an informational standpoint. The encyclopedia's physical format is generally satisfactory. The page layout is colorful and varied, with wide margins and much white space. The thin, lightweight volumes are cheaply made but should hold up reasonably well under normal use. The lettering on the spine, however, is much too small to be read comfortably at any distance.

Critical reaction to *Young Students* over the years has tended to emphasize its potential value as an inexpensive alternative to the larger encyclopedias for children and younger students, namely, the NEW BOOK OF KNOWLEDGE and BRITANNICA JUNIOR ENCYCLOPAEDIA. William A. Katz, in his *Introduction to Reference Work* (1982, vol. 1, p. 192), calls *Young Students* "a good choice after the *New Book of Knowledge,* and it certainly would be preferable to the much older and dated *Britannica Junior.*" *Booklist* (July 15, 1980, p. 1692) observes that *Young Students* "will not replace comprehensive, standard encyclopedias for children. However, its brief and well-written articles provide reliable and reasonably up-to-date information on a wide range of subjects of interest to children ages 7 to 13. It is recommended as a supplementary resource for home, elementary school, and public library children's collections." And Christine Wynar, in a review of an early version of the encyclopedia in *American Reference Books Annual* (1974, p. 27), found that "overall, this is a well-planned and well-executed set for home use and for beginners who find standard encyclopedias too imposing. It cannot substitute for the more comprehensive sets and is not intended to do so."

To Summarize: *Young Students,* a 24-volume set for elementary school students that includes a one-volume atlas and two-volume dictionary, is a colorful but superficial work. Although well organized and clearly and interestingly written, the encyclopedia lacks depth, avoids sensitive subjects of concern to young people, and includes too many inferior illustrations.

In Comparison: *Young Students,* published in 24 volumes containing approximately 1.5 million words, is intended for children and younger students in the elementary grades. The encyclopedia competes directly with three other multivolume children's sets aimed at the same audience, namely, FINDING OUT: SILVER BURDETT'S CHILDREN'S ENCYCLOPEDIA (10 volumes; 250,000 words), the NEW BOOK OF KNOWLEDGE (21 volumes; 6.8 million words), and the NEW KNOWLEDGE LIBRARY (35 volumes; 2 million words). In addition, in the past *Young Students* competed directly with the BRITANNICA JUNIOR ENCYCLOPAEDIA (15 volumes; 5.4 million words) and the OXFORD JUNIOR ENCYCLOPAEDIA (13 volumes; 3.7 million words), but these two works are now, at least temporarily, out of print. Of all of these titles, the NEW BOOK OF KNOWLEDGE is unquestionably the best. It is also the biggest and most expensive. *Young Students,* on the other hand, is affordably priced.

To Purchase the *Young Students Encyclopedia:* If you are either an individual consumer or representing an educational institution and wish to order the encyclopedia, contact the publisher, Weekly Reader Books, at P.O. Box 16615, Columbus, OH 43216 or telephone 614-771-0006. Your order will be processed immediately.

For More Information about the *Young Students Encyclopedia* See: *American Reference Books Annual,* 1974, pp. 26–27 (review by Christine L. Wynar); *Booklist,* July 15, 1980, pp. 1690–92 (unsigned review); *Introduction to Reference Work* by William A. Katz (4th ed., New York: McGraw-Hill, 1982), vol. 1: *Basic Information Sources,* pp. 191–92.

Appendixes

Appendix A: General Encyclopedia Comparison Chart

Large Encyclopedias for Adults and Older Students
(Multivolume encyclopedias containing more than 20 million words)

Title	Vols.	Words	Pages	Articles	Illustrations & Maps	Lowest Retail Price	School/ Library Price
Collier's Encyclopedia	24	21 mil	19,700	25,000	18,800	$1,099.50	$749.00[1]
Encyclopedia Americana	30	31 mil	26,690	52,000	23,695	$1,200.00	$799.00[1]
New Encyclopaedia Britannica	32	44 mil	32,000	62,000	26,300	$1,249.00	$999.00[1]

[1] Plus shipping and handling.

Medium-Sized Encyclopedias for Adults and Older Students
(Multivolume encyclopedias containing 5–20 million words)

Title	Vols.	Words	Pages	Articles	Illustrations & Maps	Lowest Retail Price	School/ Library Price
Academic American Encyclopedia	21	9 mil	9,696	28,500	17,696	$850.00	$650.00[1]
American Educator	20	5 mil	7,750	13,000	12,693	Out-of-Print	
American Peoples Encyclopedia	20	10 mil	11,125	35,000	14,342	Out-of-Print	

[1] Plus shipping and handling.

Medium-Sized Encyclopedias for Adults and Older Students
(Multivolume encyclopedias containing 5–20 million words) (continued)

Title	Vols.	Words	Pages	Articles	Illustra-tions & Maps	Lowest Retail Price	School/ Library Price
Chambers's Encyclopaedia	15	14.5 mil	12,600	28,000	4,916	Out-of-Print	
Compton's Encyclopedia	26	8.5 mil	11,000	10,000[2]	22,500	$699.00	$499.00
Encyclopedia International	20	9.5 mil	11,927	29,728	13,711	Out-of-Print	
Everyman's Encyclopaedia	12	9 mil	8,896	51,000	5,600	$157.50[3]	
Funk & Wagnalls New Encyclopedia	29	9 mil	13,024	25,000	9,492	$139.80	$199.50
Harver World Encyclopedia	20	7.5 mil	5,855	20,000	16,500	Out-of-Print	
Merit Students Encyclopedia	20	9 mil	12,300	21,000	20,770	$1,099.50	$525.00[1]
New Caxton Encyclopedia	20	6 mil	6,500	13,000	17,000	$485.00	
New Illustrated Columbia Encyclopedia	24	6.6 mil	7,522	50,515	5,000	Out-of-Print	
New Standard Encyclopedia	17	6.4 mil	10,000	17,500	12,650	$649.50	$380.70[1]
World Book Encyclopedia	22	10 mil	14,000	18,300	31,850	$499.00	$462.00

[1]Plus shipping and handling.
[2]Main articles only; the encyclopedia also includes 30,000 very brief articles (or fact entries) in the Fact-Index.
[3]Price in Canada only; the encyclopedia is not sold in the United States.

Small Encyclopedias for Adults and Older Students (One- and two-volume encyclopedias)

Title	Vols.	Words	Pages	Articles	Illustra-tions & Maps	Lowest Retail Price	School/ Library Price
Cadillac Modern Encyclopedia	1	2.5 mil	1,954	18,000	1,410	Out-of-Print	
Collins Gem Encyclopedia	2	450,000	1,125	14,000	None	$7.90	
Concise Columbia Encyclopedia	1	1 mil	943	15,000	109	$14.95[1]	
Illustrated World Encyclopedia	1	2.5 mil	1,619	7,300	2,158	Out-of-Print	
Knowledge Encyclopedia	1	300,000	415	2,500	615	$16.95	
Kussmaul Encyclopedia	Data-base[2]	3 mil	Data-base[2]	20,000	None	Contact Publisher	
Lincoln Library of Essential Information	2	3.5 mil	2,500	25,000	1,340	$139.98	
New Columbia Encyclopedia	1	6.6 mil	3,068	50,515	659	$79.50	
New Hutchinson 20th Century Encyclopedia	1	1.5 mil	1,326	15,000	1,600	Out-of-Print	
New Universal Family Encyclopedia	1	1.5 mil	1,100	25,000	1,200	$39.95	

[1]Paperback price; the encyclopedia is also available in hardcover at $29.95.
[2]The encyclopedia is published only in electronic (or online) form.

Small Encyclopedias for Adults and Older Students (One- and two-volume encyclopedias) (continued)

Title	Vols.	Words	Pages	Articles	Illustrations & Maps	Lowest Retail Price	School/Library Price
Pears Cyclopaedia	1	1.3 mil	1,050	15,000	50	$14.95	
Quick Reference Handbook of Basic Knowledge	1	750,000	895	5,000	609	$25.40	$20.00
Random House Encyclopedia	1	3 mil	2,918	26,000	13,500	$99.95	Standard Discount
University Desk Encyclopedia	1	2 mil	1,055	25,000	3,350	Out-of-Print	
Volume Library	2	3.5 mil	2,650	8,500	2,200	$109.95	

Large Encyclopedias for Children and Younger Students (Encyclopedias of three or more volumes)

Title	Vols.	Words	Pages	Articles	Illustrations & Maps	Lowest Retail Price	School/Library Price
Britannica Junior Encyclopaedia	15	5.4 mil	8,000	4,200[1]	12,866	Out-of-Print	
Charlie Brown's 'Cyclopedia	15	180,000	720	1,000	900	$38.35	
Childcraft	15	750,000	5,000	3,000	4,500	$199.00	$159.00

[1]Main articles only; the encyclopedia also includes 25,000 very brief articles in the Ready Reference Index.

Large Encyclopedias for Children and Younger Students (Encyclopedias of three or more volumes) (continued)

Title	Vols.	Words	Pages	Articles	Illustra-tions & Maps	Lowest Retail Price	School/ Library Price
Compton's Precyclopedia	16	325,000	2,944	650		$249.00	$239.00
Disney's Wonderful World of Knowledge	20	750,000	2,500	1,200	4,050	$229.50	
Finding Out: Silver Burdett's Children's Encyclopedia	10	250,000	816	1,300	2,100	$140.00	$105.00[2]
Golden Book Encyclopedia	16	600,000	1,536	1,375	6,625	Out-of-Print	
Harver Junior World Encyclopedia	16	1 mil	1,344	1,550	2,065	Out-of-Print	
New Book of Knowledge	21	6.8 mil	10,540	9,116[3]	23,546	$800.00	$499.50[2]
New Knowledge Library	35	2 mil	3,361	3,000	6,160		$299.95

[2]Plus shipping and handling.
[3]Main articles only; the encyclopedia also includes 5,000 very brief articles in the Dictionary Index.

Large Encyclopedias for Children and Younger Students (Encyclopedias of three or more volumes) (continued)

Title	Vols.	Words	Pages	Articles	Illustra- tions & Maps	Lowest Retail Price	School/ Library Price
New Talking Cassette Encyclopedia	10	100,000	NA[4]	100		$695.00	
Oxford Junior Encyclopaedia	13	3.7 mil	6,500	3,600	6,250	Out-of-Print	
Young Children's Encyclopedia	16	315,000	2,560	650	2,420	$149.50	
Young Students Encyclopedia	24	1.5 mil	3,500	2,500	6,230	$230.00	

[4]Not applicable; the encyclopedia is published only on cassette tapes.

Small Encyclopedias for Children and Younger Students (One- and two-volume encyclopedias)

Title	Vols.	Words	Pages	Articles	Illustra- tions & Maps	Lowest Retail Price	School/ Library Price
Junior Encyclopedia of General Knowledge	1	100,000	224	103	411	$9.95	
Junior Pears Encyclopaedia	1	280,000	650	1,500	342	$14.95	
Nelson's Encyclopedia for Young Readers	2	350,000	973	2,000	1,700	$34.95	

Small Encyclopedias for Children and Younger Students (One- and two-volume encyclopedias) (continued)

Title	Vols.	Words	Pages	Articles	Illustra-tions & Maps	Lowest Retail Price	School/Library Price
Purnell's Pictorial Encyclopedia	1	75,000	192	88	550	$19.95	
Rand McNally's Children's Encyclopedia	1	15,000	61	27	300	$4.95	

Appendix B: Specialized Encyclopedias

In addition to the 52 general encyclopedias described and evaluated in the foregoing, there are literally thousands upon thousands of specialized encyclopedias and encyclopedic works available to the North American consumer. Indeed, in recent years publication of specialized (or subject) encyclopedias has far outstripped general encyclopedias in terms of both quantity and quality. William A. Katz, an authority on reference materials, explains in his *Introduction to Reference Work* (1978, vol. 1, pp. 173–74): "In an editorial sense, today's subject encyclopedia holds the position the major [general] encyclopedias held in the nineteenth century; that is, it depends more upon thorough scholarship and depth of coverage than upon popularity and a large sales force. Many subject encyclopedias are examples of what can be done in the synthesis and the presentation of knowledge in a clear, understandable, and intelligent fashion. Admittedly stretching an analogy, the subject encyclopedia is the Rolls Royce of the library reference collection, whereas the general encyclopedia is the Ford or Chevrolet."

Most individual consumers naturally still prefer a general encyclopedia because of its broad coverage of all areas of knowledge. But in some instances, a specialized work might be a better buy than a general one. For example, in a home where parents and children have a strong scientific aptitude, the purchase of a substantial science encyclopedia makes good sense. Likewise, an English major at college might be better off with an encyclopedia of world literature than a general encyclopedia. In other cases, a specialized encyclopedia will serve as a valuable complement to a general work.

This section of *Best Encyclopedias* provides a selected, annotated list of more than 450 recommended specialized encyclopedias, with emphasis on standard works and the best of the newer titles. Most of the encyclopedias included here are currently in print and can be acquired through retail bookstores, book wholesalers, or directly from the publisher or distributor. (See Appendix E for addresses and telephone numbers of publishers and distributors.) The encyclopedias are grouped by subject:

Architecture
Art (General)
Astronomy and Space Science
Biology (General) and Zoology
Botany and Horticulture
Business and Economics (Includes Statistics)
Chemistry and Chemical Engineering
Computer and Electronic Sciences
Crafts and Hobbies
Decorative Arts (Includes Antiques)
Earth and Environmental Sciences (Includes Energy)
Education and Libraries
Engineering and Building Construction
Film, Radio, and Television
Food and Agriculture
Geography and Area Studies (Includes Travel)
Health and Medicine (Includes Child Care and Drugs)
History and Archaeology
Law
Literature and Language
Music
Pets and Domestic Animals (Includes Veterinary Medicine)
Photography
Physics and Mathematics
Political and Military Sciences (Includes Weapons)
Psychology and Psychiatry (Includes Parapsychology)
Religion and Philosophy (Includes Mythology)
Science and Technology (General)
Social Sciences (Includes Sociology and Anthropology)
Sports and Games
Theater and Dance
Transportation (Includes Aircraft, Automobiles, and Ships)

ARCHITECTURE

American Shelter: An Illustrated Encyclopedia of the American Home. Written by Lester Walker. Overlook Pr. (dist. by Viking Pr.), 1981. 320p. $27.95.
Presented in a popular style, this encyclopedia chronologically illustrates different dwellings found in the area covered by the United States from 300 A.D. to 1980. For those "who want to know, at a glance, the difference between Queen Anne and Second Empire" (*Choice,* March 1982, p. 898).

The Architecture Book. Written by Norval White. Knopf, 1976. 343p. Out of print (last priced at $15.00).
Library Journal (March 1, 1977, p. 595) calls White's book a "concise encyclopedia of architecture and architects that is both a useful reference

tool and a pleasure to read." It covers all major styles and periods in approximately 1,500 paragraph-length articles.

Encyclopedia of American Architecture. Written by William Dudley Hunt. McGraw-Hill, 1980. 612p. $49.95.

The 202 nontechnical articles that make up this encyclopedia treat architectural styles, types of buildings, construction materials, and prominent architects. "Although not a dynamic work, it is the only one of its kind on American architecture" (*Booklist,* December 15, 1980, p. 552).

Encyclopedia of Architectural Technology: An Encyclopedic Survey of Changing Forms, Materials, and Concepts. Edited by Pedro Guedes. McGraw-Hill, 1979. 313p. $36.50.

Aimed at both the practitioner and student of architecture, this "handsome volume, with over 500 articles by authorities in the field, approaches architecture not as art, history, or monument, but as technological development" (*Wilson Library Bulletin,* October 1979, p. 140).

The Encyclopedia of Architecture: Historical, Theoretical, and Practical. Written by Joseph Gwilt; revised by Wyatt Papworth. Reprint of 1867 ed. Crown (dist. by Outlet Books), 1982. 1,364p. $12.98.

Originally published in 1842 and revised in 1867, this is the first comprehensive architectural encyclopedia in English. The work is valuable for its copious illustrations and historical data. As *American Reference Books Annual* (1983, p. 393) observes, "If there were nothing else in this book, the list of architects, dates, and important works would be worth the modest price."

Encyclopedia of Modern Architecture. Edited by Gerd Hatje. Abrams, 1964. 336p. Out of print (last priced at $17.50).

This English translation of the German *Knaurs Lexikon der Modernen Architektur* (1963) identifies the principal people, schools, styles, materials, and trends associated with the development of modern architecture. Although currently out of print, the encyclopedia remains an important reference source.

Encyclopedia of World Architecture. Written by Henri Stierlin. Facts on File, 1977. Two vols. $80.00; $17.50 paper.

Volume 1 of this multilingual work (English, French, and German) covers the great buildings of Europe and Volume 2 Asia, the Middle East, and the Americas. "The heart and outstanding features of these volumes are the excellent plans, cross sections, and axonometrics of buildings by José Canosa" (*Choice,* October 1979, p. 999). A comparable source is Banister Fletcher's classic *A History of Architecture on the Comparative Method* (18th ed., Scribner's, 1975).

Everyman's Concise Encyclopaedia of Architecture. Written by Martin Shaw Briggs. Reprint of 1959 ed. Dutton, 1974. 372p. $17.95.

This inexpensive work includes some 2,000 short articles accompanied by good line drawings on all aspects of architecture.

A Field Guide to American Architecture. Written by Carole Rifkind. New American Library, 1980. 320p. $19.95; $9.95 paper.

"Rifkind has constructed a lucid, informed explanation of the way that architecture—residential, ecclesiastical, utilitarian, civic, and commercial—developed in the United States from 1670 to 1940" (*New York Times Book Review,* May 18, 1980, p. 45). A similar work of similar range and quality is *A Field Guide to American Houses* by Virginia and Lee McAlester (Knopf, 1984).

The World Atlas of Architecture. G.K. Hall, 1984. 408p. $75.00.
A revised and updated edition of the hugely popular *Great Architecture of the World* (published in Great Britain in 1975), this oversized volume is a colorful visual history of architecture through the ages. "The authoritative text, color illustrations, cutout reconstructions, maps, time charts, glossary, and lively overall visual appeal make this atlas an essential reference work for most people and nearly all libraries" (*American Reference Books Annual*, 1985, p. 335).

ART (GENERAL)

American Art: Painting, Sculpture, Architecture, Decorative Arts, Photography. Written by Milton W. Brown and others. Abrams, 1979. 616p. $45.00.
Encyclopedic in scope, this book broadly surveys the development of American art from the sixteenth century on. A "beautiful one-volume treatment of the visual arts in America" (*Wilson Library Bulletin*, December 1979, p. 253). The *Britannica Encyclopedia of American Art* (Encyclopaedia Britannica Educational Corp., 1973) offers similar coverage.

Artists' and Illustrators' Encyclopedia. Written by John Quick. 2nd ed. McGraw-Hill, 1977. 327p. $32.95.
Choice (April 1978, p. 212) describes this standard work as a "compact and convenient-sized handbook that will serve the practicing artist as an initial source of brief, professional information." Emphasis is on methods and materials used by the visual artist.

Dictionary of American Art. Written by Matthew Baigell. Harper & Row, 1979. 390p. $17.95; $8.95 paper.
Mainly a biographical dictionary of American artists, the book also includes readable articles on major trends and movements. An "outstanding American art history reference book" (*American Reference Books Annual*, 1981, p. 412).

Dictionary of Subjects and Symbols in Art. Written by James Hall. 2nd ed. Harper & Row, 1979. 349p. $15.95; $8.95 paper.
Alphabetical entries identify and explain the prominent mythological, religious, and literary themes of Western art. *Choice* (March 1975, p. 48) characterized the first edition (1974) as "an impressively erudite yet thoroughly useable dictionary for which students and faculty alike should be grateful."

Encyclopaedia of Drawing: Materials, Techniques and Style. Written by Clive Ashwin. North Light, 1983. 264p. $22.50.
Intended for "anyone who draws or uses drawings for whatever purpose" (introduction), this well-illustrated encyclopedia includes the history, methods, materials, and vocabulary of drawing. "To those who love drawing and want to learn more about it, *Encyclopaedia of Drawing* is a delightful book to consult" (*Booklist*, September 1, 1984, p. 50).

Encyclopedia of Painting: Painters and Painting of the World from Prehistoric Times to the Present Day. Edited by Bernard S. Myers. 4th ed. Crown, 1979. 511p. $19.95.

Myers's popular encyclopedia consists of more than 3,200 entries and 1,000 illustrations covering the history of painting in all places and times. Especially useful for students at the high school and college levels.

The Encyclopedia of Visual Arts. Edited by Lawrence Gowing. Prentice-Hall, 1983. Two vols. $100.00. (Also available from Grolier Educational Corp. in a ten-volume edition at $214.50.)

Volume 1 is a history of art and Volume 2 a biographical dictionary of artists. "Most outstanding are the quality and quantity of the illustrations and reproductions.... The combination of these two volumes provides users with much information in a useable, readable, and pleasing format" (*Choice,* June 1984, p. 1446). A comparable work is the four-volume *Random House Library of Painting and Sculpture* (Random House, 1981).

Encyclopedia of World Art. McGraw-Hill, 1959–68. 15 vols. plus supplement. $995.00 (15 vols.); $69.50 (supplement).

One of the finest subject encyclopedias ever made, the *Encyclopedia of World Art* contains approximately 1,000 scholarly articles covering the entire spectrum of the visual arts. Profusely illustrated, this multivolume work "stands alone in its field" (*Booklist,* April 15, 1969, p. 912).

Graphic Arts Encyclopedia. Written by George A. Stevenson, 2nd ed. McGraw-Hill, 1979. 483p. $38.50.

This alphabetically arranged encyclopedia provides 278 articles on the processes, equipment, and terms used in the reproduction of words and illustrations. "A well-selected bibliography, product and manufacturer information, and an index conclude this recommended ready reference for all artists, designers, and students of the graphic arts" (*American Reference Books Annual,* 1980, p. 394).

McGraw-Hill Dictionary of Art. Edited by Bernard S. Myers and Shirley D. Myers. McGraw-Hill, 1969. Five vols. $89.50.

The *McGraw-Hill Dictionary of Art* contains 15,000 entries and 2,300 illustrations covering all major art forms, periods, schools, and countries. It stands between the large 15-volume *Encyclopedia of World Art* (see above) and the many single-volume art encyclopedias. A work similar in size, scope, and quality is the five-volume *Praeger Encyclopedia of Art* (Praeger, 1971; now out of print).

The Oxford Companion to Art. Edited by Harold Osborne. Oxford Univ. Pr., 1970. 1,290p. $45.00.

"Designed both as an introductory handbook to the visual arts and as a guide to further study for the general reader, this is a welcome addition to the Oxford Companion series" (*College and Research Libraries,* July 1971, p. 310).

The Oxford Companion to Twentieth-Century Art. Edited by Harold Osborne. Oxford Univ. Pr., 1982. 656p. $45.00.

Schools, movements, techniques, and artists through the mid-1970s are identified and concisely treated. "Osborne performs a service by concentrating on lesser-known names of the period he has covered" (*Choice,* July-August 1982, p. 1542).

The Thames and Hudson Dictionary of Art and Artists. Edited by Herbert Read and others; revision editor, Nikos Stangos. Revised ed. Thames and Hudson (dist. by Norton), 1985. 352p. $19.95. (Originally published as the *Encyclopaedia of the Arts* in 1966.)

This revised and updated version of the old *Encyclopaedia of the Arts* is limited to the fine arts. "Highly recommended for both public and undergraduate libraries" (*Choice*, July-August 1985, p. 1621).

ASTRONOMY AND SPACE SCIENCE

The A-Z of Astronomy. Written by Patrick Moore. Scribner's, 1976. 192p. Out of print (last priced at $7.95).

Moore, who has written extensively in the field of astronomy, furnishes nontechnical definitions and descriptions of astronomical terms, principles, phenomena, and places in this revision of the *Amateur Astronomer's Glossary* (Norton, 1967).

Astronomy Data Book. Compiled by J. Hedley Robinson and James Muirden. 2nd ed. Wiley (a Halsted Book), 1979. 272p. $29.95.

Intended for novice or student astronomers, this handy reference "includes a wealth of information on astronomical topics as well as a chronology of important events, conversion tables, and data on radio, gamma-ray, and infrared astronomy" (*Booklist*, September 1, 1984, p. 40).

The Cambridge Encyclopedia of Astronomy. Edited by Simon Mitton. Crown, 1977. 481p. $35.00.

Cited as one of *Library Journal*'s best reference books for 1977, this thematically arranged encyclopedia provides a readable introduction to the fundamentals of astronomy. A 14-page star atlas is included. "By virtue of its superb illustrations (photographs, diagrams, charts) and the credentials of its contributors (most are affiliated with Cambridge's astronomy program), this will be a standard source for both beginners and advanced amateurs" (*American Reference Books Annual*, 1979, p. 649).

Concise Encyclopedia of Astronomy. Written by Arnold Weigert and Helmut Zimmermann. 2nd ed. Crane, Russak, 1976. 532p. $29.50.

Weigert and Zimmermann's valuable encyclopedia, an English-language edition of a German work first published in 1960, includes some 1,500 entries ranging from brief definitions of essential terms and concepts to substantial treatments of astronomical developments as well as astrophysics and space travel. "A good, well-illustrated, nontechnical reference with useful appendixes for the amateur astronomer" (*Choice*, September 1977, p. 837).

The Illustrated Encyclopedia of Astronomy and Space. Edited by Ian Ridpath. Revised ed. T.Y. Crowell (dist. by Harper & Row), 1979. 240p. $19.18.

More than 1,000 clear, concise articles accompanied by numerous tables, charts, and photographs make up this budget-priced encyclopedia. "In addition to the expected astronomical coverage, considerable space has been given to the instruments, satellites, and launch vehicles used in astronomical and space research" (*Booklist*, October 1, 1980, p. 279).

The Illustrated Encyclopedia of Space Technology: A Comprehensive History of Space Exploration. Written by Kenneth Gatland and others. Crown, 1981. 289p. $24.95.

This popularly written account of human efforts to explore space is distinguished by outstanding illustrations: "The remarkable color illustrations are found on about every fourth page in the volume. In fact, the foldouts on pages 50–57 and 170–77 are of frameable print quality" (*American Reference Books Annual*, 1982, p. 802).

The Illustrated Encyclopedia of the Universe: Exploring and Understanding the Cosmos. Written by Richard S. Lewis and others. Crown, 1983. 320p. $24.95.

Lewis, the principal author, and 11 other authorities provide 20 informative articles on the solar system. "This is a spectacular volume that illustrates man's obsession with the heavens; it is encyclopedic in its comprehensive coverage of a wide range of information" (*School Library Journal*, May 1984, p. 109).

The Larousse Guide to Astronomy. Written by David Baker. Larousse, 1978. 288p. $15.95; $9.95 paper.

American Reference Books Annual (1980, p. 611) calls this useful little work "an excellent general introduction to the world of astronomy.... The artwork in the guide is excellent and in some cases, breathtaking."

McGraw-Hill Encyclopedia of Astronomy. Edited by Sybil P. Parker. McGraw-Hill, 1983. 450p. $44.50.

The 230 articles and 393 illustrations that make up this one-volume encyclopedia also appear in the *McGraw-Hill Encyclopedia of Science and Technology* (5th ed., 1982), an expensive ($935.00) multivolume set. The *McGraw-Hill Encyclopedia of Astronomy* is a valuable source for anyone lacking ready access to the parent work.

Pictorial Guide to the Planets. Written by Joseph H. Jackson and John H. Baumert. 3rd ed. Harper & Row, 1981. 246p. $22.50.

First published in 1973 and revised twice, this standard guide offers a readable introduction to the cosmos and space exploration. In a review of the most recent edition, *American Reference Books Annual* (1982, p. 708) observes that "this new edition will serve space buffs as a good introduction to where the space sciences stand today."

BIOLOGY (GENERAL) AND ZOOLOGY

The Audubon Society Encyclopedia of Animal Life. Written by Ralph Bushsbaum and others. Clarkson N. Potter (dist. by Crown), 1982, 606p. $45.00.

An excellent single-volume alternative to the formidable and expensive 13-volume *Grzimek's Animal Life Encyclopedia* (see below). *Booklist* (December 15, 1982, p. 542) calls the Audubon Society's encyclopedia a "delight for animal lovers, zoology buffs, armchair naturalists, and browsers."

The Audubon Society Encyclopedia of North American Birds. Written by John K. Terres. Knopf, 1980. 1,109p. $60.00.

"If any person interested in North American birds were limited to possession of only a single book, this would undoubtedly be it." So says *American Reference Books Annual* (1982, p. 736) of this massive work. Other outstanding reference sources about birds include Roger Tory Peterson's *Field Guide to the Birds* (4th ed. Houghton Mifflin, 1980) and Christopher Perrins and Alex L.A. Middleton's *Encyclopedia of Birds* (Facts on File, 1985).

The Cambridge Encyclopedia of Life Sciences. Edited by Adrian Friday and David S. Ingram. Cambridge Univ. Pr., 1985. 432p. $45.00.

This heavily illustrated, thematically arranged encyclopedia covers all significant aspects of biology from microorganisms to complex plant and animal life. For high school and college level readers.

Concise Encyclopedia of Biochemistry. Edited by Thomas A. Scott and Mary Brewer. Walter de Gruyter, 1983. 516p. $29.95.

An English-language translation of the German *Brockhaus ABC Biochemie,* this specialized source contains more than 4,200 entries. "The only contemporary, comprehensive, one-volume dictionary or encyclopedia of biochemistry in English, and it is very good" (*Choice,* October 1983, p. 248). An older work is the one-volume *Encyclopedia of Biochemistry* (Reinhold, 1967) by Roger John Williams and Edwin M. Lansford.

Encyclopedia of Bioethics. Edited by Warren T. Reich. Free Pr., 1978. Four vols. $250.00. (Also available in an unabridged two-volume edition at $125.00.)

Ranging from *Abortion* to *Zygote Banking,* the 315 lengthy articles that make up this interdisciplinary encyclopedia are aimed chiefly at advanced students in the life sciences, teachers, researchers, and policymakers. "This is primarily an encyclopedia of issues and ideas rather than of events" (*Booklist,* March 15, 1983, p. 988).

The Encyclopedia of Mammals. Edited by David Macdonald. Facts on File, 1984. 943p. $45.00.

This excellent encyclopedia provides accurate, up-to-date information about all orders of mammals (roughly 4,000 species) in some 700 articles by 180 scholars. The *Times Literary Supplement* (July 20, 1984, p. 800) says "the publishers claim that the book is 'a delight to the eye and a stimulus to the mind', and so it is." Another invaluable source on the same subject is the two-volume *Walker's Mammals of the World* (4th ed. Johns Hopkins Univ. Pr., 1983).

The Encyclopedia of North American Wildlife. Written by Stanley Klein. Facts on File, 1983. 315p. $35.00.

Klein's encyclopedia covers mammals, birds, reptiles, amphibians, and fish found in the wild in the United States, Canada, and Mexico. "Written on a level suitable for older children through adult general readers, the book is an attractive, quick reference source for general collections" (*Library Journal,* January 1984, p. 76).

The Encyclopedia of Prehistoric Life. Edited by Rodney Steel and Anthony P. Harvey. McGraw-Hill, 1979. 218p. Out of print (last priced at $24.95).

Many black-and-white line drawings accompany the 370 articles by 23 specialists that make up this useful source. "This is an excellent work, unique in its field" (*American Reference Books Annual,* 1980, p. 347).

The Encyclopedia of the Biological Sciences. Edited by Peter Gray. 2nd ed. Van Nostrand, 1970 (reprinted 1981). 1,027p. $55.00.

Despite its advancing age, this large single-volume encyclopedia remains an important source of "succinct and accurate information for biologists in those fields in which they are not themselves experts" (introduction). It contains approximately 800 long, detailed, signed articles by nearly 500 contributors.

Grzimek's Animal Life Encyclopedia. Edited by Bernhard Grzimek. Van Nostrand, 1972–75. 13 vols. $500.00; $275.00 paper.

The premier animal encyclopedia, *Grzimek* originally appeared in Germany in 1967. The set, which can be used to good advantage by serious students at the high school and college levels, is authoritative and extremely well illustrated. The 21-volume *Encyclopedia of the Animal World* (dist. in North America by Farwell Promotional Books, 1979), priced at $199.95, is another multivolume work on the same subject.

Grzimek's Encyclopedia of Evolution. Edited by Bernhard Grzimek. Van Nostrand, 1976. 560p. $39.50.

Although an important reference source on its own, this single-volume work serves mainly to complement the 13-volume *Grzimek's Animal Life Encyclopedia* (see above). Along the same lines are *Grzimek's Encyclopedia of Ethology* (Van Nostrand, 1977) and *Grzimek's Encyclopedia of Ecology* (Van Nostrand, 1976).

Macmillan Illustrated Animal Encyclopedia. Edited by Philip Whitfield. Macmillan, 1984. 600p. $35.00.

This handsome, beautifully illustrated encyclopedia furnishes basic factual information about nearly 2,000 different vertebrates. "Definitely a book that will appeal to families with children and to any library that cannot afford the more expensive comprehensive volumes" (*Booklist,* May 1, 1985, p. 1246).

Marine Life: An Illustrated Encyclopedia of Invertebrates in the Sea. Written by J. David George and Jennifer J. George. Wiley, 1979. 288p. $69.95.

Intended for zoology students at the college level and serious amateur naturalists, the Georges' encyclopedia is clearly and concisely written. It is arranged phylogenetically (from sponges to lancelets) rather than alphabetically and is very well illustrated. Indeed *American Reference Books Annual* (1981, p. 675) comments that "this is doubtless the most extensive selection of color photos of marine invertebrates ever published."

The Oxford Companion to Animal Behaviour. Edited by David McFarland. Oxford Univ. Pr., 1981. 657p. $35.00.

"There is only one word to summarize this book—*excellent.* This 'companion' to animal behavior will undoubtedly become a standard reference volume and remain one for many years.... This volume should appeal to professionals and laypeople alike and is highly recommended for all libraries, especially college, university, and large public" (*Choice,* September 1982, p. 121).

Synopsis and Classification of Living Organisms. Edited by Sybil P. Parker. McGraw-Hill, 1982. Two vols. $175.00.

More than 8,000 articles by 175 leading authorities, plus some 300 pages of illustrations, make up this invaluable encyclopedic work devoted to the classification and description of all living organisms, from viruses and bacteria through invertebrates and vertebrates. A "monumental work" (*Choice,* September 1982, p. 60).

BOTANY AND HORTICULTURE

The Complete Handbook of Garden Plants. Written by Michael Wright, assisted by Sue Minter and Brian Carter. Facts on File, 1984. 544p. $18.95.
 "Compact and portable, it is crammed with information about the more than 9000 species and varieties of decorative outdoor garden plants one is likely to encounter in the temperate zones.... A hardiness map and glossaries of terms, pests, and diseases round out this unusually useful book" (*Library Journal,* May 15, 1984, p. 977).

A Dictionary of Useful and Everyday Plants and Their Common Names; Based on Material Contained in J.C. Willis: A Dictionary of the Flowering Plants and Ferns (6th Edition, 1931). Written by F.N. Howes. Cambridge Univ. Pr., 1974. 290p. $37.50.
 An expansion and updating of Willis's classic dictionary, Howes's work includes English-language botanical terminology as well as encyclopedic information about plants and their products.

Encyclopedia of American Forest and Conservation History. Edited by Richard C. Davis. Macmillan, 1983. Two vols. $150.00.
 Consisting of more than 400 substantial articles from *Afforestation* and *Air Pollution and Forests* to *Wood Preservation* and *World War II and American Forests and Forest Industry,* this specialized (albeit interdisciplinary) work is intended to be "the standard, authoritative guide and reference to the history of forestry, conservation, forest industries, and other forest-related subjects in the United States" (preface). *Booklist* (November 15, 1984, p. 427) calls the encyclopedia "an excellent set."

The Encyclopedia of Organic Gardening. Written by the staff of *Organic Gardening* magazine. Revised ed. Rodale Pr., 1978. 1,236p. $24.95.
 Long the organic gardener's bible, this work comprises more than 2,000 A-to-Z entries covering the identification, cultivation, and use of various fruits, grains, nuts, vegetables, and ornamentals. "The large print makes the clearly written text pleasant to read, and extensive cross referencing provides easy access to all of the material" (*American Reference Books Annual,* 1979, pp. 758–59).

Exotica IV: Pictorial Cyclopedia of Exotic Plants from Tropical and Near-Tropical Regions. Written by Alfred Byrd Graf. 11th ed. Scribner's, 1982. Two vols. $187.00.
 This standard work furnishes concise descriptive information and advice concerning thousands of species of exotic plants. The text is enhanced by over 400 color and 15,000 black-and-white illustrations. A companion volume is Graf's *Tropica III: Color Cyclopedia of Exotic Plants* (3rd ed. Scribner's, 1986).

Hortus Third: A Concise Dictionary of Plants Cultivated in the United States and Canada. Compiled by Liberty Hyde Bailey and Ethel Zoe Bailey; revised and expanded by the staff of the Liberty Hyde Bailey Hortorium. 3rd ed. Macmillan, 1976. 1,290p. $125.00.
 First published in 1930 and revised in 1941 and most recently in 1976, *Hortus* covers the uses, propagation, and cultivation of some 10,000 species and botanical varieties of plants found in North America. *American Reference Books Annual* (1978, p. 752) states that this work "will be of real assistance to nurserymen and home gardeners alike."

The New York Botanical Garden Illustrated Encyclopedia of Horticulture. Written by Thomas H. Everett. Garland, 1981–82. Ten vols. $525.00.

Remarkably, the work of a single person, the eminent horticulturist Thomas Everett of the New York Botanical Garden, this multivolume encyclopedia of some 3 million words covering 20,000 species is "a thorough and comprehensive study of the common and some of the more technical aspects of horticulture, and it belongs in every library that can afford it" (*Library Journal,* December 1, 1982, p. 2248).

The Oxford Encyclopedia of Trees of the World. Edited by Bayard Hora. Oxford Univ. Pr., 1981. 288p. $27.50.

"This is an informative and well-illustrated summary of the major genera of trees of the world, and is an excellent general reference source for native and exotic trees of North America" (*American Reference Books Annual,* 1983, p. 631). An older work of similar coverage and quality is Hugh Johnson's single-volume *International Book of Trees* (Simon & Schuster, 1973).

Popular Encyclopedia of Plants. Edited by Vernon H. Heywood and Stuart R. Chant. Cambridge Univ. Pr., 1982. 368p. $32.50.

Emphasizing "the main species of plants used by Man" (introduction), this encyclopedia identifies and concisely describes plants used for food, medicine, building construction, etc. "The appeal of the book lies in its beautiful, clear color photographs that appear on every page, set close to the pertinent text and giving scale" (*College and Research Libraries,* January 1983, p. 54).

Rodale's Encyclopedia of Indoor Gardening. Edited by Anne M. Halpin. Rodale Pr., 1980. 902p. $29.95.

Useful for both the beginning and advanced gardener, this Rodale reference work is a boon to those who cultivate plants indoors. "Almost everything the novice indoor gardener would wish to know is discussed: gardening with artificial lights; pests and plant diseases; or, how to care for bonsai or carnivorous plants" (*American Reference Books Annual,* 1981, p. 745).

10,000 Garden Questions Answered by 20 Experts. Edited by Marjorie J. Dietz. 4th ed. Doubleday, 1982. 1,507p. $19.95.

A handy, inexpensive, popularly written reference that treats such varied topics as soils and fertilizers, landscaping, plant pests, weeds, trees, shrubs, vines, bulbs, roses, perennials, annuals, biennials, lawns, vegetables, fruits, and house plants. Dietz is also the author of several other general books on the subject, including the *ABCs of Gardening: Outdoor and Indoor* (Doubleday, 1985).

Wyman's Gardening Encyclopedia. Written by Donald Wyman. Revised ed. Macmillan, 1977. 1,221p. $29.95.

Wyman's well-known work is arguably the best one-volume general encyclopedia on gardening currently available. Others include the *Reader's Digest Illustrated Guide to Gardening* (Norton, 1978), which lacks the depth of *Wyman,* and *Huxley's Encyclopedia of Gardening for Great Britain and America* (Universe Books, 1982) by Anthony Huxley, an authoritative source but heavily weighted toward British terminology and practice.

BUSINESS AND ECONOMICS (INCLUDES STATISTICS)

The Arnold Encyclopedia of Real Estate. Written by Alvin L. Arnold and Jack Kusnet. Warren, Gorham & Lamont, 1978. 901p. $55.00.

The *Arnold Encyclopedia* includes roughly 3,000 articles on all important aspects of real estate, from apartments to zoning. *Choice* (December 1979, p. 1283) calls it "the most comprehensive and useful one-volume real estate encyclopedia currently available." Updated each year by the *Arnold Encyclopedia of Real Estate Yearbook.*

Encyclopedia of Accounting Systems. Edited by Jerome K. Pescow. Revised ed. Prentice-Hall, 1976. Three vols. $79.50.

"This outstanding, important work illustrates, describes, and explains accounting systems for some 70 different industries, businesses, professions, and non-profit organizations ... a must book for the accountant who is faced with the accounting problems of a business or enterprise that is unfamiliar to him" (*American Reference Books Annual,* 1977, p. 385).

Encyclopedia of American Economic History: Studies of the Principal Movements and Ideas. Edited by Glenn Porter. Scribner's, 1980. Three vols. $180.00.

The 72 lengthy articles that make up this important set present "the views of many specialists on a number of aspects of the collective American economic experience as it is understood in the latter part of the 1970s" (preface). The encyclopedia is more concerned with trends and developments than specific facts and economists.

Encyclopedia of Banking and Finance. Originally written by Glenn G. Munn; revised by F.L. Garcia. 8th ed. Bankers Publishing Co., 1983. 1,024p. $89.00.

First published in 1924, this encyclopedia has become an indispensable one-volume reference for the business community. The latest edition (1983) has almost 4,000 entries, including many definitions of banking and financial terms as well as long articles on such subjects as the farm loan system. "This outstanding book belongs in all libraries with business collections" (*Library Journal,* December 1, 1983, p. 2242).

Encyclopedia of Economics. Edited by Douglas Greenwald. McGraw-Hill, 1982. 1,070p. $59.95.

Clearly written and informatively illustrated with tables, graphs, etc., this encyclopedia contains more than 300 signed articles by prominent economists on all major aspects of economics. "The encyclopedia is intended for all levels of students, but there is a great deal of sophisticated information, often in quantitative form, for advanced students as well as beginners" (*Choice,* April 1982, p. 1045).

Encyclopedia of Investments. Edited by Marshall E. Blume and Jack P. Friedman. Warren, Gorham & Lamont, 1982. 1,093p. $47.50.

This very useful work describes some 60 types of investments, both traditional (stocks, bonds, etc.) and nontraditional (art, gemstones, stamps, mortgage-backed securities, financial futures, etc.). An equally useful, complementary source is the *Investor's Encyclopedia* (Franklin Watts, 1985) by Chet Currier.

The Encyclopedia of Management. Edited by Carl Heyel. 3rd ed. Van Nostrand, 1982. 1,416p. $57.50.

Booklist (November 1, 1983, p. 412) finds this encyclopedia "a much-needed compendium of management information in compact form." A similar work is Frank Finch's *Facts on File Encyclopedia of Management Techniques* (Facts on File, 1984).

Encyclopedia of Statistical Sciences. Edited by Samuel Kotz and Norman L. Johnson. Wiley, 1982–. Eight vols. (in progress). $79.50 per vol.

Intended as an introduction to statistical concepts and applications for those who have some general knowledge of mathematics, this in-progress encyclopedia will eventually be "the most comprehensive encyclopedia in its subject yet published" (*American Reference Books Annual,* 1984, p. 340). To date, five of the projected eight volumes have appeared.

First Facts of American Labor: A Comprehensive Collection of Labor Firsts in the United States Arranged by Subject. Compiled by Philip S. Foner. Holmes & Meier, 1984. 237p. $29.75.

Choice (June 1984, p. 1444) says this source "should be purchased by college and university libraries because of Foner's commendable work in tying together so many important turning points on all aspects of labor history, from novels and academy awards to injunctions or hours of work."

International Encyclopedia of Statistics. Edited by William H. Kruskal and Judith M. Tanur. Free Pr., 1978. Two vols. $145.00.

Based on material drawn from the 17-volume *International Encyclopedia of the Social Sciences* (1968), this set contains 75 articles on statistics, 42 articles on social science subjects with particular reference to statistics, and 57 biographies of key statisticians. William A. Katz, in his *Introduction to Reference Work* (1982, vol. 1, p. 229), characterizes this encyclopedia as "a basic guide for beginners in statistics and research, of particular value to those in the social sciences and mathematics."

The Money Encyclopedia. Edited by Harvey Rachlin. Harper & Row, 1984. 672p. $25.48.

"Prepared for laypersons interested in understanding banking, finance, taxes, real estate, insurance, and estate planning, this book contains hundreds of alphabetically arranged signed articles, some lengthy and others brief, by more than 135 experts" (*Library Journal,* April 15, 1984, pp. 804–05). Other useful titles on finance for the average person are *Sylvia Porter's New Money Book for the '80s* (Avon, 1980) and Don and Joan German's *Money A to Z* (Facts on File, 1984).

Occupational Outlook Handbook. Prepared by the U.S. Bureau of Labor Statistics. U.S. Government Printing Office, published every two years since 1949. $13.00; $9.00 paper.

This standard reference source describes more than 700 occupations and industries in easy-to-understand essays that cover such points as earnings, working conditions, and opportunities for advancement. The *Occupational Outlook Quarterly* keeps the handbook up-to-date between editions.

Thorndike Encyclopedia of Banking and Financial Tables. Edited by David Thorndike. Revised ed. Warren, Gorham & Lamont, 1980. One vol. (various paging). $72.00.

Primarily for investors and bankers, this source includes all important financial and real estate tables on such subjects as interest and savings, installment loans, and mortgage rates. An updating yearbook to the encyclopedia has been published annually since 1975.

CHEMISTRY AND CHEMICAL ENGINEERING

Chemical and Process Technology Encyclopedia. Edited by Douglas M. Considine. McGraw-Hill, 1974. 1,266p. $79.50.
    An older but still relevant one-volume summary of industrial chemistry, this encyclopedia is an inexpensive alternative to the 25-volume *Kirk-Othmer Encyclopedia of Chemical Technology* (see below), the leading work in this field.

Chemical Technology: An Encyclopedic Treatment. Edited by L.W. Codd and others. Barnes & Noble, 1968–75. Eight vols. $360.00.
    This successor to the late Dr. J.F. Van Oss's classic *Warenkennis en Technologie* (*Systematic Encyclopedia of Technology*) covers the entire spectrum of chemical technology. Intended for both nonspecialists and practitioners, the set aims to describe "the sources, manufacture, processing, and uses of both natural and synthetic materials" (preface). "An essential work in this field" (*American Reference Books Annual,* 1977, p. 756).

Encyclopedia of Chemical Reactions. Written by Carl Alfred Jacobson and Clifford A. Hampel. Van Nostrand, 1946–59. Eight vols. $135.80.
    Arranged alphabetically, first by the formulas of the reactant and then by the reagents, this is the chemist's standard source for chemical reactions.

Encyclopedia of Polymer Science and Technology. Edited by Norbert M. Bikales. Wiley-Interscience, 1964–72. 16 vols. $100.00 per vol.
    "Since the first volume of this unique encyclopedia was published in 1964, its reputation has grown apace with the developments in macromolecular science and biochemistry ... an essential addition to any library serving the scientific community" (*American Reference Books Annual,* 1980, pp. 616–17).

Kingzett's Chemical Encyclopedia: A Digest of Chemistry and Its Industrial Applications. Originally edited by Charles Thomas Kingzett; revision edited by D.H. Hey. 9th ed. Van Nostrand, 1966. 1,092p. Out of print (last priced at $36.95).
    Though now out of print, *Kingzett* is still found in many library reference collections, including small ones. Intended for the nonspecialist, it remains one of the best-known encyclopedias covering the whole field of chemistry.

Kirk-Othmer Encyclopedia of Chemical Technology. Edited by Martin Grayson. 3rd ed. Wiley-Interscience, 1978–84. 25 vols. plus supplement. $4,250.00 (25 vols.); $150.00 (supplement).
    Far and away the most important reference work in the area of chemical technology, *Kirk-Othmer* has recently undergone a massive and revitalizing revision. Every article in the second edition (1963–72) has been rewritten, updated, or dropped. Happily for individuals and libraries that cannot afford the multivolume set, the publisher now offers the *Kirk-Othmer Concise Encyclopedia of Chemical Technology* (Wiley-Interscience, 1985), a one-volume abridgment at $99.95. *Choice* (June 1985, p. 1474) notes that *Kirk-Othmer* is "widely recognized as an outstanding chemical technology reference; this one-volume, concise edition maintains this reputation."

Lange's Handbook of Chemistry. Originally edited by Norbert Adolph Lange; revision edited by John A. Dean. 13th ed. McGraw-Hill, 1985. 1,470p. $45.75.

"This is a handy reference work that provides ready access to chemical and physics data used in the laboratory and manufacturing" (*Booklist,* September 1, 1984, p. 36). Another excellent desk reference for the working chemist is the *CRC Handbook of Chemistry and Physics* (published annually since 1913 by the Chemical Rubber Co.).

McGraw-Hill Encyclopedia of Chemistry. Edited by Sybil P. Parker. McGraw-Hill, 1983. 1,200p. $54.50.

Nearly 800 articles on all aspects of chemistry make up this affordable one-volume work. Note that the articles are drawn from the multivolume *McGraw-Hill Encyclopedia of Science and Technology* (5th ed., 1982).

Riegel's Handbook of Industrial Chemistry. Edited by James A. Kent. 8th ed. Van Nostrand, 1983. 979p. $59.50.

More a state-of-the-art review than a handbook, this important source covers current developments in the chemical process industry, including such diverse topics as air pollution control, wastewater technology, coal gasification, and pharmaceuticals. *American Reference Books Annual* (1984, p. 731) says *Riegel* is "a long-standing classic in the field of chemical technology."

Van Nostrand Reinhold Encyclopedia of Chemistry. Edited by Douglas M. Considine. 4th ed. Van Nostrand, 1984. 1,082p. $89.50.

Containing approximately 1,300 alphabetically arranged articles, all prepared by authorities in the field, this encyclopedia is a thorough revision of the *Encyclopedia of Chemistry* (3rd ed. Van Nostrand, 1973), edited by Clifford Hampel and Gessner Hawley. "This is one of the best, one-volume chemical encyclopedias available" (*Booklist,* September 1, 1984, p. 36).

COMPUTER AND ELECTRONIC SCIENCES

Computer Dictionary and Handbook. Written by Charles J. Sippl and Charles P. Sippl. 3rd ed. Howard W. Sams & Co., 1980. 928p. $34.95.

The Sippls' work is a basic reference that, in addition to defining essential terms, provides "a good overview and introduction to modern computer technology" (*Library Journal,* February 1, 1985, p. 60). A fourth edition is scheduled for publication in 1986.

Concise Encyclopedia of Information Technology. Written by Adrian V. Stokes. Prentice-Hall, 1983. 271p. $17.95; $9.95 paper.

Prepared and originally published in Great Britain, this encyclopedic dictionary covers the terminology of the computer and information sciences from *Abacus* to *Zoned Decimal.* "The definitions are well written and intelligible to laypersons willing, sometimes, to look up some of the technical words used in the definitions" (*Booklist,* February 1, 1984, p. 797).

Encyclopedia of Computer Science and Engineering. Edited by Anthony Ralston and Edwin D. Reilly. 2nd ed. Van Nostrand, 1983. 1,664p. $87.50.

First published in 1976 as simply the *Encyclopedia of Computer Science,* this excellent one-volume source contains some 550 articles for the nonspecialist. *Library Journal* (April 15, 1984, p. 785), when naming the encyclopedia to its list of best reference books for 1983, called it an "outstanding new edition of a highly respected and standard source."

Encyclopedia of Computer Science and Technology. Edited by Jack Belzer, Albert G. Holzman, and Allen Kent. Marcel Dekker, 1975–. 20 vols. (in progress). $99.75 per vol.

At present, 15 of the projected 20 volumes of this monumental encyclopedic survey have been published.

Encyclopedia of Computer Terms. Written by Douglas Downing. Barron's, 1983. 148p. $6.95.

"The small-scale, nonprofessional computer user will most appreciate Downing's effort. The 400 entries are very readable, in lay language, and simplified without sacrificing accuracy" (*American Reference Books Annual,* 1984, p. 616). The book also includes information about basic concepts in computing and programming techniques. Another simple, inexpensive title for the beginner is the *Encyclopedia of Computers and Electronics* (Rand McNally, 1983).

Encyclopedia of Integrated Circuits: A Practical Handbook of Essential Reference Data. Written by Walter H. Bushsbaum. Prentice-Hall, 1981. 420p. $24.95.

Anyone from hobbyists to electronics engineers interested in knowing about what integrated circuits do and the problems associated with them will find this a handy reference.

Encyclopedic Dictionary of Electronic Terms. Compiled by John F. Traister and Robert J. Traister. Prentice-Hall, 1984. 604p. $29.95.

The 1,190 entries are, according to *Choice* (November 1984, p. 409) "concise, well written, and quite long for a dictionary." Numerous illustrations enhance the printed text.

McGraw-Hill Encyclopedia of Electronics and Computers. Edited by Sybil P. Parker. McGraw-Hill, 1984. 964p. $59.50.

Most of the 477 articles that make up this valuable one-volume work derive from the multivolume *McGraw-Hill Encyclopedia of Science and Technology* (5th ed., 1982), although some are new, for example, *Electronic Publishing, Programming Languages,* and *Digital Optical Recorders. Choice* (February 1984, p. 806) finds this "a readable and well-constructed book that should prove useful to both professionals and students interested in either electronics or topics related to computers."

McGraw-Hill Personal Computer Programming Encyclopedia: Languages and Operating Systems. Edited by William J. Birnes. McGraw-Hill, 1985. 736p. $80.00.

This new work "provides quite acceptable coverage of all the major languages (and many of the minor ones) in use on microcomputers today, plus some possible future contenders" (*Library Journal,* September 1, 1985, p. 191).

Personal Computers A-Z. Written by Joel Makower. Doubleday, 1984. 185p. $15.95; $8.95 paper.

Library Journal (May 15, 1984, p. 990) describes this little book as "part primer, part encyclopedia, and part glossary, all aimed at new or potential personal computer owners." Makower explains 350 key terms, sometimes in considerable depth but always in language that can be understood by the beginning computer student.

CRAFTS AND HOBBIES

The Crafts Business Encyclopedia: How to Make Money, Market Your Product, and Manage Your Home Crafts Business. Written by Michael Scott. Revised ed. Harcourt Brace, 1979. 320p. $4.95 paper.

Scott's inexpensive guide clearly and concisely discusses such pertinent topics as insurance, taxes, accounting and bookkeeping, credit, pricing, promotion and publicity, and federal regulations. In all, there are some 375 alphabetically arranged articles.

The Encyclopedia of Crafts. Edited by Laura Torbet. Scribner's, 1980. Three vols. $100.00.

"This handsome set contains 12,000 alphabetically arranged entries covering fifty crafts, including most of the major popular crafts, such as needlework, fabric craft, stained glass, woodworking, toymaking, and jewelry" (*Wilson Library Bulletin,* February 1981, p. 464).

A Guide Book of United States Coins. Originally edited by Richard S. Yeoman; revision edited by Kenneth E. Bressett. Western, published every year since 1947. 256p. $5.95.

Known informally as the "Red Book," this standard reference provides retail price listings for all United States coins from colonial times to the present. A companion volume, also published annually, is the *Handbook of United States Coins* (Western, 1941–), a guide to the wholesale value of U.S. collector coins; it is known as the "Blue Book."

The Macmillan Encyclopedic Dictionary of Numismatics. Written by Richard G. Doty. Macmillan, 1982. 355p. $34.95.

Doty, a curator at the American Numismatic Society, covers coining processes and equipment, historically significant coins from all periods and places, and technical terminology and concepts in 422 articles accompanied by more than 650 illustrations. The work is "a comprehensive and accurate source for terms and concepts of interest to numismatics as well as amateurs" (*Booklist,* July 1984, p. 1536).

Reader's Digest Complete Guide to Needlework. Reader's Digest Association (dist. by Norton), 1979. 504p. $21.50.

Ten major needle crafts are introduced: embroidery, needlepoint, knitting, appliqué, quilting, patchwork, macramé, crochet, rugmaking, and lacework. "This tome doesn't contain creative, 'wow'-inspiring projects, though there are a few at the end of each section. Instead, it's more of a reference tool, containing the ABCs, stitches, and techniques anyone would need to start—and finish—a particular crafts project" (*Booklist,* February 15, 1980, p. 808).

Reader's Digest Crafts and Hobbies. Reader's Digest Association (dist. by Norton), 1980. 456p. $21.45.

A profusely illustrated, step-by-step guide to 37 crafts and hobbies (including leatherwork, woodworking, mosaics, batik, quilting, modeling, ceramics, jewelry, origami, and indoor gardening), this handy book "is more than a pastime for a rainy afternoon. It is an exceptional value for doers and makers, and for those who enjoy handmade objects and wish to understand how they come to be" (*School Library Journal,* March 1981, p. 164).

Scott Standard Postage Stamp Catalogue. Scott Publications, published every year since 1868. Five vols. $18.00 per vol.

Scott's encyclopedic guide to the stamps of the world is indispensable for serious collectors. A similar work in two volumes is Gibbons's annual *Stamps of the World* (Stanley Gibbons Publications, 1935–).

Stamp Collecting A to Z. Written by Walter Young. A.S. Barnes, 1981. 216p. $15.00.

"In choosing a single source for information on the subject of philately for a beginner or relatively new hobbyist, one would be tempted to select this handy guide" (*American Reference Books Annual,* 1982, p. 493). Another useful title for the beginning collector is Richard Cabeen's *Standard Handbook of Stamp Collecting* (2nd ed. T.Y. Crowell, 1979).

Standard Catalog of World Paper Money. Compiled by Albert Pick. 4th ed. Krause Publications, 1984. 832p. $40.00.

This well-known catalog, which lists prices for paper money in various conditions, is the most comprehensive work of its kind. Collectors of U.S. paper money will also be interested in Robert Friedberg's *Paper Money of the United States: A Complete Illustrated Guide with Valuations* (10th ed. Coin and Currency Institute, 1981) and Chester L. Krause and Robert F. Lemke's *Standard Catalog of U.S. Paper Money* (Krause Publications, 1981).

World Coin Encyclopedia. Written by Ewald Junge. Morrow, 1984. 297p. $19.95.

With more (1,500 as opposed to 422) but less expansive entries than Richard Doty's *Macmillan Encyclopedic Dictionary of Numismatics* (see above), Junge's well-illustrated encyclopedia covers coins from all over the world and from the earliest times. Both sources are "recommended for reference and hobby collections" (*Library Journal,* March 15, 1985, p. 53).

DECORATIVE ARTS (INCLUDES ANTIQUES)

The Collector's Complete Dictionary of American Antiques. Written by Frances Phipps. Doubleday, 1974. 640p. Out of print (last priced at $25.00).

Phipps's book, unfortunately no longer available from the publisher, "not only contains a wealth of information on objects made and used in this country during the first two centuries of its history but also, through its use of original sources, provides many valuable and fascinating insights into the life of the times" (*Booklist,* June 15, 1975, p. 1084). A number of other useful encyclopedic works on antiques exist, but paradoxically they are also all out of print: the *Collectors' Encyclopedia of Antiques* (Crown, 1973), edited by Phoebe Phillips; the *Complete Color Encyclopedia of Antiques* (2nd ed. Hawthorn, 1975), edited by L.G.G. Ramsey; Geoffrey Wills's *Concise Encyclopedia of Antiques* (Van Nostrand, 1976); James Mackay's *Encyclopedia of Small Antiques* (Harper & Row, 1975); the *Random House Collector's Encyclopedia* (Random House, 1974); and the *Random House Encyclopedia of Antiques* (Random House, 1973), edited by Ian Cameron and Elizabeth Kingsley-Rowe.

Dictionary of the Decorative Arts. Written by John Fleming and Hugh Honour. Harper & Row, 1977. 896p. $29.95.

Originally published in Great Britain under the title *Penguin Dictionary of Decorative Arts,* this work contains some 4,000 articles accompanied by more than 1,000 black-and-white illustrations. "An indispensable reference volume for anyone concerned with the visual arts" (*Publishers Weekly,* August 8, 1977, p. 55).

The Dictionary of World Pottery and Porcelain. Written by Louise Ade Boger. Scribner's, 1971. 533p. $22.50; $9.95 paper.

Intended as a "comprehensive and concise guide for the collector and student as well as the general reader" (foreword), Boger's authoritative book covers nearly 7,000 years of pottery and porcelain making in approximately 2,200 entries. Interested consumers should also check out Elisabeth Cameron's *Encyclopedia of Pottery and Porcelain: 1800–1960* (Facts on File, 1985).

Encyclopedia of Decorative Arts, 1890–1940. Edited by Philippe Garner. Van Nostrand, 1979. 320p. $35.00.

"Dozens of books have been written on the Art Noveau and Art Deco periods covered in this excellent volume. But none has succeeded until now in achieving a larger view of the two styles and their designers.... It's a feast for the eyes and for the mind—covering furniture, decorative sculpture, jewelry, glass, lighting, tablewares, pottery, posters, rugs and accessories" (*New York Times,* December 23, 1979, p. 32).

Encyclopedia of Design. Compiled by Harold H. Hart. Hart Publishing Co., 1983. 399p. $79.00; $39.00 paper.

The *Encyclopedia of Design* consists of hundreds of black-and-white illustrations from around the world that are in the public domain and therefore may be photocopied or otherwise reproduced without fee or permission. A similar work is *Designs on File* (Facts on File, 1984), a loose-leaf publication priced at $75.00.

The Encyclopedia of Furniture. Written by Joseph Aronson. 3rd ed. Crown, 1965. 484p. $15.95.

Despite its age, Aronson's encyclopedia remains a good source for furniture terms and styles. It is heavily illustrated and covers the major periods and developments. Other valuable references on this subject are *American Furniture: 1620 to the Present* (Richard Marek, 1981) by Jonathan L. Fairbanks and Elizabeth Bidwell Bates, and the *Field Guide to American Antique Furniture* (Facts on File, 1985) by Joseph T. Butler and Kathleen Eagen Johnson.

The Encyclopedia of Glass. Edited by Phoebe Phillips. Crown, 1981. 320p. $12.98.

"An excellent history of glass that acts as both a reference guide and as a collector's source book" (*Booklist,* March 1, 1982, p. 841).

The Encyclopedia of Textiles. Compiled by the Editors of *American Fabrics and Fashion Magazine.* 3rd ed. Prentice-Hall, 1980. 636p. $49.95.

Originally entitled the *AF Encyclopedia of Textiles,* this specialized reference work is for those concerned with the production and marketing of fiber and fabrics. The third edition "shows considerable updating to account for developments since 1972. There are many new illustrations, and some articles have been rewritten" (*Wilson Library Bulletin,* September 1980, p. 61).

The Encyclopedia of World Costume. Written by Doreen Yarwood. Scribner's, 1978. 471p. $32.50.

This excellent single-volume treatment of costume from the ancient world to the present day includes 650 articles (some quite lengthy) augmented by some 2,000 black-and-white drawings. An older but equally useful work is R. Turner Wilcox's *Dictionary of Costume* (Scribner's, 1968).

The Fashion Encyclopedia: An Essential Guide to Everything You Need to Know about Clothes. Written by Catherine Houck. St. Martin's Pr., 1982. 236p. $12.95 paper.

Houck's popularly written book is especially useful for home economics and design students. "With very pleasing illustrations, the encyclopedia is an excellent tool for both reference and browsing" (*Booklist,* August 1982, p. 1492).

The Oxford Companion to the Decorative Arts. Edited by Harold Osborne. Oxford Univ. Pr., 1975. 865p. $49.95.

Common and uncommon arts—costume, furniture, jewelry, leatherwork, embroidery, toymaking, landscape gardening, book production, bell-founding, lace-tatting, etc.—are covered by some 75 experts in this handy guide. "The *Companion* does not provide definitive treatment of any of its subjects, but it is an excellent starting point for the nonspecialist because of its concise, reliable coverage of a broad range of topics and useful bibliographies" (*Booklist,* June 15, 1976, p. 1486).

EARTH AND ENVIRONMENTAL SCIENCES (INCLUDES ENERGY)

The Cambridge Encyclopedia of Earth Sciences. Edited by David G. Smith. Cambridge Univ. Pr., 1982. 496p. $37.50.

Thematically arranged, this fine encyclopedia consists of 27 long, signed articles accompanied by approximately 500 illustrations. "The thorough, well-written coverage of a wide range of topics is suitable for readers on all levels.... Recommended for all libraries, and not necessarily only for the reference shelf" (*Choice,* July-August 1982, p. 1534).

Color Encyclopedia of Gemstones. Written by Joel E. Arem. Van Nostrand, 1977. 147p. $39.50.

Arem's encyclopedia, which is arranged alphabetically by mineral species, provides basic information about every known variety of gemstone. *American Reference Books Annual* (1979, p. 704) advises: "This encyclopedia is of practical interest to gemologists, but valuable also to the layman, who would do well to consult this reference before purchasing gems."

Encyclopedia of Community Planning and Environmental Management. Written by Marilyn Spigel Schultz and Vivian Loeb Kasen. Facts on File, 1984. 475p. $45.00.

Written by two urban regional planners, this 2,000-entry encyclopedia covers such interdisciplinary aspects of environmental planning as land use, economic development, flood control, landmark court cases, and major legislation in the United States and, to a lesser extent, Canada, Great Britain, and Western Europe. The encyclopedia "is well done, comprehensive, and easy to use" (*Booklist,* June 15, 1985, p. 1441).

Encyclopedia of Earth Sciences. Edited by Rhodes W. Fairbridge. Various publishers (dist. by Van Nostrand and Academic Pr.), 1966–. 15 vols. (in progress). Prices vary from $75.00 to $95.00 per vol.

The ongoing *Encyclopedia of Earth Sciences* series, a monumental endeavor under the general editorship of Rhodes Fairbridge, began in 1966 with the publication of the *Encyclopedia of Oceanography* and now includes the *Encyclopedia of Atmospheric Sciences and Astrogeology* (1967), the *Encyclopedia of Geomorphology* (1968), the *Encyclopedia of Geochemistry and Environmental Sciences* (1972), the *Encyclopedia of World Regional Geology* (1975), the *Encyclopedia of Sedimentology* (1978), the *Encyclopedia of Paleontology* (1979), the *Encyclopedia of Soil Science* (1979), the *Encyclopedia of Mineralogy* (1981), the *Encyclopedia of Beaches and Coastal Environments* (1982), and the *Encyclopedia of Applied Geology* (1984). All titles in this encyclopedic series are edited by specialists and aimed mainly at professionals and college-level students.

Encyclopedia of Environmental Science and Engineering. Edited by James R. Pfafflin and Edward N. Ziegler. 2nd ed. Gordon and Breach, 1983. Three vols. $500.00.

American Reference Books Annual (1978, p. 686) said of the first edition (1976, two vols.): "There is no doubt that this is a useful reference work. Individual articles are generally well-written and concise. The length of the articles has been limited to avoid over-specialization and to maintain readability." The expanded (three vols.) and updated second edition (1983) includes contributions by some 80 leading authorities.

Encyclopedia of Minerals. Written by Willard L. Roberts and others. Van Nostrand, 1974. 693p. $79.50.

This definitive work provides extensive data on more than 2,200 authenticated mineral species, including 1,000 full-color photomicrographs. Other important references on this subject include the *VNR Color Dictionary of Minerals & Gemstones* (Van Nostrand, 1982; also published in 1976 as part of the *Encyclopedia of Minerals and Gemstones*) and the classic *Dana's Manual of Mineralogy* (19th ed. Wiley, 1977).

Larousse Guide to Minerals, Rocks and Fossils. Written by W.R. Hamilton and others. Larousse, 1977. 320p. $15.95; $9.95.

An outstanding item for serious amateur collectors, this inexpensive guide is handsomely illustrated and intelligently organized. It covers 220 minerals, 90 rocks, and 300 fossils.

McGraw-Hill Encyclopedia of Energy. Edited by Sybil P. Parker. 2nd ed. McGraw-Hill, 1981. 838p. $49.50.

Based primarily on material drawn from the multivolume *McGraw-Hill Encyclopedia of Science and Technology* (4th ed., 1977), this collection of 300 articles is the best general source for reference information on all aspects of energy. *American Reference Books Annual* (1977, p. 684) called the first edition (1976) "superbly designed, clearly written, and amply illustrated."

McGraw-Hill Encyclopedia of Environmental Sciences. Edited by Sybil P. Parker. 2nd ed. McGraw-Hill, 1980. 858p. $46.50.

Authoritative, comprehensive, and easy to use, this encyclopedia offers an excellent one-volume overview of such environmental issues as pollution, waste management, conservation, and ecological interactions. Although based on the larger *McGraw-Hill Encyclopedia of Science and Technology* (4th ed., 1977), much of the material is new to this volume.

McGraw-Hill Encyclopedia of Ocean and Atmospheric Sciences. Edited by Sybil P. Parker. McGraw-Hill, 1980. 580p. $44.50.

Both practical and theoretical information is presented in the 236 articles and approximately 500 illustrations that make up this valuable reference source. Covered are such topics as atmospheric pollution, weather forecasting and prediction, estuarine oceanography, hydrology, marine mining, cloud physics, deep sea diving, industrial meteorology, and satellite programs. Like the other McGraw-Hill titles noted in this section, this encyclopedia derives from the *McGraw-Hill Encyclopedia of Science and Technology* (4th ed., 1977).

McGraw-Hill Encyclopedia of the Geological Sciences. Edited by Daniel N. Lapedes. McGraw-Hill, 1978. 915p. Out of print (last priced at $39.50).

Though now out of print and in need of revision, this work still furnishes an excellent one-volume encyclopedic treatment of all of the geological sciences. It too derives from the multivolume *McGraw-Hill Encyclopedia of Science and Technology* (4th ed., 1977), but also includes much original material.

Ocean World Encyclopedia. Written by Donald G. Groves and Lee M. Hunt. McGraw-Hill, 1980. 443p. $47.95.

More than 400 popularly written articles from *Abalone* to *Zooplankton* make up this attractive and informative encyclopedia. "School, public, and academic libraries that need comprehensive and convenient coverage will find this a good buy" (*Wilson Library Bulletin,* June 1980, p. 670).

The Planet We Live On: An Illustrated Encyclopedia of the Earth Sciences. Edited by Cornelius S. Hurlbut, Jr. Abrams, 1976. 527p. $40.00.

Twenty-one earth sciences from crystallography to volcanology are covered in this 1,800-entry encyclopedia for nonspecialists. "With respect to its content, this encyclopedia should appeal to high schools, public libraries of every size, and undergraduate college libraries; but because the articles are so readable, professionals on any level will find this work fascinating" (*American Reference Books Annual,* 1977, p. 690).

Volcanoes of the World: A Regional Directory, Gazetteer, and Chronology of Volcanism during the Last 10,000 Years. Compiled by Tom Simkin and others. Hutchinson Ross (dist. by Academic Pr.), 1981. 232p. $28.95.

"This complete reference will be useful for the researcher and serious student of volcanology. In addition, the format and explanatory text are clear enough for use by the interested undergraduate student or the avid layperson" (*Booklist,* June 1982, p. 1386).

EDUCATION AND LIBRARIES

ALA World Encyclopedia of Library and Information Services. Edited by Robert Wedgeworth. American Library Association, 1980. 601p. $95.00.

This 700,000-word encyclopedia consists of 452 signed articles, 144 statistical tables, and roughly 300 black-and-white illustrations. It surveys the history and current status of librarianship in 162 countries of the world, but most emphasis is placed on developments in U.S. libraries.

American Educators' Encyclopedia. Written by Edward L. Dejnozka and David E. Kapel. Greenwood, 1982. 634p. $65.00.

The best single-volume education encyclopedia currently available, Dejnozka and Kapel's book is "a convenient and reliable source of information on the names, terms, and topics most frequently used in elementary, secondary, and higher education.... A solid, basic work" (*Choice,* February 1983, p. 808).

Banned Books, 387 B.C. to 1978 A.D.. Written by Anne Lyon Haight; revised ed. by Chandler B. Grannis. 4th ed. Bowker, 1978. 196p. $14.95.

    Banned Books is chiefly a chronology of censorship from Plato's time to 1977. Much useful information is also appended, including sections on trends in censorship and pertinent U.S. laws and regulations.

The Encyclopedia of Education. Edited by Lee C. Deighton. Macmillan, 1971. Ten vols. $199.00.

    Consisting of more than 1,000 substantial articles and a fine index (in Volume 10), this outstanding, though increasingly dated, work is, in the words of William A. Katz (in his *Introduction to Reference Work,* 1982, vol. 1, p. 203), "the basic encyclopedia in education."

Encyclopedia of Educational Research. Edited by Harold E. Mitzel and others. 5th ed. Free Pr., 1982. Four vols. $275.00.

    Long recognized as one of the essential reference works in the field of education (the first edition appeared in 1940), the *Encyclopedia of Educational Research* includes 256 signed articles that succinctly summarize and evaluate the most important published research in the field at all levels. "It is notable for up-to-dateness and comprehensiveness, for its signed articles written by reputable authorities in their fields, and for its comprehensive bibliographies. It will be useful to students, faculty, counselors, and laypersons" (*Booklist,* October 1, 1983, p. 243).

Encyclopedia of Library and Information Science. Edited by Allen Kent, Harold Lancour, and Jay E. Daily. Marcel Dekker, 1968–84. 35 vols. plus two supplements. $65.00 per vol.

    Despite many flaws, this massive set provides background information on almost all library topics—and it is the "most ambitious undertaking in the professional literature of librarianship" (*American Reference Books Annual,* 1976, p. 94).

The International Encyclopedia of Education. Edited by Torsten Husen and T. Neville Postlethwaite. Pergamon, 1984. Ten vols. $1,750.00.

    Said to be "the first comprehensive and truly international scholarly review of education" (advertisement in *Choice,* June 1984, p. 1515), this expensive set contains approximately 6,000 pages, 1,500 signed articles, and 5 million words, all prepared by some 1,500 contributors and editors from over 100 countries.

The International Encyclopedia of Higher Education. Edited by Asa S. Knowles. Jossey-Bass, 1977. Ten vols. $550.00.

    Similar in size to both the ten-volume *Encyclopedia of Education* and the ten-volume *International Encyclopedia of Education* (both reviewed above), the *International Encyclopedia of Higher Education* contains roughly 1,300 articles, 6,000 pages, and 5.5 million words. "The *Encyclopedia* aims to give both the layperson and the specialist a broad overview of international aspects of higher education.... Its international approach generates much new information, and provides a new and stimulating perspective on higher education around the world" (*American Reference Books Annual,* 1979, pp. 312–13).

New Encyclopedic Dictionary of School Law. Written by Richard D. Gatti and Daniel J. Gatti. Prentice-Hall, 1983. 400p. $34.50.

    An update of the authors' *Encyclopedic Dictionary of School Law* (Prentice-Hall, 1975), this handy reference digests U.S. laws and regulations pertaining to education at both the federal and state levels. "Gatti's compilation should prove to be a useful handbook for educators and others" (*Choice,* April 1984, p. 1110).

Scholarships, Fellowships and Loans. Compiled by S. Norman Feingold and Marie Feingold. Bellman, 1982. 796p. $75.00 paper.
The Feingolds' encyclopedia of financial aid describes more than 1,350 sources of assistance for students at the college level. A similar listing is *The Scholarship Book* (Prentice-Hall, 1984) by Daniel J. Cassidy and Michael J. Alves.

Standard Education Almanac. Edited by Gerald L. Gutek. Marquis, published every year since 1968. 588p. $59.50.
This well-known title aims to be a "comprehensive reference resource providing information and viewpoints in the field of education" (preface). Limited to educational developments in the United States and Canada and containing much statistical data, the almanac covers such areas as expenditures, enrollments, staffing, curricula, performance and testing, trends, and public attitudes toward education. In a review of the 1983 edition, *American Reference Books Annual* (1984, p. 295) notes that the book "does fill a need for readily available basic information that is contained in one source."

ENGINEERING AND BUILDING CONSTRUCTION

America's Handyman Book. Compiled by the Staff of *Family Handyman Magazine.* Revised ed. Scribner's, 1983. 544p. $16.95.
This easy-to-understand guide to home maintenance and repair includes basic information about heating and cooling systems, electrical systems, plumbing, floors, roofs, etc. The text is enhanced by some 2,000 step-by-step illustrations. A comparable one-volume work is the *Reader's Digest Complete Do-It-Yourself Manual* (Norton, 1973).

Building Design and Construction Handbook. Edited by Frederick S. Merritt. 4th ed. McGraw-Hill, 1981. 1,408p. $79.50.
"For the building and construction trade, this is the standard reference book. It covers both building design and construction" (*Booklist,* September 1, 1984, p. 40). This work is encyclopedic in scope.

The Complete Handyman Do-It-Yourself Encyclopedia. Edited by Joseph Dofforn. Revised ed. H.S. Stuttman, 1983. 26 vols. $155.48.
First published in 1975 in 21 volumes, this heavily illustrated set intends to "provide the 'how-to' answers to practically any question pertaining to mechanical techniques and crafts" (introduction). Coverage includes automobile care, recreation (boating, camping, fishing, and hunting), gardening and lawn care, and home improvements and repair. A similar large set is the 18-volume *Popular Mechanics Do-It-Yourself Encyclopedia* (Revised ed. Hearst Books, 1978).

An Encyclopaedia of Metallurgy and Materials. Written by C.R. Tottle. Macdonald and Evans (dist. by Brookfield), 1984. 380p. $97.50.
Prepared and first issued in Great Britain, Tottle's encyclopedia consists of roughly 5,000 entries plus 90 pages of tables on the uses and properties of metals, alloys, plastics, and ceramics. *Choice* (October 1984, p. 254) commends the book as "a useful reference in engineering."

Engineering Formulas. Compiled by Kurt Gieck. 4th ed. McGraw-Hill, 1983. One vol. (various paging). $16.95.

This pocket-sized book of formulas used in engineering, mathematics, physics, and chemistry first appeared in English (from the German) in 1967 under the title *A Collection of Technical Formulae.* "This is a useful book for any engineering student and a quick reference source for libraries" (*American Reference Books Annual,* 1984, p. 729).

Engineering Manual: A Practical Reference of Design Methods and Data in Building Systems, Chemical, Civil, Electrical, Mechanical, and Environmental Engineering and Energy Conversion. Edited by Robert H. Perry. 3rd ed. McGraw-Hill, 1976. One vol. (various paging). $39.95.

A valuable one-volume quick reference for both students and practitioners, the *Engineering Manual* furnishes most of the basic concepts, facts, formulas, and tables needed by the engineer. The current third edition has added a section on environmental engineering.

Homeowner's Encyclopedia of House Construction. Written by Morris Krieger. McGraw-Hill, 1978. 325p. $29.95.

"For the potential house buyer, builder, or renovator, Krieger supplies technical background necessary to recognize quality construction or defects and to deal knowledgeably with repairmen or contractors" (*Booklist,* November 15, 1978, p. 516). The encyclopedia covers 53 alphabetically arranged subjects, from acoustical materials to woodframe construction. Excellent illustrations.

How to Clean Everything: An Encyclopedia of What to Use and How to Use It. Written by Alma Chestnut Moore. 3rd ed. Simon & Schuster, 1977. 239p. $6.95 paper.

Moore's *How to Clean Everything* is normally one of the most heavily used reference books in public libraries, and at $6.95 it is not beyond the reach of most individuals. An equally helpful book is Harriet Wylie's *420 Ways to Clean Everything* (Crown, 1980).

Machinery's Handbook: A Reference Book for the Mechanical Engineer, Designer, Manufacturing Engineer, Draftsman, Toolmaker, and Machinist. Written by Erik Oberg, Franklin D. Jones, and Holbrook L. Horton. 22nd ed. Industrial Pr., 1984. 2,512p. $45.00.

First published in 1914 and frequently revised (the previous edition appeared in 1979), this huge one-volume work is divided into 155 sections covering all aspects of the mechanical industries. "Libraries, engineers, hobbyists, and students will want a copy of this handbook for ready reference" (*American Reference Books Annual,* 1985, p.555).

McGraw-Hill Encyclopedia of Engineering. Edited by Sybil P. Parker. McGraw-Hill, 1983. 1,264p. $57.50.

The nearly 700 articles that make up this source were first published in the 15-volume *McGraw-Hill Encyclopedia of Science and Technology* (5th ed., 1982). "For libraries and individuals who cannot afford the full encyclopedia, this should prove to be a very useful source of engineering information" (*American Reference Books Annual,* 1984, p. 727). The only other single-volume encyclopedia covering the whole field of engineering is the now very dated *Engineering Encyclopedia* (3rd ed. Industrial Pr., 1963) by Franklin D. Jones and Paul B. Schubert.

Standard Handbook for Civil Engineers. Edited by Frederick S. Merritt. 3rd ed. McGraw-Hill, 1983. $79.95.

Merritt, who also edits the *Building Design and Construction Handbook* (see above), has expanded the third edition of this standard work to include sections on systems analysis and design, value engineering, air- and cable-supported structures, and new aspects of environmental engineering. "Highly recommended for all libraries serving civil engineering students, faculty, and professionals" (*Choice,* October 1983, p. 314).

FILM, RADIO, AND TELEVISION

Academy Awards: An Ungar Reference Index. Compiled by Richard Shale. 2nd ed. Ungar, 1982. 650p. $30.00; $14.50 paper.
   Shale's excellent book gives all nominees and winners in all categories through the early 1980s. *American Reference Books Annual* (1980, p. 463) said of the first edition (1978): "The Oscar for best book so far produced on the Academy Awards, if one were given, would undoubtedly go to this volume."

American Film Institute Catalog of Motion Pictures: Feature Films, 1921–1930. Bowker, 1971. Two vols. $125.00; *American Film Institute Catalog of Motion Pictures: Feature Films, 1961–1970.* Bowker, 1976. Two vols. $175.00.
   An ambitious, ongoing project that eventually will describe all feature films, shorts, and newsreels produced in the United States from the "beginnings" (1893) as well as major foreign film releases in the U.S., the AFI catalogs give such information as copyright date, length, color processes, cast and production credits, and plot summaries for each film covered. Additional ten-year volumes are planned, but when they will be published is not known.

The Complete Encyclopedia of Television Programs, 1947–1979. Written by Vincent Terrace. 2nd ed. A.S. Barnes, 1979. Two vols. $29.95.
   Terrace's informative encyclopedia covers nearly 3,500 network and syndicated "entertainment" programs that appeared on U.S. television between 1947 and 1979. In a review of the first edition (1976), *Choice* (June 1977, p. 516) found the set "a gold mine of trivia ... a gem beyond price."

Encyclopaedia of the Musical Film. Written by Stanley Green. Oxford Univ. Pr., 1981. 344p. $35.00.
   Coverage in this readable encyclopedia includes individual songs, performers, composers, lyricists, directors, and the like from 156 selected American and British musical films. The *New York Times Book Review* (November 15, 1981, p. 38) finds "its amusing, informative bits make the book fun to browse through." A more systematic treatment of the genre can be found in Clive Hirschhorn's *Hollywood Musical* (Crown, 1981), which covers 1,344 films.

The Film Encyclopedia. Vol. 1: *The Western* ; Vol. 2: *Science Fiction.* Written by Phil Hardy. Morrow, 1984–. Two vols. (in progress). $25.00 per vol.
   These are the first of a projected nine-volume set covering the major film genres (forthcoming volumes will cover horror, comedy, romance, war, epics, musicals, and thrillers). Information given for each film includes credits, cast, plot, and a critical note. Of the first volume *Library Journal* (February 1, 1984, p. 173) writes: "Hardy has done a remarkable job of selecting 1800 of the most important, interesting, or

arcane titles from the morass of films (the rest are covered more briefly in an appendix)."

The Film Encyclopedia: The Most Comprehensive Encyclopedia of World Cinema in a Single Volume. Written by Ephraim Katz. T.Y. Crowell (dist. by Harper & Row), 1979. 1,266p. $29.95; $14.95 paper.

"*The Film Encyclopedia* is certainly the largest one-volume film encyclopedia, and in some respects the best" (*Choice,* May 1980, p. 365). It consists of some 7,000 entries dealing with movie industry terms and personalities. Unlike Hardy's work of the same title (see above), no individual films are included.

The Great American Movie Book. Edited by Paul Michael and others. Prentice-Hall, 1980. 342p. $24.95; $9.95 paper.

Approximately 1,000 popular feature films from the sound era are described in this useful book, portions of which previously appeared in Michael's *American Movies Reference Book: The Sound Era* (Prentice-Hall, 1969) and *American Movies: A Pictorial Encyclopedia* (Garland, 1969).

Halliwell's Film Guide. Written by Leslie Halliwell. 4th ed. Scribner's, 1985. C. 1,500p. $39.95; $17.95 paper.

Halliwell's guide to more than 12,000 English-language sound and silent feature films is now firmly fixed as a standard reference. *Choice* (July-August 1978, p. 699), in a review of the first edition (1977), stated: "The combination of accurate reference data with incisive commentary on such a vast number of films makes this a uniquely valuable and enjoyable work."

Halliwell's Filmgoer's Companion. Written by Leslie Halliwell. 8th ed. Scribner's, 1984. 745p. $42.50.

Like the complementary *Halliwell's Film Guide* (see above), this one-volume work has achieved "standard reference" status among both librarians and film buffs. The *Companion* concentrates on biographies of filmmakers, directors, stars, and writers, as well as key films and movements. A note of warning: Halliwell's strong opinions and biases will irritate some readers.

The International Dictionary of Films and Filmmakers. Vol. 1: *Films* ; Vol. 2: *Directors and Filmmakers* ; Vol. 3: *Actors and Actresses* ; Vol. 4: *Writers and Production Artists.* Edited by Christopher Lyon and Susan Doll. St. James Pr., 1984–85. Four vols. $50.00 per vol.

Covering nearly 500 selected films, an equal number of filmmakers, and thousands of performers and production people, "this excellent dictionary should fill most public and academic libraries' needs for a comprehensive film reference source" (*Choice,* January 1985, p. 660).

Les Brown's Encyclopedia of Television. Written by Les Brown. New York Zoetrope, 1982. 496p. $29.95; $16.95 paper.

"This is a revised edition of the author's *New York Times Encyclopedia of Television* [1977], which has proven itself one of the most useful reference books in the field. Its brief but informative articles cover a wide range of topics from personalities and companies to technology and legal cases, mostly in regards to American television" (*Library Journal,* October 1, 1982, p. 1867).

Magill's Survey of the Cinema. Edited by Frank N. Magill. Salem Pr., 1980–82. Four vols. (1st series). $200.00; six vols. (2nd series). $300.00; three vols. (silent films). $150.00.

This impressive 13-volume series covers more than 1,500 major English-language and foreign-language feature films released since 1927. Articles on each film include a plot summary and critical notes on directing, acting, screenwriting, cinematography, and the film's place in the history of its genre.

The Motion Picture Guide. Written by Jay Robert Nash and Stanley R. Ross. CineBooks, 1985–. Ten vols. (in progress). $750.00.

The latest in a spate of multivolume sets describing films (see, for example, the *American Film Institute Catalog of Motion Pictures,* Hardy's *Film Encyclopedia,* the *International Dictionary of Films and Filmmakers,* and *Magill's Survey of the Cinema,* all reviewed above), this encyclopedic guide will eventually cover some 25,000 English-language feature films released between 1927 and 1984. *Wilson Library Bulletin* (September 1985, p. 80) is impressed: "This is destined to become a classic film reference."

The New York Times Encyclopedia of Film, 1896–1979. Edited by Gene Brown. Times Books, 1984. 13 vols. $1,500.00.

Not an encyclopedia in the traditional sense, this set is a chronologically arranged reprint from microfilm of approximately 5,500 articles on all aspects of film that have appeared in the *New York Times* between 1896 and 1979—except for reviews of films, which have been published separately in a nine-volume set entitled the *New York Times Film Reviews, 1913–1974* (Arno, 1971–75).

The Oxford Companion to Film. Edited by Liz-Anne Bawden. Oxford Univ. Pr., 1976. 767p. $39.95.

Now in need of revision, this handy one-volume, all-purpose guide to film is similar in purpose and construction to Katz's *Film Encyclopedia* and *Halliwell's Filmgoer's Companion* (both reviewed above).

Radio's Golden Years: The Encyclopedia of Radio Programs, 1930–1960. Written by Vincent Terrace. A.S. Barnes, 1981. 308p. $15.00.

Terrace, who also covers television shows in his *Complete Encyclopedia of Television Programs, 1947–1979* (see above), describes roughly 1,500 network and syndicated entertainment radio shows aired between 1930 and 1960. The encyclopedia is a "first-level reference source that will be welcomed by radio buffs and nostalgia enthusiasts" (*Booklist,* June 1, 1981, p. 1286). A comparable title is John Dunning's *Tune in Yesterday: The Ultimate Encyclopedia of Old-Time Radio, 1925–1976* (Prentice-Hall, 1976).

FOOD AND AGRICULTURE

The Cook's Encyclopedia: Ingredients and Processes. Written by Tom Stobart; edited by Millie Owen. Harper & Row, 1981. 547p. $22.07.

"Not another compilation of recipes, it is instead an encyclopedia surveying ingredients and processes in cookery" (*Wilson Library Bulletin,* March 1982, p. 542). The book, which is arranged alphabetically, contains considerable technical information, such as how various food reactions occur. A similar but more popularly written work is *Craig Claiborne's the New York Times Food Encyclopedia* (Times Books, 1985).

The Dictionary of American Food and Drink. Written by John F. Mariani. Ticknor & Fields (dist. by Houghton Mifflin), 1983. 475p. $19.95.

Mariani's encyclopedic overview of American eating and drinking customs deals with both the familiar (hamburgers, for example) and the exotic (snickerdoodles). *Library Journal* (April 15, 1984, p. 782), in naming the dictionary as one of the best reference books for 1983, says of it: "It is especially strong on the history and development of various foods, and the discussions of word derivations are delightful. Many recipes are included."

Encyclopedia of American Agricultural History. Written by Edward L. Schapsmeier and Frederick H. Schapsmeier. Greenwood, 1975. 467p. $35.00.

Intended to "provide information on all areas bearing on agricultural history" (preface) in the United States, this useful encyclopedia consists of some 2,500 articles covering pertinent legislation, agencies, publications, people, and places.

Encyclopedia of Food Science. Edited by Martin S. Peterson and Arnold H. Johnson. AVI Publishing, 1978. 1,005p. $89.50.

This technical encyclopedia of 250 substantial articles by food specialists is strictly for professionals and advanced students. Companion volumes are the *Encyclopedia of Food Engineering* (2nd ed. AVI Publishing, 1985) and the *Encyclopedia of Food Technology* (AVI Publishing, 1974).

Foods and Food Production Encyclopedia. Edited by Douglas M. Considine. Van Nostrand, 1982. 2,322p. $195.00.

The price is high but purchasers get both quantity and quality for their dollar. This massive encyclopedia contains 1.9 million words, 1,201 articles, 1,950 cross-references, 1,006 illustrations, 587 tables, and 7,500 index entries. Moreover, it is "an excellent reference work that should be of value to library collections from those in high schools to those in large research institutions. Because of its authority, currency, and comprehensive scope, it promises to be of continuing value for some time to come" (*Booklist,* September 1, 1983, p. 50).

Foods and Nutrition Encyclopedia. Written by Audrey H. Ensminger and others. Pegus Pr., 1983. Two vols. $99.00.

Similar in size and purpose to Considine's *Foods and Food Production Encyclopedia* (see above), this work includes 2,800 articles on a wide range of topics related to foods, health, agriculture, and marketing. "The language of the entries is purposely kept simple and nontechnical, although technical terms are explained when used" (*American Reference Books Annual,* 1984, p. 722).

Grossman's Guide to Wines, Beers, & Spirits. Written by Harold J. Grossman. 7th ed. Scribner's, 1983. 638p. $29.95.

Grossman's excellent book combines the best elements of an encyclopedia, pronouncing dictionary, technical manual, textbook, and browsing item. "If a library can own just a few serious books on wines and distilled spirits, it would be hard pressed to find a better choice than *Grossman's Guide* " (*American Reference Books Annual,* 1984, p. 720). Other recommended books on the subject include *Alexis Lichine's New Encyclopedia of Wine and Spirits* (4th ed. Knopf, 1985) and *Hugh Johnson's Modern Encyclopedia of Wine* (Simon & Schuster, 1983).

McGraw-Hill Encyclopedia of Food, Agriculture and Nutrition. Edited by Daniel N. Lapedes. McGraw-Hill, 1977. 732p. $43.50.

Most (but not all) of the material constituting this single-volume encyclopedia is reprinted from the multivolume *McGraw-Hill Encyclopedia of*

Science and Technology (4th ed., 1977). This is a valuable reference work for those who cannot afford or lack access to the parent set.

The New Larousse Gastronomique: The Encyclopedia of Food, Wine, and Cooking. Written by Prosper Montagne; edited by Charlotte Turgeon. Crown, 1977. 1,104p. $32.50.

This work is an updated and Americanized edition of the classic *Larousse Gastronomique,* long recognized as the bible of culinary excellence. In addition to thousands of recipes, the encyclopedia includes information about cooking terms, all types of foods and beverages, equipment, preservation, serving, etc. Approximately 1,000 illustrations complement the text.

Nutrition and Health Encyclopedia. Written by David F. Tver and Percy Russell. Van Nostrand, 1981. 569p. $29.50.

"It will please many readers to discover that in one place there is much basic information relating to the complex field of nutrition. (No more going from dictionary to data book to tables for information on food, calories, dietary requirements, etc.) The *Nutrition and Health Encyclopedia* fills a long-standing need for a compact, single-volume reference tool in this field" (*Booklist,* May 1, 1982, p. 1188). A more recent and more popularly written work is John Yudkin's *Penguin Encyclopedia of Nutrition* (Viking, 1985), also published in one volume and selling for $20.00.

Reader's Digest Eat Better, Live Better: A Commonsense Guide to Nutrition and Good Health. Reader's Digest Association (dist. by Random House), 1982. 416p. $21.50.

Written explicitly for laypeople in clear, nontechnical language, this helpful book focuses on how to buy, store, and prepare food so as to achieve the best health possible. An excellent addition to any home library.

The World Encyclopedia of Food. Written by L. Patrick Coyle, Jr. Facts on File, 1982. 790p. $40.00.

Containing more than 4,000 alphabetically arranged articles and half a million words, this readable encyclopedia covers every major food and beverage used anywhere in the world. "From folklore to nutritional facts to preparation methods to historical data, each individual article covers the gamut on the topic" (*Booklist,* February 1, 1983, p. 707).

GEOGRAPHY AND AREA STUDIES (INCLUDES TRAVEL)

The American Counties: Origins of County Names, Dates of Creation and Organization, Area, Population Including 1980 Census Figures, Historical Data, and Published Sources. Written by Joseph Nathan Kane. 4th ed. Scarecrow Pr., 1983. 546p. $39.50.

Kane's state-by-state listing provides "an invaluable wealth of information on U.S. counties and place-names and is the single most comprehensive source on the subject" (*American Reference Books Annual,* 1985, p. 149).

The Cambridge Encyclopedia of Africa. Edited by Roland Oliver and Michael Crowder. Cambridge Univ. Pr., 1981. 492p. $35.00.

Lavishly illustrated and authoritatively presented, this thematically arranged encyclopedia of Africa surveys the continent's land, people, history, nations, and problems. "There is really no other work on the market at present that is so comprehensive and useful as this handsome publication" (*Choice,* June 1982, p. 1374). An older but still viable one-volume work is the *African Encyclopedia* (Oxford Univ. Pr., 1974).

The Cambridge Encyclopedia of China. Edited by Brian Hook. Cambridge Univ. Pr., 1982. 492p. $37.50.

"A fine one-volume source of up-to-date information on China, past and present" (*Booklist,* December 15, 1982, p. 551). Another excellent reference on China is the *Encyclopedia of China Today* (3rd ed. Harper & Row, 1981) by Frederic M. Kaplan and others.

The Cambridge Encyclopedia of Latin America and the Caribbean. Edited by Simon Collier and others. Cambridge Univ. Pr., 1985. 456p. $39.50.

Edited by Latin American scholars, this colorful and informative work "should prove a boon not only for high school and university students but for the general public as well" (*Library Journal,* September 15, 1985, p. 72). Other useful, albeit dated, sources covering this area of the world are the *Encyclopedia of Latin America* (McGraw-Hill, 1974), edited by Helen Delpar, and the *Encyclopedia of Latin-American History* (Revised ed. Bobbs-Merrill, 1968; reprinted in 1981 by Greenwood) by Michael R. Martin and Gabriel H. Lovett.

The Cambridge Encyclopedia of Russia and the Soviet Union. Edited by Archie Brown and others. Cambridge Univ. Pr., 1982. 492p. $37.50.

This is another in the Cambridge series of area encyclopedias (see above), all of which are models of what a good small-volume specialized encyclopedia ought to be—authoritatively written and edited, attractively produced, impressively current, and reasonably priced. "Not only will it be a conversational coffee-table ornament, it will also command the respect of those who consult its chapters for well-written and high quality treatments of a vast array of topics" (*Choice,* September 1982, p. 49). A completely different work in practically every respect is the *Great Soviet Encyclopedia* (see below).

The Canadian Encyclopedia. Edited by James Marsh. Hurtig Publishers, 1985. Three vols. $175.00.

One of the most significant reference publications of the decade, the highly acclaimed three-volume *Canadian Encyclopedia* covers the people, places, history, land, and achievements of Canada in some 2,000 pages, 8,000 articles, 3 million words, and 1,900 illustrations and maps. It effectively complements such older encyclopedic works as the ten-volume *Encyclopedia Canadiana* (Grolier of Canada, 1957) and *Colombo's Canadian References* (Oxford Univ. Pr., 1976) by John Robert Colombo.

Collins Australian Encyclopedia. Edited by John Shaw. Collins (dist. by G.K. Hall), 1984. $49.95.

"The *Collins* work delivers essential factual information about Australia past and present while offering economy and one-volume convenience" (*Wilson Library Bulletin,* June 1985, p. 703). A more comprehensive work is the 12-volume *Australian Encyclopedia* (4th ed. Grolier of Australia, 1983).

The Columbia Lippincott Gazetteer of the World. Edited by Leon L. Seltzer. Columbia Univ. Pr., 1952. 2,148p. Plus supplement, 1961. 22p. $200.00.

The largest of the English-language geographical dictionaries, the *Columbia Lippincott Gazetteer* provides descriptive information about 130,000 place-names around the world.

Dictionary of Afro-Latin American Civilization. Written by Benjamin Nuêz with the assistance of the African Bibliographic Center. Greenwood, 1980. 525p. $45.00.

This authoritative volume consists chiefly of 4,700 short entries that describe words, phrases, events, and people significant to the life of blacks in Brazil, Jamaica, Haiti, the Anglo-French and Dutch islands, and the Spanish Caribbean. The material is "informative, clearly written, and abundantly cross-referenced" (*American Reference Books Annual,* 1982, p. 197).

Dictionary of Concepts in Human Geography. Written by Robert P. Larkin and Gary L. Peters. Greenwood, 1983. 286p. $35.00.

Roughly 100 concepts basic to the understanding of the interdisciplinary field of human geography—acculturation, agricultural revolution, frontier, geopolitics, ghetto, green revolution, infrastructure, territoriality, urbanization, etc.—are defined in encyclopedic detail. "The Larkin and Peters book would be especially helpful for faculty and students outside geography who would need general information concerning concepts and trends in this field" (*Choice,* February 1984, p. 804). A similar work covering some 550 terms is the *Dictionary of Human Geography* (Free Pr., 1981), edited by R.J. Johnston and others.

Encyclopaedia of Indian Culture. Written by Rajaram Narayam Saletore. Humanities Pr., 1981–. Five vols. (in progress). $40.50 per vol.

Saletore's in-progress encyclopedia broadly covers India and its people, customs, religions, etc. *Choice* (April 1984, p. 1117), in a review of the first two volumes, says that "those knowledgeable about and interested in the study of Indian culture will find this work interesting reading."

Encyclopedia of the Third World. Written by George Thomas Kurian. Revised ed. Facts on File, 1982. Three vols. $145.00.

First published in 1978, the *Encyclopedia of the Third World* now covers 122 countries, providing much geographical, political, economic, and social information about each, including such uncommon data as the country's percentage of population in the armed forces and the number and nationality of tourists visiting the country each year. "The format and depth of information is so good that one wishes for a companion set for developed countries to facilitate comparisons among all nations" (*Booklist,* February 15, 1983, p. 794).

The Great Soviet Encyclopedia (an English-language translation of the 3rd ed. of the 30-volume Russian *Bol'shaia Sovetskaia Entsiklopediia* published in 1969–78 in Moscow by Sovetskaia Entsiklopediia). Macmillan, 1973–. 31 vols. (in progress). $1,900.00.

A volume-by-volume translation of the Russian *Bol'shaia* (the basic school and family encyclopedia used in the U.S.S.R.; see Appendix C), this monumental—and controversial—undertaking provides readers of English with the Soviet point of view on practically every important subject, from history to art. The translation project has been severely criticized by some; for example, Harvey Einbinder, writing in *Wilson Library Bulletin* (December 1980, p. 260), observes, "Hundreds of thousands of dollars are being spent to translate this work in an apparent belief that American concern with Communist ideology and Soviet military power will ensure substantial library sales, despite the *Encyclopedia's* biased contents."

Illustrated Dictionary of Place Names: United States and Canada. Edited by Kelsie B. Harder. Van Nostrand, 1976; reprinted in 1985 by Facts on File. 631p. $19.95; $12.95 paper.

In the words of *Choice* (December 1976, p. 1272), "this compilation of 15,000 places is excellent. The names of all the provinces, states, capitals, counties, county seats, and a comprehensive selection of viable and interesting cities and towns in North America are included." A comparable source is George R. Stewart's *American Place-Names* (Oxford Univ. Pr., 1970), although it omits Canadian and Hawaiian names.

Ireland: A Cultural Encyclopedia. Edited by Brian de Breffny. Facts on File, 1983. 256p. $24.95.

Forty-five specialists on various aspects of Irish history and culture produced the approximately 600 articles that make up this fine work. The book is enhanced by some 300 carefully chosen illustrations.

Kodansha Encyclopedia of Japan. Kodansha International USA / Ltd. (dist. by Harper & Row), 1983. Nine vols. $600.00.

Like the new *Canadian Encyclopedia* (see above), this set represents national encyclopedia-making at its best. Useful to both serious students and casual readers, *Kodansha* "is an indispensable reference work on Japan. There is no other work like it, nor is anyone likely to try to match its coverage and quality for some time" (*Library Journal,* January 1984, p. 76).

Lands and Peoples. Grolier, 1985 (first published in 1929 and revised periodically). Six vols. $245.00 plus $15.00 shipping and handling; with discount to schools and libraries: $149.50 plus $4.00 shipping and handling.

Lands and Peoples, an encyclopedic set for elementary and secondary school students that covers the countries of the world continent-by-continent, goes way back, the first edition appearing in 1929. It was totally revamped in 1972 and again in 1981, when it went from seven to six volumes. The set is "recommended as a social studies reference for those who read at the fifth-grade level and above" (*Booklist,* February 1, 1985, p. 768).

The Marshall Cavendish Illustrated Encyclopedia of the World and Its People. Edited by Emrys Jones. Revised ed. Marshall Cavendish, 1986. 19 vols. $399.95 plus $10.00 shipping and handling. (Also available in the 27-volume 1st ed. from Farwell Promotional Books under the title *Encyclopedia of the World and Its People* at $199.95.)

This large, authoritative geographical encyclopedia covers all major aspects of the field, including relevant social, economic, and geological data. First published in 1978 in 27 volumes and thoroughly revised in 1986, the set comprises more than 1,300 articles accompanied by some 1,800 photographs and 250 maps.

New Zealand Encyclopedia. Edited by Gordon McLauchlan. Batemen (dist. by G.K. Hall), 1984. 656p. $39.95.

"This concisely presents a wealth of information about an often neglected part of the English-speaking world" (*Wilson Library Bulletin,* September 1985, p. 80). The 2,000 articles are readable and informative.

Reference Handbook on the Deserts of North America. Edited by Gordon L. Bender. Greenwood, 1982. 594p. $75.00.

Written by 23 specialists and covering seven major desert areas of North America, this handbook "should be on the shelves of all postsecondary academic libraries and is also highly recommended for large public libraries" (*Choice,* November 1982, p. 459).

Rolling Rivers: An Encyclopedia of America's Rivers. Edited by Richard A. Bartlett. McGraw-Hill, 1984. 416p. $29.95.
Arranged geographically, this well-edited, attractive compendium covers 117 rivers in the United States, including the Copper and Yukon in Alaska. *Rolling Rivers* "supplies a rich bed of information, though it is primarily historical rather than technical or mythical" (*Booklist*, February 1, 1984, p. 777).

Webster's New Geographical Dictionary. Revised ed. Merriam-Webster, 1984. 1,370p. $17.50.
This standard work originally appeared in 1949 as *Webster's Geographical Dictionary* ; in 1972, as the result of a major revision, it became *Webster's New Geographical Dictionary,* which is now kept up-to-date with frequent new editions. Smaller but much less expensive and much easier to handle than the massive *Columbia Lippincott Gazetteer of the World* (see above), *Webster's New Geographical Dictionary* includes basic gazetteer information about some 47,000 world place-names.

Worldmark Encyclopedia of the Nations. Edited by Moshe Y. Sachs. 6th ed. Wiley, 1984. Five vols. $199.95.
"Since its first edition in 1960, *Worldmark Encyclopedia of the Nations* has been highly acclaimed for its accurate, up-to-date, easily accessible geographic, historical, political, social, and economic data on the status of the world's nations" (*Booklist*, January 15, 1984, p. 727). The current edition covers 172 countries, plus about 60 dependencies and the United Nations and its agencies.

Worldmark Encyclopedia of the States. Edited by Moshe Y. Sachs. Harper & Row, 1981. 690p. $69.95.
Similar in format to the *Worldmark Encyclopedia of the Nations* (see above), this handy volume furnishes reliable information on each of the 50 United States, as well as U.S. dependencies. There is also a 51-page summary of the entire country. "This is a comprehensive and valuable reference aid for all ages" (*School Library Journal*, May 1982, p. 22).

HEALTH AND MEDICINE (INCLUDES CHILD CARE AND DRUGS)

The American Medical Association Family Medical Guide. Edited by Jeffrey R.M. Kunz. Random House, 1982. 831p. $29.95.
"Just about everything the layperson would want to know about health and sickness is contained in this extraordinarily thorough guide" (*Booklist*, October 15, 1982, p. 281). Numerous other recommended one-volume medical reference books for home use are available, including the *Better Homes and Gardens New Family Medical Guide* (Meredith, 1982), edited by Edwin Kiester, Jr.; the *Columbia University College of Physicians and Surgeons Complete Home Medical Guide* (Crown, 1985); Benjamin F. Miller's *Complete Medical Guide* (4th ed. Simon & Schuster, 1978); the *Good Housekeeping Family Health & Medical Guide* (Hearst Books, 1979); and the *New Illustrated Medical Encyclopedia for Home Use* (7th ed. Abrams, 1982), edited by Robert E. Rothenberg.

The Child Care Encyclopedia: A Parents' Guide to the Physical and Emotional Well-Being of Children from Birth through Adolescence. Written by Penelope Leach. Knopf, 1984. 708p. $22.95.

"Clear articles, brimming with common sense, explain problems thoroughly and treat not only the child's physical needs, but also social and emotional needs" (*Wilson Library Bulletin,* September 1984, p. 64). Leach's encyclopedia is only one of many fine single-volume works on the subject, such as the *Child Health Encyclopedia* (Delacorte, 1978); the *Encyclopedia of Baby and Child Care* (Revised ed. Warner Books, 1980) by Lendon H. Smith; *Taking Care of Your Child* (Revised ed. Addison-Wesley, 1985) by Robert H. Pantell and others; and, of course, the classic *Dr. Spock's Baby and Child Care* (Revised ed. Dutton, 1985).

The Complete Book of Medical Tests. Written by Mark A. Moskowitz and Michael E. Osband. Norton, 1984. 386p. $17.50.

More than 200 medical tests are identified and explained in this helpful book. "This volume is a valuable reference tool for consumers. It is clearly written and should increase understanding and decrease some of the fear that comes when patients are not informed" (*American Reference Books Annual,* 1985, p. 569). Comparable titles are the *Encyclopedia of Medical Tests* (Revised ed. Facts on File, 1982) by Cathey and Edward Pinckney and the *People's Book of Medical Tests* (Simon & Schuster, 1985) by David S. Sobel and Tom Ferguson.

Encyclopedia and Dictionary of Medicine, Nursing and Allied Health. Written by Benjamin Frank Miller and Claire Brackman Keane. 3rd ed. Saunders, 1983. 1,270p. $15.95 paper.

Useful for medical students as well as informed laypeople, this inexpensive reference includes 850 encyclopedic articles and more than 30,000 definitions and pronunciations of common terms used in the health field.

The Encyclopedia of Alcoholism. Written by Robert O'Brien and Morris Chafetz. Facts on File, 1982. 378p. $40.00.

"This book represents the first compilation of terms and subject matter devoted exclusively to the field of alcoholism. More than 500 entries are presented in a dictionary format which provides basic factual information on alcohol" (*Library Journal,* April 1, 1983, p. 732). The book is written in nontechnical language comprehensible to readers at the high school level and beyond.

The Encyclopedia of Drug Abuse. Written by Robert O'Brien and Sidney Cohen. Facts on File, 1984. 454p. $40.00

A companion to the *Encyclopedia of Alcoholism* (see above), this outstanding work covers the field of drugs and drug abuse in approximately 1,000 articles of varying length. "O'Brien and Cohen's reference work presents high quality coverage of the medical, social, biological, and legal issues involved with this topic" (*American Reference Books Annual,* 1985, p. 573).

Encyclopedia of Medical History. Written by Roderick E. McGrew and Margaret P. McGrew. McGraw-Hill, 1985. 400p. $34.95.

"Intended for general readers as well as historians and physicians, this unusual book provides topical access to 103 broad subjects in the history of medicine" (*Library Journal,* September 15, 1985, p. 74).

Encyclopaedia of Occupational Health and Safety. Edited by Luigi Parmeggiani. 3rd ed. International Labor Office, 1983. Two vols. $155.00.

Designed as a "source of practical information ... even for those with no specialized medical or technical knowledge" (preface), the *Encyclopaedia of Occupational Health and Safety* contains 1,150 articles prepared by 900 authorities from 60 countries that provide an overview of all significant aspects of health and safety in the work place, such as accidents, hazardous chemicals, ventilation, and lighting. The encyclopedia "should be on the reference shelves of any library servicing students of engineering, occupational medicine, nursing, health, or safety whether at graduate or undergraduate levels" (*Choice,* June 1984, pp. 1446–48).

The Essential Guide to Prescription Drugs. Written by James W. Long. 3rd ed. Harper & Row, 1982. 935p. $31.68; $9.57 paper.

Not as comprehensive but easier to use and understand than the well-known *Physicians' Desk Reference* (see below), Long's guide describes 210 generic drugs representing 1,366 brand names. Information for each drug includes manufacturers, drug family, dosage forms and strengths, how the drug works, possible side effects, and cautionary notes. A companion volume covering over-the-counter medications is David Zimmerman's *Essential Guide to Nonprescription Drugs* (Harper & Row, 1983).

The Family First Aid and Medical Guide: Emergencies, Symptoms, Treatments in the Home, on the Road, on Vacation. Written by James Bevan. Simon & Schuster, 1984. 192p. $7.95 paper.

"In addition to clear and concise information on emergency first aid, Bevan's brief book contains a wealth of general information on health and medicine in a liberally illustrated, easy-to-use format" (*Booklist,* February 15, 1985, p. 810). Another handy, inexpensive paperback guide to medical emergencies is the *American Medical Association's Handbook of First Aid and Emergency Care* (Random House, 1980) by Martha Ross Franks.

Handbook of Poisoning: Prevention, Diagnosis and Treatment. Written by Robert H. Dreisbach. 11th ed. Lange Medical, 1983. 578p. $11.00 paper.

Dreisbach's book is a standard reference on the diagnosis and treatment of acute and chronic poisoning. Emergency information appears on the inside front and back covers for quick reference.

The Human Body on File. Prepared by the Diagram Group. Facts on File, 1983. One vol. (loose-leaf; various paging). $145.00.

According to the foreword, the *Human Body on File* is intended to be used "as an atlas of anatomy, as a reference source of images for photocopying, and as a basis for examination paper illustrations." More than 1,000 black-and-white illustrations showing the various systems and parts of the human body are included. Note that any of the illustrations may be photocopied without fee or permission. "This is an excellent source for anyone studying or teaching anatomy at any basic level, particularly in K-12 and junior colleges. Since it is also a good general atlas of the human body, it may also be useful in home libraries" (*Booklist,* April 15, 1984, p. 1174). Another, much better known source on the human anatomy is *Gray's Anatomy of the Human Body* (36th ed. Saunders, 1980), edited by Roger Warwick and Peter L. Williams.

The Marshall Cavendish Illustrated Encyclopedia of Family Health: Doctor's Answers. Marshall Cavendish, 1983. 24 vols. $324.95 plus $10.00 shipping and handling.

One of the best of the large multivolume sets on health and medicine written exclusively for the layperson, this attractive, alphabetically arranged encyclopedia offers authoritative information in a question-and-answer format. "The books are easy to read, and easily comprehended language is used to explain medical procedures and concepts" (*Booklist*, February 1, 1985, p. 766). Another large, heavily illustrated set that can be recommended is the 18-volume *Family Health & Medical Library* (dist. in North America by Farwell Promotional Books, 1979), prepared by a panel of Australian doctors and medical specialists.

The Merck Manual of Diagnosis and Therapy. 14th ed. Merck & Co., 1982. 2,578p. $19.75. (Also published in a two-volume, soft-cover edition at $11.95 for Volume 1 and $6.95 for Volume 2.)

Compiled by a board of distinguished medical authorities, the *Merck Manual* has long been a standard desk reference for physicians and informed laypeople alike. Illnesses and diseases are explained in relatively nontechnical terms, symptoms and signs are noted, and diagnoses and treatments are suggested.

The New Our Bodies, Ourselves: A Book by and for Women. Compiled by the Boston Women's Health Book Collective. Simon & Schuster, 1984, 647p. $24.95; $12.95 paper.

A revision of the excellent *Our Bodies, Ourselves* (first published in 1971), this book continues to be a basic reference for anyone concerned with the health of women. "To simply call this a medical or health sourcebook is too limiting. With more than 600 pages of intense textual matter, enhanced with notable illustrations and enlightening personal quotations, it is a tour de force of difficult, and needfully controversial, women's physical and mental health issues" (*Choice*, June 1985, p. 1478). More traditional encyclopedic works on women's health include the *Better Homes and Gardens Woman's Health and Medical Guide* (Meredith, 1981), edited by Patricia J. Cooper, and *Everywoman's Health: The Complete Guide to Body and Mind* (3rd ed. Doubleday, 1985), compiled by June Jackson Christmas and others.

Physicians' Desk Reference to Pharmaceutical Specialties and Biologicals. Medical Economics, published every year since 1947. One vol. (various paging). $25.95.

Popularly known as PDR, this familiar source lists and describes some 2,500 drug products. It is a technical manual intended principally for those with medical training, and laypeople might find it difficult to use or understand. More simply written (but less comprehensive) guides include James Long's *Essential Guide to Prescription Drugs* (see above) and Joe Graedon's *People's Pharmacy* (Revised ed. St. Martin's Pr., 1985).

Prevention's New Encyclopedia of Common Diseases. Written by the Editors of *Prevention Magazine*. Rodale Pr., 1984. 1,048p. $21.95.

An updated version of the *Encyclopedia of Common Diseases* (1976), this useful work covers 141 diseases and symptoms. "The encyclopedia is well written and well indexed and presents a wealth of information in one compact volume" (*American Reference Books Annual*, 1985, p. 569).

Symptoms: The Complete Home Medical Encyclopedia. Written by Sigmund Stephen Miller. T.Y. Crowell, 1976 (reissued by Avon in 1980). 651p. $9.95 paper.

Over 600 symptoms are grouped by diseases in this authoritative but easily understood book. Comparable one-volume sources include Joan Gomez's *Dictionary of Symptoms* (Revised ed. Stein & Day, 1985) and H. Winter Griffith's *Complete Guide to Symptoms, Illness & Surgery* (Body Pr., 1985).

The World Book Illustrated Home Medical Encyclopedia. World Book, 1984. Four vols. $32.95 plus $2.45 shipping and handling.

Designed expressly for those without medical training, this excellent—and inexpensive—set covers the human body and its functions, common illnesses and symptoms, first aid and emergency care, and advice on how to achieve good health and fitness. An equally useful (and inexpensive) four-volume set is *Fishbein's Illustrated Medical and Health Encyclopedia* (H.S. Stuttman, 1983), edited by the late Morris Fishbein and selling for $39.95.

HISTORY AND ARCHAEOLOGY

Annals of America. Edited by Mortimer Adler. Encyclopaedia Britannica, 1973. 23 vols. $429.00.

Not an encyclopedia per se but a collection of documents that provide an encyclopedic sweep of the American national experience from 1493 through 1976, the set includes the full text of roughly 2,200 speeches, diaries, journals, articles, treaties, proclamations, and the like. A more affordable collection is the two-volume *Documents of American History* (9th ed. Prentice-Hall, 1974), edited by Henry Steele Commager and priced at $16.95 per volume.

The Cambridge Historical Encyclopedia of Great Britain and Ireland. Edited by Christopher Haigh. Cambridge Univ. Pr., 1985. 392p. $35.00.

"This extremely helpful reference and browsing source on Great Britain, an amalgam of the expertise of 60 contributors, is arranged into seven chronological sections, from Roman times to the post-Common Market period" (*Booklist,* October 15, 1985, p. 306).

Companion to Russian History. Written by John Paxton. Facts on File, 1983. 503p. $21.95.

Russian and Soviet history from the tenth century through the Khrushchev era is covered in approximately 2,500 brief articles in this handy, authoritative volume. "All in all, the approach is a rather popular one and because of its brevity borders on the simplistic. Nevertheless, this book can be of assistance to high school students in their homework as well as to the general public" (*American Reference Books Annual,* 1984, p. 192).

Concise Dictionary of Modern Japanese History. Compiled by Janet Hunter. Univ. of California Pr., 1984. 347p. $32.50; $10.95 paper.

Covering Japanese political and socioeconomic history from 1853 to 1980, this convenient one-volume work comprises 650 entries aimed chiefly at students in the field. For a comprehensive overview of Japanese history, see the nine-volume *Kodansha Encyclopedia of Japan* (Harper & Row, 1983), described in the "Geography and Area Studies" section of this Appendix.

Dictionary of American History. Edited by James T. Adams. Revised ed. Scribner's, 1976. Eight vols. $370.00.

Absolutely essential for practically all North American libraries and often found in the personal libraries of professors and serious students of American history, this is, in the words of reference authority William A. Katz (in his *Introduction to Reference Work,* 1982, vol. 1, p. 204), "the standard overview of American history for the layperson and the expert." Companion works are the multivolume *Dictionary of American Biography* (Scribner's, 1928–) and the *Atlas of American History* (2nd ed. Scribner's, 1984). There is also a one-volume condensation of the *Dictionary of American History* available entitled the *Concise Dictionary of American History* (Scribner's, 1983), priced at $60.00.

Dictionary of Mexican American History. Written by Matt S. Meier and Feliciano Rivera. Greenwood, 1981. 498p. $35.00.

This useful work, which covers the history of Mexican Americans from the sixteenth century to the present, "contributes valuable information in the areas of history, biography, sociology, and Chicano studies" (*Booklist,* August 1982, p. 1548).

Dictionary of the Middle Ages. Edited by Joseph R. Strayer. Scribner's 1982–. 13 vols. (in progress). $70.00 per vol.

Library Journal (February 1, 1983, p. 197), when reviewing Volume 1 of this monumental project, found it "an attractive and informative work of value to both the beginning student and the advanced scholar." Published by Scribner's under the auspices of the American Council of Learned Societies with the support of the National Endowment for the Humanities, the *Dictionary of the Middle Ages* will eventually comprise some 5,000 specially commissioned articles by 1,000 distinguished medievalists covering the period 500 to 1500 A.D. An excellent one-volume work on the same subject is Joseph Dahmus's *Dictionary of Medieval Civilization* (Macmillan, 1984).

The Discoverers: An Encyclopedia of Explorers and Exploration. Edited by Helen Delpar. McGraw-Hill, 1980. 471p. $47.95.

Two hundred alphabetically arranged articles on world exploration since the fifteenth century make up this reference. "Although biographical sketches dominate, the volume also includes explanations of geographical concepts, details of the explorations, and discussions of the impact of the discoveries on overseas expansion" (*Choice,* April 1980, p. 201).

The Encyclopedia of American Facts and Dates. Edited by Gorton Carruth. 7th ed. T.Y. Crowell (dist. by Harper & Row), 1979. 1,015p. $14.95.

This standard reference source presents the basic facts of American history chronologically in four parallel groupings. Comparable one-volume works include the *Almanac of American History* (Putnam, 1983), edited by Arthur M. Schlesinger, Jr., and *Timetables of American History* (Simon & Schuster, 1981), edited by Laurence Urdang.

Encyclopedia of American History. Edited by Richard Morris. 6th ed. Harper & Row, 1982. 1,285p. $28.80.

Acknowledged by just about everyone as the best one-volume encyclopedia of American history currently available, the latest edition of Morris's work covers events from pre-Columbian times up to 1981, including developments in such areas as space science, technology, and linguistics. An older but still valuable one-volume source is the *Oxford Companion to American History* (Oxford Univ. Pr., 1966), edited by Thomas Herbert Johnson.

Encyclopedia of Archaeological Excavations in the Holy Land. Edited by Michael Avi-Yonah and Ephraim Stern. Prentice-Hall, 1975–78. Four vols. $100.00.

"This monumental work analyzes all of the archaeological excavations done during the past 100 or more years in Palestine ... this valuable reference work is written so that the layperson can get as much from it as the scholar" (*American Reference Books Annual,* 1980, p. 160).

The Encyclopedia of Historic Places. Written by Courtlandt Canby. Facts on File, 1984. Two vols. $145.00.

"*Historic Places* has a unique emphasis and should become librarians' first choice as a source for short histories of towns, cities, countries, provinces, states, empires, battle sites, lakes, mountains, rivers, shrines, and archaeological digs" (*Wilson Library Bulletin,* June 1984, p. 753). The encyclopedia covers approximately 10,000 geographical locations.

The Encyclopedia of Southern History. Edited by Robert W. Twyman and David C. Roller. Louisiana State Univ. Pr., 1979. 1,421p. $90.00.

A model of regional encyclopedia-making, the *Encyclopedia of Southern History* provides 2,900 articles on subjects from art to zoology prepared by 1,100 scholars, mostly U.S. university professors. "This comprehensive, authoritative, and accessible work constitutes the best single reference on the American South" (*Library Journal,* May 15, 1981, p. 1044).

An Encyclopedia of World History: Ancient, Medieval and Modern, Chronologically Arranged. Edited by William L. Langer. 5th ed. Houghton Mifflin, 1972. 1,504p. $29.95.

Langer's encyclopedia attempts to cover all history from prehistoric to modern times in a single volume. It deals mainly with political, military, and diplomatic events. Another recommended one-volume reference on world history is the *Macmillan Concise Dictionary of World History* (Macmillan, 1983), compiled by Bruce Wetterau.

Famous First Facts. Compiled by Joseph Nathan Kane. 4th ed. H.W. Wilson, 1981. 1,360p. $65.00.

First published in 1933 and issued in revised and expanded editions several times since, *Famous First Facts* records more than 9,000 American "firsts," including discoveries, inventions, and happenings. A somewhat similar book is the recently published *Browser's Book of Beginnings: Origins of Everything under (and including) the Sun* (Houghton Mifflin, 1984) by Charles Panati.

Historical Dictionary of the French Revolution, 1789–1799. Edited by Samuel F. Scott and Barry Rothaus. Greenwood, 1985. Two vols. $95.00.

Ideal for serious students of European history, this alphabetically arranged reference work consists of 525 articles on the people, events, places, laws, and other aspects of the French Revolution. The publisher has also issued several other similar sources, including the *Historical Dictionary of Napoleonic France, 1799–1815* (Greenwood, 1985), edited by Owen Connelly and others; the *Historical Dictionary of Fascist Italy* (Greenwood, 1982), edited by Philip V. Cannistraro; and the *Historical Dictionary of the Spanish Civil War, 1936–1939* (Greenwood, 1982), edited by James W. Cortada.

New Cambridge Modern History. Cambridge Univ. Pr., 1957–76. 14 vols. $695.00.

An encyclopedic history that begins with the Renaissance and ends with the close of World War II, this set is renowned for its authoritative scholarship and general readability. The publisher also offers multivolume sets covering ancient and medieval history. A much less expensive and less intimidating source is Alan Palmer's *Penguin Dictionary of Modern History, 1789–1945* (2nd ed. Penguin Books, 1983).

The Princeton Encyclopedia of Classical Sites. Edited by Richard Stillwell. Princeton Univ. Pr., 1976. 1,019p. $175.00.

"The text of this huge encyclopedic dictionary contains at least 1,000,000 words and lists classical sites extending from Scotland to the Sudan and from Morocco to Pakistan.... All in all, this is an extraordinary book; nothing comparable to it exists. It should be useful especially to scholars and serious students" (*American Reference Books Annual,* 1977, p. 180).

The Reader's Encyclopedia of the American West. Edited by Howard R. Lamar. T.Y. Crowell (dist. by Harper & Row), 1977. 1,306p. $24.95.

Employing a broad definition of the region, this encyclopedia covers the people (both real and fictional), places, myths, and developments of the American West in some 2,400 signed articles. "Lamar and his 200 contributors treat the West as the evolving American culture, commencing with the colonists' penetration of the Appalachians and culminating in the contemporary movement of Americans to the frontiers of Alaska and Hawaii" (*Wilson Library Bulletin,* April 1978, p. 652).

The Timetables of History: A Horizontal Linkage of People and Events. Compiled by Bernard Grun. Revised ed. Simon & Schuster, 1982. 676p. $15.95 paper.

Based on the German *Kulturfahrplan* by Werner Stein, this chronology presents the basic facts of world history in parallel categories (science, literature, religion, music, etc.). There are a number of comparable works, including S.H. Steinberg's *Historical Tables: 58 B.C.–A.D. 1978* (10th ed. St. Martin's Pr., 1979), G.S.P. Freeman-Grenville's *Chronology of World History: A Calendar of Principal Events from 3000 BC to AD 1876* (2nd ed. Rowman and Littlefield, 1978), and James Trager's *People's Chronology: Year-by-Year Record of Human Events from Prehistory to the Present* (Holt, 1979).

LAW

An American Legal Almanac: Law in All States. Written by Joan Robinson. Oceana, 1978. 439p. $20.00.

Robinson's nontechnical guide explains the law in the United States as it pertains to marriage, divorce, children, inheritance, labor relations and workers' rights, civil rights, criminality, and other everyday topics. The book, which remains useful despite the need for an updated edition, includes numerous charts comparing state laws in various areas.

The Constitutional Law Dictionary. Written by Ralph C. Chandler and others. ABC-Clio, 1985–. Two vols. (in progress). $47.50 per vol.

Volume 1 of this projected two-volume set "focuses on concepts of constitutionalism, words and phrases common to American constitutional law, and leading case decisions rendered by the United States Supreme Court" (preface). *Wilson Library Bulletin* (May 1985, p. 623), which recommends the work, notes that the "clearly written, lengthy two-part entries define a concept or describe the facts of a case and then explain its significance and practical implications." The second volume, scheduled for 1986, will deal with governmental powers.

Corpus Juris Secundum: A Complete Restatement of the Entire American Law as Developed by All Reported Cases. West Publishing Co., 1936–74. 101 numbered vols. $3,000 (estimated price).

Cited as *C.J.S.*, this massive compilation provides an encyclopedic treatment of all legal topics based on reported court cases in the U.S. since 1658. The set is kept up-to-date by cumulative annual parts and recompiled volumes. Note that *C.J.S.* —and its equally expensive competitor, the 82-volume *American Jurisprudence* (2nd ed. Lawyers' Cooperative, 1962–74)—are intended for legal professionals; the very comprehensiveness of these sets renders them virtually inaccessible to people lacking training in the law, who will be much better served in most instances by the *Guide to American Law: Everyone's Legal Encyclopedia* (see below).

EveryWoman's Legal Guide: Protecting Your Rights at Home, in the Workplace, and in the Marketplace. Edited by Barbara A. Burnett. Doubleday, 1983. 576p. $19.95.

Called "current and thorough" by *American Reference Books Annual* (1985, p. 275), this excellent reference carefully analyzes legal questions chiefly of concern to women, such as the law on job discrimination, credit, marriage, divorce, rape, and housing. Similar works are Gayle L. Niles and Douglas H. Snider's *Women's Counsel: A Legal Guide for Women* (Arden Pr., 1984) and *Shana Alexander's State-by-State Guide to Women's Legal Rights* (Wollstonecraft Pr., 1975).

The Family Legal Advisor: A Clear, Reliable and Up-to-Date Guide to Your Rights and Remedies under the Law. Edited by Alice K. Helms. Revised ed. Crown, 1982. 496p. $14.95.

Written in a popular style, this useful one-volume legal guide for laypeople covers all major areas of U.S. law in 27 chapters. *Booklist* (November 1, 1983, p. 413) describes the book as "a compilation of brief, simple descriptions of legal concepts and laws."

The Family Legal Companion. Written by Thomas Hauser. McGraw-Hill, 1985. 240p. $15.95.

"Hauser, an attorney who writes a column on common legal matters for *McCall's* magazine, has compiled a handy collection of questions and answers under convenient subject headings" (*Booklist,* April 15, 1985, p. 1143). Although not as detailed or systematic as other single-volume legal guides for the layperson, such as the *Family Legal Advisor* (see above) or the *Reader's Digest Family Legal Guide* (see below), Hauser's book is helpful as a quick reference source in the home.

The Guide to American Law: Everyone's Legal Encyclopedia. West Publishing Co., 1983–85. 12 vols. $660.00.

This outstanding multivolume encyclopedia covers all aspects of United States law in language that can be understood by the ordinary person. Alphabetically arranged, the set "is full enough to satisfy most nonlawyers on any legal subject without being overwhelming" (*Library Journal,* September 15, 1985, p. 73). A unique work that should be found in practically all libraries regardless of type or size.

Legal Secretary's Encyclopedic Dictionary. Edited by Mary A. DeVries. 3rd ed. Prentice-Hall, 1982. 445p. $24.95.

First published in 1962 and revised in 1977 and most recently in 1982, this work introduces the neophyte to basic legal terms, concepts, and processes. *American Reference Books Annual* (1978, p. 263) wrote of the 1977 edition: "The scope of the materials included constitutes a 'how to do it' manual that could contribute not only to the career development but also to the enhancement of the multiple roles of legal secretaries."

The Oxford Companion to Law. Written by David M. Walker. Oxford Univ. Pr., 1980. 1,366 p. $49.95.

William A. Katz, in his *Introduction to Reference Work* (1982, vol. 1, p. 246), calls this book "one of the best overviews" on the subject. He goes on to say, "Compiled by a Glasgow professor of the law, the 1366 pages are inclined to focus on English law, but it does have sections on other countries, and most of the entries are as applicable to the United States and Canada as to England. It is particularly valuable for short, clear definitions and for historical background."

Paralegal's Encyclopedic Dictionary. Written by Valera Grapp. Prentice-Hall, 1979. 584p. $29.50.

Similar in concept and style to the *Legal Secretary's Encyclopedic Dictionary* (see above), the work fully defines legal terms and concepts likely to be encountered by paralegals. "This is a very valuable reference source, particularly for paralegal assistants, legal secretaries, and laypersons. It is more complete, selective, and instructional than the average law dictionary, yet not so complex as the typical legal encyclopedia" (*American Reference Books Annual,* 1981, p. 260).

Reader's Digest Family Legal Guide: A Complete Encyclopedia of Law for the Layman. Reader's Digest Association (dist. by Random House), 1981. 1,268p. $24.00.

The best of the current crop of single-volume legal guides for nonlawyers, the *Reader's Digest Family Legal Guide* covers some 2,600 topics in alphabetical order. It is both easy to use, having ample cross-references and a good index, and authoritative, the text based on contributions from the editors of West Publishing Company, the largest legal publisher in the U.S.

LITERATURE AND LANGUAGE

The Cambridge Guide to English Literature. Edited by Michael Stapleton. Cambridge Univ. Pr., 1983. 992p. $29.95.

This relatively inexpensive, handsomely produced "guide to the literature of the English-speaking world in one volume" (preface) includes more than 3,100 alphabetically arranged entries that provide basic factual information about authors, major works, prominent literary characters, and literary terms, subjects, and periods. Less detailed than the various *Oxford Companions* (see below) that cover individual national literatures, the *Cambridge Guide* has the virtue of broad coverage in a single volume.

Cassell's Encyclopedia of World Literature. Edited by John Buchanan-Brown. Revised and enlarged ed. Morrow, 1973. Three vols. Out of print (last priced at $50.00).

Originally published in two volumes in 1953, this standard reference covers all aspects of world literature regardless of time, place, or genre. Volume 1 furnishes survey articles on national literatures as well as major literary movements, terms, and forms. Volumes 2 and 3 are devoted chiefly to biographical articles. Although currently out of print, interested consumers should have little trouble acquiring a set on the secondhand book market; also, a reprint edition is quite likely in the near future.

Columbia Dictionary of Modern European Literature. Edited by Jean-Albert Bédé and William Edgerton. 2nd ed. Columbia Univ. Pr., 1980. 895p. $60.00.

The excellent *Columbia Dictionary of Modern European Literature* contains signed articles by some 500 contributors on more than 1,800 authors writing in European languages (excluding English) from the late nineteenth century to the present. "Absolutely essential for every general reference collection" (*Choice*, April 1981, p. 1069).

Crowell's Handbook of Classical Literature: A Modern Guide to the Drama, Poetry, and Prose of Greece and Rome, with Biographies of their Authors. Written by Lillian Feder. T.Y. Crowell (dist. by Harper & Row), 1964. 448p. $7.95 paper.

"Recommended as a guide for general reader, scholar, and young people" (*Library Journal*, December 1, 1964, p. 4788). A somewhat more scholarly source on the subject is Paul Harvey's *Oxford Companion to Classical Literature* (2nd ed., Oxford Univ. Pr., 1937).

Cyclopedia of Literary Characters. Edited by Frank N. Magill. Salem Pr., 1963. Two vols. $75.00.

Also published under the title *Masterplots Cyclopedia of Literary Characters,* this set lists and identifies more than 16,000 fictional characters from approximately 1,300 novels, plays, and epics drawn from world literature. "One of the virtues of the work is that editorial policy accommodates both the familiar and the arcane.... There is, overall, a nice mix of masterpieces and lesser works" (*Booklist*, May 1, 1979, p. 1393). A comparable work is William Freeman's one-volume *Dictionary of Fictional Characters* (2nd ed. The Writer, 1974).

Dictionary of Irish Literature. Edited by Robert Hogan. Greenwood, 1979. 815p. $45.00.

"A uniformly well written reference on the major and minor figures and institutions of modern Anglo-Irish literature" (*Library Journal*, September 1, 1979, p. 1684). Five hundred Irish authors who write in English or Gaelic are covered.

Dictionary of Oriental Literatures. Edited by Jaroslav Prusek. Basic Books, 1974. Three vols. Out of print (last priced at $40.00).

A unique encyclopedic overview of Oriental literature, this set includes some 2,000 signed articles that survey the major literary achievements of China, Japan, Korea, India, Pakistan, Bangladesh, Thailand, Indonesia, Egypt, Iran, Turkey, Afghanistan, and numerous other countries, including those of North Africa. *Choice* (January 1976, p. 1422) rightly observes that the "dictionary has been long needed, and is not likely to be superseded for many years," which makes its current out-of-print status all the more regrettable.

The Encyclopedia of American Journalism. Written by Donald Paneth. Facts on File, 1983. 548p. $49.95.

Over 1,000 alphabetically arranged articles covering both print and broadcast journalism make up this readable encyclopedia. "The book delivers good histories of newspapers, magazines, journalists, and court cases" (*Wilson Library Bulletin*, November 1983, p. 225).

Encyclopedia of Mystery and Detection. Edited by Chris Steinbrunner and Otto Penzler. McGraw-Hill, 1976. 436p. $14.95 paper.

Containing more than 600 articles, this encyclopedia "is a browser's delight. While differing in its content from the usual academic reference volume, its information is generally accurate. With its popular, lively style, it will appeal primarily to fans of the genre" (*Booklist,* February 15, 1977, p. 922). Another useful genre encyclopedia from the same publisher is the *Encyclopedia of Frontier and Western Fiction* (McGraw-Hill, 1983) by Jon Tuska and Vicki Piekarski.

Encyclopedia of World Literature in the 20th Century. Edited by Leonard S. Klein. 2nd ed. Ungar, 1981–84. Five vols. $300.00.

First published in four volumes between 1967 and 1975, this indispensable reference work is now available in a thoroughly revised edition. The first four volumes consist of approximately 1,700 alphabetically arranged articles that survey all important aspects of world literature in this century, including authors, genres, movements, and national developments; the final volume is an index. *Booklist* (October 15, 1985, p. 320) recommends the set for "its attention to minor as well as major literatures, its choice of authors, its qualified editor, advisers, and contributors, and its excellent index." A fine one-volume alternative to the *Encyclopedia of World Literature in the 20th Century* is Martin Seymour-Smith's *New Guide to Modern World Literature* (Harper & Row, 1985; $60.00), a revision of *Funk & Wagnalls Guide to Modern World Literature* (1973).

Encyclopedic Dictionary of the Sciences of Language. Written by Oswald Ducrot and Tzvetan Todorov; translated by Catherine Porter. Johns Hopkins Univ. Pr., 1979. 400p. $10.95 paper.

Translated from the French, this volume defines roughly 800 terms and includes 50 substantial articles. "This new translation, accessible to all American scholars, will become an indispensable research tool for those concerned with the historical development of the sciences of language or with contemporary critical theories" (*Choice,* November 1979, p. 1150).

Handbook of Russian Literature. Edited by Victor Terras. Yale Univ. Pr., 1985. 558p. $35.00.

"The combined effort of more than 100 contributors, for the most part American scholars, this handbook is a comprehensive survey in one volume of one of the world's richest national literatures" (*Booklist,* May 15, 1985, p. 1289). This excellent work effectively replaces William Harkins's *Dictionary of Russian Literature* (Philosophical Library, 1956), long a popular one-volume guide to Russian literature.

Harvard Guide to Contemporary American Writing. Edited by Daniel Hoffman. Harvard Univ. Pr., 1979. 618p. $18.50; $9.95 paper.

Not an encyclopedia in the conventional sense, this thematically arranged book is, in the words of *Library Journal* (December 15, 1979, p. 2650), "the best general survey available on post-World War II American writing." It is also a useful complement to the *Oxford Companion to American Literature* (see below).

Masterplots. Edited by Frank N. Magill. Revised ed. Salem Pr., 1976. 12 vols. $350.00.

Masterplots contains plot summaries and critical assessments of 2,010 of the world's greatest books. Says William A. Katz (in his *Introduction to Reference Work,* 1982, vol. 1, p. 233), "Plot summaries or other shortcuts to reading are often requested by students. By far the most famous name in this area is Frank N. Magill's *Masterplots,* a condensation of almost every important classic in the English language."

McGraw-Hill Encyclopedia of World Drama. Edited by Stanley Hochman, 2nd ed. McGraw-Hill, 1983. Five vols. $295.00.

The only multivolume encyclopedia on world drama in English, this outstanding set has recently been thoroughly revised and updated (the first edition appeared in 1972 in four volumes). It covers both individual playwrights and pertinent theatrical subjects, terms, movements, and styles. The set is "an invaluable reference work for theatre historians, drama critics, teachers, and actors" (*American Reference Books Annual,* 1984, p. 458). Another recent source on the subject is the one-volume *Crown Guide to the World's Great Plays* (Crown, 1984) by Joseph Shipley.

The Oxford Companion to American Literature. Written by James D. Hart. 5th ed. Oxford Univ. Pr., 1983. 896p. $49.95.

James Hart produced the first edition of the *Oxford Companion to American Literature* in 1941. An immediate success, the book has been revised four times since then, most recently in 1983. It is the standard one-volume reference on American literature, and is justly praised by practically all reviewers. For example *Booklist* (October 1, 1984, p. 204) says the latest edition "is an absolute gold mine of useful information."

The Oxford Companion to Canadian Literature. Edited by William Toye. Oxford Univ. Pr., 1984. 843p. $49.95.

"This encyclopedic reference work, by far the fullest single-volume guide to Canadian literature, contains 750 entries on individual authors, titles, periods, and numerous other subjects" (*Library Journal,* May 1, 1984, p. 889). This volume supersedes the old *Oxford Companion to Canadian History and Literature* (1967), edited by Norah Story.

The Oxford Companion to Children's Literature. Written by Humphrey Carpenter and Mari Prichard. Oxford Univ. Pr., 1984. 586p. $35.00.

"Humphrey Carpenter and Mari Prichard have produced a massive work with nearly 2,000 entries on topics ranging from fairy tales to comic strips and from Oliver Goldsmith to Judy Blume" (*American Reference Books Annual,* 1985, p. 375). A complementary work is Jon C. Stott's *Children's Literature from A to Z: A Guide for Parents and Teachers* (McGraw-Hill, 1984).

The Oxford Companion to English Literature. Edited by Margaret Drabble. 5th ed. Oxford Univ. Pr., 1985. 1,156p. $35.00.

First published in 1932, this *Oxford Companion* has been a staple item in home, public, college, and school library reference collections for more than half a century. Of the latest edition *Booklist* (August 1985, p. 1624) says, "Edited by novelist Margaret Drabble, the alphabetically arranged volume is notable not only for the encyclopedic nature of its coverage, but also for the pithiness of its prose and the ability of its contributors to succinctly place an author or work in its appropriate literary and sociocultural context."

The Oxford Companion to Spanish Literature. Edited by Philip Ward. Oxford Univ. Pr., 1978. 629p. $39.95.

This first-rate volume covers the literature of Spain as well as Spanish-speaking countries in Central and South America. Note that there are also *Oxford Companions* for French and German literatures.

Princeton Encyclopedia of Poetry and Poetics. Edited by Alex Preminger. Enlarged ed. Princeton Univ. Pr., 1975. 992p. $70.00; $16.95 paper.

More than 200 leading scholars and poets have contributed to this comprehensive guide to poetry from the earliest times to the present.

First published in 1965 and expanded in 1975, the encyclopedia treats the history and techniques of poetry, poetics and criticism, and the genre's relationship to other fields; individual poets and poems are not covered. Another quite useful source that covers the whole of poetry is the *Longman Dictionary and Handbook of Poetry* (Longman, 1985), a single-volume work by Jack Myers and Michael Simms.

The Reader's Encyclopedia. Written by William Rose Benét. 2nd ed. T.Y. Crowell (dist. by Harper & Row), 1965. 1,118p. $18.22.

Originally published in 1948, Benét's classic reference work surveys the whole of world literature in one volume. When reviewing the second edition, *Wilson Library Bulletin* (April 1965, p. 680) called the book "the most useful literary handbook in American libraries." A more recent title that covers much of the same ground is the *Harper Handbook to Literature* (Harper & Row, 1985) by Northrop Frye and others.

The Science Fiction Encyclopedia. Edited by Peter Nicholls. Doubleday, 1979. 672p. $17.95 paper.

This is the best of the several encyclopedic works on science fiction currently available. It contains some 3,000 signed articles covering all aspects of the genre, with emphasis on author biographies. Competing titles include Jeff Rovin's *Fantasy Almanac* (Dutton, 1979), the *Reader's Guide to Science Fiction* (Facts on File, 1979) by Baird Searles and others, and the *Visual Encyclopedia of Science Fiction* (Crown, 1977), edited by Brian Ash—all one-volume items.

World Press Encyclopedia. Edited by George T. Kurian. Facts on File, 1982. Two vols. $120.00.

"This excellent reference tool provides a unique, comprehensive, and thorough coverage of the state of today's fourth estate, and is invaluable for students or researchers in journalism, political history, or current events, as well as any interested reader concerned with the flow of information throughout the world" (*American Reference Books Annual,* 1983, p. 519). The encyclopedia covers the press (both print and broadcast media) in 180 countries.

Writer's Encyclopedia. Edited by Kirk Polking and others. Writer's Digest, 1983. 532p. $19.95.

Consisting of roughly 1,200 short, unsigned entries, the *Writer's Encyclopedia* covers terms, concepts, organizations, publications, etc. that relate to writing, publishing, and the media. The book "is meant to be light reading, providing general information, entertainment, and inspiration for the novice in publishing. In this it succeeds" (*American Reference Books Annual,* 1985, p. 286).

MUSIC

Britannica Book of Music. Edited by Benjamin Hadley. Doubleday, 1980. 881p. $29.95.

Based on material drawn from the *New Encyclopaedia Britannica,* this handy single-volume work contains approximately 1,500 alphabetically arranged articles on various composers and their works, musical performers, historical periods, instruments, types of music, and specialized terminology. Written in nontechnical language, "it is a very good starting point in general reference collections for readers interested in music" (*Booklist,* April 1, 1981, p. 1117).

The Complete Encyclopedia of Popular Music and Jazz, 1900-1950. Written by Roger D. Kinkle. Arlington House (dist. by Crown), 1974. Four vols. $100.00.

Said to be "the most inclusive documentation on American popular music likely to be published in a long time" (*Choice,* April 1975, p. 198), Kinkle's encyclopedia brings together a wealth of information on popular music in North America during the first half of this century. Music from the movies, Broadway, radio, television, and records is covered, along with the biographies of some 2,100 singers, composers, bandleaders, etc. Complementary one-volume works on the subject are Arnold Shaw's *Dictionary of American Pop/Rock* (Schirmer, 1983) and David Ewen's *All the Years of American Popular Music* (Prentice-Hall, 1977).

The Encyclopedia of Folk, Country & Western Music. Written by Irwin Stambler and Grelun Landon. 2nd ed. St. Martin's Pr., 1983. 902p. $50.00; $17.95 paper.

Originally published in 1969, this extensively revised and updated edition provides "a breadth of coverage for folk and country recording artists not available elsewhere" (*Library Journal,* January 1, 1983, p. 43). Note that many of the biographies in the first edition were dropped in favor of new ones in the second edition.

Encyclopedia of Music in Canada. Edited by Helmut Kallmann and others. Univ. of Toronto Pr., 1981. 1,076p. $85.00.

"In the greatest depth and breadth yet attempted (3,162 articles) it lays forth one country's musical culture in its historical and current aspects, covering all forms of music from rock to classical" (*Choice,* April 1982, p. 1045).

The Encyclopedia of the Music Business. Written by Harvey Rachlin. Harper & Row, 1981. 524p. $19.18.

Rachlin's very useful encyclopedic guide to the commercial side of music contains approximately 450 articles. "Detailed entries on copyright, performing rights, organizations, piracy of recordings and tapes, how to sell a song, and many other practical aspects of the music business highlight the book" (*Library Journal,* May 15, 1982, p. 960).

The Great Song Thesaurus. Written by Roger Lax and Frederick Smith. Oxford Univ. Pr., 1984. 665p. $75.00.

More than 10,000 of the best-known songs in the English-speaking world are described in this "unique and extremely useful reference book" (*Choice,* February 1985, p. 796). The work includes folk songs, sea chanteys, college songs, political songs, Christmas carols, and advertising jingles. A comparable title is the *Book of World-Famous Music* (Revised ed. Crown, 1971) by James J. Fuld.

Harvard Dictionary of Music. Written by Willi Apel. 2nd ed. Harvard Univ. Pr., 1969. 935p. $25.00.

Apel's encyclopedic dictionary, first published in 1944 and thoroughly revised a quarter of a century later, is an excellent single-volume source of information on serious music, although it does not cover the contemporary scene nor does it furnish biographies. Some years ago the publisher issued a condensation and expansion of Apel's work entitled the *Harvard Concise Dictionary of Music* (Harvard Univ. Pr., 1978), edited by Don Michael Randel; it includes biographies and updates the earlier book.

The International Cyclopedia of Music and Musicians. Edited by Oscar Thompson; revision editor, Bruce Bohle. 11th ed. Dodd, Mead, 1985. 2,609p. $69.95.

The most substantial and informative all-purpose one-volume music encyclopedia available in English, this indispensable work includes both long and short articles on practically all aspects of serious music, although relatively little attention is given to jazz, rock, and folk. *Booklist* (October 15, 1985, p. 321) says the *Cyclopedia* has been "long and rightly regarded as a classic."

The New College Encyclopedia of Music. Written by J.A. Westrup and F.L. Harrison; revised by Conrad Wilson. Revised ed. Norton, 1976. 608p. $12.95 paper.

Consisting of more than 6,000 concise articles on important composers, conductors, performers, genres, musical terms, instruments, individual works, and the like, the encyclopedia is an ideal quick reference source for the music student.

The New Grove Dictionary of American Music. Edited by H. Wiley Hitchcock and Stanley Sadie. Grove's Dictionaries of Music, 1986. Four vols. $450.00.

The most impressive spin-off thus far from the massive *New Grove Dictionary of Music and Musicians* (see below), this four-volume set will, according to editor Stanley Sadie, "penetrate deeper into the fabric of American musical life than was possible in a fully international work" (*Booklist,* May 15, 1982, p. 1268). The encyclopedia, scheduled for publication in September 1986, will include many articles not found in the parent set.

The New Grove Dictionary of Music and Musicians. Edited by Stanley Sadie. Grove's Dictionaries of Music, 1980. 6th ed. 20 vols. $2,100.00.

Widely heralded as "the greatest musical dictionary ever published" (*New York Review of Books,* May 28, 1981, p. 38) and "the last word on music" (*Time,* November 17, 1980, p. 110), the *New Grove* replaces the fifth edition of the old *Grove,* a nine-volume set published in 1955 (the first edition of this famous work appeared in four volumes between 1877 and 1890). The *New Grove*'s statistics are impressive: 22 million words, 18,000 pages, 22,500 articles, 4,500 illustrations, 9,500 cross-references, and 2,400 distinguished contributors. It is comprehensive, authoritative, and essential for all serious music students, teachers, and critics. As Harold Schonberg observes in the *New York Times Book Review* (December 21, 1980, p. 13), "Just about everything one would want to know about matters musical is contained in these 20 volumes."

The New Grove Dictionary of Musical Instruments. Edited by Stanley Sadie. Grove's Dictionaries of Music, 1984. Three vols. $350.00.

Although based on the 20-volume *New Grove Dictionary of Music and Musicians* (see above), this work contains much information that is new, particularly in the area of non-Western musical instruments. "Encyclopedic in scope and masterful in presentation, *The New Grove Dictionary of Musical Instruments* cannot be considered less than essential for any collection that includes music" (*Choice,* June 1985, p. 1478). A less expensive one-volume reference on the subject is *Musical Instruments of the World: An Illustrated Encyclopedia* (Facts on File, 1976; $29.95) by the Diagram Group.

The New Kobbé's Complete Opera Book. Written by Gustave Kobbé; revised by the Earl of Harewood. 9th ed. Putnam, 1976. 1,694p. $25.00.

Kobbé has long been a favorite in a crowded field. First published in 1922 and revised numerous times since, the book provides detailed plots of more than 300 operas as well as lengthy discussions of such composers as Verdi, Wagner, Rossini, and Berlioz. Worthy competitors to *Kobbé* include Robin May's *Companion to the Opera* (Hippocrene, 1977), the *Concise Oxford Dictionary of Opera* (2nd ed. Oxford Univ. Pr., 1979) by Harold Rosenthal and John Warrack, the *Encyclopedia of Opera* (Scribner's, 1976), edited by Leslie Orrey, and the *Metropolitan Opera Stories of the Great Operas* (Norton, 1984), edited by John Freeman.

The New Oxford Companion to Music. Edited by Denis Arnold. Oxford Univ. Pr., 1983. Two vols. $95.00.

Originally published as the single-volume *Oxford Companion to Music* in 1938, this standard source is now in two volumes and includes 6,600 articles covering 2,000 musical terms, 1,300 composers, 1,150 individual works, and 175 instruments. "Even though there are entries for Louis Armstrong, Bob Dylan, and reggae, the music of the conservatory and concert hall remains the focus" (*Wilson Library Bulletin,* February 1984, p. 453). Other useful Oxford reference books on music are the one-volume *Oxford Dictionary of Music* (Oxford Univ. Pr., 1985) by Michael Kennedy, which is a revision and enlargement of the third edition of the *Concise Oxford Dictionary of Music,* also a one-volume work by Kennedy; and the one-volume *Oxford Junior Companion to Music* (2nd ed. Oxford Univ. Pr., 1980) by Michael Hurd, an attractive item designed for the young reader interested in music.

The Rolling Stone Encyclopedia of Rock & Roll. Edited by Jon Pareles and Patricia Romanowski. Simon & Schuster, 1983. 704p. $19.95; $11.95 paper.

According to *Library Journal* (December 1, 1983, p. 2242), this excellent encyclopedia "leaves the competition in the dust," with more than twice as many entries as any other rock encyclopedia.

PETS AND DOMESTIC ANIMALS (INCLUDES VETERINARY MEDICINE)

The Aquarium Encyclopedia. Written by Gunther Sterba; edited by Dick Mills; translated by Susan Simpson. MIT Pr., 1983. $39.50.

A translation of the German *Lexikon der Aquaristik und Ichthyologie* (1978), the *Aquarium Encyclopedia* is a comprehensive work covering various fish species and their physiology, behavior, and diseases, plants likely to be kept in aquaria, filtering systems, water chemistry, and the like. "Sterba has done a truly monumental job in pulling together and organizing a massive amount of scattered information of interest both to amateur aquarists and professional aquatic biologists" (*Choice,* July-August 1983, p. 1571).

Black's Veterinary Dictionary. Edited by Geoffrey P. West. 14th ed. Barnes & Noble, 1982. 902p. $28.50.

"This standard reference work in the field of veterinary medicine, first published in 1928, provides reliable and up-to-date information relating to diseases and conditions of various types of animals" (*American Reference Books Annual,* 1984, p. 726). Previous editions of this British-produced work have appeared in North America under the title *Encyclopedia of Animal Care.*

The Complete Dog Book. Prepared by the American Kennel Club. 17th ed. Howell Book House, 1985. 768p. $16.95.

An indispensable reference, this latest edition of the American Kennel Club's official guide to dogs provides the history and standards of all 129 AKC-recognized breeds. Many other encyclopedic works on dogs are available, including the fine *Roger Caras Dog Book* (Holt, 1980) and *Everydog: The Complete Book of Dog Care* (Morrow, 1984) by Rowan Blogg and Eric Allan.

The Complete Encyclopedia of Horses. Written by M.E. Ensminger. A.S. Barnes, 1977. 487p. $29.50.

This outstanding work covers all important aspects of the horse, including anatomy, diseases, training, breeds, feeds, stabling, racing, riding and hunting terms, equipment, and so forth. *American Reference Books Annual* (1978, p. 742) praises the book as "the finest horse encyclopedia in print."

Encyclopedia of Aviculture: Keeping and Breeding Birds. Written by Richard Mark Martin. Arco, 1983. 227p. $14.95.

The care and breeding of wild bird species are described in this alphabetically arranged encyclopedia. The book "will be of primary use in zoo libraries and in the working collections of bird fanciers, pet-shop owners, and veterinarians ... a unique source" (*Booklist,* December 1, 1983, p. 553). An older but equally useful reference on the subject is Cyril H. Rogers' *Encyclopedia of Cage and Aviary Birds* (Macmillan, 1975).

Encyclopedia of Marine Invertebrates. Edited by Jerry G. Walls. T.F.H. Publications, 1983. 736p. $49.95.

"The text provides reliable, readable information in nontechnical language on marine invertebrates that one might want to keep and observe in a home aquarium" (*Choice,* March 1983, p. 955). Note that the publisher's initials stand for Tropical Fish Hobbyists.

The Merck Veterinary Manual: A Handbook of Diagnosis and Therapy for the Veterinarian. Edited by Otto H. Siegmund. 5th ed. Merck & Co., 1979. 1,600p. $16.50.

An essential desk reference for veterinarians and others concerned with the health of animals, this authoritative, reasonably up-to-date technical manual deals chiefly with the diagnosis and treatment of animal diseases. It is similar in purpose to *Black's Veterinary Dictionary* (see above), although *Black* has a British emphasis whereas *Merck* is oriented toward North American users.

The Pet Encyclopedia. Edited by Frank Manolson and others. Thomas Nelson, 1981. 368p. $24.95.

This all-purpose pet book "gives an overview of various animal species and breeds, care requirements and diseases of such pets as cats, dogs, horses, birds, fish, amphibians, reptiles, and insects as well as zoo and wild animals" (*American Reference Books Annual,* 1982, p. 796). Many similar titles are available, such as Frances Chrystie's *Pets: A Complete Handbook on the Care, Understanding, and Appreciation of All Kinds of Animal Pets* (3rd ed. Little, Brown, 1974) and Emil Dolensek and Barbara Burn's *Practical Guide to Impractical Pets* (Viking, 1976).

Simon and Schuster's Guide to Cats. Written by Mordecai Siegal. Simon & Schuster, 1983. 255p. $23.95; $8.95 paper.

An English-language translation of an Italian work, this encyclopedic guide to cat breeds, behavior, and care is valuable for its "200 beautiful color photographs and illustrations, the unique symbols and treatment of breed personalities, and the readability of the text" (*American Reference Books Annual,* 1985, p. 530). Another useful reference on cats is Grace Pond's *Rand McNally Pictorial Encyclopedia of Cats* (Rand McNally, 1980).

PHOTOGRAPHY

The Amateur Photographer's Handbook. Written by Aaron Sussman. 8th ed. T.Y. Crowell (dist. by Harper & Row), 1973. 562p. $15.34.

The *Amateur Photographer's Handbook* is a highly regarded one-volume encyclopedic overview of the basics of photography, including practical tips for the beginner and a glossary of terms. Although a new edition is needed, the book remains useful for both the novice and veteran photographer.

Encyclopedia of Practical Photography. Edited by John Carroll and William Broecker. Amphoto, 1977–78. 14 vols. Out of print (last priced at $159.95).

Regrettably out of print (at least for the present), this set has been called "one of the most ambitious attempts ever made to get all of photography into one set of books" (*New York Times Book Review,* December 3, 1978, p. 84). Produced by the technical and editorial staffs of Eastman Kodak and Amphoto (the American Photographic Book Company), the encyclopedia covers all aspects of photography for amateurs, hobbyists, professionals, teachers, and students.

The Focal Encyclopedia of Photography. Reprint of 1969 revised desk ed. Focal Pr., 1980. 1,699p. $30.95.

Based on the authoritative British-produced two-volume work of the same title (Revised ed., 1965), this technical reference covers photographic terms, theory, and practice. *Library Journal* (February 1, 1961, p. 586) said of the first desk edition (1960), "A good purchase for the photographer's home library." A more popular, abridged edition of the *Focal Encyclopedia* is the *Pictorial Cyclopedia of Photography* (see below).

International Center of Photography Encyclopedia of Photography. Edited by Cornell Capa. Crown, 1984. 607p. $50.00.

"This ambitious project aims to cover in one volume current information about the historical, aesthetic, communicative, scientific, technical, and commercial aspects of photography. The editors come close to realizing their goal" (*Library Journal,* December 1984, p. 2266). This outstanding new encyclopedia consists of 1,400 entries accompanied by more than 400 illustrations, including 100 technical diagrams and charts.

The Photograph Collector's Guide. Written by Lee D. Witkin and Barbara London. New York Graphic Society (dist. by Little, Brown), 1979. 438p. $35.00; $19.95 paper.

For the collector of photography (rather than the working photographer), this valuable book includes biographical information about famous photographers, a list of photographic terms and their definitions, a chronology of the history of photography, and succinct coverage of movements, organizations, and themes in the field. A "monumental addition to the literature of photography" (*Library Journal,* December 15, 1979, p. 2642).

The Photographer's Bible: An Encyclopedic Reference Manual. Written by Bruce Pinkard. Arco, 1983. 352p. $24.95.

"This A-Z encyclopedia manual combines the hardware, mechanics, techniques, personalities, aesthetics, and interpretation of photography. Entries vary in length from a one-line definition of a technical term to a three- or four-page explanation of a process or technique that tells exactly how to achieve a desired result" (*American Reference Books Annual,* 1984, p. 431).

The Photographer's Handbook: A Complete Reference Manual of Techniques, Procedures, Equipment and Style. Written by John Hedgecoe. Knopf (dist. by Random House), 1978. 352p. $18.95.

According to the preface, Hedgecoe's well-known handbook intends "to explain the full scope of photography, from the fundamentals of taking photographs, processing and printing them to the advanced aspects of such topics as composition, studio work and darkroom techniques." A less comprehensive guide for the amateur photographer by the same author is the 153-page *John Hedgecoe's Photographer's Workbook* (Simon & Schuster, 1985), which sells for only $9.95.

Photography: A Handbook of History, Materials, and Processes. Written by Charles Swedlund. 2nd ed. Holt, 1981. 368p. $23.95 paper.

This handy introductory manual to photography covers the basics of design, the camera and its lenses, the qualities and properties of light and correct exposure, film characteristics, both black-and-white and color developing and printing, etc. It is especially useful as a text in high school, college, and continuing education courses.

The Pictorial Cyclopedia of Photography. Edited by George Wakefield. 2nd ed. Focal Pr., 1979. 703p. $29.95.

First published in 1968, this abridged version of the two-volume *Focal Encyclopedia of Photography* (see above) is "tailored to the needs of the active amateur" (introduction). As the title suggests, the work is particularly well illustrated.

A World History of Photography. Written by Naomi Rosenblum. Abbeville Pr., 1984. 671p. $39.95.

Encyclopedic in scope, Rosenblum's history is "a beautiful and comprehensive survey, with a detailed text and superbly reproduced photographs" (*Booklist,* February 1, 1985, p. 782).

PHYSICS AND MATHEMATICS

Encyclopedia of Mathematics and Its Applications. Edited by Gian-Carlo Rota. Addison-Wesley (dist. by Cambridge Univ. Pr.), 1976–. 25 vols. to date (in progress). Prices vary from $32.50 to $69.50 per vol.

Each volume in this distinguished ongoing series treats a specific topic in the field (for example, Volume 2 covers the theory of partitions) and is prepared by a noted international authority. The ultimate goal is "to present the factual body of all mathematics" (editor's statement) in a manner that can be understood by the serious nonspecialist.

Encyclopedia of Physics. Edited by Rita G. Lerner and George L. Trigg. Addison-Wesley, 1981. 1,157p. $134.95.

Along with the *McGraw-Hill Encyclopedia of Physics* (see below), this is the most authoritative and up-to-date physics encyclopedia currently available. Alphabetically arranged, the work can be used with profit by physicists seeking information in the field outside their particular specialization as well as interested laypeople. Note that the one-volume *Concise Encyclopedia of Solid State Physics* (Addison-Wesley, 1983) is entirely derived from the *Encyclopedia of Physics.*

Encyclopedic Dictionary of Mathematics. Edited by Shokichi Iyanaga and Yukiyosi Kawada. MIT Pr., 1977. Two vols. $200.00; $50.00 paper.

Prepared under the auspices of the Mathematical Society of Japan and translated into English with the assistance of the American Mathematical Society, this outstanding specialized encyclopedia consists of 436 alphabetically arranged articles covering all significant aspects of mathematics. "Without a doubt, this title is unique in terms of its comprehensive, but contemporary and basic, coverage of mathematics. The price is not to be ignored, but the tool may well in the coming years stand alone in terms of its scope and purpose" (*American Reference Books Annual,* 1978, p. 629).

Encyclopaedic Dictionary of Physics: General, Nuclear, Solid State, Molecular Chemical, Metal and Vacuum Physics, Astronomy, Geophysics, Biophysics, and Related Subjects. Edited by James Thewlis. Pergamon, 1961–75. Nine vols. plus five supplements. Out of print (last priced at $430.00).

Uncontestably the best multivolume encyclopedia of physics published in recent times, Thewlis's important work is currently out of print in North America, although it can be readily consulted in any decent science library. The encyclopedia, which is written chiefly with the nonspecialist in mind, not only covers the main areas of physics but other scientific fields with a physical basis.

Handbook of Mathematical Tables and Formulas. Compiled by Richard S. Burington. 5th ed. McGraw-Hill, 1973. 500p. $24.50.

Burington states in his introduction that "this book has been constructed to meet the needs of students and workers in mathematics, engineering, physics, chemistry, science, and other fields in which mathematical reasoning, processes, and computations are required." The book includes all commonly used mathematical tables and formulas.

McGraw-Hill Encyclopedia of Physics. Edited by Sybil P. Parker. McGraw-Hill, 1983. 1,343p. $54.50.

The 760 signed articles that make up this one-volume encyclopedia are reprinted from the multivolume *McGraw-Hill Encyclopedia of Science and Technology* (5th ed., 1982). For those who lack easy access to the parent set, the *McGraw-Hill Encyclopedia of Physics* is an authoritative, up-to-date, convenient, and relatively inexpensive reference covering the field.

A New Dictionary of Physics. Edited by H.J. Gray and Alan Isaacs. Longman, 1975. 619p. $40.00.

A major revision and expansion of the *Dictionary of Physics* (1958), this work defines basic terms used in all branches of physics. Some of the entries are quite lengthy (for example, the coverage of electron microscopes runs to nearly three columns), and brief biographies of important physicists are also included. "Recommended for the graduate college library" (*Choice,* November 1977, p. 1142).

The Prentice-Hall Encyclopedia of Mathematics. Written by Beverly Henderson West and others. Prentice-Hall, 1982. 620p. $35.00.

This mathematics encyclopedia is intended strictly for students and young people at the junior and senior high school levels. Well indexed and easy to understand, the book covers the field from *Algebra* to *Zero.* A useful feature is the inclusion of math puzzles and projects. Another one-volume work on the subject for laypeople is Max Shapiro's *Mathematics Encyclopedia* (Doubleday, 1977).

The Universal Encyclopedia of Mathematics. Simon & Schuster, 1969. 598p. $12.95; $8.95 paper.

Old but still useful for high school and college students majoring in math, this affordable encyclopedia is based on the German work *Grossen Rechenduden* (1964) by Joseph Meyers. The material, topically arranged, ranges from arithmetic to calculus, followed by commonly used formulas and tables of functions with explanations.

VNR Concise Encyclopedia of Mathematics. Edited by W. Gellert and others. Van Nostrand, 1977. 760p. $22.95.

"Part one of this good one-volume mathematics encyclopedia covers traditional areas of elementary mathematics, and part two covers higher mathematics" (*Booklist,* September 1, 1984, p. 42). An English-language version of the German *Kleine Enzyklopädie der Mathematik,* this popular work is aimed principally at the serious layperson and math student and teacher.

POLITICAL AND MILITARY SCIENCES (INCLUDES WEAPONS)

The African Political Dictionary. Written by Claude S. Phillips. ABC-Clio, 1984. 254p. $30.00; $14.25 paper.

The 225 terms covered in this encyclopedic dictionary concern the political history of Africa. *Choice* (June 1984, p. 1449) notes that "all classroom instructors of African politics will acknowledge their debt to Phillips (Western Michigan University), whose knowledge of Africa goes back many years, for compiling a clear, concise, and timely reference work." A complementary work is Chris Cook and David Killingray's *African Political Facts since 1945* (Facts on File, 1983).

The American Political Dictionary. Written by Jack C. Plano and Milton Greenberg. 6th ed. Holt, 1982. 472p. $14.95 paper.

A popular reference work with students, teachers, and librarians since it first appeared in 1962, Plano and Greenberg's oft-revised dictionary of some 1,200 terms, concepts, court cases, and laws combines the best features of a specialized glossary and encyclopedia. "Each term is clearly defined and is followed by a paragraph on its historical and current significance" (*American Reference Books Annual,* 1983, p. 225). Another useful source on the subject is J.B. Whisker's *Dictionary of Concepts on American Politics* (Wiley, 1980).

Civil War Dictionary: A Concise Encyclopedia. Written by Mark M. Boatner. McKay, 1959. 974p. $25.00.

Boatner's well-known encyclopedia treats the battles, weapons, issues, and people of the American Civil War in more than 4,000 brief articles. The work also includes good map coverage of the conflict.

Dictionary of American Naval Fighting Ships. Edited by James L. Mooney. U.S. Government Printing Office, 1959–81. Eight vols. $142.00.

This "monumental achievement" (*American Reference Books Annual,* 1983, p. 751) provides both a summary of every action in which every ship commissioned in the United States Navy since its founding in 1775 was engaged and a listing of these ships by type and class. Most of the material is current as of the 1970s, and efforts are under way to keep this work up-to-date. Sources of recent information include the frequently revised *Ships and Aircraft of the U.S. Fleet* (13th ed. Naval Institute Pr., 1984) by Norman Polmar, the biennial *Combat Fleets of the World* (Naval Institute Pr., 1974–), and the classic annual *Jane's Fighting Ships* (Jane's Publishing, 1898–).

A Dictionary of Marxist Thought. Edited by Tom Bottomore. Harvard Univ. Pr., 1983. 587p. $35.00.

Largely the work of British and North American academicians, this scholarly reference offers encyclopedic coverage of the ideas and people associated with present-day Marxism. "Its articles are necessarily uneven in quality, but most are very competently and clearly written ... this work should be in every academic library and will probably be heavily used in most" (*Choice,* March 1984, p. 948). Two other excellent reference sources on the subject are Jozef Wilczynski's single-volume *Encyclopedic Dictionary of Marxism, Socialism and Communism* (Walter de Gruyter, 1981) and the eight-volume *Marxism, Communism and Western Society: A Comparative Encyclopedia* (Herder and Herder, 1972–73), edited by C.D. Kernig and currently (unfortunately) out of print.

A Dictionary of Political Thought. Written by Roger Scruton. Harper & Row, 1982. 499p. $19.18; $9.95 paper.

Scruton's dictionary contains roughly 1,200 entries that focus on concepts and ideas (such as gnosticism, macroeconomics, the right to life, and usury) rather than people, places, and events. The entries, which run from a paragraph to one or two pages in length, go well beyond the scope of typical dictionary definitions.

Encyclopedia of American Foreign Policy: Studies of the Principal Movements and Ideas. Edited by Alexander DeConde. Scribner's, 1978. Three vols. $180.00.

A collection of 95 substantial articles that deal with the fundamental policies, concepts, and issues of American foreign policy (such as the Marshall Plan, the Cold War, isolationism, and the balance of power), this outstanding set is the work of leading scholars representing a variety of political positions and ideologies. "Written for both scholars and laypersons, this *Encyclopedia* is a unique compilation that admirably complements other types of reference works in the field" (*American Reference Books Annual,* 1981, p. 251). An especially useful complementary reference is the one-volume *Dictionary of American Diplomatic History* (Greenwood, 1980) by John E. Findling.

Encyclopedia of American Political History: Studies of the Principal Movements and Ideas. Edited by Jack P. Greene. Scribner's, 1984. Three vols. $180.00.

Similar in purpose and design to the *Encyclopedia of American Foreign Policy* (see above), this set consists of 90 long survey articles covering such broad subjects as civil rights, machine politics, suffrage, separation of church and state, populism, egalitarianism, Jacksonian Democracy, federalism, and the Articles of Confederation. *Booklist* (August 1985, p. 1644) calls the encyclopedia "an impressive achievement which provides for students of U.S. political history a rare overview of the stuff of politics which many studies have ignored, viz., ideas. It not only informs but also whets one's appetite for further study in a rich field."

The Encyclopedia of Military History: From 3500 B.C. to the Present. Written by R. Ernest Dupuy and Trevor N. Dupuy. Revised ed. Harper & Row, 1977. 1,464p. $43.27.

First published in 1970 and revised in 1977, this standard source chronologically surveys world military history, noting the wars, weapons, tactics, leaders, etc. for each period. A useful supplement to the Dupuys' encyclopedia is *Harbottle's Dictionary of Battles* (3rd ed. Van Nostrand, 1979), revised by George Bruce.

Encyclopedia of the American Constitution. Edited by Leonard Levy. Macmillan, September 1986. Four vols. (in progress). $320.00.

Intended to commemorate the bicentennial of the ratification of the U.S. Constitution in 1787, this in-progress encyclopedia will, according to advanced information from the publisher, consist of 1.5 million words and 2,200 articles covering constitutional issues from abolition to zoning. It will focus on five categories dealing with the Constitution: concepts, historical subjects and periods, public acts, people, and commentaries on cases.

Encyclopedia of the American Revolution. Written by Mark M. Boatner. Revised ed. McKay, 1974. 1,290p. $9.98.

Similar in purpose and style to his *Civil War Dictionary* (see above), Boatner's *Encyclopedia of the American Revolution* covers the period from 1763 to 1783 in alphabetically arranged articles on the important people, events, and issues of the Revolution.

The Illustrated Encyclopedia of 20th Century Weapons and Warfare. Edited by Bernard Fitzsimons. Purnell, 1979. 24 vols. $466.00.

Handsomely illustrated with more than 7,000 photographs and drawings (both in color and black-and-white), this set is "a valuable and outstanding compilation of useful and authoritative information on military weapons of the twentieth century" (*American Reference Books Annual*, 1981, p. 775). Two one-volume references that cover weapons through the ages are the *Complete Encyclopedia of Arms and Weapons* (Simon & Schuster, 1982), edited by Leonid Tarassuk and Claude Blair, and *Weapons: An International Encyclopedia from 5000 B.C. to 2000 A.D.* (St. Martin's Pr., 1981) by the Diagram Group.

The International Relations Dictionary. Written by Jack C. Plano and Roy Olton. 3rd ed. ABC-Clio, 1982. 488p. $37.50; $15.00 paper.

This topically arranged encyclopedic dictionary first appeared in 1969 and was substantially revised in 1979 and 1982. It includes nearly 700 articles in which relevant terms (for example, détente) are defined and then placed in historical and political context.

The Latin American Political Dictionary. Written by Ernest E. Rossi and Jack C. Plano. ABC-Clio, 1980. 261p. $26.00; $13.50 paper.

In need of revision because of the many changes that have occurred in the area since the late 1970s, this work nevertheless continues to be a useful reference on political and governmental developments in Latin America.

The Marshall Cavendish Illustrated Encyclopedia of World War I. Edited by Peter Young. Marshall Cavendish, 1984. 12 vols. $460.00 plus $10.00 shipping and handling.

"Many books have been written on World War I, but few if any have covered the subject in as much depth or breadth, or with as many contributing experts and authorities as *The Marshall Cavendish Encyclopedia of World War I.* With its excellent illustrations, its variety of writing styles, and its clear maps and diagrams, this major historical encyclopedia on an important phase of European history is recommended for libraries of all types, as well as for homes where persons are interested in the history of Europe and the world" (*Booklist,* June 15, 1985, p. 1440).

The Marshall Cavendish Illustrated Encyclopedia of World War II. Edited by Peter Young. Revised ed. Marshall Cavendish, 1981. 12 vols. $399.95 plus $10.00 shipping and handling.

First published in 1966 and modestly revised in 1981, this set—like the Marshall Cavendish work on World War I (see above)—is a fine survey of one of the world's most devastating wars. Useful one-volume reference sources on World War II include *Louis L. Snyder's Historical Guide to World War II* (Greenwood, 1982) and the *Simon and Schuster Encyclopedia of World War II* (Simon & Schuster, 1978), edited by Thomas Parrish.

The Middle East Political Dictionary. Written by Lawrence Ziring. ABC-Clio, 1984. 452p. $37.50; $15.00, paper.

Ziring's handy one-volume work covers political parties, conflicts, movements, and issues in the extended Middle East region from Morocco to Afghanistan and Pakistan. "This valuable work should prove indispensable for both undergraduate and graduate students of the Middle East as well as general readers who seek reliable information" (*Choice,* May 1984, p. 1284).

Nuclear Weapons Databook. Written by Thomas B. Cochran and others. Ballinger, 1984. Two vols. $38.00; $19.95 per vol.

Volume 1 is entitled *U.S. Nuclear Forces and Capabilities* and Volume 2 *U.S. Nuclear Weapons Production Complex.* "The authors display an admirable degree of thoroughness and objectivity and provide a scholarly apparatus that is sufficient to permit further research ... renders a vast amount of essential data on a topic of major public interest" (*Booklist,* March 1, 1984, p. 928). Less technical but equally helpful references on the subject are Christopher Campbell's *Nuclear Weapons Fact Book* (Presidio, 1984) and the *Nuclear Almanac* (Addison-Wesley, 1984), both one-volume works.

The Presidential-Congressional Political Dictionary. Written by Jeffrey M. Elliot and Sheikh R. Ali. ABC-Clio, 1984. 365p. $28.00; $15.00 paper.

More than 300 entries grouped under 12 broad headings cover terms pertinent to the executive and legislative branches of U.S. government (such as apportionment, privileged legislation, and seniority system). Each term is fully defined and placed in political and historical context.

The Presidents: A Reference History. Edited by Henry F. Graff. Scribner's, 1984. 700p. $65.00.

This important reference provides in-depth essays on each presidential administration from Washington to Carter. "These essays represent a distillation of many years of scholarly experience and study and should be useful to both students and scholars. Written in a readable style,

without the burden of scholarly documentation, they are suitable both
for reference and general reading" (*Booklist,* January 1, 1985, p. 632).
Numerous other excellent sources on the U.S. presidents are available,
including William DeGregorio's *Complete Book of U.S.
Presidents* (Norton, 1984) and Joseph Kane's *Facts about the Presidents* (4th ed.
Wilson, 1981).

The Rand McNally Encyclopedia of Military Aircraft, 1914–1980. Edited by
Enzo Angelucci; translated by S.M. Harris. Rand McNally, 1981. 546p.
$100.00
  Library Journal (March 1, 1982, p. 553) calls this large, copiously illustrated encyclopedia "the most useful one-volume reference on military
  aircraft available." Originally published in Italy under the title *Atlante
  Enciclopedico degli Aerei Militari del Mondo dal 1914 a oggi* in 1980, the
  book covers some 800 types of military aircraft, including fighter, bomb-
  er, and reconnaissance planes. Other useful works on the subject include
  Michael J.H. Taylor's *Warplanes of the World, 1918–1939* (Scribner's,
  1981), Bill Gunston's *Illustrated Encyclopedia of Major Military Aircraft
  of the World* (Crown, 1983), and *Jane's All the World's Aircraft* (Jane's
  Publishing, 1908–).

The Soviet and East European Political Dictionary. Written by George Klein,
Barbara P. McCrea, and Jack C. Plano. ABC-Clio, 1984. 367p. $30.00;
$14.50, paper.
  Roughly 300 terms are covered in this encyclopedic dictionary.
  "Prepared by two political scientists and an East European scholar, the
  dictionary will be helpful to anyone seeking basic information on the
  topic" (*Booklist,* July 1984, p. 1527).

Spy/Counterspy: An Encyclopedia of Espionage. Written by Vincent Buranelli
and Nan Buranelli. McGraw-Hill, 1982. 361p. $27.95.
  "In approximately 400 well-written articles on organizations, persons,
  incidents, equipment, and techniques, the authors surpass spy fiction in
  engaging one's interest" (*Wilson Library Bulletin,* November 1982, p.
  254). Coverage is from Elizabethan times to the present.

World Encyclopedia of Political Systems & Parties. Edited by George E.
Delury. Facts on File, 1983. Two vols. $120.00.
  This informative encyclopedia, current as of 1982, profiles the present-
  day political scene in 169 countries and eight territories. Area specialists
  describe the electoral system and major political parties, institutions, and
  forces in each country, including a summary comment on the nation's
  political future. "This work will be especially useful in providing background material on current world trouble spots" (*Library Journal,* December 15, 1983, p. 2324).

PSYCHOLOGY AND PSYCHIATRY (INCLUDES PARAPSYCHOLOGY)

American Handbook of Psychiatry. Edited by Silvano Arieti. 2nd ed. Basic
Books, 1974–81. Seven vols. Prices vary from $42.50 to $48.00 per vol.
  A technical work mainly for professionals in the field, the *American
  Handbook of Psychiatry* is an encyclopedic survey of contemporary devel-
  opments, concepts, techniques, problems, and trends in psychiatry. The

set comprises seven titled volumes: *The Foundation of Psychiatry; Child and Adolescent Psychiatry; Sociocultural and Community Psychiatry; Adult Clinical Psychiatry; Organic Disorders and Psychosomatic Medicine; Treatment; New Psychiatric Frontiers*; and *Advances and New Directions* .

The Compact Encyclopedia of Psychological Problems. Written by Clyde M. Narramore. Zondervan, 1984. 398p. $9.95.

Narramore's book "is a hand-sized compendium of presentations of various psychological disorders. The book offers general information on psychological problems that is directed towards the layperson and the religiously oriented, but minimally trained, human relations counselor" (*American Reference Books Annual*, 1985, p. 243). Note that this work is a compact reissue of the *Encyclopedia of Psychological Problems* published in 1966.

The Dictionary of Dreams: 10,000 Dreams Interpreted. Written by Gustavus Hindman Miller. Reprint of 1901 ed. Arco, 1985. 636p. $6.95 paper.

First published in 1901 as *What's in a Dream?*, this durable work has been reprinted a number of times over the years under various titles, including *Ten Thousand Dreams Interpreted* and most recently the *Dictionary of Dreams*. The subjects of dreams—flying, falling, climbing, etc.—are covered A-to-Z.

Encyclopedia of Clinical Assessment. Edited by Robert Henley Woody. Jossey-Bass, 1980. Two vols. $69.95.

Topically arranged in 91 chapters written by specialists in the field, this two-volume encyclopedia "is intended to be a compendium of behavioral science material for the practitioner" (preface). *American Reference Books Annual* (1981, p. 700) concludes that "this work serves as a good reference source for both the academician and the practitioner on the multiple dimensions in clinical assessment."

Encyclopedia of Human Behavior: Psychology, Psychiatry, and Mental Health. Written by Robert M. Goldenson. Doubleday, 1970. Two vols. $29.95.

Aimed principally at serious general readers and students but also useful to professionals for information outside their field of specialization, the *Encyclopedia of Human Behavior* consists of approximately 1,000 substantial essays that introduce terms, concepts, theories, treatments, and people in the behavioral sciences. The set remains a valuable reference source despite its age.

Encyclopedia of Mental Health. Edited by Albert Deutsch. Franklin Watts, 1963. Six vols. Out of print; reprinted in 1970 by Scarecrow Pr. in a one-volume miniprint ed. $55.00.

This old but still useful work includes 170 articles that provide reliable reference information on mental health and illness "in simple terms that the general reader can understand" (preface).

Encyclopedia of Occultism & Parapsychology: A Compendium of Information on the Occult Sciences, Magic, Demonology, Superstitions, Spiritism, Mysticism, Metaphysics, Psychical Science, and Parapsychology, with Biographical and Bibliographical Notes and Comprehensive Indexes. Edited by Leslie Shapard. 2nd ed. Gale, 1984. Three vols. $200.00.

Originally published in two volumes in 1978, this set combines articles reprinted from two quite old encyclopedias—Lewis Spence's *Encyclopaedia of Occultism* (1920) and Nandor Fodor's *Encyclopaedia of Psychic Science* (1934)—and much new material added by Shepard. In all, the encyclopedia contains roughly 6,000 entries covering all aspects of psychical phenomena. Other less expensive, one-volume references on the subject are Nevill Drury's *Dictionary of Mysticism and the Occult* (Harper & Row, 1985) and the *Encyclopedia of the Unexplained* (McGraw-Hill, 1974), edited by Richard Cavendish.

Encyclopedia of Psychoanalysis. Edited by Ludwig Eidelberg. Free Pr., 1968. 571p. $45.00.

> The only substantive encyclopedia on the subject yet published, this standard work covers more than 600 terms in the field. Definitions are frequently followed by clinical examples and a discussion of related concepts.

Encyclopedia of Psychology. Edited by Raymond J. Corsini and Bonnie D. Ozaki. Wiley-Interscience, 1984. Four vols. $199.95.

> Standing between the much larger 12-volume *International Encyclopedia of Psychiatry, Psychology, Psychoanalysis, and Neurology* and the single-volume *Encyclopedic Dictionary of Psychology* (both reviewed below), this four-volume set contains approximately 2,000 articles prepared by some 500 experts in the field. The work is comprehensive, authoritative, up-to-date, and written for the "average intelligent layman" (preface). "A must purchase for academic libraries, this authoritative encyclopedic exposition of psychologists, theories, tests, and applications of psychology will also find favor in public libraries" (*Wilson Library Bulletin,* November 1984, p. 226).

The Encyclopedia of Sexual Behavior. Edited by Albert Ellis and Albert Arabanel. 2nd ed. Hawthorn, 1967. 1,072p. Out of print (last priced at $25.00).

> First published in 1961, this work remains the standard reference in the area of human sexuality despite its age and out-of-print status (it has been reprinted in the past and may well be again). The encyclopedia's approximately 100 articles are written with authority, clarity, and good taste.

The Encyclopedic Dictionary of Psychology. Edited by Rom Harré and Roger Lamb. MIT Pr., 1983. 718p. $80.00.

> "This highly recommended volume combines the best of both dictionary and encyclopedia.... Useful to the social science practitioner, student, and layperson, this reference tool is essential for college and university libraries" (*Choice,* April 1984, pp. 1109–10). This work is comparable in coverage and depth to the older *Encyclopedia of Psychology* (2nd ed. Continuum, 1979; 1,187p.), edited by H.J. Eysenck and others—which is not to be confused with the outstanding new four-volume *Encyclopedia of Psychology* (see above), edited by Raymond Corsini and Bonnie Ozaki.

Handbook of Child Psychology. Edited by Paul H. Mussen. 4th ed. Wiley, 1983. Four vols. $200.00.

> The first three editions (1946, 1954, and 1970) of this standard reference were entitled *Carmichael's Manual of Child-Psychology.* Now retitled and expanded to four volumes (from two in the previous edition), the set authoritatively covers the basic concerns of child growth and development, including infancy, socialization, personality, and cognitive and social development. "This updated version of *Handbook of Child Psychology* should prove to be an important reference to students, researchers, and practitioners in the field of child psychology" (*Booklist,* June 1, 1984, p. 1382).

International Encyclopedia of Psychiatry, Psychology, Psychoanalysis, and Neurology. Edited by Benjamin B. Wolman. Aesculapius Publishers and Van

Nostrand, 1977. 12 vols. plus supplement (1983). $675.00 (12 vols.); $89.00 (supplement).

A monumental achievement, this indispensable work comprises 12 volumes and 5 million words by 1,500 contributors and 300 editors and consultants. It treats all important aspects of the fields of psychology and psychiatry, including theories, procedures, issues, and people. *American Reference Books Annual* (1978, p. 697) correctly observes that "this encyclopedia will be a standard source of information in these areas for years to come."

Larousse Encyclopedia of Astrology. Written by Jean-Louis Brau; edited and translated by Helen Weaver and Allan Edmands. New American Library, 1980. 308p. $7.95 paper.

Originally published in France in 1977 and translated into English in 1980, the *Larousse Encyclopedia of Astrology* "is a lively, useful, and informative tool for practicing astrologers, students, psychologists, and even skeptics" (*American Reference Books Annual,* 1982, p. 763). Another useful work on the subject is the *New Compleat Astrologer: The Practical Encyclopedia of Astrological Science* (Revised ed. Crown, 1984) by Derek and Julia Parker.

A Reference Companion to the History of Abnormal Psychology. Written by John G. Howells and M. Livia Osborn. Greenwood, 1984. Two vols. $95.00.

"This new reference volume provides more than 4,000 alphabetically arranged references to persons, concepts, and labels that have figured in the history of psychopathology from antiquity to the present time. It thus serves a need not apparently met by any existing library resource for a combined biographical dictionary and brief encyclopedia for the field of abnormal psychology" (*Choice,* September 1984, p. 64).

RELIGION AND PHILOSOPHY (INCLUDES MYTHOLOGY)

Abingdon Dictionary of Living Religions. Edited by Keith Grim and others. Abingdon, 1981. 830p. $39.95.

One of a number of excellent one-volume comparative surveys of the world's major faiths, the *Abingdon Dictionary of Living Religions* provides more than 1,600 signed articles by 150 authorities. Equally useful references on the subject include the *Dictionary of Comparative Religion* (Scribner's, 1970), edited by S.G.F. Brandon; *Eerdmans' Handbook to the World's Religions* (Eerdmans, 1982), edited by Robert Pierce Beaver; the *Facts on File Dictionary of Religions* (Facts on File, 1984), edited by John R. Hinnells; the *Handbook of Living Religions* (Viking, 1985), also edited by John Hinnells; and *Religions of the World* (St. Martin's Pr., 1983) by Niels C. Nielsen, Jr., and others.

Dictionary of Biblical Theology. Edited by Xavier Léon-Dufour; translated by P. Joseph Cahill. 2nd ed. Seabury, 1973. 712p. Reprinted by Winston Pr. $29.95.

Originally published in France as *Vocabulaire de Théologie Biblique* in 1962 and revised some years later, this highly regarded scholarly reference emphasizes themes found in the Bible, such as anguish, conscience, dreams, responsibility, and violence. *American Reference Books Annual*

(1975, p. 542) says the "dictionary is a preeminent one for biblical theology."

Dictionary of Classical Mythology: Symbols, Attributes & Associations. Written by Robert E. Bell. ABC-Clio, 1982. 390p. $30.00.

Rather than describing the characters of mythology in alphabetical sequence (which is the format of most reference books on the subject), Bell's work covers some 1,000 topics—abandonment, cannibalism, death, fire, prudence, repentance, wine, youth, etc.—and notes the characters, places, and legends connected with each subject. "This is the single best source in English for quick reference to the symbols, attributes, and associations related to the characters found in Greek and Roman myth" (*Choice,* December 1982, p. 552).

Dictionary of the History of Ideas: Studies of Selected Pivotal Ideas. Edited by Philip P. Wiener. Scribner's, 1973–74. Five vols. $75.00 paper.

A truly interdisciplinary reference work, the *Dictionary of the History of Ideas* is an effort to "establish some sense of unity of human thought and its cultural manifestation in a world of ever-increasing specialization and alienation" (preface). The first four volumes contain some 300 lengthy articles that discuss key ideas from all major areas of knowledge; the last volume is a detailed subject and name index.

Encyclopaedia Judaica. Edited by Cecil Roth and Geoffrey Wigoder. Macmillan (dist. by Keter), 1972. 16 vols. plus supplement (1982). $395.00.

Library Journal (August 1972, p. 2562) notes that this outstanding multivolume encyclopedia represents "the latest, most comprehensive and in many ways, most authoritative summary of research in all areas of Jewish scholarship." The set, which contains roughly 25,000 articles by 1,800 authorities, is backed up by the older but still useful 12-volume *Jewish Encyclopedia* (Funk & Wagnalls, 1901–06) and the ten-volume *Universal Jewish Encyclopedia* (1939–43). There are also two excellent single-volume reference works on Judaism: the *Encyclopedic Dictionary of Judaica* (Keter, 1974), edited by Geoffrey Wigoder and designed specifically to complement *Encyclopaedia Judaica,* and the *New Standard Jewish Encyclopedia* (5th ed. Doubleday, 1977), also edited by Geoffrey Wigoder.

The Encyclopedia of American Religions. Written by J. Gordon Melton. McGrath Publishing, 1978. Two vols, plus supplement (1985, dist. by Gale). $135.00; $75.00 (supplement).

Melton, an ordained minister, has produced an invaluable reference work that identifies and describes some 1,200 religions and beliefs found in North America, including numerous cults and small sects. William A. Katz points out in his *Introduction to Reference Work* (1982, vol. 1, p. 208) that the "primary value of the work is reliable information on more obscure groups—of the 17 large categories, 10 are Christian, but 7 are not and vary from the Krishna groups to those involved with UFOs. It is particularly useful for reference, as there is an exhaustive index by names of groups, people, places, and even publications." Other major sources covering religious groups in the United States and Canada are Arthur C. Piepkorn's multivolume *Profiles in Belief: The Religious Bodies of the United States and Canada* (Harper & Row, 1977–79), Frank S. Mead's one-volume *Handbook of Denominations in the United States* (7th ed. Abingdon, 1980), and Albert M. Shulman's one-volume *Religious Heritage of America* (A.S. Barnes, 1981).

The Encyclopedia of Philosophy. Edited by Paul Edwards. Macmillan, 1967. Eight vols. Reprinted in 1973 in four vols. $200.00.

The premier reference work in the field, this encyclopedia treats Eastern and Western philosophy from ancient to modern times. The set is scholarly but its text will normally be comprehensible to the serious general reader. Useful one-volume works on the subject are Antony Flew's *Dictionary of Philosophy* (St. Martin's Pr., 1979) and the *Handbook of World Philosophy: Contemporary Developments since 1945* (Greenwood, 1980), edited by John Burr.

The Encyclopedia of Religion. Edited by Mircea Eliade. Macmillan, 1986. 16 vols. $1,200.00.

One of the newest and most impressive multivolume subject encyclopedias, this set treats the history, beliefs, and practices of both major and minor religions past and present. In all, the encyclopedia contains eight million words and 2,750 articles prepared by 1,400 authorities from around the world. The initial impression is that the *Encyclopedia of Religion* will quite likely supplant the old standard *Encyclopaedia of Religion and Ethics* (see below).

The Encyclopaedia of Religion and Ethics. Edited by James Hastings. Scribner's, 1908–27. 13 vols. Reprinted in 1985 by Fortress Pr. $499.95.

Despite its advanced age, this standard reference set remains useful today, particularly for historical information on religious beliefs and customs, ethical movements, philosophical ideas, and moral practices.

Encyclopedia of Theology: The Concise Sacramentum Mundi. Edited by Karl Rahner and others. Crossroad Publishers, 1975. 1,536p. $39.50.

A one-volume summary and update of the six-volume *Sacramentum Mundi* (Herder & Herder, 1968–70; currently out of print), this important reference source provides nearly 500 signed articles covering the central questions of modern religious thought as viewed by leading Roman Catholic theologians.

Evangelical Dictionary of Theology. Edited by Walter A. Elwell. Baker Book House, 1984. 1,204p. $29.95.

"This dictionary provides for the first time a full and balanced overview of evangelical theology" (*Library Journal,* April 15, 1985, p.39).

Funk & Wagnalls Standard Dictionary of Folklore, Mythology, and Legends. Edited by Maria Leach and Jerome Fried. Funk & Wagnalls, 1949–50. Two vols. Reprinted in 1984 by T.Y. Crowell (dist. by Harper & Row). $23.99 paper.

This well-known work furnishes encyclopedic coverage of the myths and folklore of the major cultures of the world. There is not a great deal of overlap with the more recent *Man, Myth, & Magic* (see below), a 12-volume set that also offers world coverage.

Historical Atlas of Mythology. Written by Joseph Campbell. Alfred Van Der Marck Editions (dist. by Harper & Row), 1983–. Four vols. (in progress). $75.00 per vol.

An encyclopedic history of mythology by one of the world's foremost authorities on the subject, this handsomely illustrated in-progress set will eventually comprise four titled volumes: *The Way of the Animal Powers, The Way of the Seeded Earth, The Way of the Celestial Lights,* and *The Way of Man.* In a review of the first volume *Choice* (April 1984, p. 1171) says, "Campbell begins with creation myths, moves to primitive hunters and gatherers, and culminates with the mythologies of the Great Hunt, referring to ancient and modern primitive cultures to illustrate the primacy of long-held beliefs in the development of culture. The 50 specially prepared maps help clarify for the reader this broad sweep of knowledge."

The Illustrated Bible Dictionary. Edited by Norman Hillyer and others. Tyndale House, 1980. Three vols. $99.95. (Also available from Grolier Educational Corp. at $95.00.)

The three-volume *Illustrated Bible Dictionary,* a revision and expansion of the highly regarded one-volume *New Bible Dictionary* (first published in 1962 and revised in 1965), is widely considered one of the best Bible dictionaries currently available. Prepared by some 165 biblical scholars and "written in a spirit of unqualified loyalty to Holy Scripture" (preface), the work includes articles on all the books, people, doctrines, and major words of the Bible, along with background material on the holy lands. *American Reference Books Annual* (1982, p. 564) states that "this work establishes a new standard for publishing and display techniques by which all other Bible dictionaries will henceforth be judged. This is an important new Bible dictionary."

The International Standard Bible Encyclopedia. Edited by Geoffrey W. Bromiley. Revised ed. Eerdmans, 1979–. Four vols. (in progress). $89.95.

An outstanding work of evangelical scholarship, this encyclopedia first appeared in 1915, was revised in 1929, and is now undergoing another thorough revision (at the present time, Volumes 3 and 4 are in preparation). "Intended for scholars, pastors, and laypersons, it includes articles on all persons and places mentioned in the Bible and also treats theological and ethical topics" (*American Reference Books Annual,* 1980, p. 473). Numerous other fine Bible encyclopedias are available, including *Harper's Encyclopedia of Bible Life* (3rd ed. Harper & Row, 1978) by Madeleine and J. Lane Miller, *Nelson's Bible Encyclopedia for the Family* (Thomas Nelson, 1982), the *Wycliffe Bible Encyclopedia* (Moody Pr., 1976), and the *Zondervan Pictorial Encyclopedia of the Bible* (Zondervan, 1975), a five-volume work edited by Merrill C. Tenney.

The Interpreter's Dictionary of the Bible: An Illustrated Encyclopedia Identifying and Explaining All Proper Names and Significant Terms and Subjects in the Holy Scriptures, including the Apocrypha, with Attention to Archaeological Discoveries and Researches into the Life and Faith of Ancient Times. Edited by George Arthur Buttrick. Abingdon, 1962. Four vols. plus supplement (1976). $109.00.

Like the *Illustrated Bible Dictionary* and the *International Standard Bible Encyclopedia* (both reviewed above), this set provides an authoritative and comprehensive survey of the Bible and its text (in this case the King James Version and the Revised Standard Version). The *Interpreter's Dictionary of the Bible,* which is a shortened version of the *Interpreter's Bible* (a 12-volume work published by Abingdon between 1951 and 1957), is indispensable for modern biblical study. An excellent new Bible dictionary is the single-volume *Illustrated Dictionary and Concordance of the Bible* (Macmillan, 1985), which covers some 3,500 names from the Old and New Testaments and includes almost 2,000 color illustrations. Also worthy of note is the recently revised (1985) *Harper's Bible Dictionary* (Harper and Row), which includes outlines of every book in the Bible.

Man, Myth, & Magic: The Illustrated Encyclopedia of Mythology, Religion and the Unknown. Edited by Richard Cavendish. 2nd ed. Marshall Cavendish, 1983. 12 vols. $399.95 plus $10.00 shipping and handling.

First issued in 24 very slender volumes in 1970, the revised second edition of this first-rate encyclopedia has sensibly been reduced to 12 volumes, although the amount of text remains roughly the same. Written in a popular though objective style, the set covers the beliefs and rituals of societies everywhere, with emphasis on the occult, magic, and parapsychology.

New Catholic Encyclopedia: An International Work of Reference on the Teachings, History, Organization and Activities of the Catholic Church, and on All Institutions, Religions, Philosophies and Scientific and Cultural Developments affecting the Catholic Church from Its Beginning to the Present. Prepared by the Editorial Staff of the Catholic University of America. McGraw-Hill, 1967. 15 vols. plus 2 supplements (1974 and 1979). Reprinted by the Publishers Guild. $450.00.

Comprising approximately 17,000 articles by 4,800 contributors, accompanied by 7,400 illustrations and 300 maps, the multivolume *New Catholic Encyclopedia* is an excellently produced specialized encyclopedia. In his *Introduction to Reference Work* (1982, vol. 1, p. 208), William A. Katz says of the work: "Its 17,000 articles by close to 5,000 scholars (many of whom have no affiliation with the church) are models of objectivity." A less formidable but nonetheless important reference work by the same people who produced the *New Catholic Encyclopedia* is the three-volume *Encyclopedic Dictionary of Religion* (Corpus Publications, 1979); another smaller alternative to the *New Catholic Encyclopedia* is the three-volume *New Catholic Peoples' Encyclopedia* (Revised ed. Catholic Pr., 1973).

The Oxford Dictionary of the Christian Church. Edited by F.L. Cross and E.A. Livingstone. 2nd ed. Oxford Univ. Pr., 1974, 1,518p. $60.00.

Originally published in 1957 and extensively revised in 1974, this valuable one-volume reference contains roughly 6,000 entries covering the major terms and names associated with Christianity. A complementary work is the *New International Dictionary of the Christian Church* (Zondervan, 1978), edited by J.D. Douglas.

World Christian Encyclopedia: A Comparative Study of Churches and Religions in the Modern World, A.D. 1900–2000. Edited by David B. Barrett. Oxford Univ. Pr., 1982. 1,010p. $125.00.

"From the opening chapter on the status of Christianity in the 20th century to the closing directory of religious organizations, the encyclopedia is filled with useful information.... Brilliantly produced and arranged, this will undoubtedly be a standard reference work for years to come" (*Library Journal*, June 1, 1982, p. 1084).

World Philosophy: Essay-Reviews of 225 Major Works. Edited by Frank N. Magill. Salem Pr., 1982. Five vols. $250.00.

An enlargement of Magill's earlier *Masterpieces of World Philosophy in Summary Form* (Harper & Row, 1961), this useful source summarizes basic works on philosophy from ancient to modern times. "The works selected for summarization include virtually all of the famous philosophers and most of their best-known works. The summaries are clear and intelligible to the educated lay person" (*American Reference Books Annual*, 1984, p. 499).

World Spirituality: An Encyclopedic History of the Religious Quest. Edited by Bernard McGinn and others. Crossroad Publishers, 1985–. 25 vols. (in progress). $49.50 per vol.

This new, thematically arranged set intends to cover all the world's religions. *Library Journal* (September 15, 1985, p. 74) says of the first published volume: "In less than 500 breathless pages an international array of scholars sketch significant aspects of Christian spirituality from the birth of Jesus to the 12th century in both the Eastern and Western churches.... Basic for religious and theological collections."

SCIENCE AND TECHNOLOGY (GENERAL)

Album of Science. Edited by I. Bernard Cohen. Scribner's, 1978–86. Five vols. $55.00 per vol.

Encyclopedic in scope, this impressive pictorial history of science encompasses five titled volumes, each by a distinguished authority: John E. Murdoch's *Antiquity and the Middle Ages* (1984), editor Cohen's *From Leonardo to Lavoisier, 1450–1800* (1980), L. Pearce Williams's *The Nineteenth Century* (1978), C. Stewart Gillmor's *The Physical Sciences in the Twentieth Century* (1985), and Garland Allen's *The Biological Sciences in the Twentieth Century* (1986).

Asimov's New Guide to Science. Written by Isaac Asimov. Basic Books, 1984, 940p. $29.95.

First published in 1960 as the *Intelligent Man's Guide to Science* and revised twice under the title *Asimov's Guide to Science* (1965 and 1972), this excellent work is "a summary of physical and biological science which has been interestingly and understandably written for the nonscientist" (*Choice*, March 1985, p. 1012).

The Cambridge Guide to the Material World. Written by Rodney Cotterill. Cambridge Univ. Pr., 1984. 352p. $34.50.

"Cotterill reviews much of the groundwork of the physical and biological sciences. His nonmathematical approach and considerable ability to explain things clearly will make this book a godsend to anyone who knows little or no physics, chemistry, or biology but would like a 'picture of the world at the microscopic and atomic levels'" (*Library Journal*, September 15, 1984, p. 1748).

Comparisons: Of Distance, Size, Area, Volume, Mass, Weight, Density, Energy, Temperature, Time, Speed and Number throughout the Universe. Written by the Diagram Group. St. Martin's Pr., 1980. 240p. $15.00; $9.95 paper.

"The Diagram Group's attractive, generally accurate, and usually quite effective drawings amply illustrate the gamut of measurements, from the size of animals and buildings to the temperatures of stars and planets ... this book's value lies in its illustrations of the comparisons, allowing the reader to see the differences in the objects being compared" (*Library Journal*, November 1, 1980, pp. 2315–16). A somewhat similar reference is Stuart Sandow's *Durations: The Encyclopedia of How Long Things Take* (Times Books, 1977).

Concise Encyclopedia of the Sciences. Edited by John David Yule. Facts on File, 1982. 590p. $29.95; $18.95 paper.

Some 5,500 key words in all areas of science are briefly discussed in this handy one-volume science encyclopedia, which originally appeared in Great Britain in 1978 as the *Phaidon Concise Encyclopedia of Science and Technology*.

A Dictionary of Named Effects and Laws in Chemistry, Physics and Mathematics. Written by D.W.G. Ballentyne and D.R. Lovett. 4th ed. Chapman & Hall (dist. by Methuen), 1980. 346p. $19.95 paper.
   This reference source covers equations, laws, theorems, effects, constants, etc. identified with individual scientists, such as the Van Allen Belt, Fermi Constant, and Hubble Effect.

Dictionary of the History of Science. Edited by William F. Bynum, E. Janet Browne, and Roy Porter. Princeton Univ. Pr., 1981. 494p. $48.00.
   Well produced and clearly written, this work consists of some 700 articles dealing with the key ideas of Western science developed during the past 500 years. "In this century, if not earlier, the natural and behavioral sciences have eclipsed the arts as the principal forces shaping our view of the world. This scholarly, high quality dictionary can help students, specialists, and laymen understand how those forces gained strength" (*Wilson Library Bulletin,* March 1982, p. 542).

Growing Up with Science: The Illustrated Encyclopedia of Invention. Marshall Cavendish, 1984. 25 vols. $199.95 plus $10.00 shipping and handling. (Also available from H.S. Stuttman at $149.50.)
   "This lavishly illustrated, multivolume encyclopedia for children provides a fascinating collection of articles intended to introduce young readers to the exciting world of science, technology, and invention" (*American Reference Books Annual,* 1985, p. 489). The first 22 volumes cover scientific phenomena, techniques, and discoveries in alphabetical sequence. Volume 23 is devoted to inventions, Volume 24 to inventors, and Volume 25 to hands-on projects, a glossary of terms, and an index. Another multivolume set quite similar to *Growing Up with Science* is the 20-volume *How It Works: The Illustrated Encyclopedia of Science and Technology,* also published by Marshall Cavendish (in 1977).

McGraw-Hill Concise Encyclopedia of Science and Technology. Edited by Sybil P. Parker. McGraw-Hill, 1984. 2,065p. $95.00.
   The 7,300 alphabetically arranged articles that make up this outstanding single-volume science encyclopedia are taken mainly from the multivolume *McGraw-Hill Encyclopedia of Science and Technology* (see below), although material from other McGraw-Hill reference works is also included. "The cost of this tool is eminently reasonable; the need for a single-volume encyclopedia of science, clear-cut; and the quality of this work is such that it should be an automatic purchase for all types of libraries. Individuals, as well, may wish to acquire it for their private collection" (*American Reference Books Annual,* 1985, p. 490). This volume is especially for those who lack ready access to or cannot afford the parent set (which currently retails for $935.00).

McGraw-Hill Encyclopedia of Science and Technology: An International Reference Work in Fifteen Volumes including an Index. Edited by Sybil P. Parker. 5th ed. McGraw-Hill, 1982. 15 vols. $935.00.
   Unquestionably the most important encyclopedia covering the entire spectrum of science and technology, this well-known and highly regarded set is now in its fifth edition (the first appeared in 1960). It contains more than seven million words, 12,400 pages, and 7,700 articles accompanied by 15,250 illustrations—all made readily accessible by two large indexes, one analytical and the other topical. *Booklist* (August 1983, p. 1482) notes that the encyclopedia "has truly become an authoritative and comprehensive survey of the pure and applied sciences." The set is

updated annually by the *McGraw-Hill Yearbook of Science and Technology* .

The New Book of Popular Science. Grolier, 1984. Six vols. $245.00 plus $15.00 shipping and handling; with discount to schools and libraries: $149.50 plus $4.00 shipping and handling.

Intended chiefly for students from the upper elementary grades to senior high school, the *New Book of Popular Science* contains approximately 1.4 million words, 3,000 pages, and 340 articles accompanied by 3,300 illustrations. *Booklist* (February 1, 1985, p. 770) recommends the set for libraries and "for home purchase, as it can be used, for both pleasure and profit, at a variety of levels."

The Raintree Illustrated Science Encyclopedia. Revised ed. Raintree Publications, 1984. 20 vols. $332.67. (Also available from Grolier at $249.50.)

A complete reworking of the *Encyclopedia of Nature and Science* (1974), this useful children's science encyclopedia provides roughly 3,000 articles accompanied by 4,000 full-color illustrations. "Heavily illustrated with color photographs and simple diagrams, this is a handsome, informative, and useful tool which can be used by a fourth-grade student as well as those in the upper elementary grades and junior high" (*School Library Journal,* May 1984, p. 25).

Van Nostrand's Scientific Encyclopedia. Edited by Douglas M. Considine. 6th ed. Van Nostrand, 1983. Two vols. $139.50. (Also available from the publisher in a one-volume ed. at $107.50.)

Along with the *McGraw-Hill Concise Encyclopedia of Science and Technology* (see above), this is the best small-volume general science encyclopedia for adults currently available. *American Reference Books Annual* (1984, p. 608) says of the sixth edition: "The encyclopedia remains a reliable, authoritative, and comprehensive reference tool."

SOCIAL SCIENCES (INCLUDES SOCIOLOGY AND ANTHROPOLOGY)

Dictionary of American Communal and Utopian History. Written by Robert S. Fogarty. Greenwood, 1980. 271p. $35.00.

Fogarty's book, which focuses on North American settlements and their leaders from the eighteenth to the early years of the twentieth century, "will aid the researcher concerned with America's contribution toward utopian thought and communal organization" (*American Reference Books Annual,* 1981, p. 198).

Dictionary of Demography. Written by William Petersen and Renee Petersen. Greenwood, 1985. Five vols. $350.00.

This impressive set is the most comprehensive and up-to-date reference source on the scientific study of human population currently available. Two of the volumes provide in-depth coverage of terms, concepts, and institutions in the field of demography; two others are devoted to biographical information about major demographers; and the final volume is a multilingual glossary.

A Dictionary of the Social Sciences. Edited by Julius Gould and William Kolb. Free Pr., 1964. 761p. $40.00.

Out of print for some time, now back in print, this highly regarded encyclopedic dictionary remains (despite its age) the best one-volume source on the terminology of the various social and behavioral sciences. "It defines and describes in the form of incisive essays some two thousand terms and concepts in the fields of anthropology, economics, political science, social psychology and sociology" (*College and Research Libraries,* January 1965, p. 54).

The Encyclopedia of American Crime. Written by Carl Sifakis. Facts on File, 1982. 802p. $49.95; $17.95 paper.

The *Encyclopedia of American Crime* comprises more than 1,500 brief articles on famous criminals, detectives, judges, lawyers, and criminologists as well as types of crimes, weapons, criminal slang, and so on. *Library Journal* (July 1982, p. 1341) calls the encyclopedia "the most comprehensive popular source available." A more scholarly work is the four-volume *Encyclopedia of Crime and Justice* (see below).

Encyclopedia of Anthropology. Edited by David E. Hunter and Phillip Whitten. Harper & Row, 1976. 411p. Out of print (last priced at $6.95 paper).

The only comprehensive anthropology encyclopedia of recent vintage, this work contains some 1,400 articles that treat major concepts, theories, terms, and people in the field. "It is a pioneering work that should serve the profession well as an authoritative source of information on all major aspects of anthropology" (*American Reference Books Annual,* 1977, p. 360).

Encyclopedia of Black America. Edited by W. Augustus Low and Virgil A. Clift. McGraw-Hill, 1981. 921p. $59.00; $24.95 paper.

"The *Encyclopedia of Black America* fills a need for an authoritative and comprehensive one-volume encyclopedia on Afro-American life and culture. No other current reference work matches it in range and depth of information" (*Booklist,* April 1, 1982, p. 1034). Other useful references on the subject include the *Black American Reference Book* (Prentice-Hall, 1976), edited by Mabel M. Smythe; the *Negro Almanac* (4th ed. Wiley, 1983), edited by Harry A. Ploski and James Williams; and Ellen Diggs's *Black Chronology from 4000 B.C. to the Abolition of the Slave Trade* (G.K. Hall, 1983).

The Encyclopedia of Crime and Justice. Edited by Sanford H. Kadish. Free Pr., 1983. Four vols. $300.00.

The 286 alphabetically arranged articles that make up this excellent encyclopedia include such subjects as abortion, the adversary system, arraignment, bail, confessions, forgery, jury trials, the mass media and crime, perjury, prisons, probation and parole, race and crime, treason, and victim and witness assistance programs. "This four-volume encyclopedia consists of 286 original articles written and edited by some of the best-known figures in the field of criminal justice. It is a mark of distinction that their work is as close to totally objective as possible in a field that is filled with emotionally laden issues" (*Choice,* March 1984, p. 950). A complementary source is the two-volume *International Handbook of Contemporary Developments in Criminology* (Greenwood, 1983), edited by Elmer H. Johnson.

Encyclopedia of Social Work. Edited by John B. Turner. 17th ed. National Association of Social Workers, 1977. Two vols. plus supplement (1983). $48.00 (two vols.); $14.95 (supplement).

A longtime standard reference, the *Encyclopedia of Social Work* covers the whole range of activities in the field, including articles on aging, drugs, housing, and minorities. *American Reference Books Annual* (1978, p. 336) praises the current edition as "a cornucopia of informational materials that can be put to immediate use by social work practitioners or employed as background by workers in the field of behavioral science." A new edition of the work is scheduled for 1987, after which it will be revised every ten years.

Encyclopedia of Urban Planning. Edited by Arnold Whittick. McGraw-Hill, 1974. 1,218p. Reprinted in 1980 by Krieger Publishing. $59.50.
International in scope, this valuable work provides some 400 articles on urban planning from ancient times to the present. Brief biographical profiles of leading planners are included.

Handbook of North American Indians. Edited by William C. Sturtevant. Smithsonian Institution (dist. by the U.S. Government Printing Office), 1978–. 20 vols. (in progress). Prices vary from $14.50 to $29.00 per vol.
This in-progress work is a definitive study of the history, culture, and anthropology of the aboriginal Indians (including Eskimos) of the entire North American continent. Each volume in the set covers a specific geographical region. "*Handbook of North American Indians* promises to be an invaluable source for high school, public, and academic libraries serving persons interested in North American Indians" (*Booklist,* July 1984, p. 1535). A useful one-volume reference on the subject is Barbara A. Leitch's *Concise Dictionary of Indian Tribes of North America* (Reference Publications, 1979).

The Harvard Encyclopedia of American Ethnic Groups. Edited by Stephan Thernstrom. Harvard Univ. Pr., 1980. 1,076p. $70.00.
Over 100 ethnic groups—from Acadians to Zoroastrians—are described in this outstanding reference work. Prepared by a group of distinguished scholars, the volume also includes 29 thematic essays on such topics as assimilation, intermarriage, and prejudice. Two complementary works are Stephanie Bernardo's *Ethnic Almanac* (Doubleday, 1981) and *Refugees in the United States: A Reference Handbook* (Greenwood, 1985), edited by David W. Haines.

The Illustrated Encyclopedia of Mankind. Edited by Richard Carlisle and Yvonne Deutch. Revised ed. Marshall Cavendish, 1984. 21 vols. $324.95 plus $10.00 shipping and handling.
A revision of the well-received 1978 first edition (published in 20 volumes), this encyclopedia of anthropology furnishes basic historical and ethnographic information about more than 500 social groups and cultures around the world, ranging from the Abelams to the Zulus. The set is enhanced by some 3,500 color illustrations and maps. *American Reference Books Annual* (1980, p. 347) characterized the first edition as "an important pioneering anthropological encyclopedia"; of the revised edition *American Reference Books Annual* (1985, p. 120) says, "This encyclopedic anthropological work is unique in its coverage and will be appreciated by the users."

International Encyclopedia of Population. Edited by John A. Ross. Free Pr., 1982. Two vols. $125.00.
Consisting of 129 alphabetically arranged articles by 123 specialists in the field, this two-volume set provides comprehensive coverage of the main areas of demography, including marriage, mortality, morbidity, and migration, along with such interdisciplinary topics as ecology, family

planning, and the status of women. "The *IEP* avoids excessive technicality and stresses overviews of existing knowledge. It is the first alphabetically arranged reference work devoted entirely to the field of population" (*Choice,* December 1982, p. 561). A more recent—and complementary— set is the *Dictionary of Demography* (see above).

The International Encyclopedia of Sociology: A Concise Encyclopedic Reference Work for All Students of the Social Sciences. Edited by Michael Mann. Crossroad/Continuum, 1984. 434p. $34.50.

Originally published in Great Britain as the *Macmillan Student Encyclopedia of Sociology,* this up-to-date volume contains more than 2,000 brief, signed articles covering the basic terminology and concepts of sociology. Leading sociologists also receive coverage. A quite similar one-volume reference is the older *Encyclopedia of Sociology* (Dushkin, 1974).

International Encyclopedia of the Social Sciences. Edited by David L. Sills. Free Pr., 1968. 17 vols. Reprinted in 1977 in 8 vols. $310.00; plus supplement (1979). $85.00.

A truly monumental reference work, the eight-million-word *International Encyclopedia of the Social Sciences* contains 1,716 signed articles covering all important aspects of sociology, anthropology, history, geography, political science, law, psychology, statistics, and other social and behavioral sciences. The set, which effectively replaces the old *Encyclopedia of the Social Sciences* (1930–35), is noted particularly for the interdisciplinary nature of its articles and the high caliber of its contributors. "It fills a keenly felt need of the postwar generation of students and scholars for a truly modern synthesis of all important scholarly achievements in 10 distinct and several related subfields of contemporary social science" (*Choice,* July-August 1968, p. 605). Note that a *Biographical Supplement* covering 215 contemporary social scientists appeared in 1979.

Muslim Peoples: A World Ethnographic Survey. Edited by Richard V. Weekes. 2nd ed. Greenwood, 1984. Two vols. $95.00.

This encyclopedic survey "gives an impressive overview of the languages, socioeconomic patterns, religious practices, and cultural values of different Muslim groups" (*Library Journal,* November 1, 1984, p. 2058). In all, nearly 200 ethnic or linguistic groups are covered.

The Peoples of the USSR: An Ethnographic Handbook. Written by Ronald Wixman. M.E. Sharpe, 1984. 246p. $35.00.

A Soviet counterpart to the *Harvard Encyclopedia of American Ethnic Groups* (see above), this useful work identifies and describes practically every ethnic group currently found in the Soviet Union. "Highly recommended for all academic and research reference collections" (*Choice,* September 1984, p. 72).

SPORTS AND GAMES

The Baseball Encyclopedia: The Complete and Official Record of Major League Baseball. Edited by Joseph L. Reichler. 6th ed. Macmillan, 1985. 2,733p. $39.95.

Booklist (August 1985, p. 1598) calls this comprehensive, oft-revised encyclopedia "the standard of its kind." Two formidable competitors are the *Official Encyclopedia of Baseball* (10th ed. Doubleday, 1979), edited by Hy Turkin and S.C. Thompson; and the *Sports Encyclopedia: Baseball* (6th ed. St. Martin's Pr., 1985), edited by David Neft and Richard M. Cohen.

Complete Outdoors Encyclopedia. Written by Vin T. Sparano. 2nd ed. Harper & Row, 1980. 607p. $19.18.

This handy single-volume reference covers hunting and shooting (including a section on hunting dogs), fishing, camping, boating, archery, and first aid. "Because of the wide range of information given, this volume will be of value in most libraries and in most outdoorsmen's private collections" (*American Reference Books Annual,* 1981, p. 330).

Encyclopedia of Boxing. Written by Gilbert Odd. Crown, 1984. 192p. $9.98.

Odd, a British boxing historian, covers famous fights and fighters in this inexpensive item. "Boxing fans will be delighted by this pictorial fact book" (*Booklist,* April 15, 1984, p. 1143). Another useful reference on boxing is the annual *Ring Record Book and Boxing Encyclopedia* (Ring Publications, 1941–), edited by Bert Sugar.

The Encyclopedia of Football. Edited by Roger Treat; revised ed. by Pete Palmer. 16th ed. A.S. Barnes, 1979. 738p. $17.95; $9.95 paper.

Long recognized as a standard reference work, this frequently revised encyclopedia covers the entire spectrum of professional football in the United States.

Encyclopedia of Modern Bodybuilding. Written by Arnold Schwarzenegger and Bill Dobbins. Simon & Schuster, 1985. 736p. $35.00.

"Champion bodybuilder and actor Schwarzenegger has written a comprehensive book on the sport of bodybuilding. There is a wealth of information for neophytes as well as for the accomplished" (*Library Journal,* September 1, 1985, p. 210). The text is augmented by numerous photographs, including color portraits of leading weight lifters.

Encyclopaedia of Motor-Cycle Sport. Compiled by Peter Carrick. 2nd ed. St. Martin's Pr., 1982. 240p. $14.95.

A British production but international in its coverage, the *Encyclopaedia of Motor-Cycle Sport* provides alphabetical entries on important cycle riders, manufacturers, models, types of races, individual racing events, and terms used in the sport.

Encyclopedia of Physical Education, Fitness, and Sports. Edited by Thomas K. Cureton, Jr. Brighton Publishing, 1977–81. Three vols. $38.00 per vol.

More a collection of signed articles by specialists in the field than a traditional encyclopedia, this set comprises three titled volumes: *Philosophy, Programs, and History* (1981); *Training, Environment, Nutrition, and Fitness* (1980); and *Sports, Dance, and Related Activities* (1977). "Perhaps the greatest value of this work lies in its bringing together in one place information likely to be sought by those in the field" (*American Reference Books Annual* (1983, p. 305).

The Encyclopedia of Sports. Written by Frank G. Menke; revised ed. by Pete Palmer. 6th ed. A.S. Barnes, 1977. 1,132p. Out of print (last priced at $30.00).

Despite its need for a new revision and present out-of-print status, the *Encyclopedia of Sports* remains the best single source for basic information on all major sports of the world. Arranged alphabetically by sport, each article includes the sport's history, rules, records, champions, etc. *American Reference Books Annual* (1979, p. 339) praises the current edition for its "accuracy, wide coverage, wealth of detail, and up-to-date information." A complementary one-volume work is the *Oxford Companion to World Sports and Games* (Oxford Univ. Pr., 1975), edited by John Arlott.

Golf Magazine's Encyclopedia of Golf. Edited by John M. Ross. Revised ed. Harper & Row, 1979. 439p. $19.95.
"Everything under the sun and on the green that has to do with the game, past and present, bounces between the pages like the proverbial white ball that aficionadoes pursue. We are treated to a history of golf, and to its personalities, rules, equipment, fundamentals, championship courses, and worldwide tournaments" (*American Reference Books Annual*, 1980, p. 322). Another useful, albeit aging, work on the subject is the *Encyclopedia of Golf* (Revised ed. St. Martin's Pr., 1974), compiled by Webster Evans.

The Hockey Encyclopedia: The Complete Record of Professional Ice Hockey. Written by Stan Fischler and Shirley Walton Fischler. Macmillan, 1984. 720p. $24.95.
"Any hockey enthusiast will want this encyclopedia, and any library with a sports reference collection will find it very handy" (*Booklist,* January 15, 1985, p. 702). This work supersedes *Fischlers' Ice Hockey Encyclopedia* (T.Y. Crowell, 1979) by the same authors.

McClane's New Standard Fishing Encyclopedia and International Angling Guide. Edited by A.J. McClane. Revised ed. Holt, 1974. 1,156p. $50.00.
McClane's is the most comprehensive and best-known reference work on the sport of fishing. The alphabetical entries cover fishing terms, specific fish (both freshwater and saltwater), fishing localities, biographies of important people connected with the sport, etc.

The Modern Encyclopedia of Basketball. Edited by Zander Hollander. 2nd ed. Doubleday, 1979. 624p. Out of print (last priced at $12.50 paper).
This standard reference covers both college and professional basketball. First published in 1973 and revised in 1979, it has been called "the one indispensable source on this subject for sports fans and libraries alike" (*American Reference Books Annual,* 1980, p. 316). A new edition of the encyclopedia is currently in preparation.

The Official Encyclopedia of Bridge. Edited by Harry G. Francis and the Editorial Staff of the American Contract Bridge League. 4th ed. Crown, 1984. 922p. $35.00.
Since its initial publication in 1964, this work has been the ultimate authority for the approximately 200,000 members of the American Contract Bridge League. The book admirably meets its stated objective: "to provide an official and authoritative answer to any question a reader might ask about the game of contract bridge and its leading players" (preface).

The Oxford Companion to Chess. Written by David Hooper and Kenneth Whyld. Oxford Univ. Pr., 1984. 407p. $39.95.
Encyclopedic in format, this recent addition to the *Oxford Companion* family includes definitions of key chess terms, biographies of nearly 600 grandmasters, and some 650 opening moves (which are cross-referenced to an appendix where they are charted by standard notation). *Choice* (July-August 1985, p. 1614) calls the book "a veritable gold mine of historical, sociological, and technical information on the most ancient of board games." An older (and now out-of-print) source on chess is the

Encyclopedia of Chess (2nd ed. St. Martin's Pr., 1977), compiled by Anne Sunnucks.

The Rule Book: The Authoritative, Up-to-Date, Illustrated Guide to the Regulations, History, and Object of All Major Sports. Written by the Diagram Group. St. Martin's Pr., 1983. 430p. $9.95.

The Rule Book, a revised updating of the Diagram Group's earlier *Rules of the Game: The Complete Illustrated Encyclopedia of All Sports of the World* (Paddington Pr., 1974), furnishes basic information on sports ranging from archery to yacht racing. *Choice* (September 1983, p. 66) notes that the book "should prove a useful reference in providing the average fan with basic, understandable information about a variety of sports."

The Sailing Encyclopedia. Edited by Michael W. Richey. T.Y. Crowell (dist. by Harper & Row), 1980. 288p. $29.95.

"This lovely cyclopedia covers a wide variety of topics for everyone from armchair sailors to ocean-going yachtsmen... a fascinating, informative, and attractive book to read" (*American Reference Books Annual,* 1982, p. 376).

Scarne's Encyclopedia of Card Games. Written by John Scarne. Harper & Row, 1973. 628p. $10.10 paper.

Scarne covers practically every card game ever devised in this inexpensive guide and rule book. Also included are major board, dice, tile, guessing, and parlor games, as well as a section on how to detect cheating.

Ski Magazine's Encyclopedia of Skiing. Edited by Richard Needham. 2nd ed. Harper & Row, 1979. 452p. $25.00.

This heavily illustrated encyclopedia provides essential information about the sport, including its history, equipment, techniques, terminology, associations, competitions, and people. "It is a useful reference book and is also enjoyable for browsing" (*American Reference Books Annual,* 1980, p. 327).

United States Tennis Association Official Encyclopedia of Tennis. Edited by Bill Shannon. 3rd ed. Harper & Row, 1981. 512p. $25.00.

The most comprehensive reference work on the subject, this profusely illustrated encyclopedia covers the game's history, equipment, techniques, terminology, rules, tournaments, etiquette, and players. A somewhat more informal but equally useful source is *Bud Collins' Modern Encyclopedia of Tennis* (Doubleday, 1980).

THEATER AND DANCE

The American Musical Theatre: A Chronicle. Written by Gerald Bordman. Oxford Univ. Pr., 1978. 749p. $45.00.

Bordman systematically covers the musical theater in the United States from early colonial times to mid-1978, including every musical ever produced in New York City. In all, some 3,000 shows are described. "Over the years there have been other books on musical theater, but there are none on the grand scale of this one" (*Booklist,* February 1, 1980, p. 786). Other major reference works on the subject are Stanley Green's one-volume *Encyclopedia of the Musical Theatre* (see below),

Ken Bloom's two-volume *American Song: The Complete Musical Theatre Companion* (Facts on File, 1985), Richard Lewine and Alfred Simon's one-volume *Songs of the Theater* (H.W. Wilson, 1984), David Ewen's one-volume *New Complete Book of the American Musical Theatre* (Holt, 1970), and Bordman's invaluable trilogy *American Operetta* (Oxford Univ. Pr., 1981), *American Musical Comedy* (Oxford Univ. Pr., 1982), and *American Musical Revue* (Oxford Univ. Pr., 1985), which effectively supplements his *American Musical Theatre*.

The Concise Oxford Dictionary of Ballet. Edited by Horst Koegler. 2nd ed. Oxford Univ. Pr., 1982. 459p. $14.95 paper.

Originally published in 1977, this standard reference work consists of more than 5,000 entries covering all important aspects of classical dance. Complementary titles that focus on individual ballets are the *Ballet Goer's Guide* (Random House, 1981) by Mary Clarke and Clement Crisp; Walter Terry's *Ballet Guide* (Dodd, 1976), and *Balanchine's Complete Stories of the Great Ballets* (Revised ed. Doubleday, 1977) by George Balanchine and Francis Mason.

Dictionary of the Black Theatre: Broadway, Off-Broadway, and Selected Harlem Theatre. Written by Allen Woll. Greenwood, 1983. 359p. $39.95.

This valuable reference source provides concise information about approximately 300 plays, revues, and musicals "by, about, with, for and related to blacks" (preface), as well as the leading people and organizations connected with these productions. "This is a unique, well-executed reference book and a joyous one, celebrating the black theater's past and present and raising hopes for an even greater future" (*American Reference Books Annual,* 1984, p. 464).

The Encyclopedia of the American Theatre, 1900–1975. Written by Edwin Bronner. Revised ed. A.S. Barnes, 1979. 544p. $30.00.

Plays produced on and off Broadway during the first 75 years of this century are reviewed and summarized in alphabetical sequence in this popularly written work. An equally useful title is Daniel Blum's one-volume *Pictorial History of the American Theatre, 1860–1980* (5th ed. Crown, 1981).

Encyclopedia of the Musical Theatre. Written by Stanley Green. Dodd, Mead, 1976. 488p. Reprinted in 1980 by Da Capo. $10.95 paper.

Covering the musical theater of both New York and London, Green's excellent volume furnishes basic information about some 200 musicals and their songs produced from the late nineteenth century through the mid-1970s. Biographical material on major composers, lyricists, performers, choreographers, producers, and directors is also included. This work nicely complements Gerald Bordman's *American Musical Theatre* (see above).

Illustrated Encyclopaedia of World Theatre: With 420 Illustrations and an Index of Play Titles. Edited by Martin Esslin; translated by Estelle Schmid. Thames and Hudson (dist. by Norton), 1981. 320p. $12.95.

Originally published in German in 1969 under the title *Friedrichs Theaterlexikon* and first issued in English in 1977 by Scribner's as the *Encyclopedia of World Theater,* this useful one-volume reference work consists of about 2,000 alphabetically arranged articles on all facets of theater around the world, although emphasis is clearly on the European and Anglo-American stage and its producers and performers. *Choice* (May 1978, p. 372) praised the first English-language edition, noting that "the broad coverage of this book, extending to all aspects of theater (including cabaret, music hall, circus, and other popular entertainment forms), and the handsome, useful format, which includes an index listing more than 5,000 play titles, make this an indispensable reference for all libraries."

The International Encyclopedia of Dance. Edited by the Dance Perspectives Foundation. Scribner's, 1986 (?). Five vols. (in progress). No price set.

Announced several years ago and still in preparation, this multivolume work promises to become the standard reference source in the field of dance immediately upon publication. The set will cover all aspects and types of dance, both past and present. Until the *International Encyclopedia of Dance* appears, students will have to make do with such aging and out-of-print titles as the *Dance Encyclopedia* (Revised ed. Simon & Schuster, 1967), edited by Anatole Chujoy and P.W. Manchester, and the *Encyclopedia of Dance and Ballet* (Putnam, 1977), edited by Mary Clarke and David Vaughan.

Kabuki Encyclopedia: An English-Language Adaptation of Kabuki Jiten. Adapted by Samuel L. Leiter. Greenwood, 1979. 572p. $45.00.

This work is a comprehensive guide to Kabuki, the traditional Japanese popular drama begun in the seventeenth century and of considerable interest recently among Western theatergoers. "The body of the *Kabuki Encyclopedia* is an alphabet of concise entries for actors, plays, and historical and technical terms of the Kabuki theater" (*Choice*, June 1980, p. 520). A companion work is Leiter's *Art of Kabuki: Famous Plays in Performance* (Univ. of California Pr., 1979).

The Oxford Companion to American Theatre. Written by Gerald Bordman. Oxford Univ. Pr., 1984. 734p. $49.95.

An extension of the *Oxford Companion to the Theatre* (see below), this new addition to the *Oxford Companion* series encompasses some 3,000 A-to-Z entries on the North American theater, covering such topics as specific plays, playwrights, performers, producers, individual theaters, theater issues (such as censorship), and allied performing arts (the circus, wild west shows, vaudeville, etc.). "The highly readable articles draw on social history to place the theater in context. The *Companion* is the source of choice for brief, factual information about American theater" (*Wilson Library Bulletin*, February 1985, p. 425).

The Oxford Companion to the Theatre. Edited by Phyllis Hartnoll. 4th ed. Oxford Univ. Pr., 1983. 934p. $49.95.

Long a standard reference work on the world theater (the first edition appeared in 1951 and was revised in 1957, 1967, and most recently in 1983), this invaluable one-volume reference work covers all important aspects of the legitimate theater, including excellent country-by-country surveys. For the theater generally, this volume is the best single source of information.

Stage Management: A Guidebook of Practical Techniques. Written by Lawrence Stern. 2nd ed. Allyn and Bacon, 1974. 323p. $22.95.

Somewhat dated but still useful, this well-illustrated, encyclopedic handbook of stagecraft is intended chiefly for theatrical groups in schools and communities, particularly beginners.

Theatre Backstage from A to Z. Written by Warren C. Lounsbury. Revised ed. Univ. of Washington Pr., 1973. 191p. $14.95 paper.

Originally published in 1959 as *Backstage from A to Z* and revised twice since that time, *Theatre Backstage from A to Z* aims "to present an alphabetized explanation of the terminology and methods peculiar to technical theatre" (preface). Like Lawrence Stern's *Stage Management* (see above), this work is in need of revision but remains a standard reference.

TRANSPORTATION (INCLUDES AIRCRAFT, AUTOMOBILES, AND SHIPS)

The Complete Illustrated Encyclopedia of the World's Motorcycles. Edited by Erwin Tragatsch. Holt, 1977. 320p. Out of print (last priced at $22.95).

International in scope, this well-illustrated encyclopedia of motorcycles covers roughly 2,500 makes and models manufactured from 1894 to the mid-1970s. It is "a popular book and good reference tool that should be in every public library reference collection" (*American Reference Books Annual,* 1978, p. 765). Unfortunately out of print (at least for the present), the encyclopedia is superior to George Bishop's one-volume *Encyclopedia of Motorcycling* (Putnam, 1980), which is also out of print.

Encyclopedia of American Cars, 1930–1942. Written by James H. Moloney and George H. Dammann. Crestline Publishing, 1977. 383p. $32.95; *Encyclopedia of American Cars, 1946–1959.* Written by James H. Moloney and George H. Dammann. Crestline Publishing, 1980. 416p. $29.95.

These two invaluable works provide a comprehensive history of automobiles manufactured in the United States between 1930 and 1959. Heavily illustrated, each volume includes experimental and custom-built cars that never made it into production.

Encyclopedia of Aviation. Scribner's, 1977. 218p. $5.95 paper.

A small, inexpensive alternative to the 20-volume *Illustrated Encyclopedia of Aviation* (see below), this work furnishes brief descriptions of selected civil and military aircraft, definitions of technical terms, biographies of people important in the development of aviation, and histories of major airlines—all in alphabetical order from *Aerobatics* to *Zlin.* Another handy single-volume encyclopedia on the subject is the *International Encyclopedia of Aviation* (Crown, 1977), edited by David Mondey and Juan Trippe.

The Encyclopedia of Homebuilt Aircraft. Written by Michael Markowski. TAB Books, 1979. 576p. $15.95 paper.

"Intended mainly for 'homebuilt aircraft' buffs, this thick paperback has descriptions, many photos, and plans for a variety of aircraft: hang gliders, things towed by boats, autogyros, hovercraft, amphibians, regular sailplanes, copies of World War I and World War II military craft, and the usual run of small sport planes.... For anyone interested in building planes (or only in reading about them), this is a good bet" (*American Reference Books Annual,* 1981, p. 767).

Encyclopedia of North American Railroading: 150 Years of Railroading in the United States and Canada. Written by Freeman Hubbard. McGraw-Hill, 1981. 377p. $49.95.

Hubbard's excellent encyclopedia includes articles on important people in the history of North American railroads, individual railroad companies, manufacturers of locomotives and cars, famous trains, wrecks, railroad unions, railroad slang and business terminology, and the like. "This is a delightful book to browse in and it is potentially useful as an encyclopedic reference source.... It would be useful for all libraries from high school to university and would be particularly appropriate in home libraries of railfans or persons with more than a passing interest in railroads" (*Booklist,* September 1, 1982, p. 64).

Encyclopedia of Ships and Seafaring. Edited by Peter Kemp. Crown, 1980. 256p. $30.00.

Popularly written and profusely illustrated, this encyclopedia covers the history and development of boats and ships, European exploration of the New World, warfare at sea, famous ships and people connected with the sea, diving and salvage operations, and the sea as a biological and mineral resource. The work nicely complements the *Oxford Companion to Ships and the Sea* (see below).

The Illustrated Encyclopedia of Aviation. Edited by Anthony Robinson. Marshall Cavendish, 1979. 20 vols. $149.95 plus $10.00 shipping and handling. (Also available from Farwell Promotional Books at $199.95.)

First published in Great Britain in 120 weekly parts beginning in 1977 under the title *Wings,* this set contains 480 A-to-Z articles on the history of aviation from its origins to the present time, including famous fliers, planes, air warfare, and the dynamics of flight. "All in all, there is a truly marvelous amount of information in this work, and the whole is excellently written and beautifully illustrated" (*American Reference Books Annual,* 1981, p. 766).

The Illustrated Encyclopedia of Helicopters. Written by Giorgio Apostolo. Bonanza Books (dist. by Crown), 1984. 140p. $12.95.

"Colorful illustrations of helicopters accompany descriptive entries arranged alphabetically by manufacturer in an oversize volume that helicopter enthusiasts will enjoy" (*Booklist,* January 1, 1985, p. 634). A complementary work is *Helicopters of the World* (Scribner's, 1976) by Michael J.H. Taylor and John W.R. Taylor.

The New Encyclopedia of Motor Cars, 1885 to the Present. Edited by G.N. Georgano. 3rd ed. Dutton, 1982. 688p. $45.00.

Containing approximately 2,400 illustrations, the latest edition of this standard reference work describes some 4,300 different models of cars. The book is "without doubt the most comprehensive photographic compendium on the automobile.... It is easy to use, and it contains readable brief factual entries on specific motorcars" (*American Reference Books Annual,* 1984, p. 740).

The Oxford Companion to Ships and the Sea. Edited by Peter Kemp. Oxford Univ. Pr., 1976. 971p. $39.95.

This outstanding one-volume reference offers 3,700 alphabetically arranged articles on practically all aspects of ships and the sea from earliest recorded history to the present. "It is rich in biographies, seamanship definitions, battles, famous ships, navigation terms, lore, and almost everything connected with ships and the sea except flora and fauna" (*American Reference Books Annual,* 1978, p. 779).

Silver Burdett Encyclopedia of Transport. Silver Burdett, 1983. Four vols. Prices vary from $7.96 to $14.96 per vol.

Intended for children and young students, this British-made work covers all major types of transportation. Each volume is 64 pages in length and contains brief articles accompanied by color illustrations, historical photographs, and instructional diagrams. Another well-illustrated encyclopedia covering much the same ground but designed for a somewhat older audience is the *Rand McNally Encyclopedia of Transportation* (Rand McNally, 1976).

World Encyclopedia of Civil Aircraft: From Leonardo da Vinci to the Present. Written by Enzo Angelucci; translated by S.M. Harris. Crown, 1982. 414p. $50.00

    Library Journal (February 15, 1983, p. 406) praises this reference work as "a remarkably comprehensive compendium.... Altogether, a most enjoyable and informative work." First published in Italy in 1981 under the title *Atlante Enciclopedico degli Aerei Civili del Mondo da Leonardo a oggi,* the book includes some 3,000 illustrations and covers all types of nonmilitary aircraft. Many other sources on the subject are available, including the *Complete Illustrated Encyclopedia of the World's Aircraft* (A & W Publishers, 1978), edited by David Mondey; Douglas Rolfe's *Airplanes of the World, 1490–1976* (Revised ed. Simon & Schuster, 1978); and the well-known *Jane's All the World's Aircraft* (Jane's Publishing, 1912–), an annual publication currently edited by John W.R. Taylor.

Appendix C:
Foreign-Language
Encyclopedias

This section of *Best Encyclopedias* briefly notes the most important general encyclopedias available in seven major foreign languages: Dutch, French, German, Italian, Japanese, Russian, and Spanish.

Foreign-language encyclopedias are potentially valuable sources of information for many North Americans. In his *Introduction to Reference Work* (1982, vol. 1, p. 197), William A. Katz makes these points:

> Even for users with the most elementary knowledge of the language, several of the foreign works are useful for their fine illustrations and maps. For example, the *Enciclopedia Italiana* boasts some of the best illustrations of any encyclopedia, particularly in the areas of the fine arts. A foreign encyclopedia is equally useful for viewpoint. Some American readers may be surprised to find how the Civil War, for example, is treated in the French and the German encyclopedias, and the evaluation of American writers and national heroes is sometimes equally revealing of how Europeans judge the United States. More specifically, the foreign encyclopedia is helpful for information on less known figures not found in American or British work; for foreign-language bibliographies approach; for detailed maps of cities and regions; and for other information ranging from plots of less known novels and musicals to identification of place names.

In addition, some critics believe that foreign-language encyclopedias are, in many cases, well ahead of their English-language cousins in terms of editorial and production quality. Harvey Einbinder, for example, writes in his article "Encyclopedias: Some Foreign and Domestic Developments" (*Wilson Library Bulletin*, December 1980, p. 261): "Because of commercial constraints and current editorial practices in the United States, the forefront of encyclopedia progress has passed overseas. Foreign reference works now mark the frontiers of encyclopedia synthesis."

In most instances, the encyclopedias mentioned in this section of the guide can be acquired through North American book dealers specializing in reference materials published abroad. The most prominent of these dealers is Pergamon Press, which periodically issues a comprehensive catalog entitled *Encyclopedias and Dictionaries of the World.* The most recent edition of the catalog includes descriptions and prices of approximately 1,200 major encyclopedias in some 20 languages. For price information, a copy of the catalog, or to order an encyclopedia, contact Pergamon Press, Inc. in the United States at Maxwell House, Fairview Park, Elmsford, NY 10523 or telephone 914-592-7700; in Canada write to Pergamon Press Canada Ltd., Suite 104, Consumers Road, Willowdale, Ontario M2J 1P9 or telephone 416-497-8337.

DUTCH-LANGUAGE GENERAL ENCYCLOPEDIAS

Algemene Winkler Prins Encyclopedie. Amsterdam: Elsevier, 1975–77. 14 vols.
    This popular general encyclopedia includes nearly 5,000 illustrations and maps. The set derives from the 20-volume *Grote Winkler Prins* (see below).
Grote Nederlandse Larousse Encyclopedie in Vijfentwintig Delen. Hasselt: Heideland-Orbis, 1972–79. 25 vols.
    Modeled on the French *Grand Larousse Encyclopdique* (see below), this heavily illustrated set is best known for its numerous bibliographies.
Grote Spectrum Encyclopedie. Amsterdam: Het Spectrum, 1974–79. 25 vols.
    Similar in design and tone to the innovative *Academic American Encyclopedia* (see review in the main section of this guide), the *Grote Spectrum Encyclopedie* contains 13.4 million words accompanied by some 24,000 full-color illustrations. Its text is machine-readable, with the potential for more frequent revisions in the future. The smaller 20-volume *Spectrum Compact Encyclopedie* is based on the *Grote Spectrum.*
Grote Winkler Prins: Encyclopedie in Twintig Delen. 7th ed. Amsterdam: Elsevier, 1966–75. 20 vols.
    The first six editions (1870–1954) of this venerable Dutch encyclopedia appeared under the title *Winkler Prins Encyclopedie.* The seventh edition maintains the high standard (both editorially and physically) of the earlier sets; an eighth edition is currently in progress, being issued a volume at a time.

FRENCH-LANGUAGE GENERAL ENCYCLOPEDIAS

Encyclopaedia Universalis. 2nd ed. Paris: Encyclopaedia Universalis France (a division of Encyclopaedia Britannica, Inc.), 1980. 20 vols. Available from Encyclopaedia Britannica at $1,759.00.
    First published between 1968 and 1974, this highly regarded encyclopedia was updated and reorganized in 1980. Volumes 1–16 (called the Corpus) contain some 10,000 relatively long, scholarly articles that treat

all significant areas of knowledge. Volumes 17-18 (the Symposium) include new articles that have been added to the second edition and references to information in the Corpus. And Volumes 19-20 (the Thesaurus-Index) provide both index references to the Corpus and approximately 25,000 capsule articles on specific topics. *Choice* (July-August 1973, p. 748) praised the first edition as "an outstanding foreign-language reference source."

Grand Larousse Encyclopédique en Dix Volumes. Paris: Librairie Larousse, 1960-64. Ten vols. plus two supplements (1968 and 1975).

This monumental work combines the functions of encyclopedia and dictionary, a hallmark of the *Larousse* name. Specifically, the set provides concise encyclopedic coverage of the world's knowledge as well as definitions (with quotations) of some 450,000 French words. The *Grand Larousse* is a direct descendant of the 15-volume *Grand Dictionnaire Universel du XIXe Siécle* (or the *Universal Dictionary of the Nineteenth Century*), the masterwork of Pierre Larousse published between 1865 and 1876 to "instruct all men in all things."

La Grande Encyclopédie. Paris: Librairie Larousse, 1972-78. 21 vols.

A twentieth-century revision and extension of a great nineteenth-century French encyclopedia of the same title (published in 31 volumes between 1886 and 1902), this lavishly illustrated set contains substantial signed articles that emphasize contemporary developments, particularly in the areas of science and technology. The final volume is a comprehensive index to the set.

Petit Larousse en Couleurs. Paris: Librairie Larousse, 1981. 1,665p.

A compact, frequently revised, one-volume work, the popular *Petit Larousse* is the best known of a number of small encyclopedia-dictionaries in the famous *Larousse* family of reference books, all of which derive to one degree or another from the *Grand Larousse Encyclopédique* (see above).

GERMAN-LANGUAGE GENERAL ENCYCLOPEDIAS

Das Bertelsmann Lexikon in Zehn Bänden. Gutersloh: Bertelsmann Lexikon-Verlag, 1972-76. Ten vols.

This excellent encyclopedia contains roughly 120,000 concise articles accompanied by 7,000 full-color illustrations. The set is extended by an encyclopedic work entitled *Lexikotek* (1972-76), which consists of 15 thematic volumes devoted to the major fields of knowledge, plus a one-volume world atlas.

Brockhaus Enzyklopädie in Zwanzig Bänden. 17th ed. Wiesbaden: Brockhaus, 1966-74. 20 vols. plus four supplements (1975-76).

One of the most famous and successful general encyclopedias in the world, *Brockhaus* is now in its seventeenth edition. The first edition, the work of an innovative German publisher named Friedrich Arnold Brockhaus, appeared between 1796 and 1808 under the title *Konversations-Lexikon*; later editions bore the title *Brockhaus' Konversations-Lexikon,* and the sixteenth edition (1952-63) was called *Der Grosse Brockhaus.* Numerous smaller encyclopedias derive from *Brockhaus,* including the two-volume *Der Brockhaus in Zwei Bänden*

(1977), the six-volume *Der Neue Brockhaus* (1974–75), and the twelve-volume *Der Grosse Brockhaus in Zwölf Bänden* (1977). English-language users should know that although *Brockhaus* covers all areas of knowledge, it does emphasize German history, geography, and biography.

Das Grosse Duden-Lexikon in Acht Bänden. Mannheim: Bibliographisches Institut Lexikonverlag, 1964–70. Ten vols.

This comparatively small and inexpensive encyclopedia of some 200,000 concise entries includes many biographies and reasonably good illustrations. The final volume is an atlas.

Der Grosse Herder. 5th ed. Freiburg: Herder, 1953–56. Ten vols. plus two supplements (1962).

Herder is among the foremost names in German encyclopedia publishing, along with *Brockhaus* (see above) and *Meyers* (see below). First published between 1854 and 1857, *Der Grosse Herder* (or *The Great Herder*) is noted for its short, reliable articles and fine illustrations. It is supplemented (but not supplanted) by *Der Neue Herder* (1973–75), a 14-volume work of which six volumes are arranged alphabetically and the rest topically by various scientific subjects.

Meyers Enzyklopädisches Lexikon. 9th ed. Mannheim: Bibliographisches Institut Lexikonverlag, 1971–79. 25 vols.

A well-known encyclopedia that first appeared between 1840 and 1855, *Meyers* contains 250,000 brief entries accompanied by numerous small, color illustrations. Each volume also includes several lengthy essays by 100 special contributors. Note that the incomplete eighth edition (1936–42), entitled *Meyers Neues Lexikon,* was influenced by Nazi ideology, a situation that has been corrected in the present edition.

ITALIAN-LANGUAGE GENERAL ENCYCLOPEDIAS

Dizionario Enciclopedico Italiano. Rome: Istituto della Enciclopedia Italiana, 1955–61. 12 vols. plus two supplements (1969–70).

Attractive layout and good typography characterize this encyclopedic dictionary. The brief but authoritative entries emphasize Italian people, places, culture, and words.

Enciclopedia Europea. Milan: Garzanti, 1969–80. 12 vols.

Garzanti, founded in 1938, is a well-established Italian publisher of reference books, including the 12-volume *Enciclopedia Europea,* which is "the house's pride and joy" (*Publishers Weekly,* November 19, 1979, p. 34). The set is noted for both the quantity and quality of its non-Italian contributors, such as Edward Teller, Arnold Toynbee, and Claude Levi-Strauss. Smaller general encyclopedias published by Garzanti are the five-volume *Enciclopedia Garzanti* and the two-volume *Enciclopedia Universale Garzanti.*

Enciclopedia Italiana di Scienze, Lettere ed Arti. Rome: Istituto della Enciclopedia Italiana, 1929–37. 35 vols. plus six supplements (1958–78).

Particularly valuable for its excellent illustrations and color plates, this most famous of all Italian-produced general encyclopedias includes long, signed, scholarly articles on all significant areas of knowledge, with emphasis on subjects in the arts and humanities. A few articles expound the Fascist point of view (Mussolini himself contributed to the long article *Fascismo*), but the overall impartiality of the set is not affected.

Grande Dizionario Enciclopedico UTET. 3rd ed. Turin: Unione Tipografico-Editrice, 1966–75. 20 vols.

This middle-sized adult general encyclopedia resembles the *Enciclopedia Italiana* (see above) in format, although it is less detailed, more popularly written, less impressively illustrated, and less expensive than the larger work. The final volume is a 200,000-entry index to the set.

Grande Enciclopedia Universale Curcio. Rome: Curcio, 1976–77. 20 vols.

The largest encyclopedia offered by Curcio, one of Italy's oldest and best-known publishers of reference works, the *Grande Enciclopedia Universale Curcio* is a readable, colorfully illustrated set for older students and adults.

JAPANESE-LANGUAGE GENERAL ENCYCLOPEDIAS

Dai Nihon Hyakka Jiten (Encyclopedia Japonica). Tokyo: Shṁgakukan, 1972–73. 23 vols.

Japonica (as it is known in the West) is a well-edited, handsomely illustrated adult general encyclopedia. The work contains numerous short articles on all important subjects, including places and people in North America.

Sekai Dai Hyakka Jiten. 4th ed. Tokyo: Heibonsha, 1981–82. 36 vols.

Published by Heibonsha, Japan's leading encyclopedia publisher, this major set (translated *World Encyclopedia*) has been a standard reference work in the country since the first edition appeared between 1955 and 1963. Maps make up the final two volumes.

RUSSIAN-LANGUAGE GENERAL ENCYCLOPEDIAS

Bol'shaia Sovetskaia Entsiklopediia. 3rd ed. Moscow: Sovetskaia Entsiklopediia, 1969–78. 30 vols.

The basic general encyclopedia for adults and older students in the Soviet Union, this important set first appeared in 65 volumes between 1926 and 1947, followed by a 53-volume second edition published between 1949 and 1960, and the present 30-volume third edition between 1969 and 1978. The work, although reasonably factual in most regards, exhibits a Marxist-Leninist bias in such areas as philosophy, economics, sociology, and political science (for instance, the American Declaration of Independence is portrayed as the product of a bourgeois revolution). An English-language translation is available from Macmillan under the title *Great Soviet Encyclopedia* (see Appendix B of this guide under "Geography and Area Studies" for additional information about the *Great Soviet Encyclopedia*).

Malaia Sovetskaia Entsiklopediia. 3rd ed. Moscow: Gosudarstvennoe Nauchnoe Izdatel'stvo, Bol'shaia Sovetskaia Entsiklopediia, 1958–61. 11 vols.

Translated as the *Short Soviet Encyclopedia,* this set is an abridged version of the 53-volume second edition of the famous *Bol'shaia Sovetskaia Entsiklopediia* (see above).

SPANISH-LANGUAGE GENERAL ENCYCLOPEDIAS

Diccionario Enciclopédico Espasa. 8th ed. Madrid: Espasa, 1978. 12 vols.
This very well illustrated medium-sized encyclopedic dictionary contains biographical, geographical, and lexical information, with emphasis on Spain and Hispanic America. A valuable feature is the provision of French, English, Italian, and German equivalents of key words.

Diccionario Enciclopédico Salvat Universal. Barcelona: Salvat, 1975–76. 20 vols.
Like the *Diccionario Enciclopédico Espasa* (see above), this work is an encyclopedic dictionary, combining facts and definitions in a single alphabet. It derives from the *Diccionario Salvat,* first issued between 1907 and 1913 in nine volumes.

Enciclopedia Barsa. Revised ed. Chicago: Encyclopaedia Britannica, 1985. 16 vols. $699.00.
First published in the 1950s and revised occasionally, *Enciclopedia Barsa* is intended primarily for Spanish-language students in North American secondary schools and colleges. The set emphasizes Spanish history, culture, and geography, including important places in Central and South America.

Enciclopedia Universal Ilustrada Europeo-Americana. Madrid: Espasa, 1907–33. 70 vols. plus a ten-volume supplement; annual supplements (1934–).
Usually referred to simply as *Espasa,* this monumental work provides comprehensive treatment of the world's most important knowledge in both long and short articles. The set, which currently contains more than a million entries, is particularly noted for its extensive coverage of Spanish and Hispanic American biography and geography. Consumers should be aware that the annual supplements that extend and update *Espasa* are issued quite late (for example, the 1973–74 supplement appeared in 1980). The seven-volume *Diccionario Enciclopédico Abreviado* (6th ed. Espasa, 1954–55) is an abridgment of *Espasa* .

Gran Enciclopedia Rialp GER. Madrid: Ediciones Rialp, 1971–76. 24 vols.
Gran Enciclopedia Rialp—or *GER*—is a major Spanish-language general encyclopedia prepared by an international editorial team, including some 3,500 contributors from 60 countries. It furnishes lengthy articles accompanied by 20,000 informative illustrations.

Appendix D: Encyclopedia Bibliography

This annotated bibliography directs interested readers to selected books and articles on encyclopedias. The bibliography is divided into two parts. The first part, "Evaluating Encyclopedias," covers the major sources of encyclopedia reviews. The second part, "Making and Using Encyclopedias," identifies materials concerned with the editing, content, and use of encyclopedias.

EVALUATING ENCYCLOPEDIAS

American Reference Books Annual. Edited by Bohdan S. Wynar. Littleton, CO: Libraries Unlimited, 1970–. Annual.

> *American Reference Books Annual*—or *ARBA*—aims to review all English-language reference works published or distributed in the United States each year, including both general and specialized encyclopedias. The encyclopedia reviews are usually informative, probing, and reliable.

ARBA Guide to Subject Encyclopedias and Dictionaries. Edited by Bohdan S. Wynar. Littleton, CO: Libraries Unlimited, 1986.

> A new work, this useful guide of some 500 pages contains signed reviews of roughly 1,200 specialized encyclopedias and dictionaries originally evaluated in *American Reference Books Annual* (see above) between 1970 and 1985.

Booklist: Including Reference Books Bulletin. Chicago: American Library Association, 1905–. Semimonthly.

> Formerly *Booklist and Reference and Subscription Books Reviews* (the title changed in 1983), this well-known, highly regarded book review periodical includes evaluations of both general and specialized encyclopedias available on the North American market. Most of the encyclopedia reviews are produced by the *Reference Books Bulletin* Editorial Board, a group of working librarians in the United States and Canada. The reviews, which unfortunately are not signed, tend to be lengthy and detailed but very uneven in quality.

Choice. Middletown, CT: Association of College and Research Libraries, a division of the American Library Association, 1964–. Monthly.

> *Choice* furnishes concise, critical reviews of all types of general and reference publications, including encyclopedias. The reviewers, chiefly junior-level faculty and librarians at North American colleges and univer-

sities, are now (as of September 1984) identified at the end of each review.

College and Research Libraries. Chicago: Association of College and Research Libraries, a division of the American Library Association, 1939–. Bimonthly.

Aimed specifically at academic librarians, this journal includes brief evaluative notes on recently published reference sources in its January and July issues. Normally only selected specialized encyclopedias are reviewed.

Denenberg, Herbert S. "Consumers' Guide to Buying an Encyclopedia," *Caveat Emptor,* August-September 1979, pp. 19–20.

Consumer advocate Denenberg provides very brief notes on the leading general encyclopedias in this valuable but now dated article.

"Five Multivolume Children's Encyclopedias," *Booklist,* May 15, 1983, pp. 1233–43.

Intended as a supplement to *Purchasing an Encyclopedia* (see below), this unsigned article offers substantial reviews of *Britannica Junior Encyclopaedia, Compton's Encyclopedia, Merit Students Encyclopedia,* the *New Book of Knowledge,* and the *World Book Encyclopedia.*

Guide to Reference Books. Compiled by Eugene P. Sheehy. 9th ed. Chicago: American Library Association, 1976; supplement 1980.

This indispensable guide to reference sources covers all types of encyclopedias. The annotations, however, are normally descriptive rather than critical. The basic 1976 volume also contains a useful section on encyclopedia evaluation criteria (see pages 97–99).

Instructor. Dansville, NY: Instructor Publications, Inc. 1891–. Monthly.

Major general encyclopedias for elementary and secondary school students are periodically evaluated in this magazine for teachers and school librarians. The reviews, which tend to be quite superficial, are almost always favorable.

Katz, William A. *Introduction to Reference Work.* Vol. 1: *Basic Information Sources.* 4th ed. New York: McGraw-Hill, 1982.

Katz, an internationally recognized authority on reference work, discusses encyclopedia evaluation techniques and provides critical notes on the leading encyclopedias in Chapter 6 ("Encyclopedias: General and Subject") of this frequently revised text. The two-volume *Introduction to Reference Work* is intended principally for library science students, but due to Katz's readable style, the *Basic Information Sources* volume serves the general consumer as well.

Kister, Kenneth F. *Encyclopedia Buying Guide: A Consumer Guide to General Encyclopedias in Print.* 3rd ed. New York: R.R. Bowker, 1981.

The successor to S. Padraig Walsh's *General Encyclopedias in Print* (R.R. Bowker, 1963–73), this work reviews 36 general English-language encyclopedias published or distributed in North America. First published in 1976 and revised in 1978 and 1981, *Encyclopedia Buying Guide* is now quite dated.

Library Journal. New York: R.R. Bowker, 1876–. Semimonthly.

Librarians contribute most of *LJ*'s reviews, which are customarily brief but incisive. Only important specialized and brand-new general encyclopedias are reviewed.

Purchasing an Encyclopedia: 12 Points to Consider. Chicago: American Library Association, 1979.

This unsigned 38-page pamphlet, which first appeared in *Booklist* (see above) between December 1, 1978, and February 1, 1979, under the collective title "Encyclopedias: A Survey and Buying Guide," reviews 20 general English-language encyclopedias, subjecting them to 12 evaluative criteria (such as authority, accuracy, arrangement, etc.) Unfortunately, the publication is, in the words of a review in *Library Journal* (December 15, 1979, p. 2632), an "inexcusably sloppy work."

Reference Services Review. Ann Arbor, MI: Pierian Pr., 1973–. Quarterly.
    RSR does not systematically review all or even most new encyclopedias, but those evaluations that do appear (usually in bibliographic essays) are useful.

RQ. Chicago: Reference and Adult Services Division of the American Library Association, 1960–. Quarterly.
    RQ (which stands for *Reference Quarterly*) reviews reference books, including selected new encyclopedias, in the back of each issue. The signed reviews are usually the work of academic librarians.

School Library Journal. New York: R.R. Bowker, 1954–. Ten issues per year.
    All types of materials of potential interest to school and children's librarians, including new encyclopedias, are evaluated in *SLJ*. The brief reviews are almost always by working librarians and media specialists.

"Six Multivolume Adult Encyclopedias," *Booklist,* December 1, 1982, pp. 515–32.
    Prepared as an updating supplement to *Purchasing an Encyclopedia* (see above), this unsigned article offers substantial reviews of the *Academic American Encyclopedia, Collier's Encyclopedia, Encyclopedia Americana, Funk & Wagnalls New Encyclopedia,* the *New Encyclopaedia Britannica,* and the *World Book Encyclopedia.*

Wilson Library Bulletin. New York: H.W. Wilson, 1914–. Ten issues per year.
    This general library magazine includes a regular column called "Current Reference Books" that concisely reviews new reference materials, including selected encyclopedias, both general and specialized. The reviews are readable and often provide comparative references.

MAKING AND USING ENCYCLOPEDIAS

Bennion, Bruce. "Performance Testing of a Book and Its Index as an Information Retrieval System," *Journal of the American Society for Information Science,* July 1980, pp. 264–70.
    Bennion's informative article discusses a proposed test for measuring the effectiveness of indexes using the *New Encyclopaedia Britannica* and the *Great Soviet Encyclopedia* as examples. The article is basic reading for anyone interested in accessibility of information in large reference sources.

Cheney, Frances Neel and Wiley J. Williams. *Fundamental Reference Sources.* 2nd ed. Chicago: American Library Association, 1980.
    Chapter 5 of this excellent guide to reference materials deals with encyclopedias, including detailed notes on the major titles. In addition, guidelines for evaluating an encyclopedia appear in an appendix.

Collison, Robert L. *Encyclopedias: Their History Throughout the Ages.* 2nd ed. Hafner Publishing Co., 1966.
Collison's 334-page treatise is described in a lengthy subtitle as "a bibliographical guide, with extensive historical notes, to the general encyclopedias issued throughout the world from 350 B.C. to the present day." The book is valuable as a history of encyclopedias, but it does not include reviews or much critical information.

Darnton, Robert. *The Business of Enlightenment: A Publishing History of the Encyclopédie, 1775–1800.* Harvard Univ. Pr., 1979.
Darnton records the history of Diderot's celebrated French *Encyclopédie,* incontestably the most influential encyclopedia ever published, in this invaluable book. "This is intellectual, economic, business, and social history at its best" (*Library Journal,* October 15, 1979, p. 2210).

Einbinder, Harvey. "Encyclopedias: Some Foreign and Domestic Developments," *Wilson Library Bulletin,* December 1980, pp. 257–61.
"Because of commercial constraints and current editorial practices in the United States, the forefront of encyclopedia progress has passed overseas. Foreign reference works now mark the frontiers of encyclopedia synthesis," observes Einbinder, a well-known encyclopedia critic. This article is particularly useful for its detailed discussion of specific foreign-language encyclopedias, such as the Dutch *Grote Winkler Prins,* the French *La Grande Encyclopédie,* and the German *Brockhaus Enzyklopädie* .

Engle, June L. and Elizabeth Futas. "Sexism in Adult Encyclopedias," *RQ,* Fall 1983, pp. 29–39.
This heavily documented article examines ten major general encyclopedias for evidence of sexism, finding that a "sense of male dominance" pervades the encyclopedias' language and coverage. The article also includes an extensive bibliography.

Flagg, Gordon. "Online Encyclopedias: Are They Ready for Libraries? Are Libraries Ready for Them?" *American Libraries,* March 1983, pp. 134–36.
Flagg sums up the current state of electronic encyclopedias in the library environment. His conclusion: "Online encyclopedias are here, but it's going to take more than their mere presence to get them into libraries."

Free, John. "Computerized Encyclopedias," *Popular Science,* June 1983, pp. 138–39.
The electronic version of Grolier's *Academic American Encyclopedia* is featured in this easy-to-understand article.

Graham, Beryl Caroline. "Treatment of Black American Women in Children's Encyclopedias," *Negro History Bulletin,* April 1976, pp. 596–98.
Graham analyzes eight popular general encyclopedias—*Britannica Junior Encyclopaedia, Collier's Encyclopedia, Compton's Encyclopedia, Encyclopedia Americana, Encyclopedia International, Merit Students Encyclopedia, New Book of Knowledge,* and the *World Book Encyclopedia*—to discover how they treat black American women. Her findings are not encouraging.

Grieves, Robert T. "Short Circuiting Reference Books," *Time,* June 13, 1983, p. 96.
The *Academic American Encyclopedia* is the focus of this one-page article that reports on how students in two New Jersey schools are responding to an encyclopedia in electronic form. (They like it.)

Harter, Stephen P. and Kenneth F. Kister. "Online Encyclopedias: The Potential," *Library Journal,* September 1, 1981, pp. 1600–02.

This article succinctly explains how the traditional encyclopedia in print form differs from the new electronic (or online) version, from how they are accessed to how they are sold.

Johnston, W.T. and Joy B. Trulock. "Buying an Encyclopedia," *Consumers' Research Magazine,* February 1975, pp. 12–16.

Although now over a decade old, this article remains one of the best for practical tips on how to get the best encyclopedia for your money—and how to deal with the hard-sell or dishonest encyclopedia salesperson.

Kister, Kenneth. "Encyclopedia Publishing: An Update," *Library Journal,* April 15, 1978, pp. 820–23.

Consumer trends in the encyclopedia industry are explored in this article.

Kister, Kenneth. "Encyclopedias and the Public Library: A National Survey," *Library Journal,* April 15, 1979, pp. 890–93.

Public library reference librarians—experts on how and where to find information—from all over the United States responded to a questionnaire on encyclopedia use. Not surprisingly, the *World Book Encyclopedia* was the overwhelming choice as the most effective encyclopedia currently available.

Kleinfield, N.R. "Encyclopedia with New Twist," *New York Times,* May 30, 1980, pp. 1-D; 9-D.

Kleinfield reports on the launch of the *Academic American Encyclopedia,* the newest multivolume general encyclopedia on the market, but the article also contains much useful information about the encyclopedia industry as a whole, including sales statistics.

Kraft, Linda. "Lost Herstory: The Treatment of Women in Children's Encyclopedias," *School Library Journal,* January 1973, pp. 26–35.

Similar in intent and methodology to the studies by Beryl Caroline Graham and June L. Engle and Elizabeth Futas (see above), and Edmund SantaVicca (see below), this article closely examines five leading general encyclopedias for young people for evidence of sexism. Although the particulars are now dated, the issues raised and Kraft's intelligent treatment of them render this article a small classic.

Machalaba, Daniel. "Coming Soon: Encyclopedias That Can Talk," *Wall Street Journal,* February 18, 1981, p. 29.

"Some reference companies, seeking a place in the emerging video revolution, are exploring ways to flash encyclopedia entries as text onto home television screens and, where appropriate, to add sound—bird calls, Bach fugues, even famous speeches," notes Machalaba in this short, popularly written article on how the electronic revolution is affecting the encyclopedia industry.

Mathisen, Tyler. "All about Encyclopedias," *Money,* October 1983, pp. 209–12.

This excellent consumer article discusses all the relevant questions involved when considering the purchase of an encyclopedia.

Miller, Jerome K. "Popular Encyclopedias as a Source of Information about Copyright: A Critical Comparison," *RQ,* Summer 1983, pp. 388–92.

Miller compares the treatment of the subject of copyright in five well-known general encyclopedias (the *Academic American Encyclopedia, Collier's Encyclopedia, Encyclopedia Americana,* the *New Encyclopaedia Britannica,* and the *World Book Encyclopedia*), finding that "*Collier's* appears to be best for current, nitty-gritty information about copyright and

EB3 [the *New Encyclopaedia Britannica*] is best for historical and theoretical information."

SantaVicca, Edmund F. *The Treatment of Homosexuality in Current Encyclopedias.* Ph.D. dissertation, University of Michigan, 1977. Ann Arbor, MI: University Microfilms, 1979.

Eight major general English-language encyclopedias are studied for their treatment of homosexuality in this 323-page thesis. SantaVicca scrutinizes the subject from the standpoint of accessibility and scope of information provided. Findings include the need for more coverage of female homosexuality.

Walsh, S. Padraig. *Anglo-American General Encyclopedias: A Historical Bibliography, 1703–1967.* New York: R.R. Bowker, 1968.

The late Padraig Walsh provides detailed notes on 419 general English-language encyclopedias published in North America and Great Britain between 1703 and 1967. This unique work is indispensable for serious students of encyclopedia publishing.

Whitelock, Otto V. St. "On the Making and Survival of Encyclopedias," *Choice,* June 1967, pp. 381–89.

Whitelock draws upon his longtime experience as an encyclopedia editor to survey the state of the industry. Although now 20 years old, the article remains valuable for its lucid analysis of the problems and challenges entailed in the publication of contemporary encyclopedias.

Appendix E: Encyclopedia Publishers and Distributors

This directory lists North American publishers and distributors of general and specialized encyclopedias evaluated in *Best Encyclopedias*. In the case of distributors, the publisher of the work is indicated in parentheses following the title. The directory also includes vendors of electronic (or online) encyclopedias, such as Dialog Information Services, Inc.

Abbeville Press, Inc., 505 Park Avenue, New York, NY 10022, 212-888-1969.
World History of Photography.

ABC-Clio Press, 2040 Alameda Padre Serra, P.O. Box 4397, Santa Barbara, CA 93103, 803-963-4221.
African Political Dictionary; Constitutional Law Dictionary; Dictionary of Classical Mythology; International Relations Dictionary; Latin American Political Dictionary; Middle East Political Dictionary; Presidential-Congressional Political Dictionary; Soviet and East European Political Dictionary.

Abingdon Press, 201 Eighth Avenue South, Nashville, TN 37202, 615-749-6301.
Abingdon Dictionary of Living Religions; Interpreter's Dictionary of the Bible.

Harry N. Abrams, Inc., 100 Fifth Avenue, New York, NY 10011, 212-206-7715.
American Art; The Planet We Live On.

Academic Press, Inc., 1250 Sixth Avenue (Suite 400), San Diego, CA 92101, 619-230-1840.
Encyclopedia of Earth Sciences (various volumes); *Volcanoes of the World* (published by Hutchinson Ross).

Addison-Wesley Publishing Company, Inc., One Jacob Way, Reading, MA 01867, 617-944-3700.
Encyclopedia of Mathematics and Its Applications; Encyclopedia of Physics.

Aesculapius Publishers, Inc., Ten West 66th Street (Suite 6D), New York, NY 10023, 212-595-0558.
International Encyclopedia of Psychiatry, Psychology, Psychoanalysis, and Neurology.

Allyn & Bacon, Inc., Seven Wells Avenue, Newton, MA 02159, 617-964-5530.

Stage Management.

American Library Association, 50 East Huron Street, Chicago, IL 60611, 312-944-6780.
ALA World Encyclopedia of Library and Information Services.

Arco Publishing, Inc., 215 Park Avenue South, New York, NY 10003, 212-777-6300.
Dictionary of Dreams; Encyclopedia of Aviculture; Knowledge Encyclopedia (published by Griesewood & Dempsey); *Photographer's Bible.*

Arlington House, *see* Crown Publishers, Inc.

AVI Publishing Company, Inc., 250 Post Road East, P.O. Box 831, Westport, CT 06881, 203-226-0738.
Encyclopedia of Food Science.

Avon Books, 1790 Broadway, New York, NY 10019, 212-399-4500.
Concise Columbia Encyclopedia (paperbound edition); *Symptoms: The Complete Medical Encyclopedia.*

Baker Book House, P.O. Box 6287, Grand Rapids, MI 49506, 616-676-9186.
Evangelical Dictionary of Theology.

Ballinger Publishing Company (a subsidiary of Harper & Row Publishers, Inc.), 54 Church Street, Harvard Square, Cambridge, MA 02138, 617-492-0670.
Nuclear Weapons Databook.

Bankers Publishing Company, 210 South Street, Boston, MA 02111, 617-426-4495.
Encyclopedia of Banking and Finance.

A.S. Barnes & Company, Inc., 9601 Aero Drive, San Diego, CA 92123, 619-560-5163.
Complete Encyclopedia of Horses; Complete Encyclopedia of Television Programs, 1947–1979; Encyclopedia of Football; Encyclopedia of Sports; Encyclopedia of the American Theatre, 1900–1975; Radio's Golden Years; Stamp Collecting A to Z.

Barnes & Noble Books (a division of Harper & Row Publishers, Inc.), Ten East 53rd Street, New York, NY 10022, 212-207-7000.
Black's Veterinary Dictionary; Chemical Technology.

Barron's Educational Series, Inc., 113 Crossways Park Drive, Woodbury, NY 11797, 516-921-8750.
Encyclopedia of Computer Terms.

Basic Books, Inc., Ten East 53rd Street, New York, NY 10022, 212-207-7292.
American Handbook of Psychiatry; Asimov's New Guide to Science; Dictionary of Oriental Literatures.

Bellman Publishing Company, P.O. Box 164, Arlington, MA 02174, 617-648-7243.
Scholarships, Fellowships and Loans.

Bibliographic Retrieval Services, Inc. (BRS), 1200 Route 7, Latham, NY 12110, 1-800-833-4747 (toll-free outside New York State). 518-783-7251 (New York State only).
Academic American Encyclopedia (electronic version).

Bobley Publishing Corporation, 311 Crossways Park Drive, Woodbury, NY 11797, 516-364-1800.
Illustrated World Encyclopedia.

R.R. Bowker Company, 205 East 42nd Street, New York, NY 10017, 212-916-1600.

American Film Institute Catalog of Motion Pictures; Banned Books, 387 B.C. to 1978 A.D.

Brighton Publishing Company, 131 Northwest Fourth Street, Corvallis, OR 97330,
Encyclopedia of Physical Education, Fitness, and Sports.

Brookfield Publishing Company, Old Post Road, Brookfield, VT 05036, 802-276-3162.
Encyclopedia of Metallurgy and Materials (published by Macdonald and Evans).

BRS, *see* Bibliographic Retrieval Services, Inc.

Cambridge University Press, 32 East 57th Street, New York, NY 10022, 212-688-8888.
Cambridge Encyclopedia of Africa; Cambridge Encyclopedia of China; Cambridge Encyclopedia of Earth Sciences; Cambridge Encyclopedia of Latin America and the Caribbean; Cambridge Encyclopedia of Life Sciences; Cambridge Encyclopedia of Russia and the Soviet Union; Cambridge Guide to English Literature; Cambridge Guide to the Material World; Cambridge Historical Encyclopedia of Great Britain and Ireland; Dictionary of Useful and Everyday Plants and Their Common Names; Encyclopedia of Mathematics and Its Applications (published by Addison-Wesley); *New Cambridge Modern History; Popular Encyclopedia of Plants.*

Cavendish, Marshall, *see* Marshall Cavendish Corporation.

CineBooks, 6135-A North Sheridan Road, Chicago, IL 60660, 312-274-2617.
Motion Picture Guide.

P.F. Collier, Inc., 866 Third Avenue, New York, NY 10022, 1-800-257-9500 Ext. 485 (toll-free).
Collier's Encyclopedia; Merit Students Encyclopedia.

Columbia University Press, 136 South Broadway, Irvington, NY 10533, 914-591-6471.
Columbia Dictionary of Modern European Literature; Columbia Lippincott Gazetteer of the World; Concise Columbia Encyclopedia (hardbound edition); *Concise Columbia Encyclopedia in Large Print; New Columbia Encyclopedia.*

F.E. Compton Company, *see* Encyclopaedia Britannica, Inc.

CompuServe, Inc., 5000 Arlington Centre Boulevard, P.O. Box 20212, Columbus, OH 43220, 1-800-848-8990 (toll-free outside Ohio), 614-457-8600 (Ohio only).
Academic American Encyclopedia (electronic version).

Crane, Russak & Company, Inc., Three East 44th Street, New York, NY 10017, 212-867-1490.
Concise Encyclopedia of Astronomy.

Crestline Publishing Company, 1251 North Jefferson Avenue, Sarasota, FL 33577, 813-955-8080.
Encyclopedia of American Cars, 1930–1942; Encyclopedia of American Cars, 1946–1959.

Crossroad Publishing Company, 370 Lexington Avenue, New York, NY 10017, 212-532-3650.
Encyclopedia of Theology; International Encyclopedia of Sociology; World Spirituality.

T.Y. Crowell Company, *see* Harper & Row Publishers, Inc.

Crown Publishers, Inc., One Park Avenue, New York, NY 10016, 212-532-9200.
Audubon Society Encyclopedia of Animal Life (published by Clarkson N. Potter); *Cambridge Encyclopedia of Astronomy; Complete Encyclopedia of Popular Music and Jazz, 1900–1950; Encyclopedia of Architecture; Encyclopedia of Boxing; Encyclopedia of Furniture; Encyclopedia of Glass; Encyclopedia of Painting; Encyclopedia of Ships and Seafaring; Family Legal Advisor; Illustrated Encyclopedia of Helicopters* (published by Bonanza Books); *Illustrated Encyclopedia of Space Technology; Illustrated Encyclopedia of the Universe; International Center of Photography Encyclopedia of Photography; New Larousse Gastronomique; Official Encyclopedia of Bridge; World Encyclopedia of Civil Aircraft.*

Da Capo Press, Inc., 233 Spring Street, New York, NY 10013, 212-620-8000.
Encyclopedia of the Musical Theatre (published by Dodd, Mead).

Danbury Press, *see* Grolier, Inc.

Walter de Gruyter, Inc., 200 Saw Mill River Road, Hawthorne, NY 10532, 914-747-0110.
Concise Encyclopedia of Biochemistry.

Marcel Dekker, Inc., 270 Madison Avenue, New York, NY 10016, 212-696-9000.
Encyclopedia of Computer Science and Technology; Encyclopedia of Library and Information Science.

Dialog Information Services, Inc., 3460 Hillview Avenue, Palo Alto, CA 94304, 1-800-227-1927 (toll-free outside California), 1-800-982-5838 (toll-free California only).
Academic American Encyclopedia (electronic version); *Everyman's Encyclopaedia* (electronic version).

Dodd, Mead & Company, 79 Madison Avenue, New York, NY 10016, 212-685-6464.
Encyclopedia of the Musical Theatre; International Cyclopedia of Music and Musicians.

Doubleday & Company, Inc., 245 Park Avenue, New York, NY 10017, 516-294-4400.
Britannica Book of Music; Collector's Complete Dictionary of American Antiques; Encyclopedia of Human Behavior; EveryWoman's Legal Guide; Modern Encyclopedia of Basketball; Personal Computers A-Z; Science Fiction Encyclopedia; 10,000 Garden Questions Answered by 20 Experts.

Dow Jones News/Retrieval, P.O. Box 300, Princeton, NJ 08540, 1-800-257-5114 (toll-free outside New Jersey), 609-452-2000 (New Jersey only).
Academic American Encyclopedia (electronic version).

E.P. Dutton, Two Park Avenue, New York, NY 10016, 212-725-1818.
Everyman's Concise Encyclopaedia of Architecture; New Encyclopedia of Motor Cars, 1885 to the Present.

William B. Eerdmans Publishing Company, 255 Jefferson Avenue Southeast, Grand Rapids, MI 49503, 616-459-4591.
International Standard Bible Encyclopedia.

Encyclopaedia Britannica Educational Corporation, Britannica Centre, 310 South Michigan Avenue, Chicago, IL 60604, 1-800-554-9862 (toll-free).
Annals of America; Britannica Junior Encyclopaedia (currently out of print); *Compton's Encyclopedia* (published by F.E. Compton Company); *Compton's Precyclopedia* (published by F.E. Compton Company);

Enciclopedia Barsa; Encyclopaedia Universalis; New Encyclopaedia Britannica.

Encyclopaedia Britannica, Inc., Britannica Centre, Customer Service Department, 310 South Michigan Avenue, Chicago, IL 60604, 312-347-7298.
Britannica Junior Encyclopaedia (currently out of print); *Compton's Encyclopedia* (published by F.E. Compton Company); *Compton's Precyclopedia* (published by F.E. Compton Company); *New Encyclopaedia Britannica; Young Children's Encyclopedia.*

Facts on File, Inc., 460 Park Avenue South, New York, NY 10016, 212-683-2244.
Companion to Russian History; Complete Handbook of Garden Plants; Concise Encyclopedia of the Sciences; Encyclopedia of Alcoholism; Encyclopedia of American Crime; Encyclopedia of American Journalism; Encyclopedia of Community Planning and Environmental Management; Encyclopedia of Drug Abuse; Encyclopedia of Historic Places; Encyclopedia of Mammals; Encyclopedia of North American Wildlife; Encyclopedia of the Third World; Encyclopedia of World Architecture; Human Body on File; Illustrated Dictionary of Place Names (published by Van Nostrand); *Ireland; World Encyclopedia of Food; World Encyclopedia of Political Systems & Parties; World Press Encyclopedia.*

Farwell Promotional Books (a division of Gareth Stevens, Inc.), 7221 West Greentree Road, Milwaukee, WI 53223, 414-466-7550.
Encyclopedia of the Animal World (published by Bay Books); *Encyclopedia of the World and Its People* (published by Bay Books); *Family Health & Medical Library* (published by Bay Books); *Illustrated Encyclopedia of Aviation* (published by Marshall Cavendish); *New Knowledge Library* (published by Bay Books).

Fitzhenry & Whiteside Publishers, 195 Allstate Parkway, Markham, Ontario L3R 4T8 Canada, 416-477-0030.
Everyman's Encyclopaedia (published by J.M. Dent).

Focal Press, 80 Montvale Avenue, Stoneham, MA 02180, 617-438-8468.
Focal Encyclopedia of Photography; Pictorial Cyclopedia of Photography.

Fortress Press, 2900 Queen Lane, Philadelphia, PA 19129, 1-800-822-3906 (toll-free).
Encyclopaedia of Religion and Ethics (published by Scribner's).

Free Press (a division of Macmillan Publishing Company, Inc.), 866 Third Avenue, New York, NY 10022, 212-702-2004.
Dictionary of the Social Sciences; Encyclopedia of Bioethics; Encyclopedia of Crime and Justice; Encyclopedia of Educational Research; Encyclopedia of Psychoanalysis; International Encyclopedia of Population; International Encyclopedia of Statistics; International Encyclopedia of the Social Sciences.

Frontier Press Company, P.O. Box 1098, Columbus, OH 43216, 614-864-3737.
Lincoln Library of Essential Information.

Funk & Wagnalls, Inc., 70 Hilltop Road, Ramsey, NJ 07446, 201-529-6867.
Charlie Brown's 'Cyclopedia (published by Random House); *Funk & Wagnalls New Encyclopedia.*

Gale Research Company, Book Tower, Detroit, MI 48226, 313-961-2242.
Encyclopedia of American Religions (supplement); *Encyclopedia of Occultism & Parapsychology.*

Garland Publishing, Inc., 136 Madison Avenue, New York, NY 10016, 212-686-7492.
New York Botanical Garden Illustrated Encyclopedia of Horticulture.

General Videotex Corporation, 3 Blackstone Street, Cambridge, MA 02139, 1-800-544-4005 (toll-free).
Kussmaul Encyclopedia.

Gordon & Breach Science Publications, Inc., 50 West 23rd Street, New York, NY 10010, 212-689-0360.
Encyclopedia of Environmental Science and Engineering.

Greenwood Press, 88 Post Road West, P.O. Box 5007, Westport, CT 06881, 203-226-3571.
American Educators' Encyclopedia; Dictionary of Afro-Latin American Civilization; Dictionary of American Communal and Utopian History; Dictionary of Concepts in Human Geography; Dictionary of Demography; Dictionary of Irish Literature; Dictionary of Mexican American History; Dictionary of the Black Theatre; Encyclopedia of American Agricultural History; Historical Dictionary of the French Revolution, 1789–1799; Kabuki Encyclopedia; Muslim Peoples; Reference Companion to the History of Abnormal Psychology; Reference Handbook on the Deserts of North America.

Grolier Electronic Publishing, Inc. (a subsidiary of Grolier, Inc.), 95 Madison Avenue, New York, NY 10016, 212-696-9750.
Academic American Encyclopedia (electronic version; compact disc version).

Grolier, Inc., Sherman Turnpike, Danbury, CT 06816, 1-800-243-7256 (toll-free).
Academic American Encyclopedia; Disney's Wonderful World of Knowledge (published by Danbury Press); *Encyclopedia Americana; Encyclopedia International* (published by Lexicon Publications; currently out of print); *Encyclopedia of Visual Arts; Illustrated Bible Dictionary; Lands and Peoples; New Book of Knowledge; New Book of Popular Science; Raintree Illustrated Science Encyclopedia* (published by Raintree Publications).

Grove's Dictionaries of Music, Inc., 15 East 26th Street, New York, NY 10010, 1-800-221-2123 (toll-free).
New Grove Dictionary of American Music; New Grove Dictionary of Music and Musicians; New Grove Dictionary of Musical Instruments.

G.K. Hall & Company, 70 Lincoln Street, Boston, MA 02111, 617-423-3990.
Collins Australian Encyclopedia (published by Collins); *New Zealand Encyclopedia* (published by Bateman); *World Atlas of Architecture.*

Harcourt Brace Jovanovich, Inc., 1250 Sixth Avenue, San Diego, CA 92101, 619-231-6616.
Crafts Business Encyclopedia.

Harper & Row Publishers, Inc., Ten East 53rd Street, New York, NY 10022, 212-207-7000.
Amateur Photographer's Handbook (published by T.Y. Crowell); *Complete Outdoors Encyclopedia; Cook's Encyclopedia; Crowell's Handbook of Classical Literature* (published by T.Y. Crowell); *Dictionary of American Art; Dictionary of Political Thought; Dictionary of Subjects and Symbols in Art; Dictionary of the Decorative Arts; Encyclopedia of American Facts and Dates* (published by T.Y. Crowell); *Encyclopedia of American History; Encyclopedia of Anthropology; Encyclopedia of Military History;*

Encyclopedia of the Music Business; Essential Guide to Prescription Drugs; Film Encyclopedia (published by T.Y. Crowell); *Funk & Wagnalls Standard Dictionary of Folklore, Mythology, and Legends* (published by T.Y. Crowell); *Golf Magazine's Encyclopedia of Golf; Historical Atlas of Mythology; Illustrated Encyclopedia of Astronomy and Space* (published by T.Y. Crowell); *Kodansha Encyclopedia of Japan* (published by Kodansha International); *Money Encyclopedia; Pictorial Guide to the Planets; Reader's Encyclopedia* (published by T.Y. Crowell); *Reader's Encyclopedia of the American West* (published by T.Y. Crowell); *Sailing Encyclopedia* (published by T.Y. Crowell); *Scarne's Encyclopedia of Card Games; Ski Magazine's Encyclopedia of Skiing; United States Tennis Association Official Encyclopedia of Tennis; Worldmark Encyclopedia of the States.*

Hart Publishing Company, Inc., 24 Fifth Avenue, New York, NY 10011, 212-260-2430.

Encyclopedia of Design.

Harvard University Press, 79 Garden Street, Cambridge, MA 02138, 617-495-2600.

Dictionary of Marxist Thought; Harvard Dictionary of Music; Harvard Encyclopedia of American Ethnic Groups; Harvard Guide to Contemporary American Writing.

Holmes & Meier Publications, Inc., 30 Irving Place, IUB Building, New York, NY 10003, 212-254-4100.

First Facts of American Labor.

Holt, Rinehart & Winston, Inc., 383 Madison Avenue, New York, NY 10017, 212-872-2000.

American Political Dictionary; Complete Illustrated Encyclopedia of the World's Motorcycles; McClane's New Standard Fishing Encyclopedia and International Angling Guide; Photography.

Houghton Mifflin Company, Two Park Street, Boston, MA 02108, 617-725-5000.

Dictionary of American Food and Drink (published by Ticknor & Fields); *Encyclopedia of World History.*

Howell Book House, Inc., Helmsley Building, 230 Park Avenue, New York, NY 10169, 212-986-4488.

Complete Dog Book.

Humanities Press, Inc., Atlantic Highlands, NJ 07716, 201-872-1441.

Encyclopaedia of Indian Culture.

Hurtig Publishers Ltd., 10560 105th Street, Edmonton, Alberta T5H 2W7 Canada, 403-426-2359.

Canadian Encyclopedia.

Industrial Press, Inc., 200 Madison Avenue, New York, NY 10157, 212-889-6330.

Machinery's Handbook.

International Labor Office, Washington Branch, 1750 New York Avenue Northwest, Washington, DC 20006, 202-376-2315.

Encyclopaedia of Occupational Health and Safety.

Johns Hopkins University Press, Baltimore, MD 21218, 301-338-7852.

Encyclopedic Dictionary of the Sciences of Language.

Jossey-Bass, Inc., 433 California Street, San Francisco, CA 94104, 415-433-1740.

Encyclopedia of Clinical Assessment; International Encyclopedia of Higher Education.

Alfred A. Knopf, Inc. (a subsidiary of Random House, Inc.), 201 East 50th Street, New York, NY 10022, 212-751-2600.
Audubon Society Encyclopedia of North American Birds; Child Care Encyclopedia; Photographer's Handbook.

Kodansha International USA/Ltd., *see* Harper & Row Publishers, Inc.

Krause Publications, Inc., 700 East State Street, Iola, WI 54990, 715-445-2214.
Standard Catalog of World Paper Money.

Robert E. Krieger Publishing Company, Inc., P.O. Box 9542, Melbourne, FL 32902, 305-724-9542.
Encyclopedia of Urban Planning (published by McGraw-Hill).

Lange Medical Publications, Drawer L, Los Altos, CA 94022, 415-948-4526.
Handbook of Poisoning.

Larousse & Company, Inc., 572 Fifth Avenue, New York, NY 10036, 212-575-9515.
Larousse Guide to Astronomy; Larousse Guide to Minerals, Rocks and Fossils.

Lexicon Publications, *see* Grolier, Inc.

Literary Mart, 1261 Broadway, New York, NY 10001, 212-684-0588.
Secondhand encyclopedias (write for catalog).

Little, Brown & Company, 34 Beacon Street, Boston, MA 02106, 617-227-0730.
Photograph Collector's Guide (published by the New York Graphic Society).

Longman, Inc., 1560 Broadway, New York, NY 10036, 212-764-3950.
New Dictionary of Physics.

Louisiana State University Press, Baton Rouge, LA 70893, 504-388-6666.
Encyclopedia of Southern History.

McGrath Publishing Company, P.O. Box 9001, Wilmington, NC 28402,
Encyclopedia of American Religions.

McGraw-Hill Book Company, 1221 Avenue of the Americas, New York, NY 10020, 212-512-2000.
Artists' and Illustrators' Encyclopedia; Building Design and Construction Handbook; Chemical and Process Technology Encyclopedia; The Discoverers; Encyclopedia of American Architecture; Encyclopedia of Architectural Technology; Encyclopedia of Black America; Encyclopedia of Economics; Encyclopedia of Medical History; Encyclopedia of Mystery and Detection; Encyclopedia of North American Railroading; Encyclopedia of Prehistoric Life; Encyclopedia of Urban Planning; Encyclopedia of World Art; Engineering Formulas; Engineering Manual; Family Legal Companion; Graphic Arts Encyclopedia; Handbook of Mathematical Tables and Formulas; Homeowner's Encyclopedia of House Construction; Lange's Handbook of Chemistry; McGraw-Hill Concise Encyclopedia of Science and Technology; McGraw-Hill Dictionary of Art; McGraw-Hill Encyclopedia of Astronomy; McGraw-Hill Encyclopedia of Chemistry; McGraw-Hill Encyclopedia of Electronics and Computers; McGraw-Hill Encyclopedia of Energy; McGraw-Hill Encyclopedia of Engineering; McGraw-Hill Encyclopedia of Environmental Sciences; McGraw-Hill Encyclopedia of Food, Agriculture and Nutrition; McGraw-Hill Encyclopedia of Ocean and At-

mospheric Sciences; McGraw-Hill Encyclopedia of Physics; McGraw-Hill Encyclopedia of Science and Technology; McGraw-Hill Encyclopedia of the Geological Sciences; McGraw-Hill Encyclopedia of World Drama; McGraw-Hill Personal Computer Programming Encyclopedia; New Catholic Encyclopedia; Ocean World Encyclopedia; Rolling Rivers; Spy / Counterspy; Standard Handbook for Civil Engineers; Synopsis and Classification of Living Organisms.

David McKay Company, Inc., Two Park Avenue, New York, NY 10016, 212-340-9800.
Civil War Dictionary; Encyclopedia of the American Revolution.

Macmillan Educational Company (a division of Macmillan Publishing Company, Inc.), 866 Third Avenue, New York, NY 10022, 212-702-2000.
Collier's Encyclopedia; Merit Students Encyclopedia.

Macmillan Professional Books, 866 Third Avenue, New York, NY 10022, 1-800-257-5755 (toll-free).
Collier's Encyclopedia; Merit Students Encyclopedia.

Macmillan Publishing Company, Inc., 866 Third Avenue, New York, NY 10022, 212-702-2000.
Baseball Encyclopedia; Collier's Encyclopedia; Encyclopaedia Judaica; Encyclopedia of American Forest and Conservation History; Encyclopedia of Education; Encyclopedia of Philosophy; Encylopedia of Religion; Encyclopedia of the American Constitution; Great Soviet Encyclopedia; Hockey Encyclopedia; Hortus Third; Macmillan Encyclopedic Dictionary of Numismatics; Macmillan Illustrated Animal Encyclopedia; Merit Students Encyclopedia; Wyman's Gardening Encyclopedia.

Marquis Who's Who, Inc., 200 East Ohio Street, Chicago, IL 60611, 312-787-2008.
Standard Education Almanac.

Marshall Cavendish Corporation, 147 West Merrick Road, Freeport, NY 11520, 516-546-4200.
Growing Up with Science; Illustrated Encyclopedia of Aviation; Illustrated Encyclopedia of Mankind; Man, Myth, & Magic; Marshall Cavendish Illustrated Encyclopedia of Family Health; Marshall Cavendish Illustrated Encyclopedia of the World and Its People; Marshall Cavendish Illustrated Encyclopedia of World War I; Marshall Cavendish Illustrated Encyclopedia of World War II.

Mead Data Central, 9393 Springboro Pike, P.O. Box 933, Dayton, OH 45401, 513-865-6800.
New Encyclopaedia Britannica (electronic version).

Medical Economics Books, 680 Kinderkamack Road, Oradell, NJ 07649, 201-262-3030.
Physicians' Desk Reference to Pharmaceutical Specialities and Biologicals.

Merck & Company, Inc., P.O. Box 2000, Rahway, NJ 07065, 201-574-5403.
Merck Manual of Diagnosis and Therapy; Merck Veterinary Manual.

Merriam-Webster, Inc. (a subsidiary of Encyclopaedia Britannica, Inc.), 47 Federal Street, P.O. Box 281, Springfield, MA 01101, 413-734-3134.
Webster's New Geographical Dictionary.

Merrimack Publishers' Circle, 99 Main Street, Salem, NH 03079, 617-887-2440.
Junior Pears Encyclopaedia (published by Pelham Books); *Pears Cyclopaedia* (published by Pelham Books).

Methuen, Inc., 733 Third Avenue, New York, NY 10017, 212-922-3550.
Dictionary of Named Effects and Laws in Chemistry, Physics and Mathematics (published by Chapman and Hall).

MIT Press, 28 Carleton Street, Cambridge, MA 02142, 617-253-2884.
Aquarium Encyclopedia; Encyclopedic Dictionary of Mathematics; Encyclopedic Dictionary of Psychology.

William Morrow & Company, Inc., 105 Madison Avenue, New York, NY 10016, 212-889-3050.
Cassell's Encyclopedia of World Literature; Film Encyclopedia; World Coin Encyclopedia.

National Association of Social Workers, 7981 Eastern Avenue, Silver Spring, MD 20910, 301-565-0333.
Encyclopedia of Social Work.

Thomas Nelson Publishers, P.O. Box 946, 407 Seventh Avenue South, Nashville, TN 37203, 615-889-9000.
Nelson's Encyclopedia for Young Readers; Pet Encyclopedia; Quick Reference Handbook of Basic Knowledge (published by Royal Publishers).

New American Library, 1633 Broadway, New York, NY 10019, 212-397-8000.
Field Guide to American Architecture; Larousse Encyclopedia of Astrology.

New York Graphic Society Books, *see* Little, Brown & Company.

New York Zoetrope, 80 East 11th Street, New York, NY 10003, 212-254-8325.
Les Brown's Encyclopedia of Television.

North Light Publications, P.O. Box 489, Westport, CT 06881, 203-336-4225.
Encyclopedia of Drawing.

W.W. Norton & Company, Inc., 500 Fifth Avenue, New York, NY 10110, 212-354-5500.
Complete Book of Medical Tests; Illustrated Encyclopaedia of World Theatre; New College Encyclopedia of Music; Reader's Digest Complete Guide to Needlework (published by the Reader's Digest Association); *Reader's Digest Crafts and Hobbies* (published by the Reader's Digest Association); *Thames and Hudson Dictionary of Art and Artists* (published by Thames and Hudson).

Oceana Publications, Inc., 75 Main Street, Dobbs Ferry, NY 10522, 914-693-1733.
American Legal Almanac.

Outlet Book Company (a division of Crown Publishers, Inc.), One Park Avenue, New York, NY 10016, 212-532-9200.
Encyclopedia of Architecture (published by Crown).

Oxford University Press, Inc., 200 Madison Avenue, New York, NY 10016, 212-564-6680.
American Musical Theatre; Concise Oxford Dictionary of Ballet; Encyclopaedia of the Musical Film; Great Song Thesaurus; New Oxford Companion to Music; Oxford Companion to American Literature; Oxford Companion to American Theatre; Oxford Companion to Animal Behaviour; Oxford Companion to Art; Oxford Companion to Canadian Literature; Oxford Companion to Chess; Oxford Companion to Children's Literature; Oxford Companion to English Literature; Oxford Companion to Film; Oxford Companion to Law; Oxford Companion to Ships and the Sea; Oxford Companion to Spanish Literature; Oxford Companion to the

Decorative Arts; Oxford Companion to the Theatre; Oxford Companion to Twentieth-Century Art; Oxford Dictionary of the Christian Church; Oxford Encyclopedia of Trees of the World; Oxford Illustrated Encyclopedia; Oxford Junior Encyclopedia (currently out of print); *World Christian Encyclopedia.*

Pegus Press, 648 West Sierra Avenue, P.O. Box 429, Clovis, CA 93612.
Foods and Nutrition Encyclopedia.

Pergamon Press Canada Ltd., Consumers Road (Suite 104), Willowdale, Ontario M2J 1P9 Canada, 416-497-8337.
New Caxton Encyclopedia (published by Caxton Publications); Foreign-language encyclopedias (write for catalog).

Pergamon Press, Inc., Maxwell House, Fairview Park, Elmsford, NY 10523, 914-592-7700.
Encyclopaedic Dictionary of Physics; International Encyclopedia of Education; New Caxton Encyclopedia (published by Caxton Publications); *Purnell's Pictorial Encyclopedia* (published by Purnell); Foreign-language encyclopedias (write for catalog).

Clarkson N. Potter Books, *see* Crown Publishers, Inc.

Prentice-Hall, Inc., Route 9W, Englewood Cliffs, NJ 07632, 201-592-2000.
Concise Encyclopedia of Information Technology; Encyclopedia of Accounting Systems; Encyclopedia of Archaeological Excavations in the Holy Lands; Encyclopedia of Integrated Circuits; Encyclopedia of Textiles; Encyclopedia of Visual Arts; Encyclopedic Dictionary of Electronic Terms; Great American Movie Book; Legal Secretary's Encyclopedic Dictionary; New Encyclopedic Dictionary of School Law; Paralegal's Encyclopedic Dictionary; Prentice-Hall Encyclopedia of Mathematics.

Princeton University Press, 41 William Street, Princeton, NJ 08540, 609-452-4900.
Dictionary of the History of Science; Princeton Encyclopedia of Classical Sites; Princeton Encyclopedia of Poetry and Poetics.

Proteus Enterprises, Inc., 961 West Thorndale, Bensenville, IL 60106, 312-766-5544.
Funk & Wagnalls New Encyclopedia (school and library sales only).

Publishers Guild, P.O. Box 754, Palatine, IL 60067, 312-991-0255.
New Catholic Encyclopedia (published by McGraw-Hill).

Purnell Reference Books, 205 West Highland Avenue, Milwaukee, WI 53203, 414-273-0873.
Illustrated Encyclopedia of 20th Century Weapons and Warfare.

Putnam Publishing Group, 200 Madison Avenue, New York, NY 10016, 1-800-631-8571 (toll-free).
New Kobbé's Complete Opera Book.

Raintree Publications, Inc., 205 West Highland Avenue, Milwaukee, WI 53203, 414-273-0873.
Raintree Illustrated Science Encyclopedia.

Rand McNally & Company, P.O. Box 7600, Chicago, IL 60680, 312-673-9100.
Rand McNally Encyclopedia of Military Aircraft, 1914–1980; Rand McNally's Children's Encyclopedia.

Random House, Inc., 201 East 50th Street, New York, NY 10022, 212-751-2600.

American Medical Association Family Medical Guide; Charlie Brown's 'Cyclopedia (distributed by Funk & Wagnalls); *New Universal Family Encyclopedia; Photographer's Handbook* (published by Knopf); *Random House Encyclopedia; Reader's Digest Eat Better, Live Better* (published by the Reader's Digest Association); *Reader's Digest Family Legal Guide* (published by the Reader's Digest Association).

Reader's Digest Association, Inc., 750 Third Avenue, New York, NY 10017, 212-850-7007.
Reader's Digest Complete Guide to Needlework; Reader's Digest Crafts and Hobbies; Reader's Digest Eat Better, Live Better; Reader's Digest Family Legal Guide.

Reference Book Center, 175 Fifth Avenue, New York, NY 10010, 212-677-2160.
Secondhand encyclopedias (write for catalog).

Rodale Press, Inc., 33 East Minor Street, Emmaus, PA 18049, 215-967-5171.
Encyclopedia of Organic Gardening; Prevention's New Encyclopedia of Common Diseases; Rodale's Encyclopedia of Indoor Gardening.

Royal Publishers, *see* Thomas Nelson Publishers.

St. James Press, 213 West Institute Place (Suite 305), Chicago, IL 60610, 312-944-7592.
International Dictionary of Films and Filmmakers.

St. Martin's Press, Inc., 175 Fifth Avenue, New York, NY 10010, 212-674-5151.
Comparisons; Encyclopedia of Folk, Country & Western Music; Encyclopedia of Motor-Cycle Sport; Fashion Encyclopedia; The Rule Book.

Salem Press, Inc., P.O. Box 1097, Englewood Cliffs, NJ 07632, 201-871-3700.
Cyclopedia of Literary Characters; Magill's Survey of the Cinema; Masterplots; World Philosophy.

Howard W. Sams & Company, Inc., 4300 West 62nd Street, Indianapolis, IN 46268, 317-298-5400.
Computer Dictionary and Handbook.

W.B. Saunders Company, West Washington Square, Philadelphia, PA 19105, 215-574-4808.
Encyclopedia and Dictionary of Medicine, Nursing and Allied Health.

Scarecrow Press, Inc. (a subsidiary of Grolier, Inc.), 52 Liberty Street, P.O. Box 656, Metuchen, NJ 08840, 201-548-8600.
American Counties; Encyclopedia of Mental Health (miniprint ed.).

Scott Publishing Company, Three East 57th Street, New York, NY 10022, 212-371-5700.
Scott Standard Postage Stamp Catalogue.

Charles Scribner's Sons, 597 Fifth Avenue, New York, NY 10017, 212-486-2875.
Album of Science; America's Handyman Book; A-Z of Astronomy; Dictionary of American History; Dictionary of the History of Ideas; Dictionary of the Middle Ages; Dictionary of World Pottery and Porcelain; Encyclopedia of American Economic History; Encyclopedia of American Foreign Policy; Encyclopedia of American Political History; Encyclopedia of Aviation; Encyclopedia of Crafts; Encyclopedia of Religion and Ethics; Encyclopedia of World Costume; Exotica IV; Grossman's Guide to Wines, Beers, & Spirits; Halliwell's Film Guide; Halliwell's Filmgoer's Companion; International Encyclopedia of Dance; The Presidents.

M.E. Sharpe, Inc., 80 Business Park Drive, Armonk, NY 10504, 914-273-1800.
Peoples of the USSR.

Silver Burdett Company, Morristown, NJ 07960, 1-800-631-8081 (toll-free outside New Jersey), 201-285-7700 (New Jersey only).
Silver Burdett Encyclopedia of Transport; Silver Burdett's Children's Encyclopedia (published by Grisewood & Dempsey).

Simon & Schuster, Inc., 1230 Avenue of the Americas, New York, NY 10020, 212-245-6400.
Collins Gem Encyclopedia (published by William Collins); *Encyclopedia of Modern Bodybuilding; Family First Aid and Medical Guide; How to Clean Everything; New Our Bodies, Ourselves; Rolling Stone Encyclopedia of Rock & Roll; Simon & Schuster's Guide to Cats; Timetables of History; Universal Encyclopedia of Mathematics.*

W.H. Smith Publications, Inc., 112 Madison Avenue, New York, NY 10016, 212-532-6600.
Junior Encyclopedia of General Knowledge (published by Octopus Books).

Southwestern Company, P.O. Box 820, Nashville, TN 37202, 615-790-4000.
Volume Library.

Standard Educational Corporation, 200 West Monroe Street, Chicago, IL 60606, 312-346-7440.
New Standard Encyclopedia.

Gareth Stevens, Inc., *see* Farwell Promotional Books.

H.S. Stuttman, Inc., 333 Post Road West, Westport, CT 06889, 203-226-7841.
Complete Handyman Do-It-Yourself Encyclopedia; Growing Up with Science.

TAB Books, Inc., Monterey Avenue, Blue Ridge Summit, PA 17214, 1-800-233-1128 (toll-free).
Encyclopedia of Homebuilt Aircraft.

T.F.H. Publications, 211 West Sylvania Avenue, Neptune, NJ 07753, 201-988-8400.
Encyclopedia of Marine Invertebrates.

Thames and Hudson, *see* W.W. Norton & Company, Inc.

Ticknor & Fields, *see* Houghton Mifflin Company.

Times Books, 130 Fifth Avenue, New York, NY 10011, 212-620-5900.
New York Times Encyclopedia of Film, 1896–1979.

Troll Associates, 320 Route 7, Mahwah, NJ 07430, 1-800-526-5289 (toll-free).
New Talking Cassette Encyclopedia.

Tyndale House Publications, 336 Gundersen Drive, P.O. Box 80, Wheaton, IL 60189, 312-668-8300.
Illustrated Bible Dictionary.

Frederick Ungar Publishing Company, Inc., 36 Cooper Square, New York, NY 10003, 212-473-7885.
Academy Awards; Encyclopedia of World Literature in the 20th Century.

U.S. Government Printing Office, Superintendent of Documents, Washington, DC 20402, 202-783-3238.
Dictionary of American Naval Fighting Ships; Handbook of North American Indians; Occupational Outlook Handbook

University of California Press, 2120 Berkeley Way, Berkeley, CA 94720, 415-642-6683.
Concise Dictionary of Modern Japanese History.

University of Toronto Press, 33 East Tupper Street, Buffalo, NY 14203, 416-978-2052.
Encyclopedia of Music in Canada.

University of Washington Press, P.O. Box 85569, Seattle, WA 98145, 206-543-8870.
Theatre Backstage from A to Z.

Van Nostrand Reinhold Company, Inc., 135 West 50th Street, New York, NY 10020, 212-265-8700.
Color Encyclopedia of Gemstones; Encyclopedia of Chemical Reactions; Encyclopedia of Computer Science and Engineering; Encyclopedia of Decorative Arts, 1890–1940; Encyclopedia of Earth Sciences (various volumes); *Encyclopedia of Management; Encyclopedia of Minerals; Encyclopedia of the Biological Sciences; Foods and Food Production Encyclopedia; Grzimek's Animal Life Encyclopedia; Grzimek's Encyclopedia of Evolution; Illustrated Dictionary of Place Names; International Encyclopedia of Psychiatry, Psychology, Psychoanalysis, and Neurology; Kingzett's Chemical Encyclopedia; Nutrition and Health Encyclopedia; Riegel's Handbook of Industrial Chemistry; Van Nostrand Reinhold Encyclopedia of Chemistry; Van Nostrand's Scientific Encyclopedia; VNR Concise Encyclopedia of Mathematics.*

Viking Press, Inc., 40 West 23rd Street, New York, NY 10010, 212-807-7300.
American Shelter (published by Overlook Press).

VU/TEXT Information Services, Inc., 1211 Chestnut Street, Philadelphia, PA 19107, 1-800-258-8080 (toll-free outside Pennsylvania), 215-665-3300 (Pennsylvania only).
Academic American Encyclopedia (electronic version).

Warren, Gorham & Lamont, Inc., 210 South Street, Boston, MA 02111, 617-423-2020.
Arnold Encyclopedia of Real Estate; Encyclopedia of Investments; Thorndike Encyclopedia of Banking and Financial Tables.

Webster Publishing Company Ltd., 1644 Bay View Avenue, Toronto, Ontario M4G 3C2 Canada, 416-484-6900.
Webster's New Age Encyclopedia (same as *Encyclopedia International*); *Webster's New Family Encyclopedia* (same as *Encyclopedia International*).

Weekly Reader Books, P.O. Box 16615, Columbus, OH 43216, 614-771-0006.
Young Students Encyclopedia.

West Publishing Company, 50 West Kellogg Boulevard, P.O. Box 64526, St. Paul, MN 55164, 1-800-328-9352 (toll-free).
Corpus Juris Secundum; Guide to American Law.

Western Publishing Company, 850 Third Avenue, New York, NY 10022, 212-753-8500.
Guide Book of United States Coins.

John Wiley & Sons, Inc., 605 Third Avenue, New York, NY 10158, 212-850-6418.
Astronomy Data Book; Encyclopedia of Statistical Sciences; Handbook of Child Psychology; Marine Life; Worldmark Encyclopedia of the Nations.

Wiley-Interscience (a division of John Wiley & Sons, Inc.), 605 Third Avenue, New York, NY 10158, 212-850-6418.

Encyclopedia of Polymer Science and Technology; Encyclopedia of Psychology; Kirk-Othmer Encyclopedia of Chemical Technology.

H.W. Wilson Company, 950 University Avenue, Bronx, NY 10452, 212-588-8400.

Famous First Facts.

Winston Press, 430 Oak Grove, Minneapolis, MN 55403, 612-871-7000.

Dictionary of Biblical Theology (published by Seabury).

World Book, Inc., Merchandise Mart Plaza, Chicago, IL 60654, 1-800-621-8202 (toll-free).

Childcraft; World Book Encyclopedia; World Book Illustrated Home Medical Encyclopedia.

Writer's Digest Books, 9933 Alliance Road, Cincinnati, OH 45242, 513-984-0717.

Writer's Encyclopedia.

Yale University Press, 302 Temple Street, New Haven, CT 06520, 203-436-7872.

Handbook of Russian Literature.

Zondervan Publishing House, 1415 Lake Drive Southeast, Grand Rapids, MI 49506, 616-459-6900.

Compact Encyclopedia of Psychological Problems.

Title-Subject Index

Encyclopedias and encyclopedic works reviewed in *Best Encyclopedias* appear in the index in CAPITAL LETTERS. Other encyclopedias and publications mentioned in the book are *italicized* in the index. Specialized encyclopedias are indexed by both title and subject. For example, the NEW YORK BOTANICAL GARDEN ILLUSTRATED ENCYCLOPEDIA OF HORTICULTURE can be located through the index under its title as well as the subjects "Botany," "Gardening," "Horticulture," and "Plant life." For information about encyclopedias as a type of reference work, consult the index entry "Encyclopedias—general information" and its various subheadings, such as "computerization," "sales methods and practices," "secondhand encyclopedias," etc.